For Dan, Anne, Bobby, and Scott

TABLE OF CONTENTS

The future of many organizations depends on their ability to manage projects, programs, and portfolios of projects. Skills in these areas continue to be in high demand. Colleges have responded to this need by establishing courses and degree programs in project management, and corporations are investing in continuing education to help develop effective project teams and project, program, and portfolio managers.

What makes this text different from other project management texts? First of all, people actually enjoy reading it. They like the fact that I explain concepts in a way that enables them to understand and apply them. I've taken some information and several features of my first book, *Information Technology Project Management*, now in its fifth edition, and adapted them to create a more general project management book that addresses the need for people in *all* majors and industries to understand and use good project management. This book includes many real-world examples in the "What Went Right," "What Went Wrong," "Media Snapshot," and "Best Practice" segments. People like to read about real projects that succeeded and those that failed to learn from the successes and failures of others. They also like to recognize that there are projects in all aspects of life, particularly in the media. Additional features of this text are listed under "Pedagogical Features."

I'm most excited about the fact that this book provides comprehensive samples of applying various tools and techniques to a realistic project. Many people learn best by example, so I've provided detailed examples of applying project management to a project everyone can relate to. I have never come across a textbook that presents project management concepts and then brings them to life in a fully developed sample project. I believe this approach will help many people truly understand and apply good project management.

New to the Second Edition

Building on the success of the previous edition, *Introduction to Project Management, Second Edition* introduces a uniquely effective combination of features. The main changes to the second edition include the following:

- *A Guide to Using Microsoft Project 2007* (92 pages) is included in the physical text as Appendix A. The previous Guide to Using Microsoft Project 2003 is available on the companion Web site.

- *Advice for the Project Management Professional (PMP) Exam and Related Certifications* (23 pages) is now included in Appendix B.

- Appendix C, *Resources*, now includes a detailed running case study, and additional case studies are available on the companion Web site.

- The Fissure simulation software is now an optional bundling. Instructions for using the simulation are available on the companion Web site.

- The new "Best Practice" feature enhances each chapter by providing optimal approaches to implementing project management in various industries, which helps improve project management in organizations.

- Several more advanced topics have been included, such as mind mapping (Chapters 2 and 4), critical chain scheduling (Chapter 4), resource leveling (Chapter 6), and project management maturity models (Chapter 8).

- Jeopardy games are included on the companion Web site for each chapter. You can use these as review games in class, or students can go through them on their own to help reinforce their understanding of key terms and other concepts in each chapter.

- Podcasts are also provided on the companion Web site for each chapter. Podcasts are short audio files, about five minutes long, which are designed for use on an iPod, MP3 player, or on a PC using iTunes, Windows Media Player, or other digital music players. You can listen to Podcasts on your way to class, while driving, or whenever cracking open the book isn't practical. Podcasts for each chapter include the chapter summary, quick quizzes, and key terms.

- Updated examples and references are provided throughout the text, and user feedback is incorporated.

Approach

Businesses change rapidly, and the project management field changes just as quickly to lead conceptual thinking and meet business needs. For this reason, you cannot assume that what worked even five years ago is still the best approach today. This text provides up-to-date information on how good project, program, and portfolio management can help you achieve organizational success. Five distinct features of this text include its:

- relationship to the Project Management Body of Knowledge

- bundling with Microsoft Project 2007 and VPMi software

- comprehensive samples of applying tools and techniques to a realistic project

- inclusion of templates and seamless integration of various software applications

- robust companion Web site

Use of *PMBOK® Guide Framework*

The Project Management Institute (PMI) created the *Guide to the Project Management Body of Knowledge* (the *PMBOK® Guide*) as a framework and starting point for understanding project management. The *PMBOK® Guide* is, however, just that—a guide. This text uses the *PMBOK® Guide, Third Edition* as a foundation, but goes beyond it by providing more details, highlighting additional topics, and providing a real-world context for project management. It also includes information and examples of applying project, program, and portfolio management as well as a summary of best practices in the field.

Inclusion of Microsoft Project 2007, VPMi Enterprise Project Management Software, and Optional Fissure Simulation Software

Software has advanced tremendously in recent years, and it is important for project, program, and portfolio managers and their teams to use software to help manage projects. Each copy of *Introduction to Project Management, Second Edition* includes a 60-day trial version of the leading project management software on the market—Microsoft Project 2007. Appendix A of the text includes a 92-page document, *Guide to Using Microsoft Project 2007*, which teaches you to use this powerful software in a systematic way. You do not need to buy a separate book to learn how to use Project 2007 effectively, but suggested resources are provided if you want to learn even more about the software. You also get a 120-day free trial of VPMi Express, a Web-based enterprise project management software product from Virtual Communications Services (VCS). This software automates project, program, and portfolio management and includes Microsoft Project integration. You can also purchase a special bundling of this text with a project management simulation tool developed by Fissure, a PMI Registered Education Provider. Fissure has used an expanded version of this simulation tool to help thousands of people learn how to apply various project management concepts.

Comprehensive Samples of Applying Tools and Techniques to a Realistic Project

Unlike other texts, this text shows the reader how an organization selected, initiated, planned, executed, monitored and controlled, and closed a realistic project, called the Just-In-Time Training project. It provides *over 50 sample applications* of documents, tools, and techniques such as a business case, project charter, project management plan, work breakdown structure, Gantt chart, cost baseline, Pareto chart, resource histogram, performance report, risk register, contract, lessons learned report, and so on for this project. You can also access the template files used to create them from the companion Web site for this text. As one reviewer of this text stated:

> *It comprehensively communicates what it really takes to manage a large project, including required deliverables, work products, and documentation. I haven't seen either a text or documentation in industry which communicates this subject this comprehensively or this accurately.*

(Gilbert S. Leonard, Adjunct Professor and retired project manager, Exxon Mobil Corporation)

Provides Templates and Seamless Integration of Various Software Applications

Most organizations have learned by now that they do not have to reinvent the wheel when it comes to much of the documentation required for managing projects. This text uses over 50 templates for creating various documents, spreadsheets, diagrams, and charts, and you can download these templates from the companion Web site. Various software applications are used throughout the text in a seamless fashion. Let's face it—if you're involved in project, program, or portfolio management, you have to know how to use various software tools to do your job.

Includes a Companion Web Site (www.course.com/mis/pm2/schwalbe or http://login.course.com)

A companion Web site provides you with a one-stop location to access informative links and tools to enhance your learning. Similar to other companion Web sites provided by Course Technology, this site will be a valuable resource as you access lecture notes, online quizzes, Jeopardy games, podcasts, templates, student files for Project 2007, and links to references. You can also access the author's site to see real class syllabi, samples of student projects, and other helpful links.

CoursePort: CoursePort provides a central location from which you can access Course Technology's online learning solutions with convenience and flexibility.

- Gain access to online resources including robust Student Online Companion Web sites.

- Simplify your course work by reducing human error and the need to keep track of multiple passwords.

- Take advantage of CoursePort's tailored services, including personalized homepages.

Please see the password card included in this book for instructions on how to access the CoursePort site for this text.

Organization and Content

Introduction to Project Management, Second Edition, is organized into eight chapters and three appendices. The first two chapters introduce project, program, and portfolio management and discuss different approaches for their selection. You'll read about Global Construction, Inc. and how they decided to pursue the Just-In-Time Training project. The next six chapters follow the five process groups of project management: initiating, planning (broken down into two chapters), executing, monitoring and controlling, and closing. These six chapters apply various tools and techniques in each of these process groups to the Just-In-Time Training project. Best practices are described throughout the text, with a summary in the final chapter. Appendix A provides a detailed Guide to Using Microsoft Project 2007, and Appendix B includes Advice for the Project Management Professional (PMP) Exam and Related Certifications. Appendix C provides a summary of information on the companion Web site, a list of templates, a detailed running case study, and a list of suggested resources to help you learn more about project management.

Pedagogical Features

Several pedagogical features are included in this text to enhance presentation of the materials so that you can more easily understand the concepts and apply them. Throughout the text, emphasis is placed on applying concepts to up-to-date, real-world project management.

Learning Objectives, Chapter Summaries, Quick Quizzes, Discussion Questions, Exercises, Team Projects, and Case Studies

Learning Objectives, Chapter Summaries, Quick Quizzes, Discussion Questions, Exercises, Team Projects, and Case Studies are designed to function as integrated study tools. Learning Objectives reflect what you should be able to accomplish after completing each chapter. Chapter Summaries highlight key concepts you should master. The Quick Quizzes help reinforce your understanding of important concepts in each chapter. The Discussion Questions help guide critical thinking about those key concepts. Exercises provide opportunities to practice important techniques, as do the Team Projects. The Case Studies in Appendix C and those on the companion Web site provide a robust means to apply what you have learned from the text to realistic case studies, similar to the example used throughout the text. The companion Web site also provides several additional study aids, such as lecture notes and interactive quizzes, Jeopardy games, and Podcasts for each chapter.

Opening Case and Case Wrap-Up

To set the stage, each chapter begins with an opening case related to the materials in that chapter. These scenarios spark student interest and introduce important concepts in a real-world context. As project management concepts and techniques are discussed, they are applied to the opening case and other similar scenarios. Each chapter then closes with a Case Wrap-Up—some problems are overcome and some problems require more effort—to further illustrate the real world of project management.

What Went Right? and What Went Wrong?

Failures, as much as successes, can be valuable learning experiences. Each chapter of the text includes one or more examples of real projects that went right as well as examples of projects that went wrong. These examples further illustrate the importance of mastering key concepts in each chapter.

Media Snapshots and Best Practice Features

The world is full of projects. Several television shows, movies, newspapers, Web sites, and other media highlight project results, good and bad. Relating project management concepts to all types of projects, as highlighted in the media, will help you understand and see the importance of this growing field. Why not get people excited about studying project management by showing them how to recognize project management concepts in popular television shows, movies, or other media? It is also important to study Best Practices so readers can learn how to implement project management in an optimum way.

Cartoons

Each chapter includes a cartoon, some from Dilbert and some original ones, which uses humor to illustrate concepts from the text.

Key Terms

The field of project management includes many unique terms that are vital to creating a common language and understanding of the field. Key terms are displayed in boldface and are defined the first time they appear. Definitions of key terms are provided in alphabetical order at the end of each chapter and in a glossary at the end of the text.

Application Software

Learning becomes much more dynamic with hands-on practice using the top project management software tool in the industry, Microsoft Project 2007, as well as other tools, such as spreadsheet software and Internet browsers. Each chapter offers you many opportunities to get hands-on experience and build new software skills by applying concepts to problems posed for them. In this way, the text accommodates both those who learn by reading and those who learn by doing. In addition to the exercises and team projects found at the end of chapters, several challenging projects are provided at the end of *Guide to Using Microsoft Project 2007*, available in Appendix A.

SUPPLEMENTS

The following supplemental materials are available when this text is used in a classroom setting. All of the teaching tools available with this text are provided to the instructor on CD-ROM or from *www.course.com*.

- **Electronic Instructor's Manual:** The Instructor's Manual that accompanies this textbook includes additional instructional material to assist in class preparation, including suggestions for lecture topics and additional discussion questions.

- **ExamView®:** This textbook is accompanied by ExamView, a powerful testing software package that allows instructors to create and administer printed, computer (LAN-based), and Internet exams. ExamView includes hundreds of questions that correspond to the topics covered in this text, enabling students to generate detailed study guides that include page references for further review. The computer-based and Internet testing components allow students to take exams at their computers, and also save the instructor time by grading each exam automatically.

- **PowerPoint Presentations:** This text comes with Microsoft PowerPoint slides for each chapter. These are included as a teaching aid for classroom presentation, to be made available to students on the network for chapter review, or to be printed for classroom distribution. Instructors can modify slides or add their own slides for additional topics they introduce to the class.

- **Solution Files:** Solutions to end-of-chapter questions can be found on the Instructor Resource CD-ROM and may also be found on the Course Technology Web site at *www.course.com*. The solutions are password protected.

- **Distance Learning:** Course Technology offers online WebCT and Blackboard (versions 5.0 and 6.0) courses for this text to provide the most complete and dynamic learning experience possible. When you add online content to one of your courses, you're adding a lot: automated tests, topic reviews, quick quizzes, and additional case projects with solutions. For more information on how to bring distance learning to your course, contact your local Course Technology sales representative.

- **Student Online Companion:** Visit the companion Web site for this text at *www.course.com/mis/pm2/schwalbe* for links to lecture notes, template files, interactive quizzes, Jeopardy games, podcasts, information for accessing VPMi Web-based project management software, and other helpful resources.

ACKNOWLEDGEMENTS

I never would have taken on another major book project without the help of many people. I would like to thank the staff at Course Technology for their dedication and hard work in helping me produce this book and in doing such an excellent job of marketing it. Tricia Coia, Patricia Shogren, Cathie DiMassa, and many more people did a great job in planning and executing all of the work involved in producing this book. It's amazing how many little details are involved in writing a good book, and Course Technology worked effectively to produce a high quality text.

I thank my many colleagues and experts in the field who contributed information to this book. Paul Sundby provided information on the construction industry, Mike Vinje shared best practice information, Nick Matteucci provided VPMi access, Jesse Freese provided the Fissure simulation software, Angela Jaskowiak provided feedback on the New Business Venture case study, and many other people provided input and inspiration. I really enjoy the network of project managers, authors, and consultants in this field who are passionate about improving the theory and practice of project management.

I also want to thank my students and colleagues at Augsburg College, the University of Minnesota, and corporate classes for providing input. I received many valuable comments from them on ways to improve my materials and courses. I am also grateful for the examples students provide and the questions they ask in classes. I learn new aspects of project management and teaching all the time by interacting with students, faculty, and staff.

Four faculty reviewers provided excellent feedback for me in writing this book. Gary Armstrong, Shippensburg University; Raffael Guidone, New York City College of Technology; Gilbert S. Leonard, Cy-Fair College; and Tom Norris, State University of New York at Cobleskill provided outstanding suggestions for improving the text.

Most of all, I am grateful to my family. Without their support, I never could have written this book. My wonderful husband, Dan, was very patient and supportive, as always. Our three children, Anne, Bobby, and Scott, continue to be very supportive of their mom's work. Our oldest, Anne, is now a teacher herself, teaching 9th grade English on the Rosebud Indian Reservation in South Dakota for the Teach for America program.

Bobby is a senior in college now, and he actually thinks it's cool that his mom wrote a textbook. Scott, now a freshman in high school, is glad that I can work at home a lot and likes seeing his name in print. Our children all understand the main reason why I write—I have a passion for educating future leaders of the world, including them.

As always, I am eager to receive your feedback on this book. Please send all feedback to me at schwalbe@augsburg.edu

Kathy Schwalbe, Ph.D., PMP
Augsburg College

ABOUT THE AUTHOR

Kathy Schwalbe is an Associate Professor in the Department of Business Administration at Augsburg College in Minneapolis, where she teaches courses in project management, problem solving for business, systems analysis and design, information systems projects, and electronic commerce. Kathy was also an adjunct faculty member at the University of Minnesota, where she taught a graduate-level course in project management in the engineering department. She also provides training and consulting services to several organizations and speaks at numerous conferences. Kathy's first job out of college was as a project manager in the Air Force. Kathy worked for 10 years in industry before entering academia in 1991. She was an Air Force officer, project manager, systems analyst, senior engineer, and information technology consultant. Kathy is an active member of PMI, having served as the Student Chapter Liaison for the Minnesota chapter, VP of Education for the Minnesota chapter, Editor of the ISSIG Review, member of PMI's test-writing team, and member of the OPM3 update team. She is currently the Director of Communications for PMI's Information Systems Specific Interest Group. Kathy earned her Ph.D. in Higher Education at the University of Minnesota, her MBA at Northeastern University's High Technology MBA program, and her B.S. in mathematics at the University of Notre Dame.

CHAPTER **1**

AN INTRODUCTION TO PROJECT, PROGRAM, AND PORTFOLIO MANAGEMENT

LEARNING OBJECTIVES

After reading this chapter, you will be able to:

- Understand the growing need for better project, program, and portfolio management

- Explain what a project is, provide examples of projects, list various attributes of projects, and discuss the triple constraint of project management

- Describe project management and key elements of the project management framework, including project stakeholders, project management knowledge areas, common tools and techniques, and project success factors

- Discuss the relationship between project, program, and portfolio management and their contribution to enterprise success

- Describe the project management profession, including suggested skills for project, program, and portfolio managers, the role of professional organizations such as the Project Management Institute, the importance of certification and ethics, and the growth of project and portfolio management software

OPENING CASE

Doug Armbruster, the chief executive officer (CEO) of Global Construction, Inc., was summarizing annual corporate highlights to the board of directors. When one of the board members asked what he was most proud of that year, Doug thought for a few seconds and then replied,

"Excellent question, Gabe. Honestly, I think the main reason we had record-breaking profits this year was because we have truly embraced the fact that we are a project-based organization. We have dramatically improved our ability to select and implement projects that help our company succeed. Our projects align with our business strategies, and we have consistent processes in place for getting things done. Marie Scott, our director of the Project Management Office, has done an outstanding job in making this happen. And believe me, it was not easy. It's never easy to implement changes across an entire company. But with this new capability to manage projects across the organization, I am very confident that we will have continued success in years to come."

INTRODUCTION

Many people and organizations today have a new or renewed interest in project management. In the past, project management primarily focused on providing schedule and resource data to top management in the military and construction industries. Today's project management involves much more, and people in every industry and every country manage projects. New technologies have become a significant factor in many organizations, and the use of interdisciplinary and global work teams has radically changed the work environment.

The following statistics demonstrate the significance of project management in today's society:

- A 2001 report showed that the United States spends $2.3 trillion on projects every year, and the world as a whole spends nearly $10 trillion on projects of all kinds. Projects, therefore, account for about one-fourth of the United States' and the world's gross domestic product.[1]
- In 2007, the average total annual compensation for a senior project manager was $104,776 in the United States, $111,412 in Australia, and $120,364 in the United Kingdom. The average total annual compensation of a program manager was $122,825 in the United States, $133,718 in Australia, and $165,489 in the United Kingdom. The average total compensation for a project management office (PMO) director was $134,422 in the United States, $125,197 in Australia, and $210,392 in the United Kingdom.[2]
- Project management certification continues to be one of the most popular certifications throughout the world, with over 220,000 active Project Management Professionals by the end of 2006. Certified individuals averaged a 16% pay increase from 2004 to 2005.[3]
- In the United States, the number-one reality television show in 2004, *The Apprentice,* portrayed the important role project managers play in business. Each week of the show, teams selected a project manager to lead them in accomplishing that week's project. The project manager was held partly

responsible for the team's success or failure. Whether you are trying to make money by selling lemonade, running a golf tournament, or developing a new product, project managers play a vital role to business success.

⊗ WHAT WENT WRONG?

In 1995, the Standish Group published an often-quoted study titled "The CHAOS Report" or simply "CHAOS." This prestigious consulting firm surveyed 365 information technology executive managers in the United States who managed more than 8,380 information technology application projects. As the title of the study suggests, the projects were in a state of chaos. United States companies spent more than $250 billion each year in the early 1990s on approximately 175,000 information technology application development projects. Examples of these projects included creating a new database for a state department of motor vehicles, developing a new system for car rental and hotel reservations, and implementing a client/ server architecture for the banking industry. The study reported that the overall success rate of information technology projects was only 16.2%. The surveyors defined success as meeting project goals on time and on budget. The study also found that more than 31% of information technology projects were canceled before completion, costing U.S. companies and government agencies more than $81 billion.[4]

In a more recent study, PricewaterhouseCoopers surveyed 200 companies from 30 different countries about their project management maturity and found that *over half of all projects fail*. They also found that only 2.5% of corporations consistently meet their targets for scope, time, and cost goals for all types of projects.[5] Chapter 8 includes more detailed information from this study.

Although several researchers question the methodology of the CHAOS studies, their popularity has prompted organizations throughout the world to examine their practices in managing projects. Managers are recognizing that to be successful, they need to be conversant with and use modern project management techniques. People from all types of disciplines—science, liberal arts, education, business, etc.—can benefit from basic project management principles. Individuals are realizing that to remain competitive, they must develop skills to effectively manage the professional and personal projects they undertake. They also realize that many of the concepts of project management, especially the interpersonal skills, will help them as they work with people on a day-to-day basis.

Many organizations claim that using project management provides advantages, such as:

- Better control of financial, physical, and human resources
- Improved customer relations
- Shorter development times
- Lower costs
- Higher quality and increased reliability
- Higher profit margins
- Improved productivity

- Better internal coordination
- Higher worker morale

In addition to project management, organizations are embracing program and portfolio management to address enterprise-level needs. This chapter introduces projects and project management; describes the differences between project, program, and portfolio management; discusses the role of the project, program, and portfolio manager; and provides important background information on these growing professions.

WHAT IS A PROJECT?

To discuss project management, it is important to understand the concept of a project. A **project** is "a temporary endeavor undertaken to create a unique product, service, or result."[6] Operations, on the other hand, is work done in organizations to sustain the business. Projects are different from operations in that they end when their objectives have been reached or when the project has been terminated.

Examples of Projects

Projects can be small or large and involve one person or thousands of people. They can be done in one day or take years to complete. Examples of projects include the following:

- A young couple hires a firm to design and build them a new house.
- A retail store manager works with employees to display a new clothing line.
- A college campus upgrades its technology infrastructure to provide wireless Internet access.
- A construction company designs and constructs a new office building for a client.
- A school implements new government standards for tracking student achievement.
- A group of musicians starts a company to help children develop their musical talents.
- A pharmaceutical company launches a new drug.
- A television network develops a system to allow viewers to vote for contestants and provide other feedback on programs.
- The automobile industry develops standards to streamline procurement.
- A government group develops a program to track child immunizations.

Project Attributes

As you can see, projects come in all shapes and sizes. The following attributes help define a project further:

- A *project has a unique purpose.* Every project should have a well-defined objective. For example, many people hire firms to design and build a new house, but each house, like each person, is unique.
- A *project is temporary.* A project has a definite beginning and a definite end. For a home construction project, owners usually have a date in mind when they'd like to move into their new homes.

- *A project is developed using progressive elaboration or in an iterative fashion.* Projects are often defined broadly when they begin, and as time passes, the specific details of the project become clearer. For example, there are many decisions that must be made in planning and building a new house. It works best to draft plans for owners to approve before more detailed plans are developed.
- *A project requires resources, often from various areas.* Resources include people, hardware, software, or other assets. Many different types of people and resources are needed to build a home.
- *A project should have a primary customer or sponsor.* Most projects have many interested parties, but someone must take the primary role of sponsorship. The **project sponsor** usually provides the direction and funding for the project.
- *A project involves uncertainty.* Because every project is unique, it is sometimes difficult to define the project's objectives clearly, estimate exactly how long it will take to complete, or determine how much it will cost. External factors also cause uncertainty, such as a supplier going out of business or a project team member needing unplanned time off. This uncertainty is one of the main reasons project management is so challenging.

It should not be difficult to explain the goals or purpose of a project. Unlike Dilbert, the cartoon character shown in Figure 1-1 who provides many examples of how not to manage projects, you should not have to make up words to describe a project!

DILBERT: © Scott Adams/Dist. by United Feature Syndicate, Inc.

FIGURE 1-1   Lost for words

A good project manager is crucial to a project's success. A **project manager** works with the project sponsor, the project team, and the other people involved in a project to meet project goals.

The Triple Constraint

Every project is constrained in different ways by its scope, time, and cost goals. These limitations are sometimes referred to in project management as the **triple constraint**. To create a successful project, a project manager must consider scope, time, and cost, and balance these three often-competing goals. He or she must consider the following:

- *Scope:* What work will be done as part of the project? What unique product, service, or result does the sponsor expect from the project?
- *Time:* How long should it take to complete the project? What is the project's schedule?
- *Cost:* What should it cost to complete the project? What is the project's budget?

Figure 1-2 illustrates the three dimensions of the triple constraint. Each area—scope, time, and cost—has a target at the beginning of the project. For example, a couple might initially plan to move into their new 2,000-square-foot home in six months and spend $300,000 on the entire project. These goals can be viewed as the discrete target goals, or the bull's-eye on the target. The couple will have to make many decisions along the way that might affect meeting those goals. They might need to increase the budget to meet scope and time goals or decrease the scope to meet time and budget goals. Because projects involve uncertainty and limited resources, projects rarely finish according to the discrete scope, time, and cost goals originally set. Instead of discrete target goals, it is often more realistic to set a range of goals, such as spending between $275,000 and $325,000 and having the home completed within five to seven months. These goals might mean hitting the target but not the bull's-eye.

Successful project management means meeting all three goals (scope, time, and cost)—and satisfying the project's sponsor!

Target

Scope goal

Cost goal

Time goal

FIGURE 1-2   The triple constraint of project management

Experienced project managers know that you must decide which aspect or aspects of the triple constraint are most important. If time is most important, you must often change the initial scope and/or cost goals to meet the schedule. For example, many people who plan weddings have to adjust scope and cost goals to meet their target wedding date. If scope goals are most important, you might need to adjust time and/or cost goals. For example, if a company wants to get a new drug to market, it must focus on scope goals and be willing to adjust time and cost as needed. If it is crucial to meet time and cost goals, the scope must be flexible. For example, if someone wants to move into a new home or apartment by a specific date for a specific cost, he/she must be flexible on scope goals. In any case, sponsors must provide some type of target goals for a project's scope, time, and cost.

Although the triple constraint describes how the basic elements of a project—scope, time, and cost—interrelate, other elements can also play significant roles. Quality is often a key factor in projects, as is customer or sponsor satisfaction. Some people, in fact, refer to the *"quadruple constraint"* of project management, including quality along with scope, time, and cost. Others believe that quality considerations, including customer satisfaction, must be inherent in setting the scope, time, and cost goals of a project. A project team may meet scope, time, and cost goals but fail to meet quality standards or satisfy their sponsor if they have not adequately addressed these concerns. The project manager should be communicating with the sponsor throughout the project to make sure the project meets his or her expectations.

How can you avoid the problems that occur when you meet scope, time, and cost goals but lose sight of quality or customer satisfaction? The answer is *good project management, which includes more than meeting the triple constraint.*

WHAT IS PROJECT MANAGEMENT?

Project management is "the application of knowledge, skills, tools, and techniques to project activities to meet project requirements."[7] Project managers must not only strive to meet specific scope, time, cost, and quality goals of projects, but also facilitate the entire process to meet the needs and expectations of the people involved in or affected by project activities. The Manhattan Project, which the United States military led to develop the atomic bomb, is considered to be the first project to use "modern" project management. General Leslie R. Groves was the project manager in charge of the overall management of the project's mission, schedule, and budget. Dr. Robert Oppenheimer led the technical management of this three-year, $2 billion project in the mid-1940s.

Figure 1-3 illustrates a framework to help you understand project management. Key elements of this framework include the project stakeholders, project management knowledge areas, project management tools and techniques, project success, and contribution of a portfolio of projects to the success of the entire enterprise. Each of these elements of project management is discussed in more detail in the following sections.

FIGURE 1-3 Project management framework

Project Stakeholders

Stakeholders are the people involved in or affected by project activities and include the project sponsor, project team, support staff, customers, users, suppliers, and even opponents to the project. These stakeholders often have very different needs and expectations. For example, there are several stakeholders involved in a home construction project.

- The project sponsors would be the potential new homeowners. They would be the people paying for the house and could be on a very tight budget, so they would expect the contractor to provide accurate estimates of the costs involved in building the house. They would also need a realistic idea of when they could move in and what type of home they could afford given their budget constraints. The new homeowners would have to make important decisions to keep the costs of the house within their budget. Can they afford to finish the basement right away? If they can afford to finish the basement, will it affect the projected move-in date? In this example, the project sponsors are also the customers and users for the resulting product, which is the house.

- The project manager in this example would normally be the general contractor responsible for building the house. He or she would need to work with all the project stakeholders to meet their needs and expectations.

- The project team for building the house would include several construction workers, electricians, carpenters, and so on. These stakeholders would need to know exactly what work they must do and when they need to do it. They would need to know if the required materials and equipment will be at the construction site or if they are expected to provide them. Their work would need to be coordinated because there are many interrelated factors involved. For example, the carpenter cannot put in kitchen cabinets until the walls are completed.

- Support staff might include the employers of the homeowners, the general contractor's administrative assistant, and other people who support the stakeholders. The employers of the homeowners might expect their employees to complete their work but allow some flexibility so that they can visit the building site or take phone calls related to the building of the house. The contractor's administrative assistant would support the project by coordinating meetings between the buyers, contractor, suppliers, and so on.
- Building a house requires many suppliers. The suppliers would provide the wood, windows, flooring materials, appliances, and so on. Suppliers would expect exact details on what items they need to provide, where and when to deliver those items, and so on.
- Additional stakeholders would include the city council and mayor, who would be interested in increasing revenues. Also, the local housing inspector would be a stakeholder, concerned with ensuring that everything meets specific codes and regulations.
- There might or might not be opponents to a project. In this example, there might be a neighbor who opposes the project because the workers are making so much noise that she cannot concentrate on her work at home or her sleeping children might be awakened. She might interrupt the workers to voice her complaints or even file a formal complaint. Alternatively, the neighborhood might have association rules concerning new home design and construction. If the homeowners did not follow these rules, they might have to halt construction due to legal issues.

As you can see from this example, there are many different stakeholders on projects, and they all have different interests. Stakeholders' needs and expectations are important in the beginning and throughout the life of a project. Successful project managers develop good relationships with project stakeholders to understand and meet their needs and expectations.

Project Management Knowledge Areas

Project management knowledge areas describe the key competencies that project managers must develop. The center of Figure 1-3 shows the nine knowledge areas of project management. The four core knowledge areas of project management include project scope, time, cost, and quality management. These are core knowledge areas because they lead to specific project objectives. Brief descriptions of each core knowledge area are as follows:

- **Project scope management** involves working with all appropriate stakeholders to define, gain written agreement for, and manage all the work required to complete the project successfully.
- **Project time management** includes estimating how long it will take to complete the work, developing an acceptable project schedule given cost-effective use of available resources, and ensuring timely completion of the project.
- **Project cost management** consists of preparing and managing the budget for the project.
- **Project quality management** ensures that the project will satisfy the stated and implied needs for which it was undertaken.

The four facilitating knowledge areas of project management are human resource, communications, risk, and procurement management. These are called facilitating areas because they are the processes through which the project objectives are achieved. Brief descriptions of each facilitating knowledge area are as follows:

- **Project human resource management** is concerned with making effective use of the people involved with the project.
- **Project communications management** involves generating, collecting, disseminating, and storing project information.
- **Project risk management** includes identifying, analyzing, and responding to risks related to the project.
- **Project procurement management** involves acquiring or procuring goods and services for a project from outside the performing organization.

Project integration management, the ninth knowledge area, is an overarching function that affects and is affected by all of the other knowledge areas. It involves coordinating the other knowledge areas, anticipating and dealing with issues, and making decisions each day about what is in the best interest of the entire project. Project managers must have knowledge and skills in all nine of these areas.

Project Management Tools and Techniques

Thomas Carlyle, a famous historian and author, stated, "Man is a tool-using animal. Without tools he is nothing, with tools he is all." As the world continues to become more complex, it is even more important for people to develop and use tools, especially for managing important projects. **Project management tools and techniques** assist project managers and their teams in carrying out work in all nine knowledge areas. For example, some popular time-management tools and techniques include Gantt charts, project network diagrams, and critical-path analysis. Figure 1-4 lists some commonly used tools and techniques by knowledge area. Note that a tool or technique is much more than a software package. You will learn more about several of these tools and techniques throughout this text, and examples of applying them are also provided.

A 2006 survey of 753 project and program managers was conducted to rate several project management tools. Respondents were asked to rate tools on a scale of 1–5 (low to high) based on the extent of their use and the potential of the tools to help improve project success. "Super tools" were defined as those that had high use and high potential for improving project success. Super tools that could be used more extensively include software for task scheduling (such as project management software), scope statements, requirements analyses, and lessons-learned reports. Super tools that are already extensively used include progress reports, kick-off meetings, Gantt charts, and change requests. These super tools are bolded in Figure 1-4.[8] Of course, different tools can be more effective in different situations. It is crucial for project managers and their team members to determine which tools will be most useful for their particular projects.

Knowledge area/category	Tools and techniques
Integration management	Project selection methods, project management methodologies, stakeholder analyses, project charters, project management plans, **project management software**, **change requests**, change control boards, project review meetings, **lessons-learned reports**
Scope management	**Scope statements**, **work breakdown structures**, mind maps, statements of work, **requirements analyses**, scope management plans, scope verification techniques, scope change controls
Time management	**Gantt charts**, project network diagrams, critical-path analyses, crashing, fast tracking, schedule performance measurements
Cost management	Net present value, return on investment, payback analyses, earned value management, project portfolio management, cost estimates, cost management plans, cost baselines
Quality management	Quality metrics, checklists, quality control charts, Pareto diagrams, fishbone diagrams, maturity models, statistical methods
Human resource management	Motivation techniques, empathic listening, responsibility assignment matrices, project organizational charts, resource histograms, team building exercises
Communications management	Communications management plans, **kickoff meetings**, conflict management, communications media selection, **status and progress reports**, virtual communications, templates, project Web sites
Risk management	Risk management plans, risk registers, probability/impact matrices, risk rankings
Procurement management	Make-or-buy analyses, contracts, requests for proposals or quotes, source selections, supplier evaluation matrices

FIGURE 1-4 Common project management tools and techniques by knowledge area

☑ WHAT WENT RIGHT?

Follow-up studies done by the Standish Group (see the previously quoted "CHAOS" study in the What Went Wrong? passage) showed some improvement in the statistics for information technology projects in the past decade:

- The number of successful IT projects has more than doubled, from 16% in 1994 to 35% in 2006.
- The number of failed projects decreased from 31% in 1994 to 19% in 2006.
- The United States spent more money on IT projects in 2006 than 1994 ($346 billion and $250 billion, respectively), but the amount of money wasted on challenged projects (those that did not meet scope, time, or cost goals, but were completed) and failed projects was down to $53 billion in 2006 compared to $140 billion in 1994.[9]

Even though there have been significant improvements in managing information technology projects, there is still much room for improvement in that industry as well as in many other industries. The best news is that project managers are learning how to succeed more often. "The reasons for the increase in successful projects vary. First, the average cost of a project has been more than cut in half. Better tools have been created to monitor and control progress and better skilled project managers with better management processes are being used. The fact that there are processes is significant in itself."[10]

Despite its advantages, project management is not a silver bullet that guarantees success on all projects. Some projects, such as those involving new technologies, have a higher degree of uncertainty, so it is more difficult to meet their scope, time, and cost goals. Project management is a very broad, often complex discipline. What works on one project might not work on another, so it is essential for project managers to continue to develop their knowledge and skills in managing projects. It is also important to learn from the mistakes and successes of others.

Project Success

How do you define the success or failure of a project? There are several ways to define project success. The following list outlines a few common criteria for measuring project success as applied to the sample project of building a new 2,000-square-foot home within six months for $300,000:

- The project met scope, time, and cost goals. If the home was 2,000 square feet and met other scope requirements, was completed in six months, and cost $300,000, we could call it a successful project based on these criteria. Note that the "CHAOS" studies mentioned in the What Went Wrong? and What Went Right? examples used this definition of success.

- The project satisfied the sponsor. Even if the project met initial scope, time, and cost goals, the couple paying for the house might not be satisfied. Perhaps the project manager never returned their calls and was rude to them or made important decisions without their approval. Perhaps the quality of some of the construction or materials was not acceptable. If the customers were not happy about important aspects of the project, it would be deemed a failure based on this criterion. Many organizations implement a customer satisfaction rating system for projects to measure project success.
- The results of the project met its main objective, such as making or saving a certain amount of money, providing a good return on investment (ROI), or simply making the sponsors happy. If the couple liked their new home and neighborhood after they lived there for a while, even if it cost more or took longer to build or the project manager was rude to them, it would be a successful project based on this criterion. As another example, suppose the owners actually wanted to keep the house for just a few years and then sell it for a good return. If that happened, the couple would deem the project a success, regardless of other factors involved. Note that for many projects done to meet ROI objectives, financial success cannot be determined until some time after the project is completed.

Project managers play a vital role in helping projects succeed. Project managers work with the project sponsors, the project team, and the other people involved in a project to meet project goals. They also work with the sponsor to define success for that particular project. Good project managers do not assume that their definition of success is the same as the sponsor's. They take the time to understand their sponsor's expectations. For example, if you are building a home for someone, find out what is most important:

- Meeting scope, time, and cost goals of the project to build the home
- Satisfying other needs, such as communicating in a certain way
- Being sure the project delivers a certain result, such as providing the home of the owner's dreams or a good return on investment.

The success criterion should help you develop key performance indicators needed to track project success.

PROGRAM AND PROJECT PORTFOLIO MANAGEMENT

As mentioned earlier, about one-quarter of the world's gross domestic product is spent on projects. Projects make up a significant portion of work in most business organizations or enterprises, and successfully managing those projects is crucial to enterprise success. Two important concepts that help projects meet enterprise goals are the use of programs and project portfolio management.

Programs

A **program** is "a group of related projects managed in a coordinated way to obtain benefits and control not available from managing them individually."[11] As you can imagine, it is often more economical to group projects together to help streamline management, staffing, purchasing, and other work. The following are examples of programs (Figure 1-5 illustrates the first program in the list).

- A construction firm has a program for building one hundred residential single-family homes in a particular neighborhood. Each home is a separate project for a specific homeowner—the sponsor—but the entire development is a program. A similar scenario applies to a program involving several apartment-building projects in a particular region. There would be several benefits to managing these projects under one program, such as getting planning approvals for all the homes at once, hiring workers who could work on more than one home, and purchasing common materials in bulk to earn discounts.
- A clothing firm has a program to analyze customer buying patterns. Projects under this program might include one to send out and analyze electronic surveys, one to conduct several focus groups in different geographic locations with different types of buyers, and one to develop an information system to help collect and analyze current customers' buying patterns.
- A government agency has a program for children's services, which includes a project to provide prenatal care for expectant mothers, a project to immunize newborns and young children, and a project for developmental testing for preschool children.

FIGURE 1-5   Sample program

A **program manager** provides leadership and direction for the project managers heading the projects within the program. Program managers also coordinate the efforts of project teams, functional groups, suppliers, and operations staff supporting the projects to ensure that project products and processes are implemented to maximize benefits. Program managers are responsible for more than the delivery of project results; they are change agents responsible for the success of products and processes produced by those projects.

Program managers often have review meetings with all their project managers to share important information and coordinate important aspects of each project. Many program managers worked as project managers earlier in their careers, and they enjoy sharing their wisdom and expertise with their project managers. Effective program managers recognize that managing a program is much more complex than managing a single project. They know that technical and project management skills are not enough. In addition to skills required for project managers, program managers must also possess strong business knowledge, leadership capability, and communication skills.

Project Portfolio Management

In many organizations, project managers also support an emerging business strategy of **project portfolio management** (also called **portfolio management** in this text), in which organizations group and manage projects and programs as a portfolio of investments that contribute to the entire enterprise's success. Pacific Edge Software's product manager, Eric Burke, defines project portfolio management as "the continuous process of selecting and managing the optimum set of project initiatives that deliver maximum business value."[12]

The Project Management Institute (PMI) published the *Organizational Project Management Maturity Model (OPM3): Knowledge Foundation* in 2003, which describes the importance not only of managing individual projects or programs well, but also of following organizational project management to align projects, programs, and portfolios with strategic goals. OPM3 is a standard organizations can use to measure their organizational project management maturity against a comprehensive set of best practices, as described in more detail in Chapter 8 of this text.

Portfolio managers need to understand how projects fit into the bigger picture of the organization, especially in terms of finances and business risks. They create portfolios based on meeting specific organizational goals, such as maximizing the value of the portfolio or making effective use of limited resources. Portfolio managers help their organizations make wise investment decisions by helping to select and analyze projects from a strategic perspective. Portfolio managers might or might not have previous experience as project or program managers. It is most important that they have strong financial and analytical skills and understand how projects and programs can contribute to meeting strategic goals.

Figure 1-6 illustrates the differences between project management and project portfolio management. Notice that the main distinction is a focus on meeting tactical or strategic goals. Tactical goals are generally more specific and short-term than strategic goals, which emphasize long-term goals for an organization. Individual projects often address tactical goals, whereas project portfolio management addresses strategic goals. Project management addresses questions related to how well projects are managed in terms of meeting scope, time, and costs goals and stakeholder expectations. Project portfolio management addresses questions related to what projects are being done and how well they meet organizational goals, such as making good investments and being competitive.

Project management
- Are we carrying out projects well?
- Are projects on time and on budget?
- Do project stakeholders know what they should be doing?

Project portfolio management
- Are we working on the right projects?
- Are we investing in the right areas?
- Do we have the right resources to be competitive?

FIGURE 1-6   Project management compared to project portfolio management

There can be portfolios for all types of projects. The following list outlines a few examples:

- In a construction firm, strategic goals might include increasing profit margins on large projects, decreasing costs on supplies, and improving skill levels of key workers. Projects could be grouped into these three categories for portfolio management purposes.

- In a clothing firm, strategic goals might include improving the effectiveness of information technology, introducing new clothing lines, reducing inventory costs, and increasing customer satisfaction. These might be the main categories for the firm's portfolio of projects.

- A government agency for children's services could group projects into a portfolio based on such key strategies as improving health and providing education to help make decisions on the best way to use available funds and resources.

Organizations group projects into portfolios to help them make better investment decisions, such as increasing, decreasing, discontinuing, or changing specific projects or programs based on financial performance, risks, resource utilization, and similar factors that affect business value and strategy. For example, if a construction firm has much higher profit margins on apartment buildings than single-family homes, it might choose to pursue more apartment-building projects. The firm might also create a new project to investigate ways to increase profits for single-family-home projects. On the other hand, if the company has too many projects focused on financial performance and not enough focused on improving its workforce, the portfolio manager might suggest initiating more projects to support that strategic goal.

By grouping projects into portfolios, organizations can better tie their projects to meeting strategic goals. Chapter 2 provides more information on this topic and on approaches for creating a project portfolio. Portfolio management can also help an organization do a better job of managing its human resources by hiring, training, and retaining workers to support the projects in the organization's portfolio. For example, if the construction firm needs more people with experience in building apartment buildings, it can make necessary adjustments by hiring or training current workers in the necessary skills. In summary, portfolio managers help select projects, program managers oversee groups of related projects, and project managers lead their specific projects.

THE PROJECT MANAGEMENT PROFESSION

As you can imagine, good project managers should have and continue to develop many skills. Good program and portfolio managers often need additional skills and experience in managing projects and understanding organizational strategies. This section describes some of the skills that will help you manage projects, and you will learn many more throughout this text. If you are serious about considering a career in project management, you should consider becoming a certified project management professional. You should also be familiar with some of the many project management software products available on the market today.

Suggested Skills for Project, Program, and Portfolio Managers

Project managers and their teams must develop knowledge and skills in the following areas:

- All nine project management knowledge areas
- The application area
- The project environment
- General management
- Human relations

An earlier section of this chapter introduced the nine project management knowledge areas, as well as some tools and techniques that project managers use. The application area refers to the application to which project management is applied. For example, a project manager responsible for building houses or apartment buildings should understand the construction industry, including standards and regulations important to that industry and those types of construction projects. A project manager leading a large software development project must know a lot about that application area. A project manager in education, music, the government, and so on must understand those application areas.

The project environment differs based on the organization and industry, but there are some skills that will help in most project environments. These skills include change management and understanding how organizations work within their social, political, and physical environments. Project managers must be comfortable leading and handling change, because most projects introduce changes in organizations and involve changes within the projects themselves. Project managers need to understand the organizations and industries they work in and how products are developed and how services are provided. For example, it takes different skills and behaviors to manage a project for a Fortune 100 company in the United States than it does to manage a government project for a new business in Poland or India. It also takes different skills and behaviors to manage a project in the construction industry than one in the entertainment or pharmaceutical industry.

Project managers should also possess general management knowledge and skills. They should understand important topics related to financial management, accounting, procurement, sales, marketing, contracts, manufacturing, distribution, logistics, the supply chain, strategic planning, tactical planning, operations management, organizational structures and behavior, personnel administration, compensation, benefits, career paths, and health and safety practices. On some projects, it will be critical for the project manager to have substantial experience in one or several of these general management areas. On other projects, the project manager can delegate detailed responsibility for some of these areas to a team member, support staff, or even a supplier. Even so, the project managers must be intelligent and experienced enough to know which of these areas are most important and who is qualified to do the work. They must also make and/or take responsibility for all key project decisions.

Achieving high performance on projects requires human relations—or soft—skills. Some of these soft skills include effective communication, influence within the organization to get things done, leadership, motivation, negotiation, conflict management, and problem solving. Project managers must lead their project teams by providing vision, delegating work, creating an energetic and positive environment, and setting an example of appropriate and effective behavior. Project managers must focus on teamwork skills to use their people effectively. They need to be able to motivate different types of people and develop esprit de corps within the project team and with other project stakeholders. Project managers must especially develop a good relationship with the project sponsor.

 MEDIA SNAPSHOT

In 2004, millions of people in the United States watched the first season of the reality television show called *The Apprentice,* in which contestants vied for a high-level position working for Donald Trump. (The show started its seventh season in 2007.) Each week, Trump fired one contestant and told them bluntly why they were fired or why they were spared. Trump's reasons provide insight into improving project management skills, as follows:

- Leadership and professionalism are crucial. No matter how smart you are (the first candidate fired had degrees in medicine and business), you must be professional in how you deal with people and display some leadership potential.
- Know what your sponsor expects from the project, and learn from your mistakes. Jason, the second person and first project manager fired, decided not to take the time to meet with his project sponsors, causing his team to fail their assignment. Mr. Trump wanted everyone to remember that crucial mistake.
- Trust your team and delegate decisions. Sam had several problems as a team member and project manager, but his lack of trust in and respect for and from his teammates led to his downfall.

continued

- Know the business. Restaurants often have the highest profit margins on certain items, such as drinks. Find out what's most important to your business when running projects. One team focused on increasing bar sales, which generated the most profit, and easily won the competition that week.
- Stand up for yourself. When Trump fired Kristi over two other candidates, he explained his decision by saying that Kristi didn't fight for herself, whereas the other two women did.
- Be a team player. Tammy clearly did not get along with her team, and no one supported her in the boardroom when her team lost.
- Don't be overly emotional and always stay organized. Erika had a difficult time leading her team in selling Trump Ice, and she became flustered when they did not get credit for sales because their paperwork was not done correctly. Her emotions were evident in the boardroom when she was fired.
- Work on projects and for people you believe in. Kwame's team selected an artist based on her profit potential even though he and other teammates disliked her work. The other team picked an artist they liked, and they easily outsold Kwame's team.
- Think outside the box. Troy led his team in trying to make the most money selling rickshaw rides using traditional techniques. The other team brainstormed ideas and decided to sell advertising space on the rickshaws, which was a huge success.
- There is some luck involved in project management, and you should always aim high. Nick and Amy were teamed against Bill, Troy, and Kwame to rent out a party room for the highest price. Troy's team seemed very organized and did get a couple of good bids, but Nick and Amy didn't seem to have any real prospects. They got lucky when one potential client came back at the last minute and agreed to a much higher than normal price.

Importance of Leadership Skills

In a popular study, one hundred project managers listed the characteristics they believed were critical for effective project management and the characteristics that made project managers ineffective. Figure 1-7 lists the results. The study found that effective project managers provide leadership by example, and are visionary, technically competent, decisive, good communicators, and good motivators. They also stand up to top management when necessary, support team members, and encourage new ideas. The study also found that respondents believed that *positive leadership or leading by example contributes the most to project success*. The most important characteristics and behaviors of a positive leader include being a team builder and communicator, having high self-esteem, focusing on results, demonstrating trust and respect, and setting goals.

Effective project managers	Ineffective project managers
Lead by example	Set bad examples
Are visionaries	Are not self-assured
Are technically competent	Lack technical expertise
Are decisive	Avoid or delay making decisions
Are good communicators	Are poor communicators
Are good motivators	Are poor motivators

Zimmerer, Thomas W., and Mahmoud M. Yasin. "A Leadership Profile of American Project Managers." *Project Management Journal* (March 1998), 31–38.

FIGURE 1-7 Most significant characteristics of effective and ineffective project managers

Leadership and *management* are terms often used interchangeably, although there are differences. Generally, a **leader** focuses on long-term goals and big-picture objectives while inspiring people to reach those goals. A **manager** often deals with the day-to-day details of meeting specific goals. People have expressed the difference in various ways: "Managers do things right, and leaders do the right things"; "Leaders determine the vision, and managers achieve the vision"; "You lead people and manage things."

However, project managers often take on the role of both leader and manager. Good project managers know that people make or break projects, so they must set a good example to lead their team to success. They are aware of the greater needs of their stakeholders and organizations, so they are visionary in guiding their current projects and in suggesting future ones.

Another recent study identified the 10 most important skills and competencies for effective project managers. Figure 1-8 shows the results.

1. People skills
2. Leadership
3. Listening
4. Integrity, ethical behavior, consistent
5. Strong at building trust
6. Verbal communication
7. Strong at building teams
8. Conflict resolution, conflict management06
9. Critical thinking, problem solving
10. Understands, balances priorities

Krahn, Jennifer. "Effective Project Leadership: A Combination of Project Manager Skills and Competencies in Context," PMI Research Conference Proceedings (July 2006).

FIGURE 1-8 The 10 most important skills and competencies for project managers

Respondents were also asked what skills and competencies were most important in various project situations:

- *Large projects*: Leadership, relevant prior experience, planning, people skills, verbal communication, and team-building skills were most important.
- *High uncertainty projects*: Risk management, expectation management, leadership, people skills, and planning skills were most important.
- *Very novel projects*: Leadership, people skills, having vision and goals, self confidence, expectations management, and listening skills were most important.

Notice that a few additional skills and competencies not cited in the top 10 list were mentioned when people thought about the context of a project. To be the most effective, project managers require a changing mix of skills and competencies depending on the project being delivered.

As mentioned earlier, program managers need the same skills as project managers, plus a few more. They often rely on their past experience as project managers, strong business knowledge, leadership capability, and communication skills to handle the responsibility of overseeing the multiple projects that make up their programs. It is most important that portfolio managers have strong financial and analytical skills and understand how projects and programs can contribute to meeting strategic goals.

Companies that excel in project, program, and portfolio management grow project leaders, emphasizing development of business and communication skills. Instead of thinking of leaders and managers as specific people, it is better to think of people as having leadership skills—such as being visionary and inspiring—and management skills—such as being organized and effective. Therefore, the best project, program, and portfolio managers have leadership and management characteristics; they are visionary yet focused on the bottom line. Above all else, they focus on achieving positive results.

 BEST PRACTICE

A **best practice** is "an optimal way recognized by industry to achieve a stated goal or objective."[13] Robert Butrick, author of *The Project Workout*, wrote an article on best practices in project management for the *Ultimate Business Library's Best Practice* book. He suggests that organizations need to follow basic principles of project management, including these two mentioned earlier in this chapter:

- Make sure your projects are driven by your strategy. Be able to demonstrate how each project you undertake fits your business strategy, and screen out unwanted projects as soon as possible.
- Engage your stakeholders. Ignoring stakeholders often leads to project failure. Be sure to engage stakeholders at all stages of a project, and encourage teamwork and commitment at all times. Use leadership and open communications to make things happen.[14]

Project Management Certification

Professional certification is an important factor in recognizing and ensuring quality in a profession. The Project Management Institute (PMI) is a global professional society. PMI provides certification as a **Project Management Professional (PMP)**—someone who has documented sufficient project experience and education, agreed to follow the code of ethics and professional conduct, and demonstrated knowledge of the field of project management by passing a comprehensive examination.

The number of people earning PMP certification continues to increase. In 1993, there were about 1,000 certified project management professionals. By the end of December 2006, there were 221,144 certified project management professionals.[15] Figure 1-9 shows the rapid growth in the number of people earning project management professional certification from 1993 to 2006. Although most PMPs are in the United States and Canada, the PMP credential is growing in popularity in several countries, such as Japan, China, and India.

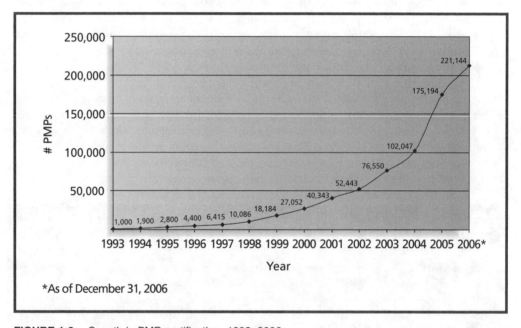

FIGURE 1-9 Growth in PMP certification, 1993–2006

Some organizations are requiring that all project managers be PMP certified. Project management certification is also enabling professionals throughout the world to share a common base of knowledge. For example, any person with PMP certification can list, describe, and use the nine project management knowledge areas, as described in PMI's *Guide to the Project Management Body of Knowledge (PMBOK® Guide)*. Sharing a common base of knowledge is important because it helps advance the theory and practice of project management. Consult PMI's Web site at *www.pmi.org* for more information on PMP certification and Appendix B of this text for details on PMP as well as other related certifications. This text focuses on PMI's project management methodology. Additional methodologies are discussed in Chapter 3.

Ethics in Project Management

Ethics, loosely defined, is a set of principles that guide our decision making based on personal values of what is "right" and "wrong." Making ethical decisions is an important part of our personal and professional lives because it generates trust and respect with other people. Project managers often face ethical dilemmas. For example, several projects involve different payment methods. If a project manager can make more money by doing a job poorly, should he or she do the job poorly? If a project manager is personally opposed to the development of nuclear weapons, should he or she refuse to manage a project that helps produce them? It is important for project managers to make decisions in an ethical manner.

In 2007, PMI developed a new Code of Ethics and Professional Conduct that applies not only to PMPs, but to all PMI members and volunteers. PMI states that it is vital to conduct work in an ethical manner. Conducting work in an ethical manner helps the profession earn the confidence of the public, employers, employees, and project team members. The Code of Ethics and Professional Conduct includes short chapters addressing vision and applicability, responsibility, respect, fairness, and honesty. The following excerpt from the code defines ethical behavior.

"As practitioners in the global project management community:

2.2.1 We make decisions and take actions based on the best interests of society, public safety, and the environment.

2.2.2 We accept only those assignments that are consistent with our background, experience, skills, and qualifications.

2.2.3 We fulfill the commitments that we undertake—we do what we say we will do.

3.2.1 We inform ourselves about the norms and customs of others and avoid engaging in behaviors they might consider disrespectful.

3.2.2 We listen to others' points of view, seeking to understand them.

3.2.3 We approach directly those persons with whom we have a conflict or disagreement.

4.2.1 We demonstrate transparency in our decision-making process.

4.2.2 We constantly reexamine our impartiality and objectivity, taking corrective action as appropriate.

4.3.1 We proactively and fully disclose any real or potential conflicts of interest to appropriate stakeholders.

5.2.1 We earnestly seek to understand the truth.

5.2.2 We are truthful in our communications and in our conduct."[16]

Project Management Software

Unlike the cobbler neglecting to make shoes for his own children, the project management and software development communities have definitely responded to the need to provide more software to assist in managing projects. The Project Management Center, a Web site for people involved in project management, provides an alphabetical directory of more than 300 project management software solutions (*www.infogoal.com/pmc*). This site and others demonstrate the growth in available project management software products, especially Web-based tools. Deciding which project management software to use has become a project in itself. This section provides a summary of the basic types of project management software available and references for finding more information.

FREE TRIAL SOFTWARE

As mentioned on the resources page in the front of this text, a 60-day evaluation copy of Microsoft Project Professional 2007 is included on the CD-ROM provided with this text. Appendix A includes a *Guide to Using Microsoft Project 2007*, which will help you develop hands-on skills using this most popular project management software tool today. You can also access a trial version of VPMi Express—a Web-based product from VCS (*www.vcsonline.com*)—by following the information provided on the resources page in the front of this text and on the companion Web site. You will see example screens from both of these products in this text. You can also download free trials of these and many other software tools.

Many people still use basic productivity software, such as Microsoft Word or Microsoft Excel, to perform many project management functions, such as determining project scope, time, and cost; assigning resources; and preparing project documentation. People often use productivity software instead of specialized project management software because they already have it and know how to use it. However, there are hundreds of project management software tools that provide specific functionality for managing projects. These project management software tools can be divided into three general categories based on functionality and price:

- *Low-end tools:* These tools provide basic project management features and generally cost less than $200 per user. They are often recommended for small projects and single users. Most of these tools allow users to create Gantt charts, which cannot be done easily using current productivity software. Top Ten Reviews listed MinuteMan ($49) and Project Kickstart ($129.95) in their list of top 10 project management software tools for 2006.[17] Several companies provide add-in features to Excel (see *www.business-spreadsheets.com*) to provide basic project management functions using a familiar software product.

- *Midrange tools:* A step up from low-end tools, midrange tools are designed to handle larger projects, multiple users, and multiple projects. All of these tools can produce Gantt charts and network diagrams, and can assist in critical-path analysis, resource allocation, project tracking, status reporting, and so on. Prices range from about $200 to $600 per user, and several tools require additional server software for using work-group features. Microsoft Project is still the most widely used project management software today, and there is also an enterprise version, as described briefly below and in Appendix A. Top Ten Reviews listed Microsoft Project as their number one choice ($599), along with Milestones ($219). A product called Copper also made the top 10 list, with a price of $999 for up to 50 users. Note that students and educators can purchase software like Microsoft Project 2007 at reduced prices from sites like *www.journeyed.com*, and anyone can download a trial version from Microsoft's Web site. You can also download trial versions of many other project management software tools from the suppliers' Web sites.
- *High-end tools:* Another category of project management software is high-end tools, sometimes referred to as enterprise project management software. These tools provide robust capabilities to handle very large projects, dispersed work groups, and enterprise functions that summarize and combine individual project information to provide project portfolio management information. These products are generally licensed on a per-user basis, integrate with enterprise database management software, and are accessible via the Internet. In mid 2002, Microsoft introduced the first version of their Enterprise Project Management software, and in 2003, they introduced the Microsoft Enterprise Project Management solution, which was updated in 2007 to include Microsoft Office Project Server 2007 and Microsoft Office Project Portfolio Server 2007. Several inexpensive, Web-based products that provide enterprise and portfolio management capabilities are also on the market. For example, VPMi Express (*www.vcsonline.com*) is available for a low monthly fee per user (see the front cover of this text for free trial information). See the Project Management Center Web site (*www.infogoal.com/pmc*) or Top Ten Reviews (*http://project-management-software-review.toptenreviews.com*) for links to many companies that provide project management software.

Figures 1-10 and 1-11 provide sample screens from two different project management software tools. Figure 1-10 shows a sample screen from Microsoft's Enterprise Project Management Solution, displaying all published projects in a company's portfolio sorted by country. This particular view shows red, yellow, or green symbols (shown in different shades of gray in the figure) indicating the status of each project in terms of meeting schedule and budget goals.

FIGURE 1-10   Sample screen from the Microsoft Enterprise Project Management Solution

Figure 1-11 shows a sample screen from VCS's VPMi Express software. This totally Web-based tool has a streamlined interface to make it easy to keep track of multiple projects. See the resources page in the front of this text and the companion Web site for this chapter for instructions on using a free trial version of VPMi Express. You will learn more about using project management software and portfolio management features in later chapters.

FIGURE 1-11 Sample screen from VPMi Express Software by VCS

By the end of the twentieth century, people in virtually every industry around the globe began to investigate and apply different aspects of project, program, and portfolio management. The sophistication and effectiveness with which organizations use these concepts and tools today is influencing the way companies do business, use resources, and respond to market requirements with speed and accuracy.

As mentioned earlier, there are many reasons to study project, program, and portfolio management. The number of projects continues to grow, the complexity of these projects continues to increase, and the profession of project management continues to expand and mature. Many colleges, universities, and companies now offer courses related to various aspects of project, program, and portfolio management. You can even earn bachelor's, master's, and doctoral degrees in project management at over 235 institutions worldwide.[18] The growing number of projects and the evidence that good project management can really make a difference continue to contribute to the growth of this field.

CASE WRAP-UP

Another board member asked the CEO to describe more about what the PMO director did to help the company become more successful at managing projects. Doug explained how Marie Scott worked with him and all of the vice presidents to reorganize several parts of the company to support their new emphasis on project, program, and project portfolio management. They formed a project team to implement a Web-based project management software tool across the enterprise. They formed another team to develop project-based reward systems for all employees. They also authorized funds for a project to educate all employees in project management and to develop a mentoring program for project, program, and project portfolio managers. Doug and Marie had successfully convinced everyone that effectively selecting and managing projects was crucial to their company's future. The board and the company's shareholders were very pleased with the results.

Chapter Summary

There is a new or renewed interest in project management today as the number of projects continues to grow and their complexity continues to increase. All types of people from all types of disciplines—science, liberal arts, education, business, etc.—can benefit from basic project management principles and skills. The success rate of information technology projects has more than doubled since 1995, but still only about one-third are successful in meeting scope, time, and cost goals. A recent global study by PricewaterhouseCoopers found that over half of all projects fail, and only 2.5% of corporations consistently meet their targets for scope, time, and cost goals for all types of projects. Using a more disciplined approach to managing projects can help organizations succeed.

A project is a temporary endeavor undertaken to create a unique product, service, or result. Projects are unique, temporary, and developed incrementally; they require resources, have a sponsor, and involve uncertainty. The triple constraint of project management refers to managing the scope, time, and cost dimensions of a project.

Project management is the application of knowledge, skills, tools, and techniques to project activities to meet project requirements. Stakeholders are the people involved in or affected by project activities. A framework for project management includes the project stakeholders, project management knowledge areas, project management tools and techniques, and project success. The nine knowledge areas are project integration management, scope, time, cost, quality, human resource, communications, risk, and procurement management. There are many tools and techniques for project management, including project management software, scope statements, requirements analyses, lessons-learned reports, progress reports, kick-off meetings, Gantt charts, and change requests. Project success can be defined in different ways, so it is important for project managers to define success for each unique project.

A program is a group of related projects managed in a coordinated way to obtain benefits and control not available from managing them individually. Project portfolio management involves organizing and managing projects and programs as a portfolio of investments that contribute to the entire enterprise's success. Portfolio management emphasizes meeting strategic goals, whereas project management focuses on tactical goals.

The profession of project management continues to grow and mature. Project, program, and portfolio managers play key roles in helping projects and organizations succeed. They must perform various duties; possess many skills; and continue to develop skills in project management, general management, and their particular application area. Soft skills, especially leadership, are particularly important for project, program, and portfolio managers. The Project Management Institute (PMI) is an international professional society that provides Project Management Professional (PMP) certification and upholds a code of ethics. Today, hundreds of project management software products are available to assist people in managing projects.

Quick Quiz

1. Approximately what percentage of the world's gross domestic product is spent on projects?

   a. 10%

   b. 25%

   c. 50%

   d. 75%

2. Which of the following is not a potential advantage of using good project management?

   a. shorter development times

   b. higher worker morale

   c. lower cost of capital

   d. higher profit margins

3. A _____ is a temporary endeavor undertaken to create a unique product, service, or result.

   a. program

   b. process

   c. project

   d. portfolio

4. Which of the following is not an attribute of a project?

   a. Projects are unique.

   b. Projects are developed using progressive elaboration.

   c. Projects have a primary customer or sponsor.

   d. Projects involve little uncertainty.

5. Which of the following is not part of the triple constraint of project management?

   a. meeting scope goals

   b. meeting time goals

   c. meeting communications goals

   d. meeting cost goals

6. _____ is the application of knowledge, skills, tools, and techniques to project activities to meet project requirements.

   a. Project management

   b. Program management

   c. Project portfolio management

   d. Requirements management

7. Project portfolio management addresses _____ goals of an organization, whereas project management addresses _____ goals.

   a. strategic, tactical

   b. tactical, strategic

   c. internal, external

   d. external, internal

8. Several individual housing projects done in the same area by the same firm might best be managed as part of a _____ .

   a. portfolio

   b. program

   c. investment

   d. collaborative

9. The most significant characteristic or attribute of an effective project manager is that he or she _____ .

   a. is a strong communicator

   b. is decisive

   c. is visionary

   d. leads by example

10. What kind of certification does the Project Management Institute provide?

    a. Microsoft Certified Project Manager (MCPM)

    b. Project Management Professional (PMP)

    c. Project Management Expert (PME)

    d. Project Management Mentor (PMM)

Quick Quiz Answers

1. B; 2. C; 3. C; 4. D; 5. C; 6. A; 7. A; 8. B; 9. D; 10. B

Discussion Questions

1. Why is there a new or renewed interest in the field of project management? How could project management be applied in your major? Do you think project management is just a passing fad?

2. What is a project, and what are its main attributes? How is a project different from what most people do in their day-to-day jobs? What is the triple constraint?

3. What is project management? Briefly describe the project management framework, providing examples of stakeholders, knowledge areas, tools and techniques, and project success factors.

4. Discuss the relationship between projects, programs, and portfolio management, and their contribution to enterprise success.

5. What are the roles of the project, program, and portfolio managers? What are suggested skills for project managers? What skills do program and portfolio managers need?

6. What role does the Project Management Institute play in helping the profession? What functions can you perform with project management software? What are some popular names of low-end, midrange, and high-end project management tools?

Exercises

Note: These exercises can be done individually or in teams in class, as homework, or in a virtual environment. Students can either write their results in a paper or prepare a short presentation to show their results.

1. Search the Internet for the terms *project management, program management,* and *project portfolio management.* Write down the number of hits that you received for each of these phrases. Find at least three Web sites that provide interesting information on one of the topics, including the Project Management Institute's Web site (*www.pmi.org*). Write a one-page paper or prepare a short presentation summarizing key information about these three Web sites.

2. Read the report by PricewaterhouseCoopers cited in Endnote 5 called "Boosting Business Performance through Programme and Project Management." Write a one- to two-page summary of the report.

3. Find an example of a real project with a real project manager. Feel free to use a project mentioned in a recent news story or a project from work or your personal life, such as a wedding, remodeling project, etc. Write a one-page paper or prepare a short presentation describing the project in terms of its scope, time, and cost goals and each of the project's attributes. Try to include information describing what went right and wrong on the project and the role of the project manager and sponsor. Also describe whether you consider the project to be a success, and why or why not. Include references and citations, if applicable.

4. Visit the Project Management Center (*www.infogoal.com/pmc*) and at least three of its links to project management software providers. Write a one-page paper or prepare a short presentation summarizing your findings.

5. Think about movies or television shows you have seen that illustrate good or bad aspects of project management. You can also search for articles and presentations on this topic. For example, the Oceans 11, 12, and 13 movies all include great planning and execution clips. Apollo 13 provides a great example of scope management and creative problem solving. The Office television show includes good examples of poor motivation techniques. Find a clip, and show it to your class, if possible, or act it out. Include discussion questions that you pose before and after the clip. Document a summary of the movie or television clip, the discussion questions, and your answers to the questions in a one- to two-page paper.

Team Projects

1. Find someone who works as a project manager or is a member of a project team. If possible, find more than one person. Prepare several interview questions, and then ask him your questions in person, via the phone, or via the Internet. Discuss the results with your team,

and then prepare a one- to two-page paper or prepare a short presentation summarizing your findings. You can use the interview guide on the companion Web site under Sample Documents, if desired.

2. Go to *www.monster.com* and search for jobs as a "project manager" or "program manager" in three geographic regions of your choice. Write a one- to two-page paper or prepare a short presentation summarizing what you found.

3. As a team, discuss projects that you are currently working on or would like to work on to benefit yourself, your employers, your family, or the broader community. Come up with at least 10 projects, and then determine if they could be grouped into programs. Write a one- to two-page paper or prepare a short presentation summarizing your results.

4. Expanding on Exercise 5 above, as a team, discuss several different movies or television shows that illustrate various aspects of project management. Select 3-4 clips, and show them to your class, if possible, or act them out. Include discussion questions that you pose before and after the clips. Document a summary of the clips, the discussion questions, and your answers to the questions in a two- to three-page paper.

Companion Web Site

Visit the companion Web site for this text (*www.course.com/mis/pm2/schwalbe* or *http://login.course.com*) to access:

- Lecture notes
- Interactive quizzes and Jeopardy games
- Template files
- Sample documents
- Podcasts
- More ideas for team projects, including real projects and case studies
- Links to additional resources related to project management

Key Terms

best practice — An optimal way recognized by industry to achieve a stated goal or objective.

ethics — A set of principles that guide our decision making based on personal values of what is "right" and "wrong."

leader — A person who focuses on long-term goals and big-picture objectives, while inspiring people to reach those goals.

manager — A person who deals with the day-to-day details of meeting specific goals.

portfolio — A collection of projects or programs and other work that are grouped together to facilitate effective management of that work to meet strategic business objectives.

program — A group of projects managed in a coordinated way to obtain benefits and control not available from managing them individually.

program manager — The person who provides leadership and direction for the project managers heading the projects within a program.

project — A temporary endeavor undertaken to create a unique product, service, or result.

project communications management — Generating, collecting, disseminating, and storing project information.

project cost management — Preparing and managing the budget for the project.

project human resource management — Making effective use of the people involved with the project.

project integration management — Coordinating the other knowledge areas, anticipating and dealing with issues, and making decisions each day about what is in the best interest of the entire project.

project management — The application of knowledge, skills, tools, and techniques to project activities to meet project requirements.

project management knowledge areas — The scope, time, cost, quality, human resource, communications, risk, procurement management, and project integration management.

Project Management Professional (PMP) — The certification provided by PMI that requires documenting project experience and education, agreeing to follow the code of ethics and professional conduct, and passing a comprehensive exam.

project management tools and techniques — The methods available to assist project managers and their teams; some popular tools in the time-management knowledge area include Gantt charts, network diagrams, critical-path analysis, and project management software.

project manager — The person responsible for working with the project sponsor, the project team, and the other people involved in a project to meet project goals.

project portfolio management — The grouping and managing of projects and programs as a portfolio of investments that contribute to the entire enterprise's success.

project procurement management — Acquiring or procuring goods and services for a project from outside the performing organization.

project quality management — Ensuring that the project will satisfy the stated and implied needs for which it was undertaken.

project risk management — Identifying, analyzing, and responding to risks related to the project.

project scope management — Working with all appropriate stakeholders to define, gain written agreement for, and manage all the work required to complete the project successfully.

project sponsor — The person who provides the direction and funding for a project.

project time management — Estimating how long it will take to complete the work, developing an acceptable project schedule given cost-effective use of available resources, and ensuring timely completion of the project.

stakeholders — The people involved in or affected by project activities.

triple constraint — The balancing of scope, time, and cost goals.

End Notes

[1] Project Management Institute, Inc., *The PMI Project Management Fact Book, Second Edition* (2001).

[2] Project Management Institute, Inc., *Project Management Salary Survey, Fifth Edition* (2007).

[3] Project Management Institute (PMI), *PMI Today* (October 2006).

[4] The Standish Group, "The CHAOS Report," (*www.standishgroup.com*) (1995).

[5] PricewaterhouseCoopers, "Boosting Business Performance through Programme and Project Management," (www.pwc.com/extweb/pwcpublications.nsf/docid/1ccdd87f4daa410c852571290051976f) (June 2004).

[6] Project Management Institute, Inc., *A Guide to the Project Management Body of Knowledge (PMBOK® Guide)* (2004), p. 5.

[7] Ibid, p. 16.

[8] Claude Besner and Brian Hobbs, "The Perceived Value and Potential Contribution of Project Management Practices to Project Success," PMI Research Conference Proceedings (July 2006).

[9] Jim Johnson, "CHAOS 2006 Research Project," CHAOS Activity News, vol. 2:issue 1, (2007).

[10] The Standish Group, "CHAOS 2001: A Recipe for Success" (2001).

[11] Project Management Institute, Inc., *A Guide to the Project Management Body of Knowledge (PMBOK® Guide)* (2004), p. 8.

[12] Eric Burke, "Project Portfolio Management," PMI Houston Chapter Meeting (July 10, 2002).

[13] Project Management Institute, Inc., *Organizational Project Management Maturity Model (OPM3) Knowledge Foundation* (2003), p. 13.

[14] Ultimate Business Library, *Best Practice: Ideas and Insights from the World's Foremost Business Thinkers*, Perseus Publishing (2003).

[15] Project Management Institute, Inc., *PMI Today* (February 2007).

[16] Project Management Institute, Inc., *PMI Today* (December 2006), p. 12-13.

[17] Top Ten Reviews, "2006 Project Management Report," (http://project-management-software-review.toptenreviews.com) (October 18, 2006).

[18] Project Management Institute, Inc., "PMI's Global Accreditation Center Assures Academic Quality", Supplement in *PMI Today* (December 2006).

CHAPTER 2

PROJECT, PROGRAM, AND PORTFOLIO SELECTION

LEARNING OBJECTIVES

After reading this chapter, you will be able to:

- Describe the importance of aligning projects with business strategy, the strategic planning process, and using a SWOT analysis

- Explain the four-stage planning process for project selection and provide examples of applying this model to ensure the strategic alignment of projects

- Summarize the various methods for selecting projects and demonstrate how to calculate net present value, return on investment, payback, and the weighted score for a project

- Discuss the program selection process and distinguish the differences between programs and projects

- Describe the project portfolio selection process and the five levels of project portfolio management

Marie Scott, the director of the Project Management Office for Global Construction, Inc., was facilitating a meeting with several senior managers throughout the company. The purpose of the meeting was to discuss a process for selecting projects, grouping them into programs, and determining how they fit into the organization's portfolio of projects. She had invited an outside consultant to the meeting to provide an objective view of the theory and practice behind project, program, and portfolio selection.

She could see that several managers were getting bored with the presentation, while others looked concerned that their projects might be cancelled if the company implemented a new approach for project selection. After the consultant's presentation, Marie had each participant write down his or her questions and concerns and hand them in anonymously for her group to review. She was amazed at the obvious lack of understanding of the need for projects to align with business strategy. How should her group respond?

ALIGNING PROJECTS WITH BUSINESS STRATEGY

Most organizations face hundreds of problems and opportunities for improvement and consider potential projects to address them. These organizations—both large and small—cannot undertake most of the potential projects identified because of resource limitations and other constraints. Therefore, an organization's overall business strategy should guide the project selection process and management of those projects.

⊗ WHAT WENT WRONG?

Unfortunately, when deciding to approve projects, many organizations lack a structured process. Mike Peterson, project management professional (PMP) and director with PricewaterhouseCoopers' Advisory Services, described an organization that decided it needed to implement a new financial system, which is often a very expensive, challenging project. "With little in the way of analysis, they selected a big-name enterprise resource planning package, and hired a boutique firm to assist with the implementation. At no time did they formally define the benefits the new system was meant to usher in; nor did they decide, exactly, which processes were to be redesigned. Their own assumptions were not articulated, timelines were never devised, nor were the key performance indicators needed to track success ever established."[1]

What was the result of this project? It was completed over budget and behind schedule, and instead of helping the company, it prevented it from closing its books for over 12 months. The company undertook a long and costly project, and ultimately failed to improve the organization's effectiveness. The company could have avoided many of the problems it encountered if it had followed a formal, well-defined process to identify and select projects.

Strategic Planning

Successful leaders look at the big picture or strategic plan of the organization to determine what projects will provide the most value. The same can be said for successful individuals. No one person can do everything, so individuals must pick projects to pursue based on their talents, interests, limitations, and so on. **Strategic planning** involves determining long-term objectives by analyzing the strengths and weaknesses of an organization, studying opportunities and threats in the business environment, predicting future trends, and projecting the need for new products and services. Strategic planning provides important information to help organizations identify and then select potential projects.

SWOT Analysis

Many people are familiar with **SWOT analysis**—analyzing **S**trengths, **W**eaknesses, **O**pportunities, and **T**hreats—which is used to aid in strategic planning. For example, a group of four people who want to start a new business in the film industry could perform a SWOT analysis to help identify potential projects. They might determine the following based on a SWOT analysis:

- Strengths:
    - As experienced professionals, we have numerous contacts in the film industry.
    - Two of us have strong sales and interpersonal skills.
    - Two of us have strong technical skills and are familiar with several film-making software tools.
    - We all have impressive samples of completed projects.

- Weaknesses:
  - None of us have accounting/financial experience.
  - We have no clear marketing strategy for products and services.
  - We have little money to invest in new projects.
  - We have no company Web site and limited use of technology to run the business.
- Opportunities:
  - A current client has mentioned a large project she would like us to bid on.
  - The film industry continues to grow.
  - There are two major conferences this year where we could promote our company.
- Threats:
  - Other individuals or companies can provide the services we can.
  - Customers might prefer working with more established individuals/ organizations.
  - There is high risk in the film business.

Based on their SWOT analysis, the four entrepreneurs outline potential projects as follows:

- Find an external accountant or firm to help run the business.
- Hire someone to develop a company Web site, focusing on our experience and past projects.
- Develop a marketing plan.
- Develop a strong proposal to get the large project the current client mentioned.
- Plan to promote the company at two major conferences this year.

Some people like to perform a SWOT analysis by using mind mapping. **Mind mapping** is a technique that uses branches radiating out from a core idea to structure thoughts and ideas. The human brain does not work in a linear fashion. People come up with many unrelated ideas. By putting those ideas down in a visual mind map format, you can often generate more ideas than by just creating lists. You can create mind maps by hand, by using sticky notes, using presentation software like PowerPoint, or by using mind mapping software.

Figure 2-1 shows a sample mind map for the SWOT analysis presented earlier. This diagram was created using MindManager software by Mindjet. (You can download a free trial of this software from *www.mindjet.com* or use a similar free tool called FreeMind available at *www.freemind.sourceforge.net*.) Notice that this map has four main branches representing strengths, weaknesses, opportunities, and threats. Icons are added to each of those main branches to more visually identify them, such as the thumbs up for strengths and thumbs down for weaknesses. Ideas in each category are added to the appropriate branch. You could also add sub-branches to show ideas under those categories. For example, under the first branch for strengths, you could start adding sub-branches to list the most important contacts you have. This mind map includes branches for project ideas related to different categories, with text markers used to identify the project names. From this visual example, you can see that there are no project ideas identified yet to address strengths or threats, so these areas should be discussed further.

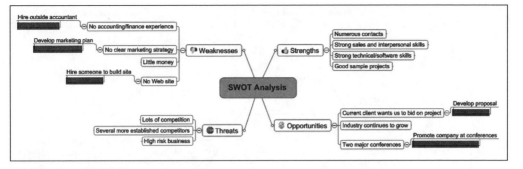

FIGURE 2-1 Mind map of a SWOT analysis to help identify potential projects

FOUR-STAGE PLANNING PROCESS FOR PROJECT SELECTION

One of the most important factors in project success is selecting the best projects to undertake. In addition to using a SWOT analysis, organizations often follow a detailed planning process for project selection. Figure 2-2 shows a four-stage planning process for selecting projects. Note the hierarchical structure of this model and the results produced from each stage. *It is very important to start at the top of the pyramid to select projects that support the organization's business strategy.* The four stages of this process include:

1. *Strategic planning*: The first step of the project selection process is to determine the organization's strategy, goals, and objectives. This information should come from the strategic plan or strategy planning meetings. For example, if a firm's competitive strategy is cost leadership, it should focus on projects that will help it retain its position as a low-cost producer.
2. *Business area analysis*: The second step is to analyze business processes that are central to achieving strategic goals. For example, could the organization make improvements in sales, manufacturing, engineering, information technology (IT), or other business areas to support the strategic plan?
3. *Project planning*: The next step is to start defining potential projects that address the strategies and business areas identified. Managers should discuss the potential projects' scope, time, and cost goals; projected benefits; and constraints as part of this process.
4. *Resource allocation*: The last step in the project planning process is choosing which projects to do and assigning resources for working on them. The amount of resources the organization has available or is willing to acquire will affect resource-allocation decisions.

Project planning stages   Results produced

Strategic planning → Determine organizational strategy, goals, and objectives

Business area analysis → Analyze how various business areas can help achieve strategic goals

Project planning → Identify potential projects to help meet strategic goals

Resource allocation → Allocate resources to selected projects

FIGURE 2-2 Pyramid for the project planning process

METHODS FOR SELECTING PROJECTS

Although people in organizations identify many potential projects as part of their strategic planning process, they also identify projects by working on day-to-day operations. For example, a project manager overseeing an apartment building project might notice that some workers are much more efficient than others. He or she might suggest a project to provide standardized training on specific skills. A marketing analyst might notice that competitors are using new forms of advertising and suggest a project to respond to this competition. It is important for organizations to encourage workers at all levels to submit project ideas because they know firsthand what problems they are encountering and what opportunities might be available.

How do senior managers decide which of the many potential projects their organization should pursue? Some projects directly support competitive strategy and are easy choices, but other project ideas require additional thought and analysis. However, organizations need to narrow down the list of potential projects to those projects that will be most beneficial. Most large organizations go through a preliminary project prioritization process annually. For example, early each fall Exxon Corporation's Information Technology (IT) organizations work with all of their internal client organizations worldwide to identify potential IT projects and resource requirements for the following year. This process takes about three weeks, followed by meetings to discuss and prioritize potential projects and agree to cut-off lines based on the availability of funds and other resources. The prioritized list of potential projects are then reviewed by senior management as part of the corporation's fall company planning and budgeting process.

Figure 2-3 provides an amusing example of strategically planning a golf tournament to achieve desired results—in this case, the elimination of incompetent management!

© Scott Adams, Inc./Dist. by UFS, Inc.

FIGURE 2-3 Example project with strategic results!

Selecting projects is not an exact science, but it is a critical part of project, program, and project portfolio management. Many methods exist for selecting from among possible projects. Common techniques are listed here and explained in the following sections:

- Focusing on competitive strategy and broad organizational needs
- Performing net present value analysis or other financial projections
- Using a weighted scoring model
- Implementing a balanced scorecard
- Addressing problems, opportunities, and directives
- Considering project time frame
- Considering project priority

In practice, organizations usually use a combination of these approaches to select projects. Each approach has advantages and disadvantages, and it is up to management to decide the best approach for selecting projects based on their particular organization. In any case, projects should first and foremost address business needs.

Focusing on Competitive Strategy and Broad Organizational Needs

When deciding what projects to undertake, when to undertake them, and to what level, managers must focus on meeting their organization's many needs. Projects that address competitive strategy are much more likely to be successful because they will be important to the organization's competitive position.

For example, a company might have a competitive strategy of cost leadership, meaning that it attracts customers primarily because its products or services are inexpensive. Wal-Mart (*www.walmart.com*) and Cub Foods (*www.cub.com*) fit into this category; a project to help reduce inventories and, thereby, costs would fit their competitive strategies. Other companies might have a particular focus for their competitive strategies, meaning that they develop products for a particular market niche. Babies "R" Us (*www .babiesrus.com*) and Ron Jon Surf Shop (*www.ronjons.com*) fit into this category; a project to help attract new customers (new parents for Babies"R"Us and new surfers for Ron Jon Surf Shop) would fit their competitive strategies.

In addition to projects that directly tie to competitive strategy, organizations might pursue projects that everyone agrees will meet broad organizational needs. These needs might involve improving the firm's IT infrastructure, improving safety, or providing faster customer service. It is often impossible to estimate the financial value of such projects, but everyone agrees that they do have a high value. As the old proverb says, "It is better to measure gold roughly than to count pennies precisely."

One method for selecting projects based on broad organizational needs is to first determine whether they meet three important criteria: need, funding, and will. Do people in the organization agree that the project needs to be done? Does the organization have the capacity to provide adequate funds to perform the project? Is there a strong will to make the project succeed? For example, many visionary chief executive officers (CEOs) can describe a broad need to improve certain aspects of their organizations, such as communications. Although they cannot specifically describe how to improve communications, they might allocate funds to projects that address this need. As projects progress, the organization must reevaluate the need, funding, and will for each project to determine if the projects should be continued, redefined, or terminated.

Performing Financial Projections

Financial considerations are often an important aspect of the project selection process, especially during tough economic times. As authors Dennis Cohen and Robert Graham put it, "Projects are never ends in themselves. Financially they are always a means to an end, cash."[2] Many organizations require an approved business case before pursuing projects, and financial projections are a critical component of the business case. Three primary methods for determining the projected financial value of projects include net present value analysis, return on investment, and payback analysis. Because project managers often deal with business executives, they must understand how to speak their language, which often boils down to understanding these important financial concepts.

Net Present Value Analysis

Net present value (NPV) analysis is a method of calculating the expected net monetary gain or loss from a project by discounting all expected future cash inflows and outflows to the present point in time. (Detailed steps to walk you through the calculation are outlined in the following paragraphs.) An organization should consider only projects with a positive NPV if financial value is a key criterion for project selection. This is because a positive NPV means the return from a project exceeds the **opportunity cost of capital**—the return available by investing the capital elsewhere. For example, is it best to put money into Project A or Project B? Projects with higher NPVs are preferred to projects with lower NPVs if all other factors are equal.

Figure 2-4 illustrates the NPV concept for two different projects. Note that this example starts discounting right away in Year 1 and uses a 10% discount rate for both projects. (The paragraphs that follow explain the discount rate.) You can use the NPV function in Microsoft Excel to calculate the NPV quickly. Detailed steps on performing this calculation manually are provided in Figure 2-5. Note that Figure 2-4 lists the projected benefits first, followed by the costs, and then the calculated cash flow amount. Notice that the sum of the **cash flow**—benefits minus costs, or income minus expenses—is the same for both projects at $5,000. The net present values are different, however, because they account for the time value of money. Money earned today is worth more than money earned in the future, primarily due to inflation. Project 1 had a negative cash flow of $5,000 in the first year, whereas Project 2 had a negative cash flow of only $1,000 in the first year.

Although both projects had the same total cash flows without discounting, these cash flows are not of comparable financial value. NPV analysis, therefore, is a method for making equal comparisons between cash flow for multiyear projects. Although this example shows both projects having the same length, NPV also works for projects of different lengths.

	A	B	C	D	E	F	G	
1	Discount rate	10%						
2								
3	**PROJECT 1**	YEAR 1	YEAR 2	YEAR 3	YEAR 4	YEAR 5	TOTAL	
4	Benefits	$0	$2,000	$3,000	$4,000	$5,000	$14,000	
5	Costs	$5,000	$1,000	$1,000	$1,000	$1,000	$9,000	
6	Cash flow	($5,000)	$1,000	$2,000	$3,000	$4,000	$5,000	
7	NPV ⟶ $2,316							
8		Formula =npv(b1,b6:f6)						
9								Note that totals
10	**PROJECT 2**	YEAR 1	YEAR 2	YEAR 3	YEAR 4	YEAR 5	TOTAL	are equal, but
11	Benefits	$1,000	$2,000	$4,000	$4,000	$4,000	$15,000	NPVs are not
12	Costs	$2,000	$2,000	$2,000	$2,000	$2,000	$10,000	because of the
13	Cash flow	($1,000)	$0	$2,000	$2,000	$2,000	$5,000	time value of
14	NPV ⟶ $3,201							money
15		Formula =npv(b1,b13:f13)						
16								
17								

FIGURE 2-4 Net present value example

Discount rate	10%					
PROJECT 1	**1**	**2**	**3**	**4**	**5**	**TOTAL**
Costs	$5,000	$1,000	$1,000	$1,000	$1,000	$9,000
Discount factor*	0.91	0.83	0.75	0.68	0.62	
Discounted costs	$4,545	$826	$751	$683	$621	**$7,427**
Benefits	$0	$2,000	$3,000	$4,000	$5,000	$14,000
Discount factor*	0.91	0.83	0.75	0.68	0.62	
Discounted benefits	0	$1,653	$2,254	$2,732	$3,105	**$9,743**
Discounted benefits - discounted costs, or NPV ⟶						**$2,316**
*Note: The discount factors are NOT rounded to two decimal places.						
They are calculated using the formula discount factor = 1/(1+discount rate)ˆyear.						
You can access this spreadsheet on the companion Web site under Sample Documents.						

FIGURE 2-5 Detailed NPV calculations

There are some items to consider when calculating NPV. Some organizations refer to the investment year(s) for project costs as Year 0 instead of Year 1 and do not discount costs in Year 0. Other organizations start discounting immediately based on their financial procedures; it is simply a matter of preference for the organization. The discount rate can also vary, based on the prime rate and other economic considerations. Financial experts in your organization will be able to tell you what discount rate to use. Some people consider it to be the rate at which you could borrow money for the project. You can enter costs as negative numbers instead of positive numbers, and you can list costs first and then benefits. For example, Figure 2-6 shows the financial calculations a consulting firm provided in a business case for an intranet project. Note that the discount rate is 8%, costs are not discounted right away (note the Year 0), the discount factors are rounded to two decimal places, costs are listed first, and costs are entered as positive numbers. The NPV and other calculations are still the same; only the format is slightly different. Project managers must be sure to check with their organization to find out its guidelines for when discounting starts, what discount rate to use, and what format the organization prefers.

			Year			
Discount rate	8%					
Assume the project is completed in Year 0			Year			
	0	1	2	3	Total	
Costs	140,000	40,000	40,000	40,000		
Discount factor	1	0.93	0.86	0.79		
Discounted costs	**140,000**	**37,200**	**34,400**	**31,600**	**243,200**	
Benefits	0	200,000	200,000	200,000		
Discount factor	1	0.93	0.86	0.79		
Discounted benefits	**0**	**186,000**	**172,000**	**158,000**	**516,000**	
Discounted benefits - costs	(140,000)	148,800	137,600	126,400	272,800	←NPV
Cumulative benefits - costs	(140,000)	8,800	146,400	272,800		
ROI ————————→ 112%						
	Payback in Year 1					

FIGURE 2-6 Intranet project NPV example

To determine NPV, follow these steps:

1. Determine the estimated costs and benefits for the life of the project and the products it produces. For example, the intranet project example assumed the project would produce a system in about six months that would be used for three years, so costs are included in Year 0, when the system is developed, and ongoing system costs and projected benefits are included for Years 1, 2, and 3.

2. Determine the discount rate. A **discount rate** is the rate used in discounting future cash flows. It is also called the capitalization rate or opportunity cost of capital. In Figures 2-4 and 2-5, the discount rate is 10% per year, and in Figure 2-6, the discount rate is 8% per year.

3. Calculate and interpret the net present value. There are several ways to calculate NPV. Most spreadsheet software has a built-in function to calculate NPV. For example, Figure 2-4 shows the formula that Excel uses: =npv(discount rate, range of cash flows), where the discount rate is in cell B1 and the range of cash flows for Project 1 are in cells B6 through F6. To use the NPV function, there must be a row in the spreadsheet (or column, depending on how it is organized) for the cash flow each year, which is the benefit amount for that year minus the cost amount. The result of the formula yields an NPV of $2,316 for Project 1 and an NPV of $3,201 for Project 2. Because both projects have positive NPVs, they are both good candidates for selection. However, because Project 2 has a higher NPV than Project 1 (38% higher), it would be the better choice between the two. If the two numbers are close, other methods should be used to help decide which project to select.

The mathematical formula for calculating NPV is:

$$NPV = \Sigma_{t=0...n}\ A_t/(1+r)^t$$

where t equals the year of the cash flow, n is the last year of the cash flow, A is the amount of cash flow each year, and r is the discount rate. If you cannot enter the data into spreadsheet software, you can perform the calculations by hand or with a simple calculator. First, determine the annual **discount factor**—a multiplier for each year based on the discount rate and year—and then apply it to the costs and benefits for each year. The formula for the discount factor is $1/(1+r)^t$, where r is the discount rate, such as 8%, and t is the year. For example, the discount factors used in Figure 2-5 are calculated as follows:

Year 0: discount factor = $1/(1+0.08)^0$ = 1
Year 1: discount factor = $1/(1+0.08)^1$ = .93
Year 2: discount factor = $1/(1+0.08)^2$ = .86
Year 3: discount factor = $1/(1+0.08)^3$ = .79

After determining the discount factor for each year, multiply the costs and benefits by the appropriate discount factor. For example, in Figure 2-6, the discounted cost for Year 1 is $40,000 * .93 = $37,200, where the discount factor is rounded to two decimal places. Next, sum all of the discounted costs and benefits each year to get a total. For example, the total discounted costs in Figure 2-6 are $243,200. To calculate the NPV, take the total discounted benefits and subtract the total discounted costs. In this example, the NPV is $516,000 – $243,200 = $272,800.

Return on Investment

Another important financial consideration is return on investment. **Return on investment (ROI)** is the result of subtracting the project costs from the benefits and then dividing by the costs. For example, if you invest $100 today and next year your investment is worth $110, your ROI is ($110 – 100)/100, or 0.10 (10%). Note that the ROI is always a percentage. It can be positive or negative. It is best to consider discounted costs and benefits for multiyear projects when calculating ROI. Figure 2-6 shows an ROI of 112%. You calculate this number as follows:

ROI = (total discounted benefits – total discounted costs)/discounted costs

ROI = (516,000 – 243,200) / 243,200 = 112%

The higher the ROI, the better; an ROI of 112% is outstanding. Many organizations have a required rate of return for projects. The **required rate of return** is the minimum acceptable rate of return on an investment. For example, an organization might have a required rate of return of at least 10% for projects. The organization bases the required rate of return on what it could expect to receive elsewhere for an investment of comparable risk. You can also determine a project's **internal rate of return (IRR)** by finding what discount rate results in an NPV of zero for the project. You can use the Goal Seek function in Excel (use Excel's Help function for more information on Goal Seek) to determine the IRR quickly. Simply set the cell containing the NPV calculation to zero while changing the cell containing the discount rate. For example, in Figure 2-4, you could set cell B7 to zero while changing cell B1 to find that the IRR for Project 1 is 27%. (Note: The Excel file for Figure 2-4 is provided on the companion Web site under Sample Documents if you want to try this out. Consult additional sources for more information on IRR and other financial concepts.)

Payback Analysis

Payback analysis is another important financial tool to use when selecting projects. **Payback period** is the amount of time it will take to recoup—in the form of net cash inflows—the total dollars invested in a project. In other words, payback analysis determines how much time will lapse before accrued benefits overtake accrued and continuing costs. Payback occurs in the year when the cumulative benefits minus costs reach zero. Figure 2-6 shows how to find the payback period. The cumulative benefits minus costs for Year 0 are ($140,000). Adding that number to the discounted benefits minus costs for Year 1 results in $8,800. Because that number is positive, the payback occurs in Year 1. Note that the year the project was undertaken in this example was called Year 0.

Creating a chart helps illustrate more precisely when the payback period occurs. Figure 2-7 charts the cumulative discounted costs and cumulative discounted benefits each year using the numbers from Figure 2-6. Note that the lines cross a little after Year 1 starts (assuming the project was done in Year 0). The cumulative discounted benefits and costs are equal to zero where the lines cross.

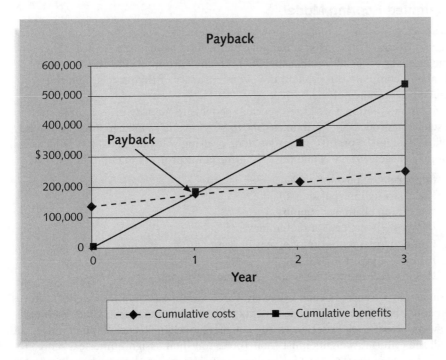

FIGURE 2-7 Charting the payback period

TEMPLATE FILES AVAILABLE

A template file charting the payback period is provided on the companion Web site for this text, as well as one for calculating NPV, ROI, and payback for a project. See Appendix C for a list of all template files.

Many organizations have certain recommendations for the length of the payback period of an investment. For example, they might require all IT projects to have a payback period of less than two years or even one year, regardless of the estimated NPV or ROI. Rhonda Hocker, CIO at San Jose–based BEA Systems, Inc., notes that the general rule at the company is that its IT projects should have a payback period of less than one year. The company also tries to limit project teams to no more than 12 people, who perform the work within four months. Given the economic climate and rapid pace of change in businesses and technology, the company has to focus on delivering positive financial results quickly.[3] However, organizations must also consider long-range goals when making major investments. Many crucial projects, such as drug development or major transportation projects, cannot achieve a payback that quickly or be completed in such a short time period.

To aid in project selection, it is important for project managers to understand the organization's financial expectations for projects. It is also important for management to understand the limitations of financial estimates, because they are just estimates.

Using a Weighted Scoring Model

A **weighted scoring model** is a tool that provides a systematic process for selecting projects based on many criteria. These criteria include such factors as meeting strategic goals or broad organizational needs; addressing specific problems or opportunities; the amount of time it will take to complete the project; the overall priority of the project; and the projected financial performance of the project.

The first step in creating a weighted scoring model is to identify criteria important to the project selection process. It often takes time to develop and reach agreement on these criteria. Holding facilitated brainstorming sessions or using software to exchange ideas can aid in developing these criteria. Some possible criteria for projects include the following:

- Supports key business objectives
- Has a strong internal sponsor
- Has strong customer support
- Uses a realistic level of technology
- Can be implemented in one year or less
- Provides a positive NPV
- Has low risk in meeting scope, time, and cost goals

Next, you assign a weight to each criterion. Once again, determining weights requires consultation and final agreement. These weights indicate how much you value each criterion or how important each criterion is. You can assign weights based on percentage, and the sum of all the criteria's weights must total 100%. You then assign numerical scores to each criterion (for example, 0 to 100) for each project. The scores indicate how much each project meets each criterion. At this point, you can use a spreadsheet application to create a matrix of projects, criteria, weights, and scores. Figure 2-8 provides an example of a weighted scoring model to evaluate four different projects. After assigning weights for the criteria and scores for each project, you calculate a weighted score for each project by multiplying the weight for each criterion by its score and adding the resulting values. For example, you calculate the weighted score for Project 1 in Figure 2-8 as:

$$25\%*90 + 15\%*70 + 15\%*50 + 10\%*25 + 5\%*20 + 20\%*50 + 10\%*20 = 56$$

	A	B	C	D	E	F
1	Criteria	Weight	Project 1	Project 2	Project 3	Project 4
2	Supports key business objectives	25%	90	90	50	20
3	Has a strong internal sponsor	15%	70	90	50	20
4	Has a strong customer support	15%	50	90	50	20
5	Uses a realistic level of technology	10%	25	90	50	70
6	Can be implemented in one year or less	5%	20	20	50	90
7	Provides a positive NPV	20%	50	70	50	50
8	Has low risk in meeting scope, time, and cost goals	10%	20	50	50	90
9	**Weighted Project Scores**	**100%**	**56**	**78.5**	**50**	**41.5**
10						
11						
12						

Weighted Score by Project

Project 4 — 41.5
Project 3 — 50
Project 2 — 78.5
Project 1 — 56

0   20   40   60   80   100

FIGURE 2-8 Sample weighted scoring model for project selection

Note that in this example, Project 2 is the obvious choice for selection because it has the highest weighted score. Creating a bar chart to graph the weighted scores for each project allows you to see the results at a glance. If you create the weighted scoring model in a spreadsheet, you can enter the data, create and copy formulas, and perform a "what-if" analysis. For example, suppose you change the weights for the criteria. By having the weighted scoring model in a spreadsheet, you can easily change the weights to update the weighted scores and charts automatically. This capability allows you to investigate various options for different stakeholders quickly. Ideally, the result should be reflective of the group's consensus, and any major disagreements should be documented. A template file for creating a weighted scoring model is provided on the companion Web site for this text.

Many readers of this text are probably familiar with a weighted scoring model because teachers often use them to determine grades. Suppose grades for a class are based on two homework assignments and two exams. To calculate final grades, the teacher would assign a weight to each of these items. Suppose Homework One is worth 10% of the grade, Homework Two is worth 20% of the grade, Test One is worth 20% of the grade, and Test Two is worth 50% of the grade. Students would want to do well on each of these items, but they would focus on performing well on Test Two because it is 50% of the grade.

You can also establish weights by assigning points. For example, a project might receive 100 points if it definitely supports key business objectives, 50 points if it somewhat supports them, and 0 points if it is totally unrelated to key business objectives. With a point model, you can simply add all the points to determine the best projects for selection without having to multiply weights and scores and sum the results.

You can also determine minimum scores or thresholds for specific criteria in a weighted scoring model. For example, suppose an organization decided that it should not consider a project if it does not score at least 50 out of 100 on every criterion. The organization can build this type of threshold into the weighted scoring model to automatically reject projects that do not meet these minimum standards. As you can see, weighted scoring models can aid in project selection decisions.

Implementing a Balanced Scorecard

Dr. Robert Kaplan and Dr. David Norton developed another approach to help select and manage projects that align with business strategy. A **balanced scorecard** is a methodology that converts an organization's value drivers—such as customer service, innovation, operational efficiency, and financial performance—to a series of defined metrics. Organizations record and analyze these metrics to determine how well projects help them achieve strategic goals.

The Balanced Scorecard Institute, which provides training and guidance to organizations using this methodology, quotes Kaplan and Norton's description of the balanced scorecard as follows:

> The balanced scorecard retains traditional financial measures. But financial measures tell the story of past events, an adequate story for industrial age companies for which investments in long-term capabilities and customer relationships were not critical for success. These financial measures are inadequate, however, for guiding and evaluating the journey that information age companies must make to create future value through investment in customers, suppliers, employees, processes, technology, and innovation.[4]

Visit *www.balancedscorecard.org* for more information on using this approach to project selection.

This site includes several examples of how organizations use this methodology. For example, the U.S. Defense Finance and Accounting Services (DFAS) organization uses a balanced scorecard to measure performance and track progress in achieving its strategic goals. Their strategy focuses on four perspectives: customer, financial, internal, and growth and learning. Figure 2-9 shows how the balanced scorecard approach ties together the organization's mission, vision, and goals based on these four perspectives. The DFAS continuously monitors this corporate scorecard and revises it based on identified priorities.

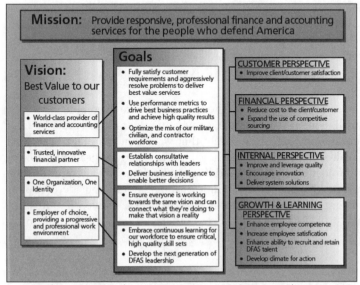

Defense Finance and Accounting Service, "DFAS Strategic Plan," Nov 2001 (http://balancedscorecard.org/files/DFAS-strategic-plan.pdf), p. 13.

FIGURE 2-9   Balanced scorecard example

Problems, Opportunities, and Directives

Another method for selecting projects is based on their response to a problem, an opportunity, or a directive, as described in the following list:

- **Problems** are undesirable situations that prevent an organization from achieving its goals. These problems can be current or anticipated. For example, users of an information system might be having trouble logging on to the system or getting information in a timely manner because the system has reached its capacity. In response, the company could initiate a project to enhance the current system by adding more access lines or upgrading the hardware with a faster processor, more memory, or more storage space.
- **Opportunities** are chances to improve the organization. For example, an organization could implement a project to train workers on important skills that will make the organization more competitive.

Project, Program, and Portfolio Selection

- **Directives** are new requirements imposed by management, government, or some external influence. For example, a college or university may have to meet a requirement to not collect or use a student's social security number.

Organizations select projects for any of these reasons. It is often easier to get approval and funding for projects that address problems or directives because the organization must respond to these categories of projects to avoid hurting the business. For example, several years ago Exxon Corporation realized that it was losing $200,000 each minute its motor fuel store point-of-sale system was down. Getting approval for a $7 million project to re-engineer this critical system was approved and given high priority. Many projects resulting from natural disasters, such as hurricanes and earthquakes, get quick approvals due to their serious nature. Many problems and directives must be resolved quickly, but managers must also consider projects that seek opportunities for improving the organization.

Project Time Frame

Another approach to project selection is based on the time it will take to complete a project or the date by which it must be done. For example, some potential projects must be finished within a specific time period, such as projects that were done to meet Year 2000 issues. If they cannot be finished by this set date, they can cause serious problems. Likewise, if there is a potential project that is only valid if it can be done by a certain time and there is no way your organization can meet the deadline, it should not be considered. Some projects can be completed very quickly—within a few weeks, days, or even minutes. However, even though many projects can be completed quickly, it is still important to prioritize them.

Project Priority

Another method for project selection is the overall priority of the project. Many organizations prioritize projects as being high, medium, or low priority based on the current business environment. For example, if it were crucial to cut operating costs quickly, projects that have the most potential to do so would be given a high priority. The organization should always complete high-priority projects first, even if a low- or medium-priority project could be finished in less time. Usually, there are many more potential projects than an organization can undertake at any one time, so it is very important to work on the most important ones first.

As you can see, organizations of all types and sizes can use many approaches to select projects. Many project managers have some say in which projects their organizations select for implementation. Even if they do not, they need to understand the motive and overall business strategy for the projects they are managing. Project managers and team members are often asked to justify their projects, and understanding many of these project selection methods can help them to do so.

PROGRAM SELECTION

After deciding which projects to pursue, organizations need to decide if it is advantageous to manage several projects together as part of a program. There might already be a program that a new project would logically fall under, or the organization might initiate a program and then approve projects for it. Recall that a program is a group of projects managed in a coordinated way to obtain benefits and control not available from managing them individually.

Focusing on Coordination and Benefits

What does it mean to manage a group of projects in a coordinated way? Project managers focus on managing individual projects. Project managers and their teams have to do many things to achieve individual project success. For example, if a project manager is in charge of building a new house for a sponsor, he or she must perform the following tasks, just to name a few:

- Work with local government groups to obtain permits
- Find and manage a land excavation firm to prepare the land
- Work with an architect to understand the house design
- Screen and hire various construction workers
- Find appropriate suppliers for the materials

If a construction firm is in charge of developing several houses in the same geographic area, it makes sense to coordinate these and other tasks for all the housing projects.

What benefits and control would be possible by managing projects as part of a program? There are several. For example, potential benefits in the housing program scenario include the following:

- *Saving money*: The construction firm can often save money by using economies of scale. It can purchase materials, obtain services, and hire workers for less money if it is managing the construction of 100 houses instead of just one house.
- *Saving time*: Instead of each project team having to perform similar work, by grouping the projects into a program, one person or group can be responsible for similar work, such as obtaining all the permits for all the houses. This coordination of work usually saves time as well as money.
- *Increasing authority*: A program manager responsible for building 100 houses will have more authority than a project manager responsible for building one house. The program manager can use this authority in multiple situations, such as negotiating better prices with suppliers and obtaining better services in a more timely fashion.

Approaches to Creating Programs

Some new projects naturally fall into existing programs, such as houses being built in a certain geographic area. As another example, many companies use IT, and they usually have a program in place for IT infrastructure projects. Projects might include purchasing new hardware, software, and networking equipment, or determining standards for IT. If a new office opens up in a new location, the project to provide the hardware, software, and networks for that office would logically fall under the infrastructure program.

Other projects might spark the need for developing a new program. For example, Global Construction, Inc., from the opening case might win a large contract to build an office complex in a foreign country. Instead of viewing the contract as either one huge project or part of an existing program, it would be better to manage the work as its own program that comprises several smaller projects. For example, there might be separate project managers for each building. Grouping related projects into programs helps improve coordination through better communications, planning, management, and control. Organizations must decide when it makes sense to group projects together. When too many projects are part of one program, it might be wise to create a new program to improve their management. Remember that the main goal of programs is to obtain benefits and control not available from managing projects separately.

MEDIA SNAPSHOT

Many people enjoy watching the extra features on a DVD that describe the creation of a movie. For example, the extended edition DVD for *Lord of the Rings: The Two Towers* includes detailed descriptions of how the script was created, how huge structures were built, how special effects were made, and how talented professionals overcame numerous obstacles to complete the three movies. Instead of viewing each movie as a separate project, the producer, Peter Jackson, decided to develop all three movies as part of one program.

"By shooting all three films consecutively during one massive production and post-production schedule, New Line Cinema made history. Never before had such a monumental undertaking been contemplated or executed. The commitment of time, resources, and manpower were unheard of as all three films and more than 1,000 effects shots were being produced concurrently with the same director and core cast."[5] At three years in the making, *The Lord of the Rings* trilogy was the largest production ever to be mounted in the Southern Hemisphere. The production assembled an international cast, employed a crew of 2,500, used over 20,000 days of extras, featured 77 speaking parts, and created 1,200 state-of-the-art computer-generated effects shots. Jackson said that doing detailed planning for all three movies made it much easier than he imagined to produce them, and the three movies were completed in less time and for less money by grouping them together. The budget for the three films was reported to be $270 million, and they grossed over $1 billion before the end of 2004.

PROJECT PORTFOLIO SELECTION

Projects and programs have existed for a long time, as has some form of project portfolio management. There is no simple process for deciding how to create project portfolios, but the goal of project portfolio management is clear: to help maximize business value to ensure enterprise success. You can measure business value in several ways, such as in market share, profit margins, growth rates, share prices, and customer or employee satisfaction ratings. Many factors are involved in ensuring enterprise success. Organizations cannot only pursue projects that have the best financial value. They must also consider resource availability (including people, equipment, and cash); risks that could affect success; and other concerns (potential mergers, public relations, balancing investments, and so on) that affect enterprise success.

Focusing on Enterprise Success

Project managers strive to make their projects successful and naturally focus on doing whatever they can to meet the goals of their particular projects. Likewise, program managers focus on making their programs successful. Project portfolio managers and other senior managers, however, must focus on how all of an organization's projects fit together to help the entire enterprise achieve success. That might mean canceling or putting several projects on hold, reassigning resources from one project to another, suggesting changes in project leadership, or taking other actions that might negatively affect individual projects or programs to help the organization as a whole. For example, a university might have to close a campus in order to provide quality services at other campuses. Running any large organization is complex, as is project portfolio management.

☑ WHAT WENT RIGHT?

Many companies have seen great returns on investment after implementing basic ideas of project portfolio management. For example, Jane Walton, the project portfolio manager for IT projects at Schlumberger, saved the company $3 million in one year by simply organizing the organization's 120 IT projects into one portfolio. Before then, all IT projects and their associated programs were managed separately, and no one looked at them as a whole. Manufacturing companies used project portfolio management in the 1960s, and Walton anticipated the need to justify investments in IT projects just as managers have to justify capital investment projects. She found that 80% of the organization's projects overlapped, and 14 separate projects were trying to accomplish the same thing. By simply looking at all IT projects and programs together, Schlumberger could make better strategic business decisions. The company canceled several projects and merged others to reduce the newly obvious redundancy.[6]

Mercy Health Partners' chief information officer, Jim Albin, says project portfolio management helped his company improve its IT services and reduce costs by $4 million. It also helped encourage business area leaders to make decisions about how IT resources were used, not the IT department.[7] A crucial part of project portfolio management is looking at the big picture and not focusing on individual departments. Strategic business needs must drive portfolio management.

Recall that project portfolio management focuses on strategic issues while individual projects often focus on tactical issues. Portfolios should be formed and continuously updated to help the organization as a whole make better strategic decisions. Organizations normally put all projects into one portfolio, but then often break it down into more detailed sub-portfolios, often set up by major departments or other categories. Several companies create a separate portfolio for IT projects. It is often difficult to measure the financial value of many IT projects, yet these projects are often a large investment and have a strong effect on other business areas. For example, if you have to update your financial system to meet new government regulations, such as the 2002 Sarbanes-Oxley Act, where would it fit in your enterprise project portfolio? (After several major corporate scandals, the Sarbanes-Oxley Act was passed to help restore public confidence in the financial reporting of publicly traded companies in the United States. Companies have spent millions of dollars to be compliant with this act.) You have to do it to stay in business, but you can't generate a positive return on investment from that particular project.

 BEST PRACTICE

Many organizations rely on effective new product development (NPD) to increase growth and profitability, yet according to Robert Cooper of McMaster University and the New Product Development Institute in Ontario, Canada, only one in seven product concepts comes to fruition. Why is it that some companies, like Proctor & Gamble, Johnson and Johnson, Hewlett Packard, and Sony are consistently successful in NPD? Because they use a disciplined, systematic approach to NPD projects based on best practices, including focusing NPD on business strategy.

Cooper's study compared companies that were the best at performing NPD with those that were the worst. For example:

- 65.5% of companies performing the best at NPD align projects with business strategy.
- 46% of companies performing the worst at NPD align projects with business strategy.
- 65.5% of best performing NPD companies have their resource breakdown aligned to business strategy.
- 8% of worst performing companies do.

It's easy for a company to say that its projects are aligned with business strategy, but assigning its resources based on that strategy is a measurable action that produces results. Best performing NPD companies are also more customer-focused in identifying new product ideas and put a project manager in charge of their NPD projects:

- 69% of best performing NPD companies identify customer needs and problems based on customer input.
- 15% of worst performing companies do.
- 80% of best performing companies have an identifiable NPD project manager.
- 50% of worst performing companies do.[8]

These best practices apply to all projects:

- Align projects *and* resources with business strategy.
- Focus on customer needs when identifying potential projects.
- Assign project managers to lead the projects.

Sample Approach for Creating a Project Portfolio

Figure 2-10 illustrates one approach for project portfolio management in which there is one large portfolio for the entire organization. Sections of the portfolio are then broken down to improve the management of projects in each particular sector. For example, Global Construction might have the main portfolio categories shown in the left part of Figure 2-10 (marketing, materials, IT, and HR (human resources)) and divide each of those categories further to address their unique concerns. The right part of this figure shows how the IT projects could be categorized in more detail to assist in their management. For example, there are three basic IT project portfolio categories:

1. *Venture*: Projects in this category would help transform the business. For example, Global Construction might have an IT project to provide Webcams and interactive Web-based reporting on construction sites that would be easily accessible by its customers and suppliers. This project could help transform the business by developing more trusting partnerships with customers and suppliers, who could know exactly what is happening with their construction projects.

2. *Growth*: Projects in this category would help the company grow in terms of revenue. For example, Global Construction might have an IT project to provide information on its corporate Web site in a new language, such as Chinese or Japanese. This capability could help the company grow its business in those countries.

3. *Core*: Projects in this category must be accomplished to run the business. For example, an IT project to provide computers for new employees would fall under this category.

Note that the core category of IT projects is labeled as nondiscretionary costs. This means that the company has no choice in whether to fund these projects; it must fund them to stay in business. Projects that fall under the venture or growth category would be discretionary costs because the company can use its own discretion in deciding whether to fund them. Also note the arrow in the center of Figure 2-10. This arrow indicates that the risks, value, and timing of projects normally increase as you go from core to growth to venture projects. However, some core projects can also be high risk, have high value, and require good timing.

FIGURE 2-10 Sample project portfolio approach

Five Levels of Project Portfolio Management

As you can imagine, it takes time to understand and apply project portfolio management. You can develop and manage a project portfolio in many ways. Just as projects are unique, so are project portfolios.

An organization can view project portfolio management as having five levels, from simplest to most complex, as follows:

1. Put all of your projects in one list. Many organizations find duplicate or unneeded projects after they identify all the projects on which they are working.

2. Prioritize the projects in your list. It's important to know which projects are most important to an organization so that resources can be applied accordingly.

3. Divide your projects into several categories based on types of investment. Categorizing projects helps you see the big picture, such as how many projects are supporting a growth strategy, how many are helping to increase profit margins, how many relate to marketing, and how many relate to materials. Organizations can create as many categories as they need to help understand and analyze how projects affect business needs and goals.

4. Automate the list. Managers can view project data in many different ways by putting key information into a computerized system. You can enter the project information in spreadsheet software such as Excel. You might have headings for the project name, project manager, project sponsor, business needs addressed, start date, end date, budget, risk, priority, key deliverables, and so on. You can also use more sophisticated tools to help perform project portfolio management, such as enterprise project management software, as described in Chapter 1.

5. Apply modern portfolio theory, including risk-return tools that map project risks. Figure 2-11 provides a sample map to assist in evaluating project risk versus return, or business value. Each bubble represents a project, and the size of the bubble relates to its approved budget (that is, the larger bubbles have larger budgets). Notice that there are not and should not be projects in the lower-right quadrant, which is the location of projects that have low relative value and high risk. As described in Chapter 1, many project portfolio management software products are available on the market today to help analyze portfolios. Consult references on portfolio theory and project portfolio management software for more details on this topic.

It is important for organizations to develop a fair, consistent, and logical process for selecting projects, programs, and portfolios. Studies show that one of the main reasons people quit their jobs is because they feel they do not make a difference. After employees understand how their work fits into the big picture, they can work more effectively to help themselves and their entire organizations succeed.

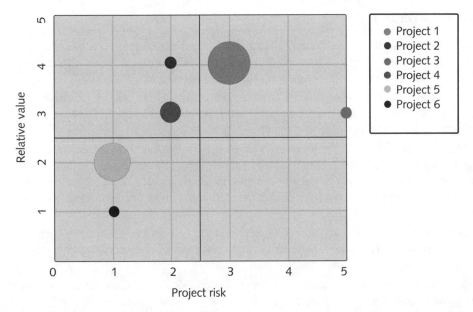

FIGURE 2-11   Sample project portfolio risk map

CASE WRAP-UP

Marie and her team summarized the inputs from the meeting and discussed them with their CEO, Doug Armbruster, and other senior managers. They felt people were nervous that the company might not be doing well and that their jobs were in jeopardy. They discussed options for how to proceed and decided that it was important for the CEO to explain the importance of aligning projects with business strategy. Doug and his staff put together a memo and presentation to explain that the company was doing very well, and that they had no intentions of either letting anyone go or cutting major programs. On the contrary, they had far more projects to pursue than they possibly could, and they believed that using project portfolio management would help them select and manage projects better. After everyone heard this information, they were much more open to working with Marie's group to improve their project, program, and portfolio management processes.

Chapter Summary

An organization's overall business strategy should guide the project selection process and management of those projects. Many organizations perform a SWOT analysis to help identify potential projects based on their strengths, weaknesses, opportunities, and threats.

The four-stage planning process helps organizations align their projects with their business strategy. The four stages of this model, from highest to lowest, are strategic planning, business area analysis, project planning, and resource allocation.

Several methods are available for selecting projects. Financial methods include calculating and analyzing the net present value, return on investment, and payback period for projects. You can also use a weighted scoring model; implement a balanced scorecard; address problems, opportunities, and directives; or consider project time frame or project priority to assist in project selection.

After determining what projects to pursue, it is important to decide if projects should be grouped into programs. The main criteria for program selection are the coordination and benefits available by grouping projects together into a program.

There is no simple process for deciding how to create project portfolios, but the goal of project portfolio management is to help maximize business value to ensure enterprise success. There are five levels of complexity for project portfolio managing, ranging from simply putting all projects in one list to applying modern portfolio theory to analyze risks and returns of a project portfolio.

Quick Quiz

1. Which of the following is not part of a SWOT analysis?

    a. strengths

    b. weaknesses

    c. opportunities

    d. tactics

2. A large company continues to be successful by providing new products and services for its market niche of brides. What is its main competitive strategy?

    a. cost leadership

    b. quality

    c. focus

    d. customer service

3. The last step in the four-stage planning process for projects is _____ .

    a. resource allocation

    b. project planning

    c. business area analysis

    d. strategic planning

4. It is very important to start at the top of the four-stage planning process pyramid to select projects that support the organization's _____ .

   a. vision

   b. business strategy

   c. financial position

   d. culture

5. Which of the following statements is false concerning the financial analysis of projects?

   a. The higher the net present value the better.

   b. A shorter payback period is better than a longer one.

   c. The required rate of return is the discount rate that results in an NPV of zero for the project.

   d. ROI is the result of subtracting the project costs from the benefits and then dividing by the costs.

6. A _____ is a methodology that converts an organization's value drivers—such as customer service, innovation, operational efficiency, and financial performance—into a series of defined metrics.

   a. balanced scorecard

   b. weighted scoring model

   c. net present value analysis

   d. directive

7. Which of the following is not a major benefit of grouping projects into programs?

   a. increasing revenues

   b. increasing authority

   c. saving money

   d. saving time

8. A college approved a project to provide discounts for faculty, students, and staff to use the city's new light-rail system. Under what existing program might this project naturally fit?

   a. academic enrichment program

   b. fund-raising program

   c. entertainment program

   d. transportation program

9. The goal of project portfolio management is to help maximize business value to ensure _____ .

   a. profit maximization

   b. enterprise success

   c. risk minimization

   d. competitive advantage

10. Many organizations find duplicate or unneeded projects after they perform which step in project portfolio management?

    a. prioritizing the projects in their list

    b. dividing the projects into several categories based on type of investment

    c. putting all projects in one list

    d. applying modern portfolio theory, including risk-return tools that map project risk

Quick Quiz Answers

1. D; 2. C; 3. A; 4. B; 5. C; 6. A; 7. A; 8. D; 9. B; 10. C

Discussion Questions

1. Why is it important to align projects to business strategy? What is SWOT analysis? How can you use a mind map to create a SWOT analysis and generate project ideas?

2. What are the stages called in the four-stage planning process for project selection? How does following this process assist in selecting projects that will provide the most benefit to organizations?

3. When should you use net present value analysis to evaluate projects? How do you decide which projects to pursue using net present value analysis? How do return on investment and payback period relate to net present value?

4. What are three main benefits of grouping projects into programs?

5. What are the five levels of project portfolio management?

Exercises

Note: These exercises can be done individually or in teams, in class, as homework, or in a virtual environment. Students can either write their results in a paper or prepare a short presentation to show their results.

1. Perform a financial analysis for a project using the format provided in Figure 2-6. Assume the projected costs and benefits for this project are spread over four years as follows: Estimated costs are $100,000 in Year 1 and $25,000 each year in Years 2, 3, and 4. (*Hint*: Just change the years in the template file from 0, 1, 2, 3, and 4 to 1, 2, 3, 4, and 5. The discount factors will automatically be recalculated.) Estimated benefits are $0 in Year 1 and $80,000 each year in Years 2, 3, and 4. Use an 8% discount rate. Use the business case financials template provided on the companion Web site to calculate and clearly display the NPV, ROI, and year in which payback occurs. In addition, write a paragraph explaining whether you would recommend investing in this project based on your financial analysis.

2. Create a weighted scoring model to determine which project to select. Assume the criteria are cost, strategic value, risk, and financials, with weights of 15%, 40%, 20%, and 25%, respectively. Enter values for Project 1 as 90, 70, 85, and 50; Project 2 as 75, 80, 90, and 70; and Project 3 as 80 for each criterion. Use the weighted scoring model template provided on the companion Web site to create the model, calculate the weighted score, and graph the results.

3. Search the Internet to find a real example of how a company or organization uses a structured process to aid in project, program, and/or project portfolio selection. As an alternative, document the process you followed to make a major decision where you had multiple options, such as what college or university to attend, what job to take, where to live, what car to buy, etc. Write a one-page paper or prepare a short presentation summarizing your findings.

4. Search the Internet for software that helps organizations perform strategic planning, project selection, or project portfolio management. Summarize at least three different tools and discuss whether or not you think these tools are good investments in a one- to two-page paper. Cite your references.

Team Projects

1. Find someone who has been involved in the project selection process within an organization. Prepare several interview questions, and then ask him your questions in person, via the phone, or via the Internet. Be sure to ask if he uses any of the project selection tools discussed in this chapter (that is, financial analysis, weighted scoring models, balanced scorecard, and so on). Discuss the results with your team, and then prepare a one- to two-page paper or prepare a short presentation summarizing your findings.

2. Search the Internet to find two good examples of how organizations group projects into programs and two examples of how they create project portfolios. Write a one- to two-page paper or prepare a short presentation summarizing your results, being sure to cite your references.

3. Develop criteria that your class could use to help select what projects to pursue for implementation by your class or another group. For example, criteria might include benefits to the organization, interest level of the sponsor, interest level of the class, and fit with class skills and timing. Determine a weight for each criterion, and then enter the criteria and weights into a weighted scoring model, similar to that shown in Figure 2-8. (You can use the template for a weighted scoring model provided on the companion Web site.) Then review the list of projects you prepared in Chapter 1, Team Project 3, and enter scores for at least five of those projects. Calculate the weighted score for each project. Write a one- to two-page paper or prepare a short presentation summarizing your results.

4. Using your college, university, or an organization your team is familiar with, create a mind map of a SWOT analysis, including at least three branches under each category. Also add sub-branches with at least four potential project ideas. You can create the mind map by hand, or try using software like MindManager (free trial available at *www.mindjet.com*) or FreeMind (available at *www.freemind.sourceforge.net*).

5. As a team, discuss other methods you could use to select class projects. Be sure to review the other methods described in this chapter (besides a weighted scoring model). Document your analysis of each approach as it applies to this situation in a two- to three-page paper or 10 minute presentation.

Companion Web Site

Visit the companion Web site for this text (*www.course.com/mis/pm2/schwalbe* or *http://login.course.com*) *to access:*

- Lecture notes
- Interactive quizzes and Jeopardy games
- Template files
- Sample documents
- Podcasts
- More ideas for team projects, including real projects, and case studies
- Links to additional resources related to project management

Key Terms

balanced scorecard — A methodology that converts an organization's value drivers to a series of defined metrics.

cash flow — Benefits minus costs, or income minus expenses.

directives — The new requirements imposed by management, government, or some external influence.

discount factor — A multiplier for each year based on the discount rate and year.

discount rate — The rate used in discounting future cash flows.

internal rate of return (IRR) — The discount rate that results in an NPV of zero for a project.

mind mapping — A technique that uses branches radiating out from a core idea to structure thoughts and ideas.

net present value (NPV) analysis — A method of calculating the expected net monetary gain or loss from a project by discounting all expected future cash inflows and outflows to the present point in time.

opportunities — Chances to improve the organization.

opportunity cost of capital — The return available by investing the capital elsewhere.

payback period — The amount of time it will take to recoup, in the form of net cash inflows, the total dollars invested in a project.

problems — Undesirable situations that prevent the organization from achieving its goals.

required rate of return — The minimum acceptable rate of return on an investment.

return on investment (ROI) — (Benefits minus costs) divided by costs.

strategic planning — The process of determining long-term objectives by analyzing the strengths and weaknesses of an organization, studying opportunities and threats in the business environment, predicting future trends, and projecting the need for new products and services.

SWOT analysis — Analyzing Strengths, Weaknesses, Opportunities, and Threats.

weighted scoring model — A technique that provides a systematic process for basing project selection on numerous criteria.

End Notes

[1] Mike Peterson, "Why Are We Doing This Project?" Projects@Work, (*www.projectsatwork. com*) (February 22, 2005).

[2] Dennis J. Cohen and Robert J. Graham, *The Project Manager's MBA*. San Francisco: Jossey-Bass, (2001), p. 31.

[3] Marc L. Songini, "Tight Budgets Put More Pressure on IT," *Computer World* (December 2, 2002).

[4] The Balanced Scorecard Institute, "What Is a Balanced Scorecard?" (*www.balancedscorecard. org*) (February 2003).

[5] The Compleat Sean Bean Web Site, "Lord of the Rings" (February 23, 2004).

[6] Scott Berinato, "Do the Math," *CIO Magazine* (October 1, 2001).

[7] Joshua Weinberger, "Voice of Experience: Mercy Health Partners CIO Jim Albin," *Baseline Magazine* (October 1, 2003).

[8] Robert G. Cooper, "Winning at New Products: Pathways to Profitable Intervention," PMI Research Conference Proceedings (July 2006).

CHAPTER **3**

INITIATING PROJECTS

LEARNING OBJECTIVES

After reading this chapter, you will be able to:

- Describe the five project management process groups, map them to the project management knowledge areas, discuss other project management methodologies and why organizations often develop their own, and understand the importance of top management commitment and organizational standards in project management

- Discuss the initiating process used by Global Construction, Inc., including pre-initiating tasks, breaking large projects down into smaller projects, and initiating tasks

- Identify project stakeholders and perform a stakeholder analysis

- Prepare a business case to justify the need for a project

- Create a project charter to formally initiate a project

- Describe the importance of holding a good project kick-off meeting

- Develop a preliminary project scope statement to help understand project requirements

OPENING CASE

Marie Scott worked with other managers at Global Construction, Inc. to decide what projects their firm should undertake to meet business needs. Construction is a low-margin, very competitive industry, and productivity improvements are crucial to improving shareholder returns. After participating in several strategic planning and project selection workshops, one of the opportunities the company decided to pursue was just-in-time training. Several managers pointed out that Global Construction was spending more than the industry average on training its employees, especially in its sales, purchasing, engineering, and information technology departments, yet productivity for those workers had not improved much in recent years. They also knew that they needed to transfer knowledge from many of their retiring workers to their younger workers. Global Construction, Inc. still offered most courses during work hours using an instructor-led format, and the course topics had not changed in years. Several managers knew that their competitors had successfully implemented just-in-time training programs so that their workers could get the type of training they needed when they needed it. For example, much of the training was provided over the Internet, so employees could access it anytime, anywhere. Employees were also able to ask questions of instructors as well as experts within the company at any time via the Internet to help them perform specific job duties. In addition, experts documented important knowledge and let other workers share their suggestions. Management believed that Global Construction could reduce training costs and improve productivity by successfully implementing a project to provide just-in-time training on key topics and promote a more collaborative working environment.

Mike Sundby, the vice president of human resources, was the project's champion. After successfully completing a Phase I Just-In-Time Training study to decide how they should proceed with the overall project, Mike and his directors selected Kristin Maur to lead Phase II of the project. Kristin suggested partnering with an outside firm to help with some of the project's technical aspects. Mike asked Kristin to start forming her project team and to prepare important initiating documents, including a business case, a stakeholder analysis, a project charter, and a preliminary scope statement for the project. He was also looking forward to participating in the official kick-off meeting.

PROJECT MANAGEMENT PROCESS GROUPS

Recall from Chapter 1 that project management consists of nine project management knowledge areas: project integration, scope, time, cost, quality, human resource, communications, risk, and procurement management. Another important concept to understand is that projects involve five project management process groups: initiating, planning, executing, monitoring and controlling, and closing. Applying these process groups in a consistent, structured fashion increases the chance of project success. This chapter briefly describes each project management process group and then describes the initiating process in detail through a case study based on Global Construction's Just-In-Time Training project. Subsequent chapters describe the other process groups and apply them to the same project.

Project management process groups progress from initiating activities to planning activities, executing activities, monitoring and controlling activities, and closing activities. A **process** is a series of actions directed toward a particular result. All projects use the five process groups as outlined in the following list:

- **Initiating processes** include actions to begin or end projects and project phases. To initiate a project such as the Just-In-Time Training project, someone must develop a project charter and hold a kick-off meeting to officially start the project. This chapter will describe these and other initiating tasks in detail.

- **Planning processes** include devising and maintaining a workable scheme to ensure that the project meets its scope, time, and cost goals as well as organizational needs. There are often many different plans to address various project needs as they relate to each knowledge area. For example, as part of project scope management for the Just-In-Time Training project, the project team will develop a scope statement to plan the work that needs to be done to develop and provide the products and services produced as part of the project. As part of project time management, the project team will create a detailed schedule that lets everyone know when specific work will start and end. As part of procurement management, the project team will plan for work that will be done by external organizations to support the project. Chapters 4 and 5 describe the planning tasks in detail.

- **Executing processes** include coordinating people and other resources to carry out the project plans and produce the deliverables of the project or phase. A **deliverable** is a product or service produced or provided as part of a project. For example, a project to construct a new office building would include deliverables such as blueprints, cost estimates, progress reports, the building structure, windows, plumbing, and flooring. The Just-In-Time Training project would include deliverables such as a training needs survey, training materials, and classes. Chapter 6 describes executing tasks in detail.

- **Monitoring and controlling processes** measure progress toward achieving project goals, monitor deviation from plans, and take corrective action to match progress with plans and customer expectations. For example, the main objective of the Just-In-Time Training project is to provide training to help employees be more productive. If the first training course does not improve productivity or meet other customer expectations, the project team should take corrective action to deliver more suitable training courses. As another example, if the project team continues to miss deadlines in the schedule for the Just-In-Time Training project, the project manager should lead the team in taking corrective action, such as developing a more realistic schedule or securing additional resources to help meet deadlines. Chapter 7 describes monitoring and controlling tasks in detail.

- **Closing processes** include formalizing acceptance of the project or phase and bringing it to an orderly end. Administrative tasks are often involved in this process group, such as archiving project files, closing out contracts, documenting lessons learned, and receiving formal acceptance of the deliverables. It is also important to plan for a smooth transition of the results of the project to the responsible operational group. For example, after the Just-In-Time Training project is completed, the training department will need to schedule and provide courses developed as part of the project. The planning for this transition should be done as part of the closing process group. Chapter 8 describes closing tasks in detail.

The process groups are not isolated events. For example, project managers must perform monitoring and controlling processes throughout the project's life span. The level of activity and length of each process group varies for every project. Normally, executing tasks require the most resources and time, followed by planning tasks. Initiating and closing tasks are usually the shortest (at the beginning and end of a project or phase, respectively), and they require the least amount of resources and time. However, every project is unique, so there can be exceptions.

Many people ask for guidelines on how much time to spend in each process group. In his 2006 book, *Alpha Project Managers: What the Top 2% Know That Everyone Else Does Not*, Andy Crowe collected data from 860 project managers in various companies and industries in the United States. He found that the best or "alpha" project managers spent more time on every process group than their counterparts except for execution, as follows:

- Initiating: 2% vs. 1%
- Planning: 21% vs. 11%
- Executing: 69% vs. 82%
- Controlling: 5% vs. 4%
- Closing: 3% vs. 2%[1]

This breakdown suggests that the most time should be spent on executing, followed by planning. Note the importance of spending a fair amount of time on planning, which should lead to less time spent on execution.

Note that process groups apply to entire projects as well as to project phases. A **phase** is a distinct stage in project development, and most projects have distinct phases. For example, the Just-In-Time Training project includes phases called study or feasibility, course design and development, course administration, and course evaluation. In this case, the study or feasibility phase is done as a separate project. The other phases were done in a second, larger project. To ensure that they continue to meet current organizational needs, projects should pass successfully through each phase before continuing.

Mapping the Process Groups to the Knowledge Areas

You can map the process group into the nine project management knowledge areas. For example, project integration management includes the following seven processes:

- Develop a project charter and develop a preliminary project scope statement (during the initiating process group).
- Develop a project management plan (during the planning process group).

- Develop and manage project execution (during the executing process group).
- Monitor and control project work and integrated change control (during the monitoring and controlling process group).
- Close the project (during the closing process group).

Based on the *PMBOK® Guide,* Third Edition, there are 44 total processes in project management. Figure 3-1 provides a big-picture view of the relationships among these processes, the time in which they are typically completed, and the knowledge areas into which they fit.

Knowledge area	Project management process groups				
	Initiating	Planning	Executing	Monitoring and Controlling	Closing
Project integration management	Develop project charter; develop preliminary project scope statement	Develop project management plan	Direct and manage project execution	Monitor and control project work; integrate change control	Close project
Project scope management		Plan scope; define scope; create WBS		Verify scope; control scope	
Project time management		Define activities; sequence activities; estimate activity resources; estimate activity durations; develop schedule		Control schedule	
Project cost management		Estimate cost; plan cost budget		Control cost	
Project quality management		Plan for quality assurance	Perform quality assurance	Perform quality control	
Project human resource management		Develop human resources plan	Acquire project team; develop project team	Manage project team	
Project communications management		Plan for communications	Distribute information	Report performance; manage stakeholders	

FIGURE 3-1 Project management process groups and knowledge area mapping

Knowledge area	Project management process groups				
	Initiating	Planning	Executing	Monitoring and Controlling	Closing
Project risk management		Develop risk management plan; identify risks; perform qualitative risk analysis; perform quantitative risk analysis; plan risk response		Monitor and control risk	
Project procurement management		Plan purchases and acquisitions; plan contracting	Request seller responses; select sellers	Administer contracts	Close contracts

PMBOK® Guide, Third Edition, p. 70

FIGURE 3-1   Project management process groups and knowledge area mapping (continued)

This chapter describes in detail the processes followed and the outputs produced while initiating the Just-In-Time Training project. For example, key outputs of initiating described in this chapter include the following:

- Stakeholder analysis
- Business case for the project
- Project charter
- Kick-off meeting
- Preliminary scope statement

You can also access templates to help create these and other documents on the companion Web site for this text, as summarized in Appendix C. A **template** is a file with a preset format that serves as a starting point for creating various documents so that the format and structure do not have to be re-created. The remaining chapters of this text follow a similar format to describe the processes and outputs used for the Just-In-Time Training project for planning, executing, monitoring and controlling, and closing. To help you visualize outputs for each process group, Figure 3-2, shown later in the chapter, summarizes the outputs for the initiating process group. Similar figures or tables are provided in the following chapters as well.

Several organizations use PMI's information as a foundation for developing their own project management methodologies, as described in the next section. Notice in Figure 3-1 that the majority of project management processes occur as part of the planning process group. Because each project is unique, project teams are always trying to do something that has not been done before. To succeed at unique and new activities, project teams must do a fair amount of planning. Recall, however, that the most time and money is normally spent on executing because that is where the project's products and/or services (for example, the buildings for a construction project, the training courses for a training project, and so on) are produced. It is good practice for organizations to determine how project management will work best in their own organizations.

Developing a Project Management Methodology

Some organizations spend a great deal of time and money on training efforts for general project management skills, but after the training, a project manager might still not know how to tailor their project management skills to the organization's particular needs. Because of this problem, some organizations develop their own internal project management methodologies. The *PMBOK® Guide* is a **standard** that describes best practices for *what* should be done to manage a project. A **methodology** describes *how* things should be done.

Besides using the *PMBOK® Guide* as a basis for a project management methodology, many organizations use others, such as the following:

- *PRojects IN Controlled Environments (PRINCE2)*: Originally developed for information technology projects, PRINCE2 was released in 1996 as a generic project management methodology by the U.K. Office of Government Commerce (OCG). It is the defacto standard in the U.K. and is used in over 50 countries. (See *www.prince2.com* for more information.) PRINCE2 defines 45 separate sub-processes and organizes these into eight process groups as follows:

  1. Starting Up a Project
  2. Planning
  3. Initiating a Project
  4. Directing a Project
  5. Controlling a Stage
  6. Managing Product Delivery
  7. Managing Stage Boundaries
  8. Closing a Project

- *Rational Unified Process (RUP) framework*: RUP is an iterative software development process that focuses on team productivity and delivers software best practices to all team members. According to RUP expert Bill Cottrell, "RUP embodies industry-standard management and technical methods and techniques to provide a software engineering process particularly suited to creating and maintaining component-based software system solutions."[2] Cottrell explains that you can tailor RUP to include the PMBOK process groups, since several customers asked for that capability. There are several other project management methodologies specifically for software development projects such as Joint Application Development (JAD), Rapid Application Development (RAD), and Extreme Programming. (See Web sites like *www.ibm.com/software/awdtools/rup* for more information.)
- *Six Sigma*: Many organizations have projects underway that use Six Sigma methodologies. The work of many project quality experts contributed to the development of today's Six Sigma principles. In their book, The Six Sigma Way,

authors Peter Pande, Robert Neuman, and Roland Cavanagh define Six Sigma as "a comprehensive and flexible system for achieving, sustaining and maximizing business success. Six Sigma is uniquely driven by close understanding of customer needs, disciplined use of facts, data, and statistical analysis, and diligent attention to managing, improving, and reinventing business processes."[3] Six Sigma's target for perfection is the achievement of no more than 3.4 defects, errors, or mistakes per million opportunities. The two main methodologies used on Six Sigma projects: DMAIC (Define, Measure, Analyze, Improve, and Control) is used to improve an existing business process, and DMADV (Define, Measure, Analyze, Design, and Verify) is used to create new product or process designs to achieve predictable, defect-free performance. (See Web sites like *www.isixsigma.com* for more information.)

Many organizations tailor a standard or methodology to meet their unique needs. For example, if organizations use the *PMBOK® Guide* as the basis for their project management methodology, they still have to do a fair amount of work to adapt it to their work environment.

For example, the *PMBOK® Guide* lists *what* information a project charter, as described later in this chapter, should address:

- Requirements that satisfy customer, sponsor, and other stakeholder needs, wants, and expectations
- Business needs, a high-level project description, or product requirements that the project is undertaken to address
- Project purpose or justification
- Assignment of a project manager and designation of his or her authority level
- Summary milestone schedule
- Stakeholder influences
- Identification of functional organizations and their participation
- Organizational, environmental, and external assumptions
- Organizational, environmental, and external constraints
- Business case justifying the project, including return on investment
- Summary budget or money allocated for the project

However, the *PMBOK® Guide* does not provide information on *how* the previously listed project charter requirements should be created, when, or by whom. Also, many organizations prefer that project charters be fairly short documents. They create a separate document with business case information, only if it is required for the project, instead of including it in a project charter. (As the name implies, a **business case** is a document that provides justification for investing in a project.) Some organizations list different project management requirements based on the dollar value of a project. For example, a project estimated to cost less than $50,000 might not require a business case. A project estimated to cost more than $1 million might need an extensive business case signed off by the Chief Financial Officer. Successful organizations have found that they need to develop and follow a customized, formal project management process that describes not only what needs to be done, but also how it should be done in their organizations. They also must involve key stakeholders and ensure that projects are aligned with organizational needs.

☑ WHAT WENT RIGHT?

William Ibbs and Justin Reginato completed a five-year study to help quantify the value of project management. Among their findings are the following points:

- Organizations with more mature project management practices have better project performance, which result in projects completed on time and within budget much more often than most projects.
- Project management maturity is strongly correlated with more predictable project schedule and cost performance.
- Organizations that follow good project management methodologies have lower direct costs of project management (6–7 percent) than those that do not (11–20 percent).[4]

Another study published by the Centre for Business Practices shows that creating value for stakeholders is the key to project and organizational success. Organizations that stress shareholders, customers, and employees outperform those that do not. "Over an 11-year period, the former increased revenues by an average of 682% versus 166% for the latter, expanded their workforces by 282% versus 36%, grew their stock prices by 901% versus 74%, and improved their net incomes by 756% versus 1%."[5]

Part of creating and following a project management methodology includes the creation and use of templates. Companies that excel in project management know that it does not make sense to reinvent the wheel by having every project manager decide how to create standard documents, such as project charters and business cases. They also know that top management commitment and organizational standards are crucial for project success.

The Importance of Top Management Commitment

Without top management commitment, many projects will fail. Some projects have a senior manager called a **champion** who acts as a key proponent for a project. Projects are part of the larger organizational environment, and many factors that might affect a project are out of the project manager's control. Top management commitment is crucial for the following reasons:

- Project managers need adequate resources. The best way to kill a project is to withhold the required money, human resources, and/or visibility for the project. If project managers have top management commitment, they will also have adequate resources and be able to focus on completing their specific projects.
- Project managers often require approval for unique project needs in a timely manner. For example, a project team might have unexpected problems and need additional resources halfway through the project, or the project manager might need to offer special pay and benefits to attract and retain key project personnel. With top management commitment, project managers can meet these specific needs in a timely manner.

- Project managers must have cooperation from people in other parts of the organization. Because most projects cut across functional areas, top management must help project managers deal with the political issues that often arise in these types of situations. If certain functional managers are not responding to project managers' requests for necessary information, top management must step in to encourage functional managers to cooperate.
- Project managers often need someone to mentor and coach them on leadership issues. Many project managers come from technical positions and are inexperienced as managers. Senior managers should take the time to pass on advice on how to be good leaders. They should encourage new project managers to take classes to develop leadership skills and allocate the time and funds for them to do so.

The Need for Organizational Standards

Another problem in most organizations is not having standards or guidelines to follow that could help in performing project management functions. These standards or guidelines might be as simple as providing standard forms or templates for common project documents, examples of good project documentation, or guidelines on how the project manager should perform certain tasks, such as holding a kick-off meeting or providing status information. Providing status information might seem like common sense to senior managers, but many new project managers have never given a project status report and are not used to communicating with a wide variety of project stakeholders. Top management must support the development of these standards and guidelines and encourage or even enforce their use.

Some organizations invest heavily in project management by creating a project management office or center of excellence. A **project management office (PMO)** is an organizational entity created to assist project managers in achieving project goals. Some organizations develop career paths for project managers. Some require that all project managers have some type of project management certification and that all employees have some type of project management training. The implementation of all of these standards demonstrates an organization's commitment to project management and helps them ensure project success.

Many people learn best by example. The following section describes an example of how Global Construction applied initiating processes to the Just-In-Time Training project. It uses some of the ideas from the *PMBOK® Guide* and additional ideas to meet the unique needs of this project and organization. Several templates illustrate how project teams prepare various project management documents. You can download these templates from the companion Web site for this text.

BEST PRACTICE

It is very important to follow best practices while initiating projects, especially to avoid major scope problems. Senior management must take an active role in following these best practices:

1. Keep the scope realistic. Don't make projects so large that they can't be completed. Break large projects down into a series of smaller ones.

2. Involve users from the start. Assign key users to the project team, invite them to important meetings, and require their signatures on key documents. Assign a manager from the operations group most affected by the project as the project manager. Also assign a champion to help promote the project.

3. Use off-the-shelf hardware and software whenever possible. Many people enjoy using the latest and greatest technology, but business needs, not technology trends, must take priority.

4. Follow good project management processes. As described in this chapter and others, there are several standards and methodologies for managing projects. Senior managers should define them and enforce their use as appropriate on their projects.

INITIATING PROCESS FOR GLOBAL CONSTRUCTION'S JUST-IN-TIME TRAINING PROJECT

Figure 3-2 illustrates the process that Global Construction will follow for initiating the Just-In-Time Training project. Notice that several tasks are completed *before* the project initiation starts. First, the project is approved through a formal project selection process and is given the go-ahead. Second, senior managers perform several activities as part of pre-initiating, as described in the following section. Finally, initiating begins as the project manager works with the team and other stakeholders to hold a kick-off meeting for the project and produce a stakeholder analysis, a business case, a project charter, and a preliminary scope statement.

Pre-initiating Tasks

It is good practice to lay the groundwork for a project before it officially starts. After a project is approved, senior managers should meet to accomplish the following tasks:

- Determine the scope, time, and cost constraints for the project
- Identify the project sponsor
- Select the project manager
- Meet with the project manager to review the process and expectations for managing the project
- Determine if the project should be divided into two or more smaller projects

FIGURE 3-2 Initiating process summary

Why is it necessary to perform these last two tasks? Many organizations have organizational processes and procedures in place for managing projects. It is very important for project managers to understand them as well as the expectations for the project. For example, will there be formal management reviews for the project, and if so, how often will they be held? Are there any regulations, standards, or guidelines related to the project? Is there historical information or are there reports on lessons learned from past projects that might apply to the project? Senior managers should also share their wisdom with project managers to get the project off to a good start. For example, they might recommend key people who would be good team members for the project or offer suggestions based on personal experiences.

Many people know from experience that it is easier to successfully complete a small project than a large one. It often makes sense to break large projects down into two or more smaller projects. For Global Construction's Just-In-Time Training project, senior management decided to use this approach. They knew that when scope, time, and cost goals for a large project were unclear, it would help to have a Phase I project to clarify the situation. For a large training project, there is often a study project done first before investing in a larger project.

Lucy Camarena, training director, would sponsor the study project, called the Just-In-Time Training Phase I project. Mike Sundby, the vice president of human resources, would act as the project champion. Lucy assigned one of her senior staff members, Ron Ryan, to manage the project. The scope, time, and cost goals and a summary of the approach and assumptions are provided in Figure 3-3.

Senior managers were satisfied with the results of the Phase I project, but they realized that they did not want someone from the HR department to lead the Phase II project. Instead, they wanted a manager from one of their key operating divisions—such as sales,

Scope Goals:

- Investigate and document the training taken in the last two years by all internal employees.
- Determine what courses were taken, the cost of all training, the process for approving/assigning training, and the evaluation of the training by participants, if available.
- Survey employees to get their input on what training they believe they'll need in the next two years, and how they want to receive that training (instructor-led in-house; instructor-led through a local college, university, or training company; Web-based; CD-ROM). Also hold focus groups to verify training needs.
- Recommend how to provide the most valuable training for Global Construction employees in the next two years.
- Determine the scope, time, and cost goals for the development and implementation of the Just-In-Time Training Phase II project.

Time Goals: Three months
Cost Goals: $50,000

Approach/Assumptions:

- All of the costs would be for internal labor.
- All managers and employees would receive information about this study project.
- A response rate of 30 percent would be acceptable for the survey.
- The project team would do extensive research to back up their recommendations.
- The team would also provide detailed monthly reports and presentations to a steering committee.
- The final deliverables would include a one-hour final presentation and a comprehensive project report documenting all of the information and recommendations.

FIGURE 3-3 Summary information for Just-In-Time Training Phase I project

engineering, or purchasing—to lead the project. It was important to have buy-in for this new training program from the operating groups, and a strong project manager from one of those areas would likely have more respect and influence than one from HR. Someone from operations would also know firsthand what type of training people in operations would need. HR posted the position internally, and a selection committee decided that Kristin Maur, a former purchasing specialist and now a sales manager, was the best person to lead the Just-In-Time Training Phase II project.

Senior managers at Global Construction knew that it was good practice to have experienced managers from operations lead projects that were critical to the operational areas. They also knew that they needed support from several senior managers in the operating divisions as well as other areas, such as IT. So they asked key managers from several divisions to be on a project steering committee to oversee the project. As its name implies, a project steering committee steers a project in the right direction by overseeing it and providing guidance to the project manager. The people on the steering committee are important stakeholders on the project.

Now that important pre-initiating tasks were completed, Kristin Maur was ready to tackle important tasks to initiate the Just-In-Time Training project.

Initiating Tasks

The main tasks normally involved in project initiation are as follows:

- Identifying and understanding project stakeholders
- Preparing a business case for the project
- Creating the project charter
- Holding a kick-off meeting
- Developing a preliminary scope statement

For the Just-In-Time Training Phase I project, Ron Ryan led his small team in doing all of the initiating activities except for creating a business case. Global Construction only requires a formal business case for projects over a certain dollar amount (over $50,000 in this case) or when the sponsor requests it. The company also requires a stakeholder analysis and a project kick-off meeting as outputs of the initiating process. The following sections of this chapter describe each of these outputs in detail for the larger Just-In-Time Training Phase II project.

IDENTIFYING AND UNDERSTANDING PROJECT STAKEHOLDERS

Recall from Chapter 1 that project stakeholders are the people involved in or affected by project activities. Stakeholders can be internal to the organization or external.

- Internal project stakeholders generally include the project sponsor, project team, support staff, and internal customers for the project. Other internal stakeholders include top management, other functional managers, and other project managers. Because organizations have limited resources, projects affect top management, other functional managers, and other project managers by using some of the organization's limited resources.
- External project stakeholders include the project's customers (if they are external to the organization), competitors, and suppliers, and other external groups that are potentially involved in or affected by the project, such as government officials and concerned citizens.

Because the purpose of project management is to meet project requirements and satisfy stakeholders, it is critical that project managers take adequate time to identify, understand, and manage relationships with all project stakeholders. A tool to help accomplish these tasks is a stakeholder analysis.

Preparing a Stakeholder Analysis

A **stakeholder analysis** provides information on key stakeholders to help manage relationships with them. The type of information included in a stakeholder analysis includes the following:

- Names and organizations of key stakeholders
- Their roles on the project
- Unique facts about each stakeholder
- Their level of interest in the project
- Their influence on the project
- Suggestions for managing relationships with each stakeholder

It is helpful to start preparing a stakeholder analysis during initiation and adding information to it during the planning process.

How does a project manager identify key project stakeholders and find out more about them? The best way is by asking around. There might be formal organizational charts or biographies that can provide some information, but the main goal of the stakeholder analysis is to help project managers manage relationships with key stakeholders. Talking to other people who have worked with those stakeholders usually provides the best information. For example, in this case, Kristin Maur knew who some of the key stakeholders were but did not know any of them well. It did not take her long, however, to get the information she needed.

Because a stakeholder analysis often includes sensitive information, it should *not* be part of the official project plans, which are normally available for all stakeholders to review. In many cases, only project managers and a few other team members should be involved in preparing the stakeholder analysis. In most cases, the analysis is not even written down, and if it is, its distribution is strictly limited.

Sample Stakeholder Analysis

Figure 3-4 provides an example of a stakeholder analysis that Kristin Maur could use to help her manage the Just-In-Time Training Phase II project (referred to without the Phase II from now on). It is important for project managers to take the time to perform a stakeholder analysis of some sort to identify and try to meet stakeholder needs and expectations. In addition, as new stakeholders are added to the project and more information is provided, the analysis should be updated. Early in this project, for example, all of the stakeholders are internal to the company; later on, however, there will be external stakeholders as well.

Stakeholder Analysis
July 3, 2009

Project Name: Just-In-Time Training Project

KEY STAKEHOLDERS					
	Mike Sundby	**Lucy Camarena**	**Ron Ryan**	**Mohamed Abdul**	**Julia Portman**
Organization	VP of HR	Training director	Senior HR staff member	Senior programmer/ analyst	VP of IT
Role on project	Project champion	Project sponsor	Led the Phase I project	Project team member	Project steering committee member
Unique facts	Outgoing, demanding, focuses on the big picture; MBA with emphasis on organizational design	Very professional, easy to work with but can stretch out discussions; Ph.D. in education	Old-timer; jealous that he wasn't asked to lead Phase II project	Excellent technical skills, English his second language, weak people skills, not excited about a training project	Thinks the company is way behind in applying IT, especially for training; wary of many suppliers
Level of interest	Very high	Very high	High	Medium	High
Level of influence	Very high; can call the shots	Very high; subject matter expert	Medium; he could sabotage the project	High; needs strong IT support for project to succeed	High; people listen to her at steering committee meetings
Suggestions on managing relationship	Keep informed, ask for advice as often as needed	Make sure she reviews work before showing to managers	Ask Lucy to talk to him to avoid problems, ask him to be available for advice	Help him see the project's importance, encourage his creativity	Compliment her a lot, ask for additional IT support as needed

FIGURE 3-4 Sample stakeholder analysis

PREPARING A BUSINESS CASE FOR THE PROJECT

Successful organizations initiate projects to meet business needs, and a common business need is to spend money wisely. As stated previously, a business case is a document that provides justification for investing in a project. As described in the opening case, Global Construction believed they could reduce training costs and improve productivity by successfully implementing a project to provide just-in-time training on key topics.

The Phase I project provided a wealth of information to help write a business case for the Phase II project. Kristin and Lucy reviewed this information carefully and worked together to create the business case. They also had one of the company's financial managers review the information for accuracy.

Contents of a Business Case

Like most project documents, the contents of a business case will vary to meet individual project needs. Typical information included in a business case includes the following:

- Introduction/Background
- Business Objective
- Current Situation and Problem/Opportunity Statement
- Critical Assumptions and Constraints
- Analysis of Options and Recommendation
- Preliminary Project Requirements
- Budget Estimate and Financial Analysis
- Schedule Estimate
- Potential Risks
- Exhibits

Because this project is relatively small and is for an internal sponsor, the business case is not as long as many other business cases. The following section shows the initial business case for the Just-In-Time Training project.

Sample Business Case

Kristin reviewed all of the information created from the Phase I project and drafted a business case. She reviewed it with her sponsor, Lucy (the training director) and had Peter from finance review the financial section. Peter told Kristin to be very conservative by not including any benefit projections that were based on productivity improvements. She still estimated that the project would have a 27 percent discounted return on investment and payback in the second year after implementing the new training program. The resulting business case, including a detailed financial analysis, is provided in Figure 3-5.

Business Case
July 11, 2009

Project Name: Just-In-Time Training Project

1.0 Introduction/Background

Global Construction employs 10,000 full-time employees in 10 different counties and 15 states in the United States. They spend an average of $1,000 per employee for training (not including tuition reimbursement), which is higher than the industry average. However, the productivity of workers—especially in the sales, purchasing, engineering, and information technology departments—has not improved much in recent years. In the fast-paced, ever-changing construction market, training employees about new products, new technologies, and soft skills across a globally dispersed company with different populations is a challenge. By redesigning training, Global Construction can reduce training costs and improve productivity.

2.0 Business Objective

Global Construction's strategic goals include continuing growth and profitability. The company must have a highly skilled workforce to continue to compete in a global environment. Current training programs, however, are expensive and outdated. We can reduce costs by providing more targeted and timely training to our employees and by taking advantage of new technologies and business partnerships. Global Construction can also increase profits by improving productivity, especially by improving supplier management and negotiation skills.

3.0 Current Situation and Problem/Opportunity Statement

Global Construction has not updated its training approach or course offerings in the past five years. Most training is provided on-site during business hours and uses a traditional instructor-led approach with little or no technology involved. Department managers often request slots for various courses, but then they send whoever is available to the course because the department has already paid for it. Therefore, there is often a mismatch between skills needed by employees and the skills taught in a course. The current training is expensive and ineffective. Many employees would like training in key subjects that are currently not provided and that would use more modern approaches and technologies. If the training is directly related to their jobs or interests, employees are willing to take it on their own time, if needed. Survey results indicated that employees are most in need of training in supplier management, negotiating skills, project management, Six Sigma (a quality management methodology), and software applications (for example, spreadsheet and Web development tools).

4.0 Critical Assumptions and Constraints

This project requires strong participation and cooperation from a wide variety of people. A project steering committee will be formed to provide close oversight and guidance. Some of the requested training will be outsourced, as will development of unique courses. The project will include investigating and taking advantage of new training technologies, such as multimedia and Web-based

FIGURE 3-5 Sample business case

courses that workers can take on their own time. Employees will also be able to contact instructors and internal experts via the Internet for guidance in performing current work tasks as part of this project.

5.0 Analysis of Options and Recommendation

There are three options for addressing this opportunity:

1. Do nothing. The business is doing well, and we can continue to conduct training as we have in the past.

2. Instead of providing any internal training, give each employee up to $1,000 to spend on outside training as approved by his or her supervisor. Require employees to stay with the company for one year after using training funds or return the money.

3. Design and implement a new training program as part of this project.

Based on the financial analysis and discussions with key stakeholders, we believe that option 3 is the best option.

6.0 Preliminary Project Requirements

The main requirements of this project include the following:

1. Based on survey results, the only current training that does not need to change is the Six Sigma training. No changes will be made in that area. The tuition reimbursement program will also continue as is.

2. Training for improving supplier management and negotiating skills, especially international negotiations, has the highest priority because these areas are the most important to the business today and will continue to be so for the next few years. Internal staff will work with outside firms to develop a customized approach to this training that takes advantage of internal experts and new technologies.

3. Demand is also high for training in project management and software applications. The project team will analyze several approaches for this training, including in-house courses, courses offered by local colleges/universities, and computer-based/online courses. They will develop and implement the best combination of approaches for these courses.

4. The project will include updating the corporate intranet site to explain the new training program, to allow employees to sign up for and evaluate courses, and to track training demand and expenses.

5. The project team will develop an approach for measuring the effect of training on productivity on an annual basis.

7.0 Budget Estimate and Financial Analysis

A preliminary estimate of costs for the entire project is $1,000,000. Half of the cost is for internal labor, $250,000 is for outsourced labor, and $250,000 is for outsourced training programs. These are preliminary estimates that will be revised as more details become known. Projected benefits are estimated very conservatively. Because the average amount spent on training last year was $1,000/employee, we assumed only a 10 percent or $100-per-employee reduction. This number is also very conservative, especially because much of the new training will be provided outside of work hours, and we are not including lost employee hours in the estimate.

FIGURE 3-5 Sample business case (continued)

Exhibit A summarizes the projected costs and benefits, and shows the estimated net present value (NPV), return on investment (ROI), and year in which payback occurs. It also lists assumptions made in performing this preliminary financial analysis. All of the financial estimates are very encouraging. The estimated payback is in the second year after implementing the new training program. The NPV is $505,795, and the discounted ROI based on a three-year implementation is 27 percent.

8.0 Schedule Estimate

The sponsor would like to see the entire project completed within one year. Courses will be provided as soon as they are available. The impact of training on productivity will be assessed one year after training is completed and annually thereafter.

9.0 Potential Risks

There are several risks involved with this project. The foremost risk is a lack of interest in the new training program. Employee input is crucial for developing the improved training and for realizing its potential benefits on improving productivity. There are some technical risks in developing courses using advanced technologies. There are also risks related to outsourcing much of the labor and actual course materials/instruction. The main business risk is investing the time and money into this project and not realizing the projected benefits.

10.0 Exhibits

Exhibit A: Financial Analysis

Discount rate	8%					
Assume the project is completed in Year 1						
			YEAR			
	1	2	3	4	TOTAL	
Costs	1,000,000	400,000	400,000	400,000		
Discount factor*	0.93	0.86	0.79	0.74		
Discounted costs	925,926	342,936	317,533	294,012	1,880,406	
Benefits	–	1,000,000	1,000,000	1,000,000		
Discount factor	0.93	0.86	0.79	0.74		
Discounted benefits	–	857,339	793,832	735,030	2,386,201	
Discounted benefits - costs	(925,926)	514,403	476,299	441,018	505,795	← NPV
Cumulative benefits - costs	(925,926)	(411,523)	64,777	505,795		
* Rounded to two decimal places.						
ROI ——————————→	27%					
			Payback in Year 3			
Assumptions						
Costs for the project are based on the following:						
Internal labor costs: $500,000						
Outsourced labor costs: $250,000						
Outsourced training costs: $250,000						
After implementation, maintenance costs are estimated at 40% of total development cost						
Benefits are estimated based on the following:						
$100/employee/year X 10,000 employees						
No benefits are included for increased productivity						

FIGURE 3-5 Sample business case (continued)

CREATING A PROJECT CHARTER

After top management determines which projects to pursue, it is important to let the rest of the organization know about these projects. Management needs to create and distribute documentation to authorize project initiation. This documentation can take many different forms, but one common form is a project charter. A **project charter** is a document that formally recognizes the existence of a project and provides a summary of the project's objectives and management. It authorizes the project manager to use organizational resources to complete the project. Ideally, the project manager will play a major role in developing the project charter.

Instead of project charters, some organizations initiate projects using a simple letter of agreement, whereas others use much longer documents or formal contracts. When Global Construction initiates a building project for an outside organization, it still creates a separate charter and attaches it to the contract, which is usually a much longer, more complex document. (You will see an example of a contract for outsourced work for this project in Chapter 5.) A crucial part of the project charter is the sign-off section, where key project stakeholders sign the document to acknowledge their agreement on the need for the project.

Contents of a Project Charter

Contents of a project charter will also vary to meet individual project needs. Typical information included in a project charter includes the following:

- Project Title and Date of Authorization
- Project Start Date
- Project Finish Date
- Other Schedule Information (if available)
- Budget Information
- Project Manager (name and contact information)
- Project Objectives (brief description of what the main objectives are for the project)
- Approach (description of how the project objectives will be met, list of important assumptions, and often references to related documents)
- Roles and Responsibilities (names, roles, positions, and contact information)
- Sign-off
- Comments (allows stakeholders to document important information they want to add)

Project charters are normally short documents. Some are only one-page long, whereas others might be several pages long. The following section shows the project charter for the Just-In-Time Training project.

Sample Project Charter

Kristin drafted a project charter and had the project team members review it before showing it to Lucy. Lucy made a few minor changes, which Kristin incorporated, and then all the key stakeholders who would be working on the project signed the project charter. Figure 3-6 shows the final project charter. Note that Lucy stated her concern about totally changing most training and terminating several contracts with local trainers. Also note that Tim

Nelson, director of supplier management, wanted to be heavily involved in deciding how to provide the supplier management training. Kristin knew that she would have to consider these concerns when managing the project.

Project Charter
July 16, 2009

Project Title: Just-In-Time Training Project
Project Start Date: July 1, 2009   **Projected Finish Date:** June 30, 2010

Budget Information: The firm has allocated $1,000,000 for this project. Approximately half of these costs will be for internal labor, whereas the other half will be for outsourced labor and training programs.

Project Manager: Kristin Maur, (610) 752-4896, kristin_maur@globalconstruction.com

Project Objectives: Develop a new training program that provides just-in-time training to employees on key topics, including supplier management, negotiating skills, project management, and software applications (spreadsheets and Web development). Reduce the training cost per employee by 10 percent, or $100 per employee per year. Develop an approach for measuring productivity improvements from this approach to training on an annual basis.

Approach:

- Terminate all internal training courses except the Six Sigma training after new courses are developed.
- Communicate to all employees the plans to improve internal training and let them know that tuition reimbursement will continue as is.
- Work closely with internal managers and employees to determine the best approaches for providing training in supplier management, negotiating skills, project management, and software applications.
- Research existing training, and work with outside experts to develop several alternatives for providing each training topic.
- Develop and implement new training.
- Take advantage of new training approaches and technologies, and encourage employees to take some training during nonworking hours.
- Encourage experts within the company to mentor other workers on current job duties.
- Determine a way to measure the effectiveness of the training and its impact on productivity on an annual basis.

Roles and Responsibilities:

Name and Signature	Role	Position	Contact Information
Mike Sundby *Mike Sundby*	Project champion	VP of HR	mike_sundby@globalconstruction.com
Lucy Camarena *Lucy Camarena*	Project sponsor	Training director	lucy_camarena@globalconstruction.com
Kristin Maur *Kristin Maur*	Project manager	Project manager	kristin_maur@globalconstruction.com
Julia Portman *Julia Portman*	Steering committee member	VP of IT	julia_portman@globalconstruction.com

FIGURE 3-6 Sample project charter

Tim Nelson Tim Nelson	Steering committee member	Supplier management director	tim_nelson@globalconstruction.com
Mohamed Abdul Mohamed Abdul	Team member	Senior programmer/ analyst	mohamed_abdul@globalconstruction.com
Kim Johnson Kim Johnson	Team member	Curriculum designer	kim_johnson@globalconstruction.com
Etc.			

Comments: (Handwritten or typed comments from above stakeholders, if applicable)

"I am concerned about people's reactions to canceling most internal training and totally changing most training classes. I also hate to terminate some contracts with local training firms we've used for several years. We should try to get some of them involved in this project." Lucy

"I want to review all of the information related to providing the supplier management training. We need to make something available quickly." Tim

FIGURE 3-6 Sample project charter (continued)

Because many projects fail because of unclear requirements and expectations, starting with a project charter makes sense. If project managers are having difficulty obtaining support from project stakeholders, for example, they can refer to what everyone agreed to in the project charter. After the charter is completed, it is good practice to hold an official kick-off meeting for the project.

MEDIA SNAPSHOT

Many people enjoy watching television shows like *Changing Rooms* or *Trading Spaces*, in which participants have two days and $1,000 to update a room in their neighbor's house. Because the time and cost are set, it's the scope that has the most flexibility. Examples of some of the work completed include new flooring, light fixtures, paint, new shelves, and artwork to brighten up a dull room.

Designers on these shows often have to change initial scope goals due to budget or time constraints. For example, designers often go back to local stores to exchange such items as lights, artwork, or fabric for less-expensive items to meet budget constraints. Or they might describe a new piece of furniture they want the carpenter to build, but the carpenter changes the design or materials to meet time constraints. Occasionally, designers can buy more expensive items or have more elaborate furniture built because they underestimated costs and schedules for their original items.

continued

Another important issue related to project scope management is meeting customer expectations. Who wouldn't be happy with a professionally designed room at no cost to them? Although most homeowners are very happy with work done on the show, some are obviously disappointed. Unlike most projects in which the project team works closely with the customer, homeowners have little say in what is done and cannot inspect the work along the way. They walk into their newly decorated room with their eyes closed. Modernizing a room can mean something totally different to a homeowner than it does to an interior designer. For example, one woman was obviously shocked when she saw her bright orange kitchen with black appliances. Another couple couldn't believe there was moss on their bedroom walls. What happens when the homeowners don't like the work that's been done? The FAQ section of tlc.com says, "Everyone on our show is told upfront that there's a chance they won't like the final design of the room. Each applicant signs a release acknowledging that the show is not responsible for redecorating a room that isn't to the owner's taste." Too bad you can't get sponsors for most projects to sign a similar release form. It would make project management much easier!

HOLDING A PROJECT KICK-OFF MEETING

Experienced project managers know that it is crucial to get projects off to a great start. Holding a good kick-off meeting is an excellent way to do this. A **kick-off meeting** is a meeting held at the beginning of a project so that stakeholders can meet each other, review the goals of the project, and discuss future plans. The kick-off meeting is often held after the business case and project charter are completed, but it could be held sooner, as needed.

Purpose of the Kick-Off Meeting

Project kick-off meetings are often used to get support for a project and clarify roles and responsibilities. If there is a project champion, as there is for this project, he or she should speak first at the kick-off meeting and introduce the project sponsor and project manager. If anyone seems opposed to the project or unwilling to support it, the project champion—an experienced senior manager—should be able to handle the situation.

As discussed earlier in the chapter, there is normally a fair amount of work done before an official kick-off meeting for a project. At a minimum, the project manager and sponsor should have met several times, and other key stakeholders should have been involved in developing the project charter. The project manager should make sure the right people are invited to the kick-off meeting and send out an agenda in advance. For a small project, a kick-off meeting might be an informal meeting of the project team held in a social environment. The main idea is to get the project off to a good start.

Sample Kick-Off Meeting Agenda

All project meetings with major stakeholders should include an agenda. Figure 3-7 provides the agenda that Kristin provided for the Just-In-Time Training project kick-off meeting. Notice the main topics in an agenda:

- Meeting objective
- Agenda (lists in order the topics to be discussed)

- A section for documenting action items, who they are assigned to, and when each person will complete the action
- A section to document the date and time of the next meeting

---

Kick-Off Meeting
July 16, 2009

Project Name: Just-In-Time Training Project

Meeting Objective: Get the project off to an effective start by introducing key stakeholders, reviewing project goals, and discussing future plans

Agenda:
- Introductions of attendees
- Review of the project background
- Review of project-related documents (i.e., business case, project charter)
- Discussion of project organizational structure
- Discussion of project scope, time, and cost goals
- Discussion of other important topics
- List of action items from meeting

Action Item	Assigned To	Due Date

Date and time of next meeting:

FIGURE 3-7 Sample kick-off meeting agenda

It is good practice to focus on results of meetings, and having sections for documenting action items and deciding on the next meeting date and time on the agenda helps to do so. It is also good practice to document meeting minutes, focusing on key decisions and action items, and to send them to all meeting participants and other appropriate stakeholders within a day or two of a meeting. If there is a project Web site or other place for storing project information, the meeting minutes should be stored there.

DEVELOPING A PRELIMINARY SCOPE STATEMENT

A **scope statement** is a document used to develop and confirm a common understanding of the project scope. It describes in detail the work to be accomplished on the project and is an important tool for preventing **scope creep**—the tendency for project scope to continually increase. It is helpful to create a *preliminary,* or initial, scope statement during project initiation so that the entire project team can start important discussions and work related to the project scope. As described in Chapter 4, a more detailed scope statement is prepared later in the project's life span as part of planning. There are usually several versions of the scope statement, and each one becomes more detailed as the project progresses and more information becomes available.

(X) WHAT WENT WRONG?

There are many examples of poor scope management in the software industry. A highly publicized example is Nike's now infamous i2 supply-chain management problem. A software glitch from the $400 million project cost Nike more than $100 million in lost sales; depressed its stock price by 20 percent; triggered several class-action lawsuits; and caused its chairman, president, and CEO, Phil Knight, to lament, "This is what you get for $400 million...a speed bump." [6]

The Nike disaster provides a classic example of spending too much money on too much software and consulting, with too little to show for the effort. The company also moved too quickly in implementing new software without knowing how it might affect its older legacy systems. Nike has since recovered from this major software disaster and learned to be more patient in understanding and managing the scope of software projects.

Many projects fail due to poor scope management. Communications are an important part of this problem. It is often difficult for people to explain what they want and for all project stakeholders to remain on the same page when it comes to meeting scope goals. Figure 3-8 provides a version of a popular cartoon illustrating this problem. Even a project as simple as creating a tire swing can have many scope problems.

Contents of a Scope Statement

Scope statements, like project charters, also vary by project type. Complex projects have very long scope statements, whereas smaller projects have shorter scope statements. Items often described in a preliminary scope statement include, as a minimum, the product or service requirements and characteristics, a summary of all major deliverables, and the project success criteria.

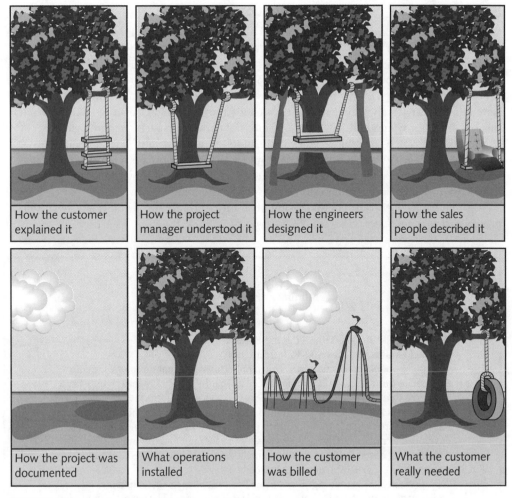

How the customer explained it	How the project manager understood it	How the engineers designed it	How the sales people described it
How the project was documented	What operations installed	How the customer was billed	What the customer really needed

FIGURE 3-8   A swing is a swing is a swing?

The preliminary and subsequent scope statements should expand on information provided in the business case and project charter. Many scope statements also refer to other documents, such as specifications for particular products or relevant policies, procedures, or standards. Project managers must decide what aspects of scope are most important to define early in the project and document them in the preliminary scope statement. They should also establish a process for ensuring that everyone agrees on project scope throughout the project and a process for handling scope changes. For example, the project team could deliver prototypes of certain deliverables to make sure they are on track toward meeting customer needs.

Sample Sections of a Preliminary Scope Statement

Kristin and her team knew that it was crucial to provide effective training on all of the topics listed in their charter: supplier management, negotiating skills, project management, and software applications. They knew that training for improving supplier management and negotiating skills, especially international negotiations, had the highest priority. They also believed that the scope of this part of the project was the most difficult. The business case stated that internal staff would work with outside firms to develop a customized approach to this training that would take advantage of internal experts and new technologies.

Kristin had some experience working in supplier management, but she had no experience negotiating with foreign suppliers. She met with Tim Nelson, director of supplier management, to get his views on how to begin defining the scope of that part of the project. Figure 3-9 provides part of the preliminary scope statement.

As you can see, substantial effort should go into initiating projects. It is crucial to get projects off to a good start.

Preliminary Scope Statement
July 23, 2009

Project Name: Just-In-Time Training Project
Product Characteristics and Requirements
1. Supplier management training: The supplier management director estimates the need to train at least 100 employees each year in supplier management. There should be three levels of courses: an executive course, an introductory course, and an advanced course. Course materials should be developed as a joint effort among internal experts, outside training firms, and key suppliers. A partnership should be developed to maximize the effectiveness of the training and minimize development costs. Different delivery methods should be explored, including instructor-led, CD-ROM, and Web-based.
2. Negotiating skills training: Employees from supplier management and other departments would benefit from this training. There should be several courses offered, including a basic course, a course tailored to negotiating contracts, and a course tailored to international negotiations.

FIGURE 3-9   Sample section of preliminary scope statement

Deliverables:

1. Supplier management training:

    1.1. Needs assessment: A study will be conducted to determine the learning objectives for the executive, introductory, and advanced courses. Study results will be documented in a report about 20–30 pages long

    1.2. Research of existing training: A short study will identify current training courses and materials available. Study results will be documented in a report about 10–20 pages long, plus attachments and references.

    1.3. Partnerships: Partnership agreements will be made to get outside training organizations and suppliers to work on developing and providing training. The legal department will assist in developing these partnerships.

    1.4. Course design and development.

    1.5. Pilot course.

    Etc.

Project Success Criteria: Our sponsor has stated that the project will be a success if the new training courses are all available within one year, if the average course evaluations are at least 3.0 on a 1–5 scale, and if the company reduces its training costs per employee by 10 percent each year.

FIGURE 3-9   Sample section of preliminary scope statement (continued)

CASE WRAP-UP

Kristin was pleased with work completed in initiating the Just-In-Time Training project, as were the project sponsor and other key stakeholders. Kristin met weekly with the project steering committee to review project progress. She found the committee to be very helpful, especially when dealing with several challenges they encountered. For example, it was difficult finding a large enough conference room for the kick-off meeting and setting up the Webcast to allow other stakeholders to participate in the meeting. She was also a bit nervous before running the meeting, but Lucy and Mike, the project sponsor and champion, helped her relax and stepped in when people questioned the need for the project. There were also indications that several key departments would not be represented at the kick-off meeting, but Mike made sure that they were. Kristin could see how important senior management support was on this project, in particular for obtaining buy-in from all parts of the organization.

Chapter Summary

The five project management process groups are initiating, planning, executing, monitoring and controlling, and closing. These processes occur at varying levels of intensity throughout each phase of a project, and specific outcomes are produced as a result of each process.

Mapping the main activities of each project management process group into the nine project management knowledge areas provides a big picture of what activities are involved in project management. Some organizations develop their own project management methodologies, often using the standards found in the *PMBOK® Guide* as a foundation. It is important to tailor project management methodologies to meet the organization's particular needs.

Global Construction's Just-In-Time Training project demonstrates the process of initiating a project. After a project is approved, senior managers often meet to perform several pre-initiating tasks, as follows:

- Determining the scope, time, and cost constraints for the project
- Assigning the project sponsor
- Selecting the project manager
- Meeting with the project manager to review the process and expectations for managing the project
- Determining if the project should be broken down into two or more smaller projects

The main tasks normally involved in project initiation are the following:

- Identifying and understanding project stakeholders
- Preparing a business case for the project
- Creating the project charter
- Holding a kick-off meeting
- Developing a preliminary scope statement

Descriptions of how each of these tasks was accomplished and samples of related outputs are described in the chapter.

Quick Quiz

1. In which of the five project management process groups is the most time and money usually spent?
   a. initiating
   b. planning
   c. executing
   d. monitoring and controlling
   e. closing

2. In which of the five project management process groups are activities performed that relate to each knowledge area?

   a. initiating

   b. planning

   c. executing

   d. monitoring and controlling

   e. closing

3. The best or "alpha" project managers spend more time on every process group than other project managers except for which one?

   a. initiating

   b. planning

   c. executing

   d. monitoring and controlling

4. What document provides justification for investing in a project?

   a. project charter

   b. business case

   c. preliminary scope statement

   d. stakeholder analysis

5. What document formally recognizes the existence of a project and provides direction on the project's objectives and management?

   a. project charter

   b. business case

   c. preliminary scope statement

   d. stakeholder analysis

6. What is a crucial part of the project charter—a section in which key project stakeholders acknowledge their agreement on the need for the project?

   a. project objectives

   b. approach

   c. roles and responsibilities

   d. sign-off

7. Which project document should not be made available to all key project stakeholders due to its sensitive nature?

   a. project charter

   b. business case

   c. preliminary scope statement

   d. stakeholder analysis

8. All project meetings with major stakeholders should include _____ .

   a. an agenda

   b. food

   c. name tags

   d. all of the above

9. The tendency for project scope to increase is called _____ .

   a. gold-plating

   b. incremental planning

   c. scope creep

   d. analysis paralysis

10. Which of the following is not usually included in a preliminary scope statement?

    a. project success criteria

    b. product characteristics and requirements

    c. deliverables

    d. roles and responsibilities

Quick Quiz Answers

1. C; 2. B; 3. C; 4. B; 5. A; 6. D; 7. D; 8. A; 9. C; 10. D

Discussion Questions

1. Briefly describe what happens in each of the five project management process groups (initiating, planning, executing, monitoring and controlling, and closing). On which process should team members spend the most time? Why? Why is it helpful to follow a project management methodology?

2. What pre-initiating tasks were performed for the Just-In-Time Training project? Does it make sense to do these tasks? What are the main initiating tasks?

3. What is the main purpose of performing a stakeholder analysis? When should it be done, and who should see the results?

4. Describe the purpose of a business case and its main contents.

5. Why should projects have a project charter? What is the main information included in a project charter?

6. Discuss the process for holding a project kick-off meeting. Who should attend? What key topics should be on the agenda?

7. Why is it important to develop a preliminary project scope statement during project initiation?

Exercises

1. Find an example of a large project that took more than a year to complete, such as a major construction project. You can ask people at your college, university, or work about a recent

project, such as a major fund raising campaign, information systems installation, or building project. You can also find information about projects online such as the Big Dig in Boston (*www.masspike.com/bigdig*), the Patronas Twin Towers in Malaysia and many other building projects (*www.greatbuildings.com*), etc. Why was the project initiated? Describe some of the pre-initiating and initiating tasks completed for the project. Write a one-page paper or prepare a short presentation summarizing your findings.

2. Review the business case for the Just-In-Time Training project. Do you think there is solid business justification for doing this project? Why or why not? What parts of the business case do you think could be stronger? How? Rewrite a section that you believe can be improved. Write a one-page paper or prepare a short presentation summarizing your findings.

3. Search the Internet for "project charter." Find at least three good references that describe project charters. Write a one-page paper or prepare a short presentation summarizing your findings.

4. Review the preliminary scope statement for the Just-In-Time Training project. How does this document help clarify what work will be done on the project? How is the description of the products different from the listing of deliverables? Is the success criteria clear for this project? What questions do you have about the scope of the project? Write a one-page paper or prepare a short presentation summarizing your ideas.

Team Projects

1. Your organization has decided to initiate a project to raise money for an important charity. Assume that there are 1,000 people in your organization. Use the pre-initiating tasks described in this chapter to develop a strategy for how to proceed. Be creative in describing your organization; the charity; the scope, time, and cost constraints for the project; and so on. Document your ideas in a one- to two-page paper or a short presentation.

2. You are part of a team in charge of a project to help people in your company (500 people) lose weight. This project is part of a competition, and the top "losers" will be featured in a popular television show. Assume that you have six months to complete the project and a budget of $10,000. Develop a project charter for this project using the sample provided in this chapter. Be creative in developing detailed information to include in the charter.

3. Using the information you developed in Team Project 1 or 2, role-play the kick-off meeting for this project. Follow the sample agenda provided in this chapter.

4. Perform the initiating tasks for the New Business Venture case study provided in Appendix C or for one of the cases on the companion Web site. If you are working on a real team project, perform the applicable pre-initiating and initiating tasks for that project. Prepare a business case, if applicable; a project charter; and key parts of a preliminary scope statement.

5. As a team, research two different project management methodologies (other than using the *PMBOK® Guide*), such as PRINCE2, RUP, Six Sigma, etc. Summarize your findings in a two- to three-page paper or a short presentation. Try to include examples of projects managed using each methodology.

Companion Web Site

Visit the companion Web site for this text (*www.course.com/mis/pm2/schwalbe* or *http://login. course.com*) to access:

- Lecture notes
- Interactive quizzes and Jeopardy games
- Template files
- Sample documents
- Podcasts
- More ideas for team projects, including real projects and case studies
- Links to additional resources related to project management

Key Terms

business case — A document that provides justification for investing in a project.

champion — A senior manager who acts as a key proponent for a project.

closing processes — The actions that involve formalizing acceptance of the project or phase and bringing it to an orderly end.

deliverable — A product or service produced or provided as part of a project.

executing processes — The actions that involve coordinating people and other resources to carry out the project plans and produce the deliverables of the project.

initiating processes — The actions to begin or end projects and project phases.

kick-off meeting — A meeting held at the beginning of a project so that stakeholders can meet each other, review the goals of the project, and discuss future plans.

methodology — A plan that describes how things should be done to manage a project.

monitoring and controlling processes — The actions taken to measure progress toward achieving project goals, monitor deviation from plans, and take corrective action.

phase — A distinct stage in project development.

planning processes — The actions that involve devising and maintaining a workable scheme to ensure that the project meets its scope, time, and cost goals as well as organizational needs.

process — A series of actions directed toward a particular result.

project charter — A document that formally recognizes the existence of a project and provides a summary of the project's objectives and management.

project management office (PMO) — An organizational entity created to assist project managers in achieving project goals.

project management process groups — The progression from initiating activities to planning activities, executing activities, monitoring and controlling activities, and closing activities.

PRojects IN Controlled Environments (PRINCE2) — A project management methodology with eight process groups developed in the U.K.

Rational Unified Process (RUP) framework — A project management methodology that uses an iterative software development process that focuses on team productivity and delivers software best practices to all team members.

scope creep — The tendency for project scope to continually increase.

scope statement — A document used to develop and confirm a common understanding of the project scope.

Six Sigma — A comprehensive and flexible system for achieving, sustaining, and maximizing business success; uniquely driven by close understanding of customer needs, disciplined use of facts, data, and statistical analysis, and diligent attention to managing, improving, and reinventing business processes.

stakeholder analysis — A document that provides information on key stakeholders to help manage relationships with them.

standard — A document that describes best practices for what should be done to manage a project.

template — A file with a preset format that serves as a starting point for creating various documents so that the format and structure do not have to be re-created.

End Notes

[1] Andy Crowe, *Alpha Project Managers: What the Top 2% Know That Everyone Else Does Not*, Velociteach Press (2006).

[2] Bill Cottrell, "Standards, compliance, and Rational Unified Process, Part I: Integrating RUP and the PMBOK," *IBM Developerworks* (May 10, 2004).

[3] Peter S. Pande, Robert P. Neuman, and Roland R. Cavanagh, *The Six Sigma Way*. New York: McGraw-Hill (2000), p. xi.

[4] William Ibbs and Justin Reginato, *Quantifying the Value of Project Management*, Project Management Institute (2002).

[5] AST Group, "Can You Quantify the Value of Enterprise Project Management in Your Organisation?" *ITWeb Tech Forum* (March 17, 2005).

[6] Christopher Koch, "Nike Rebounds: How (and Why) Nike Recovered from its Supply Chain Disaster," *CIO Magazine* (June 15, 2004).

CHAPTER 4

PLANNING PROJECTS, PART I (PROJECT INTEGRATION, SCOPE, TIME, AND COST MANAGEMENT)

LEARNING OBJECTIVES

After reading this chapter, you will be able to:

- Describe the importance of creating plans to guide project execution, and list several planning tasks and outputs for project integration, scope, time, and cost management

- Discuss project integration management planning tasks, and explain the purpose and contents of a team contract and a project management plan

- Explain the project scope management planning tasks, and create a scope management plan, scope statement, work breakdown structure (WBS), and WBS dictionary

- Describe the project time management planning tasks, and prepare a project schedule based on activity and milestone lists, activity sequencing, durations, and resources

- Discuss the project cost management planning tasks, and create a cost estimate and cost baseline

OPENING CASE

Kristin Maur continued to work with her project team and other key stakeholders on the Just-In-Time Training project. She knew that it was crucial to do a good job in planning all aspects of the project, and she strongly believed that execution would be much smoother if they had good plans to follow. She also knew that it was important to involve the people who would be doing the work in actually planning the work, and that planning was an iterative process. Involving key people in the planning process and keeping the plans up to date had been her main challenges on past projects, so Kristin focused proactively on those areas.

Kristin and her team were fortunate to have many templates to use in developing several planning documents. They could also review examples of planning documents from past and current projects available on Global Construction's intranet site and use project management software to enter key planning data. Kristin also found that the project steering committee that had been set up during project initiation gave her very helpful advice. Several experienced members warned her to be thorough in planning but not to become bogged down in too much detail.

INTRODUCTION

Many people have heard the following sayings:

- If you fail to plan, you plan to fail.
- If you don't know where you're going, any road will take you there.
- What gets measured gets managed.

All of these sayings emphasize the fact that planning is crucial to achieving goals. Successful project managers know how important it is to develop, refine, and follow plans to meet project goals, and they know how easy it is to become sidetracked if they do not have good plans to follow. They also know that people are more likely to perform well if they know what they are supposed to do and when.

Project Planning Should Guide Project Execution

Planning is often the most difficult and unappreciated process in project management. Often, people do not want to take the time to plan well, but theory and practice show that good planning is crucial to good execution. *The main purpose of project planning is to guide project execution.* To guide execution, plans must be realistic and useful, so a fair amount of time and effort must go into the project planning process.

Recall from Chapter 3 that project planning involves devising and maintaining a workable scheme to ensure that the project meets its scope, time, and cost goals as well as organizational needs. Also, recall that planning includes tasks related to each of the nine project management knowledge areas. This chapter describes the types of planning performed in four of the knowledge areas—project integration, scope, time, and cost management—and summarizes the planning done for Global Construction's Just-In-Time Training project. Chapter 5 focuses on planning done as part of the other five knowledge areas—quality, human resource, communications, risk, and procurement management.

Summary of Planning Tasks and Outputs

The *PMBOK® Guide* lists over 50 documents that project teams can produce as part of project planning. Other experts suggest even more potential planning documents. Every project is unique, so project managers and their teams must determine which planning outputs are needed for their projects and how they should be created.

Figure 4-1 summarizes the project planning outputs for integration, scope, time, and cost management that Global Construction will use for the Just-In-Time Training project. (See the *PMBOK® Guide* for their lists and descriptions of the many inputs, outputs, and tools and techniques for project planning.) All of these planning documents, as well as other project-related information, will be available to all team members on a project Web site. Global Construction has used project Web sites for several years, and everyone agrees that they significantly facilitate communications.

Knowledge area	Outputs
Project integration management	Team contract Project management plan
Project scope management	Scope management plan Scope statement Work breakdown structure (WBS) WBS dictionary

FIGURE 4-1 Planning outputs for project integration, scope, time, and cost management

Knowledge area	Outputs
Project time management	Activity list and attributes
	Milestone list
	Network diagram (showing activity dependencies)
	Activity resource requirements
	Activity duration estimates
	Project schedule (in Gantt chart format)
Project cost management	Cost estimate
	Cost baseline

FIGURE 4-1 Planning outputs for project integration, scope, time, and cost management (continued)

The following sections describe planning tasks and outputs in the first four knowledge areas and then provide examples of applying them to the Just-In-Time Training project at Global Construction. You can consider many of these planning tasks as following a chronological order, especially for the scope, time, and cost tasks. You need to plan the project scope and determine what activities need to be done before you can develop a detailed project schedule. Likewise, you need a detailed project schedule before you can develop a cost baseline. Of course, human resource planning and appointment to the project team must also be accomplished at the start of a project as part of project human resource management. As noted earlier, there are many interdependencies between various knowledge areas and process groups.

PROJECT INTEGRATION MANAGEMENT PLANNING TASKS

Project integration management involves coordinating all the project management knowledge areas throughout a project's life span. The main planning tasks performed as part of project integration management include creating a team contract and developing the project management plan.

Team Contracts

Global Construction believes in using **team contracts** to help promote teamwork and clarify team communications. After core project team members have been selected, they meet to prepare a team contract. The process normally includes reviewing a template and then working in small groups of three to four people to prepare inputs for the team contract. Creating smaller groups makes it easier for everyone to contribute ideas. Each group then shares their ideas on what the contract should contain, and then they work together to form one project team contract. Ideally, the contract should be finished in a one- to two-hour meeting. The project manager should attend the meeting and act as a coach or facilitator, observing the different personalities of team members and seeing how well they work together. It is crucial to emphasize the importance of the project team throughout the project's life cycle. The team contract should provide the groundwork for how the project team will function.

Sample Team Contract

Figure 4-2 shows the team contract created for the Just-In-Time Training project. Notice that the main topics covered include the following:

- Code of conduct
- Participation
- Communication
- Problem solving
- Meeting guidelines

Everyone involved in creating the team contract should sign it. As new project team members are added, the project manager should review ground rules with them and have them read and sign the contract as well.

Project Management Plans

To coordinate and integrate information across all project management knowledge areas and across the organization, there must be a good project management plan. A **project management plan**, which is a deliverable for the project integration management knowledge area, is a document used to coordinate all project planning documents and to help guide a project's execution and control. Plans created in the other knowledge areas are subsidiary parts of the overall project management plan. Project management plans facilitate communication among stakeholders and provide a baseline for progress measurement and project control, as discussed in detail in Chapter 7. A **baseline** is a starting point, a measurement, or an observation that is documented so that it can be used for future comparison. The project management plan briefly describes the overall scope, time, and cost baselines for the project. Specific plans in each of those knowledge areas provide more detailed baseline information. For example, the project management plan might provide a high-level budget baseline for the entire project, whereas the cost baseline prepared as part of the project cost management knowledge area (explained later in this chapter) provides detailed cost projections by WBS by month.

Project management plans should be dynamic, flexible, and receptive to change when the environment or project changes. These plans should greatly assist the project manager in leading the project team and assessing project status. Just as projects are unique, so are project plans. For a small project involving a few people over a couple of months, a project charter, team contract, scope statement, and Gantt chart might be the only project planning documents needed; there would not be a need for a separate project management plan. A large project involving 100 people over three years would benefit from having a detailed project management plan and separate plans for each knowledge area. It is important to tailor all planning documentation to fit the needs of specific projects. Because all project plans should help guide the completion of the particular project, they should be only as detailed as needed for each project.

Team Contract
July 9, 2009

Project Name: Just-In-Time Training Project

Project Team Members' Names and Sign-Off:

Name	Date
Kristin Maur	**July 9, 2009**
Etc.	

Code of Conduct: As a project team, we will:
- Work proactively, anticipating potential problems and preventing their occurrence.
- Keep other team members informed of information related to the project.
- Focus on what is best for the entire project team.

Participation: We will:
- Be honest and open during all project activities.
- Provide the opportunity for equal participation.
- Be open to new approaches and consider new ideas.
- Let the project manager know well in advance if a team member has to miss a meeting or may have trouble meeting a deadline for a given task.

Communication: We will:
- Keep discussions on track and have one discussion at a time.
- Use the telephone, e-mail, a project Web site, instant messaging, and other technology to assist in communicating.
- Have the project manager or designated person facilitate all meetings and arrange for phone and videoconferences, as needed.
- Work together to create the project schedule and related information and enter actuals, issues, risks, and other information into our enterprise project management system by 4 p.m. every Friday.

Problem Solving: We will:
- Only use constructive criticism and focus on solving problems, not blaming people.
- Strive to build on each other's ideas.
- Bring in outside experts when necessary.

Meeting Guidelines: We will:
- Plan to have a face-to-face meeting of the entire project team every Tuesday morning.
- Arrange for telephone or videoconferencing for participants as needed.
- Hold other meetings as needed.
- Develop and follow an agenda for all meetings.
- Record meeting minutes and send them out via e-mail within 24 hours of all project meetings, focusing on decisions made and action items and issues from each meeting.

FIGURE 4-2 Sample team contract

There are, however, common elements to most project management plans, as follows:

- Introduction/overview of the project
- Project organization
- Management and technical processes
- Work to be performed
- Schedule information
- Budget information
- References to other project planning documents

Sample Project Management Plan

Figure 4-3 provides partial information from the initial project management plan for Global Construction's Just-In-Time Training project. Of course, the actual document would be longer because this is a one-year, $1 million project involving many different stakeholders, including outside suppliers. The document would also be updated as needed. It is important to mark the date and version number on the document to avoid confusion. Also note that project organization varies on projects, so it is helpful to provide a high-level project organizational chart in the project management plan. On some projects, the project sponsor and project champion are the same person, but not always. Projects that cross functional boundaries, as the Just-In-Time Training project does, often benefit from having a high-level project champion, such as a vice president, from a key functional area.

Project Management Plan Version 1.0
September 17, 2009

Project Name: Just-In-Time Training Project

Introduction/Overview of the Project

Global Construction employs 10,000 full-time employees in 10 different counties and 15 U.S. states. The company spends, on average, $1,000 per employee for training (not including tuition reimbursement), which is higher than the industry average. By redesigning training, Global Construction can reduce training costs and improve productivity. The main goal of this project is to develop a new training program that provides just-in-time training to employees on key topics, including supplier management, negotiating skills, project management, and software applications.

Project Organization

The basic organization of the project is provided in Figure 1. The project sponsor, Lucy Camarena, will have the final say on major decisions, with consultation from the project steering committee and the project champion, Mike Sundby. The project sponsor should have time to thoroughly review important project information and provide timely feedback to the project manager. The project manager in this case reports to the project sponsor, and the team leaders and supplier project managers report to the project manager.

FIGURE 1   Project organizational chart

Management and Technical Processes

Management Processes:

1. Management Review Process: The project steering committee will meet at least monthly to provide inputs and review progress on this project.
2. Progress Measurement Process: The project steering committee will review project progress during project review meetings, and they can also review information as needed by viewing reports on the enterprise project

FIGURE 4-3   Sample project management plan

management software system. Earned value data will be provided for this project and available on a weekly basis in the system. Post-project progress will also be measured to see if the project met its goals. These goals include reducing the training cost per employee by $100/person/year and receiving positive results from survey participants on the effectiveness of the training.

3. Change Approval Process: See Attachment 1 based on corporate standards.
4. Supplier Management Process: See Attachment 2 based on corporate standards.

Technical Processes:

1. Enterprise Project Management Software: All tasks, costs, resources, issues, and risks will be tracked for this project using our enterprise project management software. Data must be entered on at least a weekly basis to provide timely information.
2. Supplier Evaluation: The project team will coordinate with the purchasing department to follow our standard procedures for selecting and working with suppliers. See Attachment 2 for corporate standards.
3. Productivity Improvement: The project team will work with the finance and quality assurance departments to develop and implement a system to measure improvements in employee productivity that result from this new training program. The finance department will report on this information annually, beginning one year after the first new training course is offered.

Work to Be Performed

Summary: Research, develop or purchase, and implement a new just-in-time training program covering the topics of supplier management, negotiating skills, project management, and software applications, and determine a way to measure the effectiveness of the training and its impact on productivity on an annual basis. See the scope statement, WBS, and other scope documents for further details.

Schedule Information

The entire project will be completed in one year, with a projected completion date of June 30, 2010. See the project schedule and other time management documents for further details.

Budget Information

The total budget for this project is $1,000,000. Approximately half of these costs will be for internal labor, whereas the other half will be for outsourced labor and training programs. See the cost estimate and cost baseline for further details.

References to Other Project Planning Documents

All current project plans created for this project are provided in Appendix A. Initial documents and revisions are available on the project Web site.

FIGURE 4-3 Sample project plan (continued)

PROJECT SCOPE MANAGEMENT PLANNING TASKS

Project scope management involves defining and controlling what work is or is not included in a project. The main planning tasks performed as part of project scope management include scope planning, scope definition, and creating the WBS. The main documents produced are a scope management plan, scope statement, WBS, and WBS dictionary.

Scope Planning and the Scope Management Plan

A project's size, complexity, importance, as well as other factors affect how much effort is spent on scope planning. The main output of scope planning is a **scope management plan**, which is a document that includes descriptions of how the team will prepare the scope statement, create the WBS, verify completion of the project deliverables, and control requests for changes to the project scope. Key inputs to the scope management plan include the project charter, preliminary scope statement, and current project management plan, as described previously. Additional inputs include policies and procedures related to scope management and historical information about previous projects. Environmental factors, such as marketplace conditions, also affect project scope planning.

Sample Scope Management Plan

Kristin and her team had already created a project charter and a preliminary scope statement as part of project initiation. The project sponsor and other key stakeholders had reviewed and approved both of these documents. Kristin continued to work with her team to decide how they would prepare the more detailed scope statement and WBS. It was also important to document how the team would verify completion of project deliverables and manage change requests related to the project scope. (Change requests are used to formally document changes to project plans, as described more fully in Chapter 7.) Figure 4-4 shows an abbreviated version of a scope statement for the Just-In-Time Training project. As with other planning documents, Krisin's team would update it as needed.

Scope Definition and the Scope Statement

Good scope definition is crucial to project success because it helps improve the accuracy of time, cost, and resource estimates; defines a baseline for performance measurement and project control; and aids in communicating clear work responsibilities. Work that is not included in the scope statement should not be done. The main techniques used in scope definition include analyzing products, identifying alternative approaches to doing the work, understanding and analyzing stakeholder needs, and using expert judgment. The main output of scope definition is the scope statement.

As described in Chapter 3, the project team develops a preliminary scope statement during project initiation. The preliminary project scope statement should provide basic scope information, and subsequent scope statements should clarify and provide information that is more specific. Although contents vary, scope statements should include, at a minimum, a description of the project, including its overall objectives and justification; detailed descriptions of all project deliverables; characteristics and requirements of products and services produced as part of the project; and project success criteria. It should also reference supporting documents, such as product specifications and corporate policies, which often affect how products or services are produced.

Scope Management Plan
July 17, 2009

Project Name: Just-In-Time Training Project

Introduction

The purpose of this document is to provide suggestions and guidance for preparing several important scope management documents related to the Just-In-Time Training project at Global Construction.

Preparing the Scope Statement

The preliminary scope statement will provide the basis for preparing more detailed scope statements. It is also important to review the scope statement with key stakeholders, especially the project sponsor, potential suppliers, and users of the project deliverables. The scope statement will become longer and more detailed as the project progresses. To limit the length and complexity of the scope statement, it is best to reference and include several attachments, such as product descriptions (usually documented by suppliers) specifications, and corporate standards. Each version of the scope statement should be clearly labeled and dated to ensure that everyone uses the most recent version. Changes and additions will be highlighted and communicated to affect personnel. The scope statement will be available on the password-protected project Web site.

Creating the Work Breakdown Structure (WBS)

The project team should work together to create the WBS. The project sponsor and project steering committee should review the WBS to ensure that it includes all of the work required to complete the project. The project team should review WBSs of similar projects, review corporate guidelines for creating WBSs, and focus on determining all of the deliverables required for the project. The tasks required to complete each deliverable should also be determined. These tasks should include product- and process-related tasks. A general guideline to follow for determining the level of detail is that the lowest level of the WBS should normally take no longer than two weeks to complete. The WBS can be revised as needed, and the sponsor and steering committee must approve these revisions.

Verifying Completion of Project Deliverables

The project manager will work with the sponsor and steering committee to develop a process for verifying successful completion of project deliverables. In general, the project sponsor will be responsible for verifying the completion of major deliverables. The contract administrator will also be involved in verifying successful completion of deliverables received from outside sources. Contracts will include clauses describing the scope verification process.

Managing Requests for Changes to Project Scope

All requests for changes to project scope that may have significant effects on meeting project requirements must follow the formal change-control procedures specified in Attachment 1. A change request form will be completed and reviewed by the appropriate group. It is crucial to follow these procedures to prevent scope creep.

FIGURE 4-4 Sample scope management plan

Sample Scope Statement

Kristin worked closely with her team to develop the first full version of the scope statement, reviewing information from the preliminary scope statement and meeting several times with key stakeholders to develop a thorough document. Part of the scope statement is shown in Figure 4-5. Note that the scope statement documents the product characteristics and requirements, summarizes the deliverables, and describes project success criteria. Kristin knew that this document would change as they finalized more details of the project scope. Note that some details have been added and changes have been made since the preliminary scope statement (Figure 3-9) was completed. For example, class size has been added, more information on the needs assessment and survey has been provided, and the success criteria has been changed slightly.

As more information becomes available and decisions are made related to project scope—such as specific products that will be purchased or changes that have been approved—the project team should update the project scope statement. Different iterations of the scope statement should be named Version 1.0, Version 2.0, and so on. These updates might also require changes to the scope management plan. For example, if the team decides to purchase products or services for the project from a supplier with whom it has never worked, the scope management plan should include information on working with that new supplier.

An up-to-date project scope statement is an important document for developing and confirming a common understanding of the project scope. It describes in detail the work to be accomplished on the project and is an important tool for ensuring customer satisfaction and preventing scope creep.

Creating the Work Breakdown Structure

A **work breakdown structure (WBS)** is a deliverable-oriented grouping of the work involved in a project that defines the total scope of the project. In other words, the WBS is a document that breaks all the work required for the project into discrete tasks, and groups those tasks into a logical hierarchy. Because most projects involve many people and many different deliverables, it is important to organize and divide the work into logical parts based on how the work will be performed. The WBS is a foundation document in project management because it provides the basis for planning and managing project schedules, costs, resources, and changes. Because the WBS defines the total scope of the project, some project management experts believe that work should not be done on a project if it is not included in the WBS. Therefore, it is crucial to develop a good WBS.

Scope Statement, Version 1.0
August 1, 2009

Project Title: Just-In-Time Training Project

Project Justification
Strategic planning initiatives identified the opportunity to improve productivity and reduce costs by changing Global Construction's approach to internal training. The project team will develop a new training program that provides just-in-time training to employees on key topics, including supplier management, negotiating skills, project management, and software applications.

Product Characteristics and Requirements
1. Supplier management training: The supplier management director estimates the need to train at least 100 employees each year in supplier management. There should be three levels of courses: an executive course, an introductory course, and an advanced course. Course materials should be developed as a joint effort among internal experts, outside training experts, if needed, and key suppliers. This training must be tailored to meet business needs. A partnership might be developed to maximize the effectiveness of the training and minimize development costs. Different delivery methods should be explored, including instructor-led, CD-ROM, and Web-based. About half of employees would prefer an instructor-led approach, and about half would prefer a self-paced course they could take at their convenience.
2. Negotiating skills training: Employees from supplier management and other departments would benefit from this training. There should be several courses offered, including a basic course, a course tailored to negotiating contracts, and a course tailored to international negotiations. Different delivery methods should be explored, including instructor-led, CD-ROM, and Web-based.
Etc.

Deliverables
Project Management-Related Deliverables: Team contract, project management plan, scope management plan, scope statement, WBS, etc.

Product-Related Deliverables:
1. Supplier management training:
      1.1. Needs assessment: A study will be conducted to determine the learning objectives for the executive, introductory, and advanced courses. A detailed survey will be included as part of the study. One survey will be done to assess all training needs (i.e. supplier management, negotiating skills, etc.). Results will be documented in a report about 20-30 pages long and provided in hard copy and presentation format to all project steering committee members. Results will also be stored on the project Web site.
      1.2. Research of existing training: A study will be done to identify current training courses and materials available. Study results will be documented in a report about 10-20 pages long, plus attachments and references. This report will be provided in hard copy format to all project steering committee members and stored on the project Web site.
      1.3. Partnerships: Partnership agreements will be explored to get outside training organizations and suppliers to work on developing and providing training. Product descriptions or descriptions of current courses provided that could meet our training needs will be documented. The legal department will assist in delivering these partnerships.
      1.4. Course development: Appropriate materials will be developed for each course. Materials could take various formats, including written, video, CD-ROM, and Web-based.

FIGURE 4-5 Sample scope statement

Materials should include interactivity to keep learners engaged. Stakeholders from related departments will be actively involved in reviewing the new course materials.

    1.5. Pilot course: A pilot course will be provided for the introductory supplier management course. Feedback from the pilot course will be incorporated into future courses. Instructor-led classes will initially be designed for 20 participants. Changes to this number might be made as needed.

2. Negotiating skills training:

    2.1. Needs assessment: A study will be conducted to determine the learning objectives for the basic negotiations, contract negotiations, and international negotiations courses.

    2.2. Research of existing training: A study will be done to identify current training courses and materials available.

Etc.

Project Success Criteria

Our sponsor has stated that the project will be a success if the new training courses are all available within one year, if the average course evaluations are at least 3.0 on a 1-5 scale, and if the company recoups the cost of the project in reduced training costs within two years after project completion.

FIGURE 4-5 Sample scope statement (continued)

A WBS is often depicted in a graphical format, similar to an organizational chart. The name of the entire project is the top box, called level 1, and the main groupings for the work are listed in the second tier of boxes, called level 2. This level numbering is based on PMI's *Practice Standard for Work Breakdown Structure, Second Edition (2006)*. Each of those boxes can be broken down into subsequent tiers of boxes to show the hierarchy of the work. Project teams often organize the WBS around project products, project phases, or other logical groupings. People often like to create a WBS in a graphical format first to help them visualize the whole project and all of its main parts. You can also show a WBS in tabular form as an indented list of tasks showing the groupings of the work. Note that the term "task" is used to describe each level of work in the WBS. For example, in Figure 4-6, the following items can be referred to as tasks: the level 2 item called Concept, the level 3 item below that called Define Requirements, and the level 4 item below that called Define User Requirements. Tasks that are decomposed into smaller tasks are called summary tasks.

Figure 4-6 shows a sample WBS in both chart and tabular form. Notice that both of these formats show the same information. Many documents, such as contracts, use the tabular format. Project management software also uses this format. The WBS becomes the contents of the Task Name column in Microsoft Project, and the hierarchy or level of tasks is shown by indenting and numbering tasks within the software. The numbering shown in the tabular form on the left in Figure 4-6 coincides with numbering done in Microsoft Project and other sources. The numbering shown in the tabular form on the right in Figure 4-6 is based on PMI's *Practice Standard for Work Breakdown Structures, Second Edition*. Be sure to check with your organization to see what numbering scheme they prefer to use for work breakdown sturctures.

In Figure 4-6, the lowest level of the WBS is level 4. A **work package** is a task at the lowest level of the WBS. In Figure 4-6, tasks 1.2.1, 1.2.2, 1.2.3, and 1.2.4 based on numbering on the left are work packages. The other tasks would probably be broken down further. However, some tasks can remain at a level 3 in the WBS. Some might be broken down to

Level 1 - Entire Project

Level 2

Chart form →

Level 3

Level 4

Tabular form with Microsoft Project Numbering

1.0 Concept
    1.1 Evaluate current systems
    1.2 Define requirements
        1.2.1 Define user requirements
        1.2.2 Define content requirements
        1.2.3 Define system requirements
        1.2.4 Define server owner requirements
    1.3 Define specific functionality
    1.4 Define risks and risk management
        approach
    1.5 Develop project plan
    1.6 Brief Web development team
2.0 Web site design
3.0 Web site development
4.0 Roll out
5.0 Support

Tabular form with PMI Numbering

1.1 Concept
    1.1.1 Evaluate current systems
    1.1.2 Define requirements
        1.1.2.1 Define user requirements
        1.1.2.2 Define content requirements
        1.1.2.3 Define system requirements
        1.1.2.4 Define server owner requirements
    1.1.3 Define specific functionality
    1.1.4 Define risks and risk management
        approach
    1.1.5 Develop project plan
    1.1.6 Brief Web development team
1.2 Web site design
1.3 Web site development
1.4 Roll out
1.5 Support

FIGURE 4-6   WBS in chart and tabular form

level 5 or 6, depending on the complexity of the work. It also represents the level of work that the project manager monitors and controls. You can think of work packages in terms of accountability and reporting. If a project has a relatively short time frame and requires weekly progress reports, a work package might represent work completed in one week or less. On the other hand, if a project has a very long time frame and requires quarterly progress reports, a work package might represent work completed in one month or more. A work package might also be the procurement of a specific product or products, such as an item or items purchased from an outside source.

The sample WBS shown here seems somewhat easy to construct and understand. *Nevertheless, it is very difficult to create a good WBS.* To create a good WBS, you must understand both the project and its scope, and incorporate the needs and knowledge of the stakeholders. The project manager and the project team must decide as a group how to organize the work and how many levels to include in the WBS. Many project managers have found that it is better to focus on getting the top levels done well to avoid being distracted by too much detail.

Many people confuse tasks on a WBS with specifications. Tasks on a WBS represent work that needs to be done to complete the project. For example, if you are creating a WBS to redesign a kitchen, you might have level 2 categories called design, purchasing, flooring, walls, cabinets, and appliances. Under flooring, you might have work packages to remove the old flooring, install the new flooring, and install the trim. You would not have items like "12' by 14' of light oak" or "flooring must be durable" on a WBS.

Another concern when creating a WBS is how to organize it so that it provides the basis for the project schedule. You should focus on what work needs to be done, not when it will be done. In other words, the tasks do not have to be developed as a sequential list of steps. If you do want some time-based flow for the work, you can create a WBS using the project management process groups of initiating, planning, executing, controlling, and closing as level 2 in the WBS. By doing this, not only does the project team follow good project management practice, but the WBS tasks can be mapped more easily against time.

MEDIA SNAPSHOT

Few events get more media attention than the Olympic Games. Imagine all the work involved in planning and executing an event that involves thousands of athletes from around the world with millions of spectators. The 2002 Olympic Winter Games and Paralympics took five years to plan and cost more than $1.9 billion. PMI awarded the Salt Lake Organizing Committee (SLOC) the Project of the Year award for delivering world-class games that, according to the International Olympic Committee, "made a profound impact upon the people of the world."[1]

Four years before the Games began, the SLOC used a Primavera software-based system with a cascading color-coded WBS to integrate planning. A year before the Games, they added a Venue Integrated Planning Schedule to help the team integrate resource needs, budgets, and plans. For example, this software helped the team coordinate different areas involved in controlling access into and around a venue, such as roads, pedestrian pathways, seating and safety provisions, and hospitality areas, saving nearly $10 million.[2]

Approaches to Developing Work Breakdown Structures

Because it is difficult to create a good WBS, this section describes several approaches you can use to develop them. These approaches include:

- Using guidelines
- The analogy approach
- The top-down approach
- The bottom-up approach
- The mind-mapping approach

Using Guidelines

If guidelines for developing a WBS exist, it is very important to follow them. Some organizations—for example, the U.S. Department of Defense (DOD)—prescribe the form and content for WBSs for particular projects. Many DOD projects require contractors to prepare their proposals based on the DOD-provided WBS. For example, a large contract for purchasing hardware and software might prescribe a WBS with level 2 WBS items that included hardware, off-the-shelf software, software development, training, project management, and the like. The hardware item could include several level 3 items, such as servers, laptops, printers, network hardware, and so on. Many government projects include project management as a level 2 item to make sure that work is not forgotten.

The Analogy Approach

Another approach for constructing a WBS is the analogy approach, where you use a similar project's WBS as a starting point. For example, many organizations have sample WBSs from past projects. Many software products, like Project 2007, include several templates for WBSs for various types of projects that can be used as a starting point for creating a new WBS. (See Appendix A for information on using templates.) While starting with a WBS from a similar project can save a lot of time, it is important that project managers and their teams address their unique project needs and how work will be done when creating their WBSs.

The Top-down Approach

Most project managers consider the top-down approach of WBS construction to be conventional. To use the top-down approach, start with the largest items of the project and break them into their subordinate items. This process involves refining the work into greater and greater levels of detail. For example, Figure 4-6 shows how work was broken down to level 4 for part of the intranet project. After breaking down or decomposing the top-level items, resources should then be assigned at the work-package level. The top-down approach is best suited to project managers and teams who have vast technical insight and a big-picture perspective.

The Bottom-up Approach

In the bottom-up approach, team members first identify as many specific tasks related to the project as possible. They then aggregate the specific tasks and organize them into summary activities, or higher levels in the WBS. For example, a group of people might be responsible for creating a WBS to create a brand new product. They could begin by listing detailed tasks they think they would need to do in order to create the product and then group the tasks into categories. Then, they would group these categories into higher-level categories. Some people have found that writing all possible tasks down on sticky notes and then placing them on a wall helps them see all the work required for the project and develop logical groupings for performing the work. The bottom-up approach can be very time consuming, but it can also be a very effective way to create a WBS. Project teams often use the bottom-up approach for projects that represent entirely new products or approaches to doing a job, or to help create buy-in and synergy with a project team.

Mind Mapping

Some project managers like to use mind mapping to help develop WBSs. As described in Chapter 2, mind mapping is a technique that uses branches radiating out from a core idea to structure thoughts and ideas. This more visual, less structured approach to defining and then grouping tasks can unlock creativity among individuals and increase participation and morale among teams. You can create mind maps by hand, by using sticky notes, using presentation software like PowerPoint, or by using mind mapping software.

Figure 4-7 shows a diagram that uses mind mapping to create a WBS for an information technology upgrade project. This figure was created using MindManager software by Mindjet (www.mindjet.com). The circle in the center represents the entire project. Each of the four main branches radiating out from the center represents the main tasks or level 2 items for the WBS. Different people at the meeting creating this mind map might have different roles in the project, which could help in deciding the tasks and WBS structure. For example, the project manager would want to focus on all of the project management tasks, and he or she might also know that they will be tracked in a separate budget category. People who are familiar with acquiring or installing hardware and software might focus on that work, and so on. Branching off from the main task called "Update inventory" are two subtasks, "Perform physical inventory" and "Update database." Branching off from the "Perform physical inventory" subtask are three further subdivisions, labeled Building A, Building B, and Building C, and so on. The team would continue to add branches and items until they have exhausted ideas on what work needs to be performed.

FIGURE 4-7 Sample mind-mapping technique for creating a WBS

After discovering WBS items and structure using the mind-mapping technique, you could then translate the information into chart or tabular form, as described earlier. A feature of MindManager software is that you can export your map into Microsoft Project. The WBS is entered in the Task List column, with the structure automatically created based on the mind map. Figure 4-8 shows the resulting Project 2007 file for the information technology upgrade project.

Mind mapping can be used for developing WBSs using the top-down or bottom-up approach or a combination of the two. For example, you could conduct mind mapping for an entire project by listing the whole project in the center of a document, adding the main

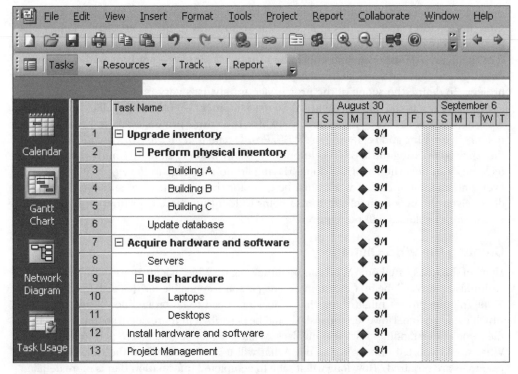

FIGURE 4-8 Project 2007 file with WBS generated from a mind map

categories on branches radiating out from the center, and then adding branches for appropriate subcategories. You could also develop a separate mind-mapping diagram for each major deliverable and then merge them to create one large diagram for the entire project. You can also add items anywhere on a mind-mapping document without following a strict top-down or bottom-up approach. After the mind-mapping documents are complete, you can convert them into a chart or tabular WBS form.

Sample WBS

The Just-In-Time Training project team decided to use the project management process groups for the level 2 tasks in its WBS, following a top-down approach. They also reviewed WBSs of similar projects as they created theirs. (Remember that the process groups include initiating, planning, executing, monitoring and controlling, and closing.) The level 3 tasks under "Executing" (where the products and services of the project are produced) included course design and development, course administration, course evaluation, and stakeholder communications. The project team knew that they had to have strong communications to make the project a success, so they created a separate WBS level 3 category for communications under "Executing." They focused on the product deliverables they had to produce in breaking down the course design and development task by having level 4 categories based on the types of courses: supplier management, negotiating skills, project management, and software applications.

Figure 4-9 shows part of the initial WBS Kristin and her team created. You will see this same information later in this chapter as the task names in the Gantt chart. Some tasks have been broken down into more detail while others have not. For example, section 4 and 5 in the figure, "Monitoring and controlling" and "Closing" are not broken down in more detail. Recall that the scope statement should list and describe all the work required for the project. To define the scope of the project accurately, it is very important to ensure consistency between the project charter, scope statement, WBS, Gantt chart, and related documents. It is also very important to involve the entire project team and other stakeholders in creating and reviewing the WBS. *People who will do the work should help to plan the work* by creating the WBS. It is important to let workers be creative and know that they have a say in how their work is done. Having group meetings to develop a WBS helps everyone understand *what* work must be done for the entire project and *how* it should be done, given the people involved. It also helps to identify where coordination between different work packages will be required.

Creating the WBS Dictionary

Many of the tasks listed on a WBS can be rather vague. What exactly does WBS item 3.1.1.1.2, "Administer survey" mean, for example? The person responsible for this task for the Just-In-Time Training project might think that it does not need to be broken down any further, which could be fine. However, the task should be described in more detail so that everyone has the same understanding of what it involves. What if someone else has to perform the task? What would you tell him or her to do? What will it cost to complete the task? How many resources are required? How long will it take to complete? Information that is more detailed is needed to answer these and other questions. Of course you must use common sense in deciding how much documentation is needed. For a simple task, verbal instructions might be sufficient.

A **WBS dictionary** is a document that describes WBS tasks in detail. The format of the WBS dictionary can vary based on project needs. It might be appropriate to have just a short paragraph describing each work package. For a more complex project, an entire page or more might be needed for the work-package descriptions. Some projects might require that each WBS item describe the responsible person or organization, resource requirements, estimated costs, and other information. Other projects might not require a WBS entry for every single WBS task.

Work Breakdown Structure (WBS) for the Just-In-Time Training Project
August 1, 2009

1. Initiating
   1.1. Prepare stakeholder analysis
   1.2. Prepare business case
   1.3. Create project charter
   1.4. Hold project kick-off meeting
   1.5. Develop preliminary scope statement
2. Planning
   2.1. Project integration management
       2.1.1. Create team contract
       2.1.2. Develop project management plan
   2.2. Project scope management
       2.2.1. Develop scope statement
       2.2.2. Create WBS and WBS dictionary
   2.3. Project time management
   2.4. Project cost management
   2.5. Project quality management
   2.6. Project human resources management
   2.7. Project communications management
   2.8. Project risk management
   2.9. Project procurement management
3. Executing
   3.1. Course design and development
       3.1.1. Supplier management training
           3.1.1.1. Needs assessment
               3.1.1.1.1. Develop survey
               3.1.1.1.2. Administer survey
               3.1.1.1.3. Analyze survey results
           3.1.1.2. Research of existing training
           3.1.1.3. Partnerships
               3.1.1.3.1. Research potential partners for providing training
               3.1.1.3.2. Meet with potential partners
               3.1.1.3.3. Develop partnership agreements
           3.1.1.4. Course development
               3.1.1.4.1. Develop executive course
               3.1.1.4.2. Develop introductory course
               3.1.1.4.3. Develop advanced course
           3.1.1.5. Pilot course
               3.1.1.5.1. Plan pilot course
               3.1.1.5.2. Hold pilot course
               3.1.1.5.3. Prepare report on pilot course
               3.1.1.5.4. Review results of pilot course
       3.1.2. Negotiating skills training
       3.1.3. Project management training
       3.1.4. Software applications training
   3.2. Course administration
   3.3. Course evaluation

FIGURE 4-9   Sample WBS

```
        3.4. Stakeholder communications
            3.4.1.  Communications regarding project and changes to training
                3.4.1.1.    Prepare e-mails, posters, memos, and other information
                3.4.1.2.    Plan and hold meetings
                3.4.1.3.    Prepare information for the corporate intranet
            3.4.2.  Communications regarding productivity improvements
    4.  Monitoring and controlling
    5.  Closing
```

FIGURE 4-9   Sample WBS (continued)

Sample WBS Dictionary Entry

The project manager should work with his or her team and sponsor to determine the level of detail needed in the WBS dictionary. Project teams often review WBS dictionary entries from similar tasks to get a better idea of how to create these entries. They should also decide where this information will be entered and how it will be updated. For the Just-In-Time Training project, Kristin and her team will enter all of the WBS dictionary information into their enterprise project management system. Figure 4-10 provides an example of one of the entries.

WBS Dictionary Entry
August 1, 2009

Project Title: Just-In-Time Training Project
WBS Item Number: 3.1.1.1.2
WBS Item Name: Administer survey
Description: The purpose of the survey for the supplier management training is to determine the learning objectives for the executive, introductory, and advanced supplier management courses (see WBS item 3.1.1.1.1 for additional information on the survey itself). The survey will be administered online using the standard corporate survey software. After the project steering committee approves the survey, the IT department will send it to all employees of grade level 52 or higher in the purchasing, accounting, engineering, IT, sales, marketing, manufacturing, and HR departments. The project champion—Mike Sundby, VP of Human Resources—will write an introductory paragraph for the survey. Department heads will mention the importance of responding to this survey in their department meetings and will send an e-mail to all affected employees to encourage their inputs. If the response rate is less than 25 percent one week after the survey is sent out, additional work may be required.

FIGURE 4-10   Sample WBS dictionary entry

The approved project scope statement and its associated WBS and WBS dictionary form the **scope baseline**. Performance in meeting project scope goals is based on the scope baseline.

PROJECT TIME MANAGEMENT PLANNING TASKS

Project time management involves the processes required to ensure timely completion of a project. The main planning tasks performed as part of project time management are activity definition, activity sequencing, activity resource estimating, activity duration estimating, and schedule development. The main documents produced are an activity list and attributes, a milestone list, a network diagram, the activity resource requirements, the activity duration estimates, and a project schedule. Samples of these documents are provided later in this section.

Activity Definition

Project schedules grow out of the basic documents that initiate a project. The project charter often mentions planned project start and end dates, which serve as the starting points for a more detailed schedule. The project manager starts with the project charter and then develops a project scope statement and WBS, as discussed in the previous section. Using this information with the scope statement, WBS, WBS dictionary, project management plan, and other related information, the project team begins to develop a schedule by first clearly defining all the activities it needs to perform.

Creating the Activity List and Attributes

The **activity list** is a tabulation of activities to be included on a project schedule. The list should include the activity name, an activity identifier or number, and a brief description of the activity. The **activity attributes** provide schedule-related information about each activity, such as predecessors, successors, logical relationships, leads and lags, resource requirements, constraints, imposed dates, and assumptions related to the activity. The activity list and activity attributes should be in agreement with the WBS and WBS dictionary. Recall that a work package is the lowest level task in a WBS. Activities in the activity list are based on the detailed work required to complete each work package.

The goal of the activity definition process is to ensure that project team members have a complete understanding of all the work they must do as part of the project scope so that they can start scheduling the work. For example, one of the work packages in the WBS for the Just-In-Time Training project is "Prepare report on pilot course." The project team would have to understand what that means before it can make schedule-related decisions. How long should the report be? Does it require a survey or extensive research to produce it? What skill level does the report writer need to have? Further defining the task will help the project team determine how long it will take to do and who should do it.

The WBS is often expanded during the activity definition process as the project team members further define the activities required for performing the work. For example, the task "Prepare report on pilot course" might be broken down into several subtasks describing the steps involved in producing the report, such as developing a survey, administering the survey, analyzing the survey results, conducting interviews, writing a draft report, editing the report, and finally producing the report.

To avoid too much detail, some people prefer *not* to include these additional schedule-related activities in the WBS. They keep the lowest level of the WBS at the previously defined work package and describe detailed activities separately in the activity list and schedule. With most project management software, however, it is easy to include *all* the activity data in one place and then view information at whatever level of detail is desired. In this example, the activity list refers to the lowest level of work described for the project.

The project team should review the activity list and activity attributes with project stakeholders. If they do not, they could produce an unrealistic schedule and deliver unacceptable results. For example, if a project team simply estimated that it would take one day for the "Prepare report on pilot course" task and had an intern or trainee write a two-page report to complete that task, the result could be a furious sponsor who expected extensive research, surveys, and a 50-page report. Clearly defining the work and having a realistic schedule for all activities is crucial to project success.

Sample Activity List and Attributes

Kristin and her team developed an activity to assist in developing the project schedule. Figure 4-11 provides a sample entry in the activity list. Notice the detailed information provided, such as the predecessors, successors, resource requirements, and assumptions. As you can see from this sample, Kristin and her team would have to work closely with other stakeholders to define this information.

Creating a Milestone List

To ensure that all major activities are accounted for, project teams often create a milestone list. A **milestone** is a significant event on a project. It often takes several activities and a lot of work to complete a milestone, but the milestone itself is like a marker to help in identifying necessary activities. There is usually no cost or duration associated with a milestone. Milestones are also useful tools for setting schedule goals and monitoring progress, and project sponsors and senior managers often focus on major milestones when reviewing projects. For example, milestones for many projects include sign-off of key documents; completion of specific products; and completion of important process-related work, such as awarding a contract to a supplier. Milestone names are generally written in past tense, such as "Contract awarded."

Sample Milestone List

Kristin and her team reviewed the draft WBS and activity list to develop an initial milestone list. They reviewed the list with their sponsor and other key stakeholders. Project teams often estimate completion dates for milestones early in the scheduling process and adjust them after going through additional time management planning steps such as activity sequencing, activity resource estimating, duration estimating, and schedule development. Figure 4-12 shows part of the milestone list for the Just-In-Time Training project. This section focuses on the milestones related to the needs assessment for supplier management training (WBS item 3.1.1.1). Kristin knew her team had to complete this survey early in the project and that the results would affect many of the other tasks required for the project.

Activity List and Attributes
August 1, 2009

Project Name: Just-In-Time Training Project
WBS Item Number: 3.1.1.1.2
WBS Item Name: Administer survey
Predecessors: 3.1.1.1.1 Develop survey
Successors: 3.1.1.1.3 Analyze survey results
Logical Relationships: finish-to-start
Leads and Lags: None
Resource Requirements: IT personnel, corporate survey software, corporate Intranet
Constraints: None
Imposed dates: None
Assumptions: The survey for the supplier management training will be administered online using the standard corporate survey software. It should include questions measured on a Likert scale. For example, a question might be as follows: "I learned a lot from this course." Respondents would enter 1 for Strongly Agree, 2 for Agree, 3 for Undecided, 4 for Disagree, or 5 for Strongly Disagree. There should also be several open-ended questions, such as "What did you like most about the pilot course? What did you like least about the pilot course?" After the project steering committee approves the survey, the IT department will send it to all employees of grade level 52 or higher in the purchasing, accounting, engineering, IT, sales, marketing, manufacturing, and HR departments. The project champion—Mike Sundby, VP of Human Resources— will write an introductory paragraph for the survey. Department heads will mention the importance of responding to this survey in their department meetings and will send an e-mail to all affected employees to encourage their inputs. If the response rate is less than 25 percent one week after the survey is sent out, additional work may be required, such as a reminder e-mail to follow-up with people who have not responded to the survey.

FIGURE 4-11 Sample activity list and attributes

Her team might need to see all the milestones provided in Figure 4-12, but the steering committee might only need to see the last milestone, "Survey results reported to steering committee." The steering committee might focus on other milestones, including the project kick-off meeting, results of the pilot course, dates for each training class provided as part of the project, results of the course evaluations, and projected end date for the project. Using project management software, such as Project 2007, makes it easy to filter information and create reports so that different people can focus on their own tasks and milestones. See Appendix A for more details on using Project 2007.

```
                            Milestone List
                            August 1, 2009

Project Name: Just-In-Time Training Project

Milestone                                   Initial Estimated Completion Date*
Draft survey completed                      8/3/09
Survey comments submitted                   8/8/09
Survey sent out by IT                       8/10/09
Percentage of survey respondents reviewed   8/17/09
Survey report completed                     8/22/09
Survey results reported to steering committee 8/24/09
*Note: Dates are in U.S. format. 8/3/09 means August 3, 2009.
```

FIGURE 4-12 Sample milestone list

BEST PRACTICE

Many people use the SMART criteria to help define milestones. The SMART criteria are guidelines suggesting that milestones should be:

- Specific
- Measureable
- Assignable
- Realistic
- Time-framed

For example, completing the draft survey, as listed in Figure 4-12 is specific, measurable, and assignable if everyone knows what should be in the draft survey, how and to whom it should be distributed, and who is responsible for creating the survey. Completing the draft survey is realistic and able to be time-framed if it is an achievable event and scheduled for completion at an appropriate time.

You can also use milestones to help reduce schedule risk by following these best practices:

- Define milestones early in the project and include them in the Gantt chart to provide a visual guide.
- Keep milestones small and frequent.
- The set of milestones must be all-encompassing.
- Each milestone must be binary, meaning it is either complete or incomplete.
- Carefully monitor the milestones on the critical path (described later in this chapter).[3]

Activity Sequencing

After defining project activities, the next step in project time management is activity sequencing. Activity sequencing involves reviewing the activity list and attributes, project scope statement, and milestone list to determine the relationships or dependencies between activities. It also involves evaluating the reasons for dependencies and the different types of dependencies.

A **dependency** or **relationship** relates to the sequencing of project activities or tasks. For example, does a certain activity have to be finished before another one can start? Can the project team do several activities in parallel? Can some overlap? Determining these relationships or dependencies between activities has a significant impact on developing and managing a project schedule.

There are three basic reasons for creating dependencies among project activities:

- **Mandatory dependencies** are inherent in the nature of the work being performed on a project. They are sometimes referred to as hard logic because their relationships are unavoidable. For example, you cannot hold training classes until the training materials are ready, the training materials cannot be created until the objectives of the course are determined, and so on.
- **Discretionary dependencies** are defined by the project team. For example, a project team might follow good practice and not start detailed design work until key stakeholders sign off on all of the analysis work. Discretionary dependencies are sometimes referred to as soft logic and should be used with care because they might limit later scheduling options.
- **External dependencies** involve relationships between project and non-project activities. The installation of new software might depend on delivery of new hardware from an external supplier. Even though the delivery of the new hardware might not be in the scope of the project, it should have an external dependency added to it because late delivery will affect the project schedule.

As with activity definition, it is important that project stakeholders work together to define the activity dependencies that exist on their project. If you do not define the sequence of activities and estimate their durations, you cannot use some of the most powerful schedule tools available to project managers: network diagrams and critical path analysis. The main output of activity sequencing is a network diagram.

Network Diagrams

Network diagrams are the preferred technique for showing activity sequencing. A **network diagram** is a schematic display of the logical relationships among, or sequencing of, project activities. Some people refer to network diagrams as PERT charts. PERT is described later in this section. Figure 4-13 shows a sample network diagram for Project X, which uses the arrow diagramming method (ADM), or activity-on-arrow (AOA) approach. (Note: This approach is shown first because the diagrams are easier to understand and create. Its main limitation is that it can only show finish-to-start dependencies, as described later in this section.)

Note the main elements on this network diagram. The letters A through J represent activities with dependencies that are required to complete the project. These activities come from the WBS and activity definition process described earlier. The arrows represent the activity sequencing, or relationships between tasks. For example, Activity A must be done before Activity D, Activity D must be done before Activity H, and so on.

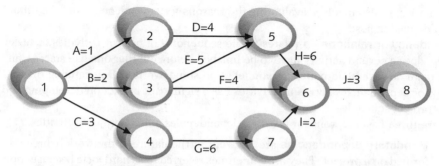

Note: Assume all durations are in days; A=1 means Activity A has a duration of 1 day.

FIGURE 4-13   Activity-on-arrow (AOA) network diagram for Project X

The format of this network diagram uses the **activity-on-arrow (AOA)** approach, or the **arrow diagramming method (ADM)**—a network diagramming technique in which activities are represented by arrows and connected at points called nodes to illustrate the sequence of activities. A **node** is simply the starting and ending point of an activity. The first node signifies the start of a project, and the last node represents the end of a project.

Keep in mind that the network diagram represents activities that must be done to complete the project. It is not a race to get from the first node to the last node. *Every* activity on the network diagram must be completed for the project to finish. It is also important to note that not every single item on the WBS needs to be on the network diagram; only activities with dependencies need to be shown on the network diagram. However, some people like to have start and end milestones and to list every activity. It is a matter of preference. For projects with hundreds of activities, it might be simpler to include only activities with dependencies on a network diagram.

Assuming you have a list of the project activities and their start and finish nodes, follow these steps to create an AOA network diagram:

1. Find all of the activities that start at Node 1. Draw their finish nodes, and draw arrows between Node 1 and each of those finish nodes. Put the activity letter or name on the associated arrow. If you have a duration estimate, write that next to the activity letter or name, as shown in Figure 4-13. For example, A = 1 means that the duration of Activity A is one day, week, or other standard unit of time. Also be sure to put arrowheads on all arrows to signify the direction of the relationships.

2. Continue drawing the network diagram, working from left to right. Look for bursts and merges. **Bursts** occur when two or more activities follow a single node. A **merge** occurs when two or more nodes precede a single node. For example, in Figure 4-13, Node 1 is a burst because it goes into Nodes 2, 3, and 4. Node 5 is a merge preceded by Nodes 2 and 3.

3. Continue drawing the AOA network diagram until all activities are included on the diagram.
4. As a rule of thumb, all arrowheads should face toward the right, and no arrows should cross on an AOA network diagram. You might need to redraw the diagram to make it look presentable.

Even though AOA network diagrams are generally easy to understand and create, a different method is more commonly used: the precedence diagramming method. The **precedence diagramming method (PDM)** is a network diagramming technique in which boxes represent activities. It is particularly useful for visualizing different types of time dependencies. AOA diagrams can only show the most common type of dependency, finish-to-start.

Figure 4-14 illustrates the types of dependencies that can occur among project activities, based on a Help screen from an older version of Microsoft Project. After you determine the reason for a dependency between activities (mandatory, discretionary, or external), you must determine the type of dependency. Note that the terms "activity" and "task" are used interchangeably, as are "relationship" and "dependency." The four types of dependencies, or relationships, between activities include the following:

- *Finish-to-start:* A relationship in which the "from" or predecessor activity must finish before the "to" or successor activity can start. For example, you cannot provide training until after the training materials are available. Finish-to-start is the most common type of relationship, or dependency, and AOA network diagrams use only finish-to-start dependencies.
- *Start-to-start:* A relationship in which the "from" activity cannot start until the "to" activity is started. For example, as soon as you start a project review meeting, you can start documenting attendees, serving refreshments, taking minutes, and so on.
- *Finish-to-finish:* A relationship in which the "from" activity must be finished before the "to" activity can be finished. One task cannot finish before another finishes. For example, quality control efforts cannot finish before production finishes, although the two activities can be performed at the same time.
- *Start-to-finish:* A relationship in which the "from" activity must start before the "to" activity can be finished. This type of relationship is rarely used, but it is appropriate in some cases. For example, an organization might strive to stock raw materials just in time for the manufacturing process to begin. A delay in the start of the manufacturing process should delay completion of stocking the raw materials. Another example is when an employee cannot leave his/her current job until a replacement is found.

Figure 4-15 illustrates Project X (shown originally in Figure 4-13) using the precedence diagramming method. Notice that the activities are placed inside boxes, which represent the nodes on this diagram. Arrows show the relationships between activities. For example, Activity D has a relationship of depedency with Activity A. This figure was created using Microsoft Project, which automatically places additional information inside each node. Each task box includes the start and finish date, labeled "Start" and "Finish"; the task ID number, labeled "ID"; the task's duration, labeled "Dur"; and the names of resources, if any, assigned to the task, labeled "Res." The border of the boxes for tasks on

Task dependencies

The nature of the relationship between two linked tasks. You link tasks by defining a dependency between their finish and start dates. For example, the "Contact caterers" task must finish before the start of the "Determine menus" task. There are four kinds of task dependencies in Microsoft Project:

Task dependency	Example	Description
Finish-to-start (FS)	A → B	Task (B) cannot start until task (A) finishes.
Start-to-start (SS)	A / B	Task (B) cannot start until task (A) starts.
Finish-to-finish (FF)	A / B	Task (B) cannot finish until task (A) finishes.
Start-to-finish (SF)	A / B	Task (B) cannot finish until task (A) starts.

FIGURE 4-14   Task dependency types

the critical path (discussed later in this section) appears automatically in red in the Microsoft Project network diagram view. In Figure 4-15, the boxes for critical tasks have a thicker border and are not shaded.

FIGURE 4-15   Precedence diagramming method (PDM) network diagram for Project X

Although the AOA diagram might seem easier to understand, the precedence diagramming method is used more often than AOA network diagrams. Its main advantage is that it allows you to show different types of dependencies among tasks, whereas AOA network diagrams use only finish-to-start dependencies.

Kristin and her team reviewed all the project activities and determined which ones had dependencies. They also determined which tasks could be overlapped (or have "lead" time) and which needed some "lag" time, or a gap in time. See Appendix A for more information on lead and lag time. For example, they wanted to wait 30 days after holding the first supplier management course before holding the second one, which meant they needed to create a dependency with 30 days of lag time between the two courses. If the first class was held earlier or later than planned, the date for the second course would automatically adjust to follow it 30 days later. They entered the information into Project 2007 to begin building a detailed Gantt chart for the project, as described later in this section. The Project 2007 file would be integrated with their enterprise project management system to have all information in one place.

Activity Resource Estimating

Before you can estimate the duration for each activity, you must have a good idea of the quantity and type of resources (people, equipment, and materials) that will be assigned to each activity. It is important that the people who help determine what resources are necessary include people who have experience and expertise in similar projects and with the organization performing the project.

Important questions to answer in activity resource estimating include the following:

- How difficult will it be to do specific activities on this project?
- Is there anything unique in the project's scope statement that will affect resources?
- What is the organization's history in doing similar activities? Has the organization done similar tasks before? What level of personnel did the work?
- Does the organization have appropriate people, equipment, and materials available for performing the work? Are there any organizational policies that might affect the availability of resources?
- Does the organization need to acquire more resources to accomplish the work? Would it make sense to outsource some of the work? Will outsourcing increase or decrease the amount of resources needed and when they will be available?

It is important to thoroughly brainstorm and evaluate alternatives related to resources, especially on projects that involve people from multiple disciplines and companies. Because most projects involve many human resources and the majority of costs are for salaries and benefits, it is often effective to solicit ideas from different people and to address resource-related issues early in a project. The resource estimates should also be updated as more detailed information becomes available.

Sample Activity Resource Requirements

A key output of the resource estimating process is documentation of activity resource requirements. This list can take various formats. For the Just-In-Time Training project, Kristin met with her team, her sponsor, and the project steering committee, as needed, to discuss resource requirements for the project. They also discussed which training might be best to outsource, which would be best to perform with internal resources, and which should use both internal and external resources. They entered important resource information for each task in their enterprise project management software.

Figure 4-16 provides an example of one of the resource requirement entries for the activity described earlier in the WBS dictionary entry called "Administer survey."

Activity Resource Requirements
August 1, 2009

Project Name: Just-In-Time Training Project
WBS Item Number: 3.1.1.1.2
WBS Item Name: Administer survey
Description: Internal members of our IT department will perform this task. The individuals must be knowledgeable in using our online survey software so that they can enter the actual survey into this software. They must also know how to run a query to find the e-mail addresses of employees of grade level 52 or higher in the purchasing, accounting, engineering, IT, sales, marketing, manufacturing, and HR departments.

FIGURE 4-16   Sample activity resource requirements information

Activity Duration Estimating

After working with key stakeholders to define activities, determine their dependencies, and estimate their resources, the next process in project time management is to estimate the duration of activities. It is important to note that **duration** includes the actual amount of time spent working on an activity *plus* elapsed time. For example, even though it might take one workweek or five workdays to do the actual work, the duration estimate might be two weeks to allow extra time needed to obtain outside information or to allow for resource availability. Do not confuse duration with **effort**, which is the number of workdays or work hours required to complete a task. A duration estimate of one day could be based on eight hours of work or 80 hours of work. Duration relates to the time estimate, not the effort estimate. Of course, the two are related, so project team members must document their assumptions when creating duration estimates and update the estimates as the project progresses.

The outputs of activity duration estimating include updates to the activity attributes, if needed, and duration estimates for each activity. Duration estimates are provided as a discrete number, such as four weeks; as a range, such as three to five weeks; or as a three-point estimate. A **three-point estimate** is an estimate that includes an optimistic, most likely, and pessimistic estimate, such as three weeks, four weeks, and five weeks, respectively. The optimistic estimate is based on a best-case scenario, whereas the pessimistic estimate is based on a worst-case scenario. The most likely estimate, as it sounds, is an estimate based on a most likely or expected scenario.

A three-point estimate is required for performing PERT estimates. **Program Evaluation and Review Technique (PERT)** is a network analysis technique used to estimate project duration when there is a high degree of uncertainty about the individual activity duration estimates. By using the PERT weighted average for each activity duration estimate, the total project duration estimate accounts for the risk or uncertainty in the individual activity estimates. To use PERT, you calculate a weighted average for the duration estimate of each project activity using the following formula:

$$\text{PERT weighted average} = \frac{\text{optimistic time} + 4 \times \text{most likely time} + \text{pessimistic time}}{6}$$

Sample Activity Duration Estimates

Many project teams use one discrete estimate—the most likely estimate—to estimate activity durations. For example, Kristin's team could enter these discrete estimates into their enterprise project management system. If Kristin's project team used PERT to determine the schedule for the Just-In-Time Training project, they would have to collect numbers for the optimistic, most likely, and pessimistic duration estimates for each project activity. For example, suppose the person assigned to administer the survey for the supplier management training estimated that it would take two workdays to do this activity. Without using PERT, the duration estimate for that activity would be two workdays. Suppose an optimistic time estimate for this activity is one workday, and a pessimistic time estimate is nine workdays. Applying the PERT formula, you get the following:

$$\text{PERT weighted average} = \frac{1 \text{ workday} + 4 \times 2 \text{ workdays} + 9 \text{ workdays}}{6} = 3 \text{ workdays}$$

Instead of using the most likely duration estimate of two workdays, the project team would use three workdays. The main advantage of PERT is that it attempts to address the risk associated with duration estimates. Because many projects exceed schedule estimates, PERT might help in developing schedules that are more realistic.

PERT also has disadvantages: It involves more work because it requires several duration estimates, and there are better probabilistic (based on probability) methods for assessing schedule risk, such as Monte Carlo simulations. To perform a Monte Carlo simulation, in addition to the three-point estimate, you also collect probabilistic information for each activity duration estimate. For example, Kristin would ask the person assigned to administer the survey for the supplier management training what the probability was of completing that activity between the optimistic and most likely times (one and two days, in this example). If he estimated only a 10 percent probability, Kristin would know that a two-day estimate or even a three-day estimate might be unrealistic. For this project, however, Kristin and her team decided to enter realistic discrete estimates for each activity instead of using PERT or a Monte Carlo simulation. She stressed that people who would do the work should provide the estimate, and they should have 50 percent confidence in meeting each estimate. If some tasks took longer, some took less time, and some were exactly on target, they should still meet their overall schedule.

Schedule Development

Schedule development uses the results of all the preceding project time management processes to determine the start and end dates of project activities and of the entire project. There are often several iterations of all the project time management processes before a project schedule is finalized. The ultimate goal of schedule development is to create a realistic project schedule that provides a basis for monitoring project progress for the time dimension of the project. Project managers must lead their teams in creating realistic schedules and then following them during project execution.

☑ WHAT WENT RIGHT?

Chris Higgins used the discipline he learned in the Army to transform project management into a cultural force at Bank of America. Higgins learned that taking time on the front end of a project could save significant time and money on the back end. As a quartermaster in the Army, when Higgins's people had to pack tents, he devised a contest to find the best way to fold a tent and determine the precise spots to place the pegs and equipment for the quickest possible assembly. Higgins used the same approach when he led an interstate banking initiative to integrate incompatible check processing, checking account, and savings account platforms in various states.

Law mandated that the banks solve the problem in one year or less. Higgins's project team was pushing to get to the coding phase of the project quickly, but Higgins held them back. He made the team members develop a realistic project schedule that included adequate time to analyze, plan, and document requirements for the system in detail. It turned out that they needed six months just to complete that work. However, the discipline up front enabled the software developers on the team to do all of the coding in only three months, as planned, and the project was completed on time.[4]

The main output of the schedule development process is the project schedule, which is often displayed in the form of a Gantt chart.

Gantt charts provide a standard format for displaying project schedule information by listing project activities and their corresponding start and finish dates in a calendar format. Figure 4-17 shows a simple Gantt chart for Project X, described earlier, created with Project 2007. Recall that this example only uses finish-to-start dependencies and no lead or lag time. See Appendix A for examples and instructions for using other types of dependencies.

Recall that the activities on the Gantt chart should coincide with the activities on the WBS, the activity list, and the milestone list. Before showing a Gantt chart for the Just-In-Time Training project, it is important to explain a fundamental concept that assists project teams in developing and meeting project schedules: critical path analysis.

FIGURE 4-17 Gantt chart for Project X

Critical Path Analysis

Many projects fail to meet schedule expectations. **Critical path method (CPM)**—also called **critical path analysis**—is a network diagramming technique used to predict total project duration. This important tool will help you combat project schedule overruns. A **critical path** for a project is the series of activities that determine the *earliest* time by which the project can be completed. It is the *longest* path through the network diagram and has the least amount of slack or float. **Slack** or **float** is the amount of time an activity may be delayed without delaying a succeeding activity or the project finish date. There are normally several tasks done in parallel on projects, and most projects have multiple paths through a network diagram. The longest path or the path containing the critical tasks is what is driving the completion date for the project. Remember that you are not finished with the project until you have finished *all* the tasks.

Calculating the Critical Path

To find the critical path for a project, you must first develop a good network diagram as described earlier, which requires a good activity list based on the WBS. To create a network diagram, you must determine the dependencies of activities and also estimate their durations. Calculating the critical path involves adding the durations for all activities on each path through the network diagram. The longest path is the critical path.

Figure 4-18 shows the AOA network diagram for Project X again. Note that you can use either the AOA or the precedence diagramming method to determine the critical path on projects. Figure 4-18 shows all of the paths—a total of four—through the network diagram. Note that each path starts at the first node (1) and ends at the last node (8) on the AOA network diagram. This figure also shows the length or total duration of each path through the network diagram. These lengths are computed by adding the durations of each activity on the path. Because path B-E-H-J at 16 days has the longest duration, it is the critical path for the project.

What does the critical path really mean? *The critical path shows the shortest time in which a project can be completed.* If one or more of the activities on the critical path takes longer than planned, the whole project schedule will slip *unless* the project manager takes corrective action.

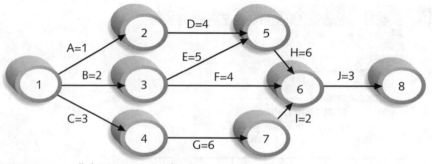

Note: Assume all durations are in days.

Path 1:   A-D-H-J   Length = 1+4+6+3 = 14 days
Path 2:   B-E-H-J   Length = 2+5+6+3 = 16 days
Path 3:   B-F-J   Length = 2+4+3 = 9 days
Path 4:   C-G-I-J   Length = 3+6+2+3 = 14 days

Because the critical path is the longest path through the network diagram, Path 2, B-E-H-J, is the critical path for Project X.

FIGURE 4-18   Critical path calculation for Project X

Project teams can be creative in managing the critical path. For example, Joan Knutson, a well-known author and speaker in the project management field, often describes how a gorilla helped Apple computer complete a project on time. Team members worked in an area with cubicles, and whoever was in charge of a task currently on the critical path had a big, stuffed gorilla on top of his or her cubicle. Everyone knew that that person was under the most time pressure, so they tried not to distract him or her. When a critical task was completed, the person in charge of the next critical task received the gorilla (see Figure 4-19).

FIGURE 4-19   Who's stuck with the gorilla this week?

Growing Grass Can Be on the Critical Path

People are often confused about what the critical path is for a project or what it really means. Some people think the critical path includes the most critical activities. However, the critical path focuses on the time dimension of a project. The fact that its name includes the word "critical" does *not* mean that it includes all critical activities in terms of scope, quality, resources, or other areas. For example, Frank Addeman, executive project director at Walt Disney Imagineering, explained in a keynote address at the May 2000 PMI-ISSIG Professional Development Seminar that growing grass was on the critical path for building Disney's Animal Kingdom theme park. This 500-acre park required special grass for its animal inhabitants, and some of the grass took years to grow. The project manager did not assign his top people to watching grass grow! He did use this information, however, to delay the start of other more expensive activities to make effective use of resources. Another misconception is that the critical path is the shortest path through the network diagram. In areas such as transportation modeling, multiple network diagrams are drawn in which identifying the shortest path is the goal. For a project, however, each task or activity must be done in order to complete the project. It is not a matter of choosing the shortest path.

Other aspects of critical path analysis may cause confusion. Can there be more than one critical path on a project? Does the critical path ever change? In the Project X example, suppose that Activity A has a duration estimate of three days instead of one day. This new duration estimate would make the length of Path 1 equal to 16 days. Now the project has two paths of the longest duration, so there are two critical paths. Therefore, there *can* be more than one critical path on a project. Project managers should closely monitor performance of activities on the critical path to avoid late project completion. If there is more than one critical path, project managers must keep their eyes on all of them.

The critical path on a project can change as the project progresses. For example, suppose everything is going as planned at the beginning of the project. In this example, suppose Activities A, B, C, D, E, F, and G from Figure 4-18 all start and finish as planned. Then suppose Activity I runs into problems. If Activity I takes more than four days, it will cause path C-G-I-J to be longer than the other paths, assuming they progress as planned. This change would cause path C-G-I-J to become the new critical path. Therefore, the critical path can change on a project.

Using Critical Path Analysis to Make Schedule Trade-Offs

It is important to know what the critical path is throughout the life of a project so that the project manager can make trade-offs. If the project manager knows that one of the tasks on the critical path is behind schedule, he needs to decide what to do about it. Should the schedule be renegotiated with stakeholders? Should more resources be allocated to other items on the critical path to make up for that time? Is it okay if the project finishes behind schedule? By keeping track of the critical path, the project manager and his team take a proactive role in managing the project schedule.

It is common for stakeholders to want to shorten a project schedule estimate. Your team may have done its best to develop a project schedule by defining activities, determining sequencing, and estimating resources and durations for each activity. The results of this work may have shown that your team needs 10 months to complete the project. Your sponsor might ask if the project can be done in eight or nine months. Rarely do people ask you to take longer than you suggested. By knowing the critical path, the project manager and his team can use several duration compression techniques to shorten the project schedule. One technique is to reduce the duration of activities on the critical path. The project manager can shorten the duration of critical path activities by allocating more resources to those activities or by changing their scope.

Crashing is a technique for making cost and schedule trade-offs to obtain the greatest amount of schedule compression for the least incremental cost. For example, suppose one of the items on the critical path for the Just-In-Time Training project was to design and develop an advanced course for supplier management. If this task is yet to be done and was originally estimated to take four weeks based on key people working 25 percent of their time on this task, Kristin could suggest that people work 50 percent of their time to finish the task faster. This change might cost some additional money if people had to work paid overtime, but it could shorten the project end date by two weeks. By focusing on tasks on the critical path that could be finished more quickly for either no extra cost or a small cost, the project schedule could be shortened. The main advantage of crashing is shortening the time it takes to finish a project. The main disadvantage of crashing is that it often increases total project costs. If used too often, however, crashing can affect staff negatively by lowering morale or causing burnout.

Another technique for shortening a project schedule is fast tracking. **Fast tracking** involves doing activities in parallel that you would normally do in sequence. For example, Kristin's project team may have planned not to start any of the work on the negotiating skills training until they finished most of the work on the supplier management training. Instead, they could consider performing several of these tasks in parallel to shorten the schedule. As with crashing, the main advantage of fast tracking is that it can shorten the time it takes to finish a project. The main disadvantage of fast tracking is that it can end up lengthening the project schedule, because starting some tasks too soon often increases project risk and results in rework.

Importance of Updating Critical Path Data

In addition to finding the critical path at the beginning of a project, it is important to update the schedule with actual data. After the project team completes activities, the project manager should document the actual duration of each of those activities. He or she should also document revised estimates for activities in progress or yet to be started. These revisions often cause a project's critical path to change, resulting in a new estimated completion date for the project. Again, proactive project managers and their teams stay on top of changes so that they can make informed decisions and keep stakeholders informed of, and involved in, major project decisions.

Critical Chain Scheduling

Another more advanced scheduling technique that addresses the challenge of meeting or beating project finish dates is an application of the Theory of Constraints called critical chain scheduling. The **Theory of Constraints (TOC)** is a management philosophy developed by Eliyahu M. Goldratt and discussed in his books *The Goal* and *Critical Chain*. The

Theory of Constraints is based on the fact that, like a chain with its weakest link, any complex system at any point in time often has only one aspect or constraint that limits its ability to achieve more of its goal. For the system to attain any significant improvements, that constraint must be identified, and the whole system must be managed with it in mind. **Critical chain scheduling** is a method of scheduling that considers limited resources when creating a project schedule and includes buffers to protect the project completion date.

An important concept in critical chain scheduling is the availability of scarce resources. Some projects cannot be done unless a particular resource is available to work on one or several tasks. For example, if a television station wants to produce a show centered around a particular celebrity, it must first check the availability of that celebrity. As another example, if a particular piece of equipment is needed full time to complete each of two tasks that were originally planned to occur simultaneously, critical chain scheduling acknowledges that you must either delay one of those tasks until the equipment is available or find another piece of equipment in order to meet the schedule. Other important concepts related to critical chain scheduling include multitasking and time buffers.

Multitasking occurs when a resource works on more than one task at a time. This situation occurs frequently on projects. People are assigned to multiple tasks within the same project or different tasks on multiple projects. For example, suppose someone is working on three different tasks, Task 1, Task 2, and Task 3, for three different projects, and each task takes 10 days to complete. If the person did not multitask, and instead completed each task sequentially, starting with Task 1, then Task 1 would be completed after day 10, Task 2 would be completed after day 20, and Task 3 would be completed after day 30, as shown in Figure 4-20. However, because many people in this situation try to please all three people who need their tasks completed, they often work on the first task for some time, then the second, then the third, then go back to the first task, and so on, as shown in Figure 4-21. In this example, the tasks were all half-done one at a time, then completed one at a time. Task 1 is now completed at the end of day 20 instead of day 10, Task 2 is completed at the end of day 25 instead of day 20, and Task 3 is still completed on day 30. This example illustrates how multitasking can delay task completions. Multitasking also often involves wasted setup time, which increases total duration.

FIGURE 4-20   Three Tasks without Multitasking

Critical chain scheduling assumes that resources do not multitask or at least minimize multitasking. Someone should not be assigned to two tasks simultaneously on the same project when critical chain scheduling is in effect. Likewise, critical chain theory suggests that projects be prioritized so people working on more than one project at a time know which tasks take priority. Preventing multitasking avoids resource conflicts and

FIGURE 4-21 Three Tasks with Multitasking

wasted setup time caused by shifting between multiple tasks over time. In fact, a 2006 cover story for Time Magazine discussed the negative affects of multi-tasking, especially with the advent of new technologies. "Decades of research (not to mention common sense) indicate that the quality of one's output and depth of thought deteriorate as one attends to ever more tasks. Some are concerned about the disappearance of mental downtime to relax and reflect."[5]

An essential concept to improving project finish dates with critical chain scheduling is to change the way people make task estimates. Many people add a safety or **buffer**, which is additional time to complete a task, to an estimate to account for various factors. These factors include the negative effects of multitasking, distractions and interruptions, fear that estimates will be reduced, Murphy's Law, and so on. **Murphy's Law** states that if something can go wrong, it will. Critical chain scheduling removes buffers from individual tasks and instead creates a **project buffer**, which is additional time added before the project's due date. Critical chain scheduling also protects tasks on the critical chain from being delayed by using **feeding buffers**, which are additional time added before tasks on the critical chain that are preceded by non-critical-path tasks.

Figure 4-22 provides an example of a network diagram constructed using critical chain scheduling. Note that the critical chain accounts for a limited resource, X, and the schedule includes use of feeding buffers and a project buffer in the network diagram. The tasks marked with an X are part of the critical chain, which can be interpreted as being the critical path using this technique. The task estimates in critical chain scheduling should be shorter than traditional estimates because they do not include their own buffers. Not having task buffers should mean less occurrence of **Parkinson's Law**, which states that work expands to fill the time allowed. In other words, if you included a buffer in a task estimate and you did not need it, you would still use it. The feeding and project buffers protect the date that really needs to be met—the project completion date.

As you can see, critical chain scheduling is a fairly complicated yet powerful tool that involves critical path analysis, resource constraints, and changes in how task estimates are made in terms of buffers. Several organizations have reported successes with this approach. Some consider critical chain scheduling one of the most important new concepts in the field of project management.

Critical chain

Critical chain

Critical chain

Project buffer

Completion date

X = Tasks done by limited resource
FB = Feeding buffer

FIGURE 4-22 Example of Critical Chain Scheduling[6]

Sample Project Schedule

Kristin worked with her team to define project activities, determine activity sequencing, describe activity resources, estimate activity durations, and make schedule trade-offs to perform all of the work required for the project within one year, as desired by the project sponsor.

Figure 4-23 provides part of the resulting Gantt chart the team will use to guide their project schedule. To fit the information on one page, the executing tasks have been collapsed, which means that you cannot see the tasks under that category but you can expand them on the computer screen. Notice that the items in the Task Name column come from the WBS, and duration estimates are entered in the "Duration" column. Also notice the flow between the initiating, planning, executing, monitoring and controlling, and closing tasks. Dependencies between activities are shown by the entries in the "Pred" (short for Predecessors) column and the arrows connecting symbols on the Gantt chart. You can download and review the entire Project 2007 file from the companion Web site for this text and learn how to use Project 2007 by reading Appendix A, the *Guide to Using Microsoft Project 2007*.

Figure 4-24 shows another view of the Gantt chart for the Just-In-Time Training project, showing all of the summary tasks (represented by thick black lines) and milestones (represented by black diamonds). Note that the milestones include the schedule items that the project manager and the project steering committee would be most interested in monitoring and controlling to make sure the project stays on schedule. You will learn more about monitoring and controlling projects in Chapter 7.

By using project management software like Project 2007, you can easily see different levels of detail in the schedule information. Also note that Kristin decided to include a

Task Name	Duration	Start	Finish	Predecessors
⊟ 1 Initiating	16 days	Wed 7/1/09	Wed 7/22/09	
1.1 Prepare stakeholder analysis	3 days	Wed 7/1/09	Fri 7/3/09	
1.2 Prepare business case	5 days	Mon 7/6/09	Fri 7/10/09	2
1.3 Create project charter	3 days	Mon 7/13/09	Wed 7/15/09	3
1.4 Hold project kickoff meeting	0 days	Wed 7/15/09	Wed 7/15/09	4
1.5 Develop preliminary scope statement	5 days	Thu 7/16/09	Wed 7/22/09	4
⊟ 2 Planning	53 days	Mon 7/6/09	Wed 9/16/09	
⊟ 2.1 Project integration management	53 days	Mon 7/6/09	Wed 9/16/09	
2.1.1 Create team contract	3 days	Mon 7/6/09	Wed 7/8/09	2
2.1.2 Develop project management plan	50 days	Thu 7/9/09	Wed 9/16/09	
⊟ 2.2 Project scope management	10 days	Thu 7/23/09	Wed 8/5/09	
2.2.1 Develop scope statement	7 days	Thu 7/23/09	Fri 7/31/09	6
2.2.2 Create WBS and WBS dictionary	3 days	Mon 8/3/09	Wed 8/5/09	12
2.3 Project time management	10 days	Thu 8/6/09	Wed 8/19/09	13
2.4 Project cost management	10 days	Thu 8/6/09	Wed 8/19/09	13
2.5 Project quality management	10 days	Thu 8/6/09	Wed 8/19/09	13
2.6 Project human resource management	10 days	Thu 8/6/09	Wed 8/19/09	13
2.7 Project communications management	10 days	Thu 8/20/09	Wed 9/2/09	14
2.8 Project risk management	10 days	Thu 8/20/09	Wed 9/2/09	14
2.9 Project procurement management	20 days	Thu 8/20/09	Wed 9/16/09	14
⊞ 3 Executing	207.5 days?	Fri 7/17/09	Tue 5/4/10	
4 Monitoring and Controlling	237 days	Thu 7/2/09	Fri 5/28/10	
5 Closing	21 days	Tue 5/4/10	Tue 6/1/10	81
6 Project buffer	20 days	Wed 6/2/10	Tue 6/29/10	
7 Project must be completed by date	0 days	Wed 6/30/10	Wed 6/30/10	

Collapsed symbol

FIGURE 4-23   Sample project schedule

project buffer to account for unexpected factors. This buffer (shown as the second to last item in the Task Name column in Figure 4-23) will help ensure that the project is completed on time. Kristin has learned from past projects that no matter how well you try to schedule everything, it can still be a challenge to finish on time without a mad rush at the end. For this reason, she decided to include a 20-day project buffer, which the project steering committee thought was an excellent idea.

FIGURE 4-24   Sample Gantt chart showing summary tasks and milestones

PROJECT COST MANAGEMENT PLANNING TASKS

Project cost management includes the processes required to ensure that a project team completes a project within an approved budget. The main planning tasks performed as part of project cost management are cost estimating and cost budgeting. Cost estimating involves developing an approximation or estimate of the costs of the resources needed to complete a project. Cost budgeting involves allocating the overall cost estimate to individual tasks over time to establish a baseline for measuring performance. The main documents produced include a cost estimate and a cost baseline.

Cost Estimating

Project teams normally prepare cost estimates at various stages of a project, and these estimates should be fine-tuned as time progresses. Before management approves a project, someone must develop a rough estimate of what it will cost to complete the project. After the project manager and team are assigned to a project, they normally prepare a more detailed cost estimate. If this estimate is substantially different from the initial budgeted amount, the project manager should negotiate with the project sponsor to increase or decrease the budget, or to make changes to the scope or time goals to meet cost constraints. As more detailed information becomes available, the project team should update the cost estimates and continue negotiating with the sponsor to meet project goals.

In addition to creating cost estimates, it is also important to provide supporting details for the estimates. The supporting details include the ground rules and assumptions used in creating the estimate, the description of the project (including references to the scope statement, WBS, and so on) that was used as a basis for the estimate, and details on the cost estimation tools and techniques used to create the estimate. These supporting details should make it easier to prepare an updated estimate or similar estimate as needed.

A large percentage of total project costs are often labor costs. Many organizations estimate the number of people or hours they need for major parts of a project over the life cycle of the project. They also determine the labor rate to apply based on the category of labor. It is important to work with people in the organization's finance and accounting departments to determine these labor rates and apply the appropriate amounts for benefits and overhead so that total labor costs are included in the estimate.

Cost Estimation Tools and Techniques

As you can imagine, developing a good cost estimate is difficult. Fortunately, several tools and techniques are available to assist in creating them. Three commonly used techniques for creating estimates include the following:

1. **Analogous estimates**, also called **top-down estimates**, use the actual cost of a previous, similar project as the basis for estimating the cost of the current project. This technique requires a good deal of expert judgment and is generally less costly than others are, but it can also be less accurate. Analogous estimates are most reliable when the previous projects are similar in fact, not just in appearance.

2. **Bottom-up estimates** involve estimating individual activities and summing them to get a project total. The size of the individual activities and the experience of the estimators drive the accuracy of the estimates. If a detailed WBS is available for a project, the project manager could have each person responsible for a work package develop his own cost estimate for that particular work package. The project manager would then add all of the cost estimates to create cost estimates for each higher-level WBS item and finally for the entire project. This approach can increase the accuracy of the cost estimate, but it can also be time intensive and, therefore, expensive to develop.

3. **Parametric modeling** uses project characteristics (parameters) in a mathematical model to estimate project costs. A parametric model might provide an estimate of $5 per square foot for flooring, for example, based on the type of flooring, total square feet required, and location of the job. Parametric models are most reliable when the historical information used to create the model is accurate, the parameters are readily quantifiable, and the model is flexible in terms of the size of the project.

Sometimes it makes sense to use more than one approach for creating a cost estimate, and sometimes more than one approach is used on different parts of a project. For example, a project team might develop an analogous estimate and a parametric model for an entire project or a key part of the project, such as software development, and compare the results. If the estimates were far apart, the team would need to collect more information to develop a better estimate.

Sample Cost Estimate

Every cost estimate is unique, just as every project is unique. This section includes a step-by-step approach for developing the major parts of the cost estimate for the Just-In-Time Training project. Of course, this example is much shorter and simpler than a real cost estimate would be, but it illustrates an easy-to-follow process and uses several of the tools and techniques described earlier.

It is important to first clarify and document the ground rules and assumptions for the estimate. For the Just-In-Time Training project cost estimate, these include the following:

- This project was preceded by a project that provided valuable information, such as the training taken in the last two years by all internal employees, the cost of all training, the process for approving/assigning training, the evaluation of the training by participants, what training employees would need in the next two years, how they would like to take the training (that is, instructor-led in-house; instructor-led through a local college, university, or training company; online; and so on).

- There is a WBS for the project, as described earlier. The level 2 and some of the level 3 categories are shown as follows:

1. Initiating
2. Planning
3. Executing
   3.1 Course design and development
   3.2 Course administration

      3.3 Course evaluation

      3.4 Stakeholder communications

4. Monitoring and controlling

5. Closing

- Costs must be estimated by WBS and by month. The project manager will report progress on the project using earned value analysis, which requires this type of estimate.
- Costs will be provided in U.S. dollars. Because the project length is one year, inflation will not be included.
- There will be a project manager who spends three-quarters of her time on the project, and three core team members assigned to the project half-time. Two of the team members will be from the training department and one will be from the supplier management department. Additional internal resources from various departments will support the project as needed and charge their time to the project.
- The project steering committee members' time is not directly charged to the project. Internal labor costs include a 40 percent overhead charge as well as a 30 percent benefits charge. For example, if the direct labor rate is $30/hour, the burdened rate, or the rate including benefits and overhead, is $30*1.3* 1.4=$55 (rounded to the nearest whole-dollar amount).
- The project cost estimate does not include any hardware, software, or facilities that will be used to develop and administer the courses.
- The project team should purchase training materials and related products and services from qualified suppliers to take advantage of their expertise and to reduce internal costs. Estimates are based on analogous projects and will be updated as contracts are awarded.
- Labor costs for employees to cover their salaries while they attend training classes are not included in this estimate.
- Because several risks are related to this project, the estimate includes 10 percent of the total estimate as reserves.
- A computer model of the project estimate will be developed to facilitate the changing of inputs, such as labor rates or the number of labor hours for various activities.

Fortunately, the project team can easily access cost estimates and actual information from similar projects. A great deal of information is available from the Phase I project, and the team can talk to supplier personnel from the past project to help them develop the estimate.

Because the estimate must be provided by WBS monthly, Kristin and her team reviewed the draft of the project schedule and made further assumptions. They decided first to estimate the cost of each WBS task and then determine when the work would be performed, even though costs might be incurred at times other than when the work was actually performed. Their budget expert had approved this approach for the estimate. Further assumptions and information for estimating the costs for each WBS category are as follows:

1. *Initiating*: The team used the actual labor costs charged to the project for project initiation activities.
2. *Planning*: The team used actual labor costs to date and added the projected hours and costs per hour to develop this part of the estimate.
3. *Executing*:
   3.1 *Course design and development:* The team used labor hour and rate estimates for internal and external staff, plus estimates for purchasing existing course materials for each course (that is, supplier management, negotiating skills, project management, and software applications). Some of the purchased costs were based on the number of students using the materials each year. The majority of project costs should be applied to this category.
   3.2 *Course administration:* Estimates were made based on the number of courses and number of people expected to take each course using various delivery methods (that is, instructor-led, CD-ROM, Web-based).
   3.3 *Course evaluation:* The team estimated labor hours and rates.
   3.4 *Stakeholder communications:* The team estimated labor hours and rates.
4. *Monitoring and controlling:* The team estimated labor hours and rates.
5. *Closing:* The team estimated labor hours and rates.
6. *Reserves:* As directed, reserved costs were estimated at 10 percent of the total estimate.

The project team developed a cost model using the preceding information. Figure 4-25 shows a spreadsheet that summarizes the costs by WBS based on that information. There are columns for entering the number of labor hours and the costs per hour. Several tasks are estimated using this approach. There are also some short comments within the estimate, such as reserves being 10 percent of the total estimate. With this computerized model, you can easily change input variables, such as number of hours or cost per hour, to revise the estimate.

It is very important to have several people review the project cost estimate, including the ground rules and assumptions. It is also helpful to analyze the total dollar value as well as the percentage of the total amount for each major WBS category. For example, a senior executive could quickly look at the Just-In-Time Training project cost estimate and decide whether the costs are reasonable and whether the assumptions are well documented. In this case, Global Construction had budgeted $1 million for the project, so the estimate was right in line with that amount. The WBS level 2 and 3 tasks also seem to be at appropriate percentages of the total cost based on similar past projects. In some cases, a project team might also be asked to provide a range estimate for each task instead of one discrete amount.

After the total cost estimate is approved, Kristin's team can then allocate costs for each month based on the project schedule and when costs will be incurred. Many organizations also require that the estimated costs be allocated into certain budget categories, such as compensation or travel.

WBS Categories	Internal Labor	$/hour	Internal $ Total	External Labor	$/hour	External $ Total	Total Labor	Non-labor $	Total Cost
1. Initiating	200	$ 65	$ 13,000			$ -	$ 13,000		$ 13,000
2. Planning	600	$ 60	$ 36,000			$ -	$ 36,000		$ 36,000
3. Executing			$ -			$ -	$ -		$ -
3.1 Course design and development			$ -			$ -	$ -		$ -
3.1.1 Supplier management training	600	$ 60	$ 36,000	600	$ 150	$90,000	$ 126,000	$ 100,000	$ 226,000
3.1.2 Negotiating skills training	300	$ 55	$ 16,500	300	$ 150	$45,000	$ 61,500	$ 50,000	$ 111,500
3.1.3 Project management training	400	$ 60	$ 24,000	400	$ 150	$60,000	$ 84,000	$ 50,000	$ 134,000
3.1.4 Software applications training	400	$ 60	$ 24,000	400	$ 150	$60,000	$ 84,000	$ 50,000	$ 134,000
3.2 Course administration	400	$ 55	$ 22,000	300	$ 250	$75,000	$ 97,000	$ 80,000	$ 177,000
3.3.Course evaluation	300	$ 55	$ 16,500			$ -	$ 16,500		$ 16,500
3.4 Stakeholder communications	300	$ 55	$ 16,500			$ -	$ 16,500		$ 16,500
4. Monitoring and Controlling	500	$ 55	$ 27,500			$ -	$ 27,500		$ 27,500
5. Closing	200	$ 55	$ 11,000			$ -	$ 11,000		$ 11,000
Subtotal									$ 903,000
Reserves			$ -			$ -	$ -		90,300.0
Total	4,200		243,000	2,000		330,000	573,000	330,000	$ 993,300

Assumptions

Internal labor rates include benefits and overhead. Average hourly rates are based on skill levels and departments of stakeholders.
External labor rates are based on historical averages; may change as contracts are awarded.
Non-labor costs include purchasing licenses for using training materials, books, CD/ROMs, travel expenses, etc.
Non-labor costs may change as contracts are awarded.
Reserves are calculated by taking 10% of the total estimate.

FIGURE 4-25 Sample cost estimate

Cost Budgeting

Project cost budgeting involves allocating the project cost estimate to tasks over time. These tasks are based on the work breakdown structure for the project. The WBS, therefore, is a required input to the cost budgeting process. Likewise, the project scope statement, WBS dictionary, activity cost estimates and supporting detail, project schedule, and other plans provide useful information for cost budgeting.

The main goal of the cost budgeting process is to produce a cost baseline. A **cost baseline** is a time-phased budget that project managers use to measure and monitor cost performance. Estimating costs for each major project activity over time provides project managers and top management with a foundation for project cost control using earned value management, as described in Chapter 7. See the *Guide to Using Microsoft Project 2007* in Appendix A for information on using Project 2007 for cost control.

Sample Cost Baseline

The Just-In-Time Training project team used the cost estimate from Figure 4-25 along with the project schedule and other information to allocate costs for each month. Figure 4-26 provides an example of a cost baseline for this project. Again, it is important for the team to document the assumptions they made when developing the cost baseline and have several experts review it. The cost baseline should also be updated as more information becomes available.

WBS Categories	Month												Total Cost
	1	2	3	4	5	6	7	8	9	10	11	12	
1. Initiating	13,000												$ 13,000
2. Planning	6,000	16,000	8,000	1,000	1,000	1,000	1,000	1,000	1,000				$ 36,000
3. Executing			-			-	-						$ -
3.1 Course design and development			-			-	-						$ -
3.1.1 Supplier management training			5,000	73,667	73,667	73,667							$226,000
3.1.2 Negotiating skills training			5,000	35,500	35,500	35,500							$111,500
3.1.3 Project management training			5,000	43,000	43,000	43,000							$134,000
3.1.4 Software applications training			5,000	43,000	43,000	43,000							$134,000
3.2 Course administration						17,000	53,333	53,333	53,333				$177,000
3.3.Course evaluation							3,000	3,000	3,000	7,500			$ 16,500
3.4 Stakeholder communications		1,500	1,500	1,500	1,500	1,500	1,500	1,500	1,500	1,500	1,500	1,500	$ 16,500
4. Monitoring and Controlling	1,000	2,000	2,000	2,000	3,000	3,500	3,000	3,000	2,000	3,000	2,000	1,000	$ 27,500
5. Closing											8,000	3,000	$ 11,000
Subtotal													$903,000
Reserves*			-			-	-					90,300	$ 90,300
Total	20,000	19,500	31,500	199,667	200,667	218,167	61,833	61,833	60,833	12,000	11,500	95,800	993,300

*Reserves are all entered in month 12

FIGURE 4-26 Sample cost baseline

CASE WRAP-UP

Kristin learned a lot by leading her team during the planning phase of the Just-In-Time Training project. She did her best to get key stakeholders involved, including those who had little experience in planning. She could see that some people jumped to the planning details right away while others wanted to do as little planning as possible. She continued to consult members of the project steering committee for their advice, especially in helping everyone see how crucial it was to understand and document the scope, time, and cost of the project to provide a good baseline for measuring progress.

Chapter Summary

Successful project managers know how important it is to develop, refine, and follow plans to meet project goals. It is important to remember that the main purpose of project plans is to guide project execution. Planning is done in all nine project management knowledge areas. This chapter summarizes the planning tasks and outputs for integration, scope, time, and cost management.

Planning tasks for integration management include developing a team contract and a project management plan. Samples of these documents are provided for the Just-In-Time Training project.

Planning tasks for scope management include creating a scope management plan, a scope statement, a WBS, and a WBS dictionary. Samples of these documents are provided for the Just-In-Time Training project.

Planning tasks for time management include developing a project schedule by creating an activity list, a milestone list, network diagrams, activity resource requirements, and activity duration estimates. Samples of these documents are provided for the Just-In-Time Training project. It is also important to understand critical path analysis to make schedule trade-off decisions. Critical chain scheduling can also help in scheduling when there are scarce resources involved in a project.

Planning tasks for cost management include developing a project cost estimate and a cost baseline. Samples of these documents are provided for the Just-In-Time Training project.

Quick Quiz

1. What can project teams create to help promote teamwork and clarify team communications?
   a. a project Web site
   b. a team-building plan
   c. a team roster
   d. a team contract

2. The main purpose of project planning is to:
   a. obtain funding for the project
   b. guide project execution
   c. clarify roles and responsibilities
   d. keep senior managers informed

3. Project teams develop a _____ to coordinate all other project plans.
   a. strategic plan
   b. project management plan
   c. master plan
   d. project Web site

4. A _____ is a deliverable-oriented grouping of the work involved in a project that defines the total scope of the project.

   a. contract

   b. Gantt chart

   c. WBS

   d. network diagram

5. A _____ is a task at the lowest level of the WBS that represents the level of work that the project manager uses to monitor and control the project.

   a. WBS dictionary

   b. budget item

   c. line item

   d. work package

6. What is the first step in planning a project schedule?

   a. developing a budget

   b. developing an activity list

   c. assigning resources to the project

   d. determining activity sequencing

7. What is the most common type of dependency between activities?

   a. finish-to-start

   b. start-to-finish

   c. start-to-start

   d. finish-to-finish

8. The _____ method is a network diagramming technique used to predict total project duration.

   a. PERT

   b. Gantt chart

   c. critical path

   d. crashing

9. What cost estimating technique uses project characteristics in a mathematical model to estimate project costs?

   a. parametric modeling

   b. fast-track estimating

   c. analogous estimating

   d. critical chain

10. A _____ is a time-phased budget that project managers use to measure and monitor cost performance.

   a. cost baseline

   b. cost estimate

   c. life-cycle budget

   d. cash flow analysis

Quick Quiz Answers

1. D; 2. B; 3. B; 4. C; 5. D; 6. B; 7. A; 8. C; 9. A; 10. A

Discussion Questions

1. Why does having good plans help project teams during project execution? Why is it difficult to develop good plans?

2. What are the main planning tasks performed as part of project integration management? What are the main documents created, and what are some of their main contents?

3. What are the main planning tasks performed as part of project scope management? What are some approaches for creating a WBS? Why is it important to develop a good WBS? What do you think about the scope planning documents prepared by the Just-In-Time Training project team? Do they seem too broad or too detailed in certain areas?

4. What are the main planning tasks performed as part of project time management? What is the critical path for a project, and why is it important to know which tasks are on the critical path? When should you consider critical chain scheduling?

5. What are the main planning tasks performed as part of project cost management? What is the difference between a cost estimate and a cost baseline? Why is it important to have clear ground rules and assumptions for a cost estimate?

Exercises

1. Find an example of a large project that took more than a year to complete, such as a major construction project. You can ask people at your college, university, or work about a recent project, such as a major fund raising campaign, information systems installation, or building project. You can also find information about projects online such as the Big Dig in Boston (www.masspike.com/bigdig), the Patronas Twin Towers in Malaysia and many other building projects (www.greatbuildings.com), etc. Describe some of the tasks done in planning the integration, scope, time, and cost aspects of the project. Write a one-page paper or prepare a short presentation summarizing your findings.

2. Review the sample scope statement in Figure 4-5. Assume you are responsible for planning and then managing the course development for the introductory supplier management course. What additional information would you want to know to develop a good schedule and cost estimate, and why? Write a one-page paper or prepare a short presentation summarizing your response.

3. Create a WBS for building a new house by using the mind mapping approach. Assume that the WBS Level 2 categories include managing the project, finding property, securing a loan,

designing the entire home, building the entire home, and providing landscaping and external items, including a hot tub and swimming pool. Break at least two Level 2 items down to
Level 4. Try to use MindManager software from www.mindjet.com, if possible. You can also
create the mind map by hand or using similar mind-mapping software.

4. Consider Figure 4-27. All duration estimates are in days, and the network proceeds from
Node 1 to Node 9. (*Note*: Instructors should see the Instructor's Manual for similar exercises.)

Activity	Initial node	Final node	Duration estimate
A	1	2	2
B	2	3	2
C	2	4	3
D	2	5	4
E	3	6	2
F	4	6	3
G	5	7	6
H	6	8	2
I	6	7	5
J	7	8	1
K	8	9	2

FIGURE 4-27 Network diagram data for a small project

a. Draw an AOA network diagram representing the project. Put the node numbers in circles
   and draw arrows from node to node, labeling each arrow with the activity letter and estimated duration.

b. Identify all the paths on the network diagram and note how long they are, using
   Figure 4-18 as a guide for how to represent each path.

c. What is the critical path for this project, and how long is it?

d. What is the shortest possible time it will take to complete this project?

e. Enter the information into Project 2007. See the *Guide to Using Microsoft Project 2007*
   in Appendix A for detailed instructions on using this software. View the network diagram and task schedule table to see the critical path and float or slack for each activity.
   Print the Gantt chart and network diagram views and the task schedule table. Write a
   short paper that interprets this information for someone unfamiliar with project time
   management.

5. Create a cost estimate/model for redecorating a room using spreadsheet software. Assume
   you have one month and $5,000 to spend. Develop a WBS for the project and create a cost
   model based on your WBS. Document the assumptions you made in preparing the estimate and provide explanations for key numbers.

Team Projects

1. Your organization initiated a project to raise money for an important charity. Assume that there are 1,000 people in your organization. Also assume that you have six months to raise as much money as possible, with a goal of $100,000. Develop a scope statement, WBS, and Gantt chart for the project. Be creative in deciding how you will raise the money and the major work packages required to complete the project. Assume that the only costs are volunteer labor, so you do not need to prepare a cost estimate.

2. You are part of a team in charge of a project to help people in your company (500 people) lose weight. This project is part of a competition, and the top "losers" will be featured in a popular television show. Assume that you have six months to complete the project and a budget of $10,000. Develop a scope statement, WBS, Gantt chart, and cost estimate for the project.

3. Using the information you developed in Project 1 or 2, role-play a meeting to review one of these planning documents with key stakeholders. Determine who will play what role (project manager, team member from a certain department, senior managers, and so on). Be creative in displaying different personalities (a senior manager who questions the importance of the project to the organization, a team member who is very shy or obnoxious).

4. Perform the planning tasks through cost (tasks 1–5) for the New Business Venture case study provided in Appendix C or for one of the cases on the companion Web site. If you are working on a real team project, perform the applicable integration, scope, time, and cost planning tasks for that project. At a minimum, prepare a team contract, a project management plan, a scope statement, a WBS, a Gantt chart, and a cost estimate. Remember to be thorough in your planning so that your execution goes smoothly.

5. As a team, find at least six examples of Gantt charts for various types of projects. Discuss the similarities and differences between how the WBSs are structured, how durations and dependencies are entered, etc. Also discuss the quality of these examples. Document your results in a two- to three-page paper or a 15–20 minute presentation. Include screen shots of the files and citations for where and when you found them in an appendix.

Companion Web Site

Visit the companion Web site for this text (*www.course.com/mis/pm2/schwalbe* or *http://login.course.com*) to access:

- Lecture notes
- Interactive quizzes and Jeopardy games
- Template files
- Sample documents
- Podcasts
- More ideas for team projects, including real projects and case studies
- Links to additional resources related to project management

Key Terms

activity attributes — Information that provides schedule-related information about each activity, such as predecessors, successors, logical relationships, leads and lags, resource requirements, constraints, imposed dates, and assumptions related to the activity.

activity list — A tabulation of activities to be included on a project schedule.

activity-on-arrow (AOA) approach, or the **arrow diagramming method (ADM)** — A network diagramming technique in which activities are represented by arrows and connected at points called nodes to illustrate the sequence of activities.

analogous estimates, or **top-down estimates** — The estimates that use the actual cost of a previous, similar project as the basis for estimating the cost of the current project.

baseline — A starting point, a measurement, or an observation that is documented so that it can be used for future comparison; also defined as the original project plans plus approved changes.

bottom-up estimates — Cost estimates created by estimating individual activities and summing them to get a project total.

buffer — Additional time to complete a task, added to an estimate to account for various factors.

burst — An occurence when two or more activities follow a single node on a network diagram.

cost baseline — A time-phased budget that project managers use to measure and monitor cost performance.

crashing — A technique for making cost and schedule trade-offs to obtain the greatest amount of schedule compression for the least incremental cost.

critical chain scheduling — A method of scheduling that takes limited resources into account when creating a project schedule and includes buffers to protect the project completion date.

critical path — The series of activities that determine the *earliest* time by which the project can be completed; it is the *longest* path through the network diagram and has the least amount of slack or float.

critical path method (CPM), or **critical path analysis** — A network diagramming technique used to predict total project duration.

dependency, or **relationship** — The sequencing of project activities or tasks.

discretionary dependencies — The dependencies that are defined by the project team.

duration — The actual amount of time spent working on an activity *plus* elapsed time.

effort — The number of workdays or work hours required to complete a task.

external dependencies — The dependencies that involve relationships between project and non-project activities.

fast tracking — A schedule compression technique where you do activities in parallel that you would normally do in sequence.

feeding buffers — Additional time added before tasks on the critical path that are preceded by non-critical-path tasks.

Gantt charts — A standard format for displaying project schedule information by listing project activities and their corresponding start and finish dates in a calendar format.

mandatory dependencies — The dependencies that are inherent in the nature of the work being performed on a project.

merge — A situation when two or more nodes precede a single node on a network diagram.

milestone — A significant event on a project.

multitasking — When a resource works on more than one task at a time.

Murphy's Law — If something can go wrong, it will.

network diagram — A schematic display of the logical relationships among, or sequencing of, project activities.

node — The starting and ending point of an activity on an activity-on-arrow network diagram.

parametric modeling — A technique that uses project characteristics (parameters) in a mathematical model to estimate project costs.

Parkinson's Law — Work expands to fill the time allowed.

precedence diagramming method (PDM) — A network diagramming technique in which boxes represent activities.

Program Evaluation and Review Technique (PERT) — A network analysis technique used to estimate project duration when there is a high degree of uncertainty about the individual activity duration estimates.

project buffer — The additional time added before a project's due date to account for unexpected factors.

project management plan — A document, which is a deliverable for the project integration management knowledge area, used to coordinate all project planning documents and to help guide a project's execution and control.

scope baseline — The approved project scope statement and its associated WBS and WBS dictionary.

scope management plan — A document that includes descriptions of how the team will prepare the project scope statement, create the WBS, verify completion of the project deliverables, and control requests for changes to the project scope.

slack or **float** — The amount of time an activity may be delayed without delaying a succeeding activity or the project finish date.

team contract — A document created to help promote teamwork and clarify team communications.

Theory of Constraints (TOC) — A management philosophy that states that any complex system at any point in time often has only one aspect or constraint that is limiting its ability to achieve more of its goal.

three-point estimate — An estimate that includes an optimistic, most likely, and pessimistic estimate.

work breakdown structure (WBS) — A deliverable-oriented grouping of the work involved in a project that defines the total scope of the project.

work breakdown structure (WBS) dictionary — A document that describes detailed information about WBS tasks.

work package — A task at the lowest level of the WBS.

End Notes

[1] Ross Foti, "The Best Winter Olympics, Period," *PM Network* (January 2004) p. 23.

[2] Ibid, p. 23.

[3] Luc K. Richard, "Reducing Schedule Risk, Parts 1 and 2," (*www.Gantthead.com*) (November 10, 2003 and January 31, 2005).

[4] Kathleen Melymuke, "Spit and Polish," *ComputerWorld* (February 16, 1998).

[5] Claudia Wallis, "The Multitasking Generation," *Time Magazine* (March 19, 2006).

[6] Goldratt, Eliyahu, *Critical Chain*. Great Barrington, MA: The North River Press, 1997, p. 218.

CHAPTER 5

PLANNING PROJECTS, PART 2 (PROJECT QUALITY, HUMAN RESOURCE, COMMUNI-CATIONS, RISK, AND PROCUREMENT MANAGEMENT)

LEARNING OBJECTIVES

After reading this chapter, you will be able to:

- List several planning tasks and outputs for project quality, human resource, communications, risk, and procurement management

- Discuss the project quality management planning tasks, and explain the purpose and contents of a quality management plan, project dashboard, quality metrics, and quality checklists

- Explain the project human resource management planning tasks, and create a project organizational chart, responsibility assignment matrix, resource histogram, and staffing management plan

- Describe the project communications management planning tasks, and describe the importance of using a project communications management plan and project Web site

- Discuss the project risk management planning tasks, and explain how a risk management plan, a probability/impact matrix, a risk register, and risk-related contractual agreements are used in risk management planning

- Discuss the project procurement management planning tasks, and explain a make-or-buy analysis, procurement management plans, requests for proposal/quote, contract statements of work, and supplier evaluation matrices

OPENING CASE

Kristin and her team continued to plan various aspects of the Just-In-Time Training project. About half of her project's budget was allocated for external labor and outsourced training programs, but Kristin and her team were still unsure about what sources to use for most of the training. Kristin had worked with many construction suppliers before, but she had never had to select or negotiate contracts with educational consultants or training companies. She knew that developing and providing quality training courses was very important to this project; however, she also knew that successfully planning the human resource, communications, risk, and procurement management dimensions were also important—especially because the project involved so many different stakeholders. Because some of the plans in these areas might affect the initial scope, time, and cost plans, Kristin knew that she had to focus on project integration management to pull all these plans together and effectively lead the team in preparing and then executing these plans.

Fortunately, Global Construction had well-defined processes for planning all aspects of projects, and the project steering committee provided helpful advice, especially in the areas in which Kristin had little experience, such as risk and procurement management. She also relied heavily on her team members and other stakeholders to help create all the initial plans for the project. Because they knew that many of the plans would require updates, they built in flexibility as much as possible.

INTRODUCTION

Everyone knows that it is important to effectively plan the scope, time, and cost dimensions of a project and to develop the overall project management plan as part of integration management. However, some project managers neglect planning in the other knowledge areas—quality, human resource, communications, risk, and procurement management. It is important to skillfully plan *all* of these areas because they are all crucial to project success. This chapter summarizes key information on planning in these knowledge areas and specific actions that Kristin and her team took. The next chapter, which covers executing projects, shows how plans provide the basis for executing tasks.

SUMMARY OF PLANNING TASKS AND OUTPUTS

Figure 5-1 shows the project planning outputs for quality, human resource, communications, risk, and procurement management that Global Construction will use on the Just-In-Time Training project. As mentioned in Chapter 4, these planning documents, as well as other project-related information, will be available to all team members on a project Web site.

Knowledge area	Outputs
Project quality management	Quality management plan Project dashboard Quality metrics descriptions Quality checklist
Project human resource management	Project organizational chart Responsibility assignment matrix Resource histogram Staffing management plan
Project communications management	Communications management plan Project Web site
Project risk management	Risk management plan Probability/impact matrix Risk register Risk-related contractual agreements
Project procurement management	Make-or-buy analysis Procurement management plan Requests for proposal/quote Contract statement of work Supplier evaluation matrix

FIGURE 5-1 Planning outputs for project quality, human resource, communications, risk, and procurement management

The following sections describe planning tasks in the quality, human resource, communications, risk, and procurement management knowledge areas, and then provide examples of applying them to the Just-In-Time Training project at Global Construction. You can download templates for creating these planning documents and access the sample Web site and the documents provided in this chapter from the companion Web site for this text.

PROJECT QUALITY MANAGEMENT PLANNING TASKS

Project quality management ensures that the project will satisfy the stated or implied needs for which it was undertaken. Key outputs produced as part of project quality management include a quality management plan, quality metrics, and quality checklists. Before describing these outputs, it is important to understand what quality is and why it is an important part of project management.

The International Organization for Standardization (ISO) defines **quality** as "the degree to which a set of inherent characteristics fulfill requirements" (ISO9000:2000). Other experts define quality based on conformance to requirements and fitness for use. **Conformance to requirements** means that the project's processes and products meet written specifications. For example, Kristin's project team might write specifications stating that a course must cover certain topics and be written in English, Chinese, and Japanese. As part of quality management, Kristin's team would verify that the training vendors meet those written requirements. **Fitness for use**, on the other hand, means that a product can be used as it was intended. For example, a training vendor might develop a course in English and then translate it into Chinese and Japanese, but the translations might be faulty, causing confusion to learners. These translated courses, then, would not be fit for use, even though they might have met the written specifications.

Recall that project management involves meeting or exceeding stakeholder needs and expectations. To understand what quality means to the stakeholders, the project team must develop good relationships with them—especially the main customer for the project. *After all, the customer ultimately decides that the quality level is acceptable.* Many projects fail because the project team focuses only on meeting the written requirements for the main products being produced and ignores other stakeholder needs and expectations for the project.

Quality, therefore, must be considered on an equal level of importance with project scope, time, and cost. If a project's stakeholders are not satisfied with the quality of the project management or the resulting products or services, the project team will need to adjust scope, time, and cost to satisfy stakeholder needs and expectations. Meeting only written requirements for scope, time, and cost is not sufficient.

Quality Planning and the Quality Management Plan

Quality planning includes identifying which quality standards are relevant to the project and how best to satisfy those standards. It also involves designing quality into the products and services of the project as well as the processes involved in managing the project. It is important to describe important factors that directly contribute to meeting customer requirements. Organizational policies related to quality, the scope statement, product descriptions, and related standards and regulations are all important inputs to the quality planning process.

The quality management plan describes how the project management team will implement quality policies. Like other project plans, its format and contents vary based on the particular project and organizational needs. It can be a long, formal document or short and informal.

Sample Quality Management Plan

Kristin and her team worked together to create a quality management plan for the Just-In-Time Training project (see Figure 5-2). The primary purpose of the plan was to ensure that all the products and services produced as part of the project are of known quality and sufficient quantity to meet customer expectations.

Quality Management Plan
August 20, 2009

Project Name: Just-In-Time Training Project

Introduction

The main goal of this project is to develop a new training program that provides just-in-time training to employees on key topics, including supplier management, negotiating skills, project management, and software applications.

Quality Standards

The standards that apply to this project are summarized as follows:

1. Survey standards: See Attachment 1 for corporate standards for developing and administering surveys to employees. Quantitative and qualitative information will be collected. Quantitative data will use a 5-point Likert scale as much as possible. A corporate expert on surveys will review the survey before it is administered.

2. Supplier selection standards: See Attachment 2 for corporate standards regarding supplier selection. Past performance and developing partnerships will be key issues for this project.

3. Training standards: See Attachment 3 for corporate standards regarding training. The training provided as part of this project will be available in several formats, including instructor-led, CD-ROM, and Web-based. Employees will have access to CD-ROM and Web-based training at any time to meet individual and business needs on a just-in-time manner.

Etc.

Metrics

Metrics measure quality performance. Several metrics apply to this project, and more may be developed as the project progresses. The project team will use a few key metrics, as follows:

1. Survey response rate: For the survey to be successful, a response rate of at least 25 percent must be achieved.

2. Course evaluations: All course participants must complete a course evaluation. In addition to evaluations on more detailed topics, there will be an overall course rating. The average course rating should be 3.0 or better on a 5.0 scale.

Etc.

Problem Reporting and Corrective Action Processes

Project plans will include clear roles and responsibilities for all stakeholders. The person responsible for an individual task should report problems to appropriate managers (see the project organizational chart) and work with them to determine and implement corrective actions. Major problems should be brought to the attention of the project manager, who should elevate problems that might affect project success—including meeting scope, time, cost, and quality goals—to the project steering committee and then the project sponsor. It is crucial to address problems as early as possible and develop several alternative solutions.

Supplier Quality and Control

The project manager will closely monitor work performed by suppliers, with assistance from our supplier management department. The contract must clearly state quality standards, metrics, etc.

Etc.

FIGURE 5-2 Sample quality management plan

Quality Metrics

A **metric** is a standard of measurement. Metrics allow organizations to measure their performance in certain areas and to compare them over time or with other organizations. Examples of common metrics used by organizations include failure rates of products produced, availability of goods and services, and customer satisfaction ratings.

Individual projects also have metrics. Before deciding on the metrics to use for a particular project, it is important to clarify the project goals, business case for the project, and success criteria. Knowing this information, you can then decide what data will give you the information you need, and how to collect it.

For example, the Just-In-Time Training project's success criteria, as documented in the scope statement, included metrics based on:

- *Time*: Completing the project within one year
- *Customer satisfaction*: Achieving an average course evaluation of at least 3.0 on a 5.0 scale
- *Cost reduction*: Recouping the cost of the project in reduced training costs within two years after project completion

Global Construction's senior management, therefore, should collect and analyze data to ensure these metrics, as well as other metrics related to the project, are being met, such as how well they are meeting general scope, time, and cost goals. Many organizations use charts to keep track of metrics, such as a **project dashboard**—a graphical screen summarizing key project metrics.

 BEST PRACTICE

Dragan Milosevic, author of the Project Management Toolbox, has done several studies to investigate what companies that excel in project delivery capability do differently from others. After analyzing data from hundreds of companies, he found four key practices these best-performing companies follow:

1. They build an integrated project management toolbox. In other words, they use several standard and advanced project management tools. They tailor these tools to their organizations and provide employees with lots of templates.

2. They grow competent project leaders, emphasizing business and soft skills. These organizations identify good project leaders and provide training, mentoring, and a career path for them.

3. They develop streamlined, consistent project delivery processes. Project management methodologies are well defined and followed.

4. And probably the hardest of all, they install a sound but comprehensive set of project performance metrics. It is difficult defining, measuring, and tracking metrics across an organization, but in order to improve project delivery capability, these metrics are crucial.[1]

Sample Project Dashboard and Quality Metrics Description

Figure 5-3 provides a sample project dashboard that could be used on the Just-In-Time Training Project. Most dashboards use red, yellow, and green to indicate the status of each metric, where green indicates the metric is on target, yellow means it is slightly off target/caution, and red indicates the metric is off target/problem area. (This example uses different shades of purple.) It also describes how the metric is measured and explains the reason for the status rating. You will learn more about earned value charts, a tool for measuring overall scope, time, and cost goals, in Chapter 7.

Just–In–Time Training Project Dashboard
January 20, 2010

Metric Name	Description	Status	How measured	Explanation
Scope	Meeting project scope goals	◑	Earned value chart	On target
Time	Completing the project within one year	◑	Earned value chart	On target
Cost	Staying within budget – under $1 million	○	Earned value chart	A little over budget
Survey response	Must be at least 25%	○	Surveys received/sent	Got 33% response
Customer satisfaction	Average course rating of at least 3.0/5.0	○	Course evaluations	Goal part of success criteria
	–Number of course evaluations received	38	Feed from online system	All course participants must complete
	–Average course rating	2.7	Feed from online system	CD/ROM course had low ratings
Cost reduction	Recoup investment within two years	N/A	Cost/employee for training	Can't measure until project is completed
Courses developed	Meeting milestones for development	◑	Milestone dates	Course development on target
Number of people trained	Meeting goals of people trained	○	Filling scheduled classes	Last minute cancellations

◑ = on target
○ = slightly off target/caution
● = off target/problem area

FIGURE 5-3 Sample Project Dashboard

As mentioned in the sample quality management plan, two important metrics related to the Just-In-Time Training project include the survey response rate and course evaluation ratings. Figure 5-4 provides more information on these metrics.

Quality Checklists

A **checklist** is a list of items to be noted or consulted. Checklists help project teams verify that a set of required topics or steps has been covered or performed. A single project can have many different checklists. For example, there can be checklists related to interviewing project team members, selecting suppliers, reviewing important documents, ensuring a room is ready for training, and so on.

```
Quality Metrics Description
August 20, 2009

Project Name: Just-In-Time Training Project
The following quality metrics apply to this project:
1. Survey response rate: In order for the survey to be successful, a response rate of
   at least 25 percent must be achieved. Most surveys will be administered online
   using the standard corporate survey software, which can track the response
   rate automatically. If the response rate is less than 25 percent one week after
   the survey is sent out, the project manager will alert the project steering
   committee to determine corrective action.
2. Course evaluations: All course participants must complete a course evaluation
   so that their training can be tracked in our corporate professional development
   system. In addition to evaluations on more detailed topics, there will be an
   overall course rating. The average course rating should be at least 3.0, with 5.0
   being the highest score. Surveys should include questions measured on a
   Likert scale. For example, a question might be as follows: "My overall
   evaluation of this course is _____." Respondents would select 1 for Poor,
   2 for Fair, 3 for Average, 4 for Good, or 5 for Excellent.
Etc.
```

FIGURE 5-4   Sample quality metrics description

Sample Quality Checklist

Kristin and her team developed several checklists for their project and used others that were already available on the corporate intranet. Figure 5-5 is a sample checklist that the company uses for ensuring that training rooms are in proper order.

```
Quality Checklist
August 20, 2009

Project Name: Just-In-Time Training Project
Checklist Purpose: Ensure the training classroom is in proper order.
   ☐   Tables and chairs are arranged in a U-shape and properly aligned.
   ☐   Room has been cleaned and is free of trash.
   ☐   Whiteboards are clean.
   ☐   Projection system is in working order.
   ☐   Overhead, flip chart, or other ordered equipment is available.
   ☐   Supplies are readily available (i.e., markers, sticky notes, name plates)
   ☐   Food and beverages have been ordered.
```

FIGURE 5-5   Sample quality checklist

PROJECT HUMAN RESOURCE MANAGEMENT PLANNING TASKS

Many corporate executives have said, "People are our most important asset." People determine the success and failure of organizations and projects. Project human resource management is concerned with making effective use of the people involved with a project. Key outputs produced as part of project human resource management planning include developing a project organizational chart, a responsibility assignment matrix, a resource histogram, and a staffing management plan. Chapter 6, which covers project execution, includes much more information on project human resource management, as Kristin encounters some problems related to this topic. Planning human resources effectively will help her face these challenges.

Project Organizational Charts

After identifying the important skills and types of people needed to staff a project, the project manager should work with top management and project team members to create an organizational chart for the project. Similar to a company's organizational chart, a **project organizational chart** is a graphic representation of how authority and responsibility is distributed within the project. The size and complexity of the project determines how simple or complex the organizational chart is.

Sample Project Organizational Chart

Figure 5-6 shows a project organizational chart that Kristin put together. After supplier project managers and other personnel were assigned, Kristin would fill in more of the chart. Notice that Kristin has a direct reporting line to the project sponsor, and the project team leaders and supplier project managers would report to her. Also note that the project steering committee and project sponsor have a strong role on the project. Sometimes, dotted lines are used to represent indirect reporting relationships.

Responsibility Assignment Matrices

A **responsibility assignment matrix (RAM)** is a matrix that maps the work of the project as described in the work breakdown structure (WBS) to the people responsible for performing the work. A RAM allocates work to responsible and performing organizations, teams, or individuals, depending on the desired level of detail. For smaller projects, it is best to assign WBS activities to individuals. For larger projects, it is more effective to assign the work to organizational units or teams. In addition to using a RAM to assign detailed work activities, you can use a RAM to define general roles and responsibilities on projects. This type of RAM can include the stakeholders in the project. The project team should decide what to use as categories in the RAM and include a key to explain those categories. For example, a RAM can show whether stakeholders are accountable for (A) or just participants (P) in part of a project, and whether they are required to provide input (I), review (R), or sign off (S) on parts of a project. This simple tool enables the project manager to efficiently communicate the roles of project team members and expectations of important project stakeholders.

FIGURE 5-6 Sample project organizational chart

Sample Responsibility Assignment Matrix

Some organizations, including Global Construction, use **RACI charts**—a type of responsibility assignment matrix that shows **R**esponsibility (who does the task), **A**ccountability (who signs off on the task or has authority for it), **C**onsultation (who has information necessary to complete the task), and **I**nformed (who needs to be notified of task status/results) roles for project stakeholders. Figure 5-7 shows a RACI chart that Kristin developed for the supplier management training part of the project. Jamie and Mohamed were early members of the project team, and Supplier A represents the supplier who would be selected to provide the supplier management training courses. Notice that the RACI chart lists tasks vertically and individuals or groups horizontally, and that each intersecting cell contains at least one of the letters R, A, C, or I. For the first task, needs assessment, Kristin is accountable for getting it done, Jamie is responsible for doing the work, Mohamed is providing information in a consultative role, and Supplier A will be informed about it. Each task may have multiple R, C, or I entries, but there can only be one A entry to clarify which particular individual or group has accountability for each task (only one A in a matrix row). One person can also have multiple roles for each task, such as being responsible and accountable. (Note that some people switch the meaning of the R and A. It is important to clarify people's roles on projects.)

Just-In-Time Training Project RACI Chart
August 20, 2009

Tasks	Kristin	Jamie	Mohamed	Supplier A
Needs assessment	A	R	C	I
Research of existing training	I	A, R	C	I
Partnerships	A, R	I	I	C
Course development	A	C	C	R
Pilot course	A	C	I	R
Course administration	I	A	R	I
Course evaluation	I	A	R	I
Stakeholder communications	A, R	R	C	C

R: Responsible
A: Accountable
C: Consulted
I: Informed

FIGURE 5-7 Sample RACI chart

Resource Histograms

A **resource histogram** is a column chart that shows the number of resources required for or assigned to a project over time. In planning project staffing needs, senior managers often create a resource histogram in which columns represent the number of people (or person hours, if preferred) needed in each skill category, such as managers, IT specialists, and HR specialists. By stacking the columns, you can see the total number of people needed each month. After resources are assigned to a project, you can view a resource histogram for each person to see how his or her time has been allocated. You can create resource histograms using spreadsheets or project management software. See Appendix A for information on using Project 2007 to view resource allocations.

Sample Resource Histogram

Kristin worked with other managers to estimate how many internal resources they would need for the Just-In-Time Training project over time. They decided that in addition to herself (the project manager, or PM), they would require people from human resources (HR), supplier management (SM), information technology (IT), the project management office (PMO), and the contracting department. After contracts were written, Kristin could request a similar resource histogram from each supplier to review overall staffing for the project. Figure 5-8 is the resulting resource histogram for internal resources, showing the total number of people, or head count, by month. For example, it shows the need for a project manager (PM) .75 time for all 12 months, 1 HR person (or several HR people part-time, adding up to 1 total person) for all 12 months, etc. If needed, Kristin could also develop a similar chart showing the estimated number of hours per month. She could also use resource histograms to see where people might be overallocated, as described in Chaper 7.

Type of Resource	Meaning	Month											
		1	2	3	4	5	6	7	8	9	10	11	12
PM	Project Manager	0.75	0.75	0.75	0.75	0.75	0.75	0.75	0.75	0.75	0.75	0.75	0.75
HR	Human Resources	1	1	1	1	1	1	1	1	1	1	1	1
SM	Supplier Management	0.5	0.5	0.5	0.5	0.5	0.5	0.5	0.5	0.5	0.5	0.5	0.5
IT	Information Technology	0.25	0.5	0.5	0.5	0.25	0.25	0.25	0.25	0.25	0.25	0.25	0.25
Contracting	Contracting	0	0	0.25	0.25	0.25	0.25	0.25	0.25	0.25	0.25	0.25	0.25
PMO	Project Management Office	0	0.5	0.5	0.5	0.5	0	0	0	0	0	0	0
Miscellaneous	Miscellaneous	0.25	0.25	0.25	0.25	0.25	0.5	0.5	0.5	0.5	0.25	0.25	0.25

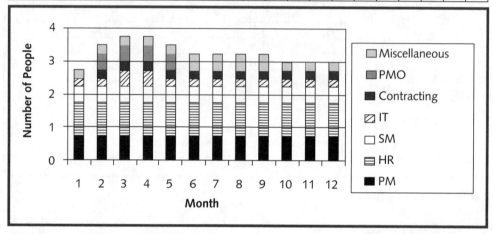

FIGURE 5-8   Sample resource histogram

Staffing Management Plans

A **staffing management plan** describes when and how people will be added to and removed from a project. The level of detail can vary based on the type of project. The staffing management plan describes the number of and types of people needed to work on the project. It also describes how these resources will be acquired, trained, rewarded, and reassigned after the project, and so on. All these issues are important to meeting the needs of the project, the employees, and the organization.

Sample Staffing Management Plan

Figure 5-9 provides part of a staffing management plan that Kristin created for the Just-In-Time Training project.

Staffing Management Plan
August 20, 2009

Project Name: Just-In-Time Training Project

Introduction

The main goal of this project is to develop a new HR program that provides just-in-time training to employees on key topics, including supplier management, negotiating skills, project management, and software applications.

Staffing Requirements

This project will require the following internal staff:

- Project manager (PM) (assigned 3/4 time)
- Project team members from the HR department (two people assigned half-time) to help with all project training
- Project team member from the supplier management (SM) department (assigned half-time) to assist with supplier management training
- Information technology (IT) department staff to help with technical support and software applications training
- Project management (PMO) staff to help with project management training
- Contracting department staff to assist in administering project contracts

See the resource histogram in Attachment A for projected staffing needs over time.

Staff Assignments

The project manager will work through functional managers to assign individuals to the project. The project manager will interview potential candidates to determine suitability. If particular expertise is required for part of the project, the functional managers will plan to make experts available. Employees will be paid overtime if needed.

Training, Rewards, and Reassignment

Ideally, people assigned to this project will have appropriate experience or be willing to learn quickly on the job. The project manager will do his or her best to provide a challenging and enjoyable work environment. Assignment to the project will not affect an individual's salary, but the project manager will write a performance evaluation and recommend appropriate rewards. If an individual is not performing as expected, the project manager will work with him or her and the appropriate functional manager to determine reassignment.

Attachment A: Resource histogram

FIGURE 5-9   Sample staffing management plan

PROJECT COMMUNICATIONS MANAGEMENT PLANNING TASKS

Many experts agree that the greatest threat to the success of any project is a failure to communicate. Many project managers say that 90% of their job is communicating. Yet many project managers fail to take the time to plan for project communications. Even though having a plan does not guarantee that all communications will flow smoothly, it certainly helps.

⊗ WHAT WENT WRONG?

An amusing example of miscommunication comes from a director of communications at a large firm:

I was asked to prepare a memo reviewing our company's training programs and materials. In the body of the memo in one of the sentences, I mentioned the *"pedagogical approach"* used by one of the training manuals. The day after I routed the memo to the executive committee, I was called into the HR director's office, and told that the executive vice president wanted me out of the building by lunch. When I asked why, I was told that she wouldn't stand for perverts (pedophiles?) working in her company. Finally, he showed me her copy of the memo, with her demand that I be fired—and the word *"pedagogical"*—circled in red. The HR manager was fairly reasonable, and once he looked the word up in his dictionary and made a copy of the definition to send back to her, he told me not to worry. He would take care of it. Two days later, a memo to the entire staff came out directing us that no words that could not be found in the local Sunday newspaper could be used in company memos. A month later, I resigned. In accordance with company policy, I created my resignation memo by pasting words together from the Sunday paper.[2]

Project communications management involves generating, collecting, disseminating, and storing project information. Key outputs produced for the Just-In-Time Training project include a communications management plan and a project Web site.

Communications Management Plans

Because project communication is so important, every project should include a **communications management plan**—a document that guides project communications. The communications management plan will vary with the needs of the project, but some type of written plan should always be prepared. The communications management plan should address the following items:

- Stakeholder communications requirements
- Information to be communicated, including format, content, and level of detail
- Identification of who will receive the information and who will produce it
- Suggested methods or guidelines for conveying the information
- Description of the frequency of communication
- Escalation procedures for resolving issues
- Revision procedures for updating the communications management plan
- A glossary of common terminology used on the project

Sample Communications Management Plan

Kristin and her team drafted a communications management plan (Figure 5-10) for the Just-In-Time Training project. The project steering committee reviewed it and provided suggestions on how to keep communication lines open. They advised Kristin to stress the importance of communications with *all* project stakeholders. They also mentioned the fact that people communicate in different ways and recommended that her team not be afraid of overcommunicating by providing the same information in multiple formats. The steering committee noted that it is not enough to provide formal documents; Kristin and her team should use face-to-face communications, e-mails, phone calls, and other communications media to ensure optimal communications. Recall that the WBS for this project included an item called stakeholder communications to ensure good project communications.

Communications Management Plan Version 1.0
August 28, 2009

Project Name: Just-In-Time Training Project
   1. Stakeholder communications requirements:
Because this project involves many people from all over the company as well as outside suppliers, the project team will use surveys, interviews, checklists, and other tools and techniques to determine the communications requirements for various stakeholders. Employees will have specific communications needs in that several training programs are being totally changed, and they will likely be uncomfortable with that change. Suppliers will have communications needs to ensure that they are developing courses that will meet our organization's needs. Internal experts providing content will have communications needs related to providing useful information, and so on.
   2. Communications summary:
The following table summarizes various stakeholders; communications required; the delivery method or format of the communications; who will produce the communications; and when they will be distributed, or the frequency of distribution. All communications produced will be archived and available on the project Web site. As more communications items are defined, they will be added to this list. The project team will use various templates and checklists to enhance communications. The team will also be careful to use the appropriate medium (that is, face-to-face meeting, phone, e-mail, hard copy, Web site, and so on) and follow corporate guidelines for effective communications.

Stakeholders	Communications Name	Delivery Method/Format	Producer	Due/Frequency
Project steering committee	Weekly status report	Hard copy and short meeting	Kristin Maur	Wednesdays at 9 a.m.
Sponsor and champion	Monthly status report	Hard copy and short meeting	Kristin Maur	First Thursday of month at 10 a.m.
Affected employees	Project announcement	Memo, e-mail, intranet site, and announcement at department meetings	Lucy Camarena and Mike Sundby	July 1, 2009
Project team	Weekly status report	Short meeting	All team members	Tuesdays at 2 p.m.

FIGURE 5-10 Sample communications management plan

Planning Projects, Part 2 (Project Quality, Human Resource, Communications, Risk, and Procurement Management)

   3. **Guidelines:**
   - Make sure people understand your communications. Use commonsense techniques to check comprehension, such as having them explain what you mean in their own words. Don't overuse/misuse e-mail or other technologies. Short meetings or phone calls can be very effective.
   - Use templates as much as possible for written project communications. The project Web site includes a link to all project-related templates.
   - Use the titles and dates of documents in e-mail headings, and have recipients acknowledge receipt.
   - Prepare and post meeting minutes within 24 hours of a meeting.
   - Use checklists for reviewing product requirements, conducting interviews, and so on.
   - Use corporate facilitators for important meetings, such as kick-off meetings and supplier negotiations.

   4. **Escalation procedures for resolving issues:**
   Issues should be resolved at the lowest level possible. When they cannot be resolved, affected parties should alert their immediate supervisors of the issues. If it is critical to the project or extremely time sensitive, the issue should be brought directly to the project manager. If the project manager cannot resolve an issue, he or she should bring it to the project steering committee or appropriate senior management, as required.

   5. **Revision procedures for this document:**
   Revisions to this plan will be approved by the project manager. The revision number and date will be clearly marked at the top of the document.

   6. **Glossary of common terminology:**

   actual cost—The total direct and indirect costs incurred in accomplishing work on an activity during a given period.

   baseline—The original project plan plus approved changes.

   bid—A document prepared by sellers providing pricing for standard items that have been clearly defined by the buyer.
   Etc.

FIGURE 5-10   Sample communications management plan (continued)

Project Web Sites

In the past few years, more and more project teams have started posting all or part of their project information to project Web sites. Project Web sites provide a centralized way of delivering project documents and other communications. Some project teams also create **blogs**—easy-to-use journals on the Web that allow users to write entries, create links, and upload pictures, while allowing readers to post comments to particular journal entries. Project teams can develop project Web sites using Web-authoring tools, such as Microsoft FrontPage or SharePoint Designer 2007 or Macromedia Dreamweaver; enterprise project management software, if available; or a combination of the two approaches. Part of the Web site might be open to outside users, whereas other parts might be accessible only by certain stakeholders. It is important to decide if and how to use a project Web site to help meet project communications requirements.

Sample Project Web Site

Kristin and her team entered detailed project information into the company's enterprise project management software. From within that system, Kristin could control who could and could not see various types of information. In addition, she worked with her team and the IT department to create a simple project Web site using a project Web site template of Microsoft FrontPage. This site would be available on the corporate intranet. Kristin's team felt it was important to let all employees access basic information about the project. Figure 5-11 shows the home page of the Web site for the Just-In-Time Training project. It includes summary information, such as project objectives, new information, and key milestones. It also includes links to information on team members, the project schedule, the project archive, a search feature, a discussions feature, and contact information.

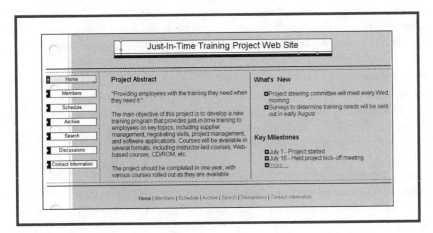

FIGURE 5-11   Sample project Web site

PROJECT RISK MANAGEMENT PLANNING TASKS

Although it is a frequently overlooked aspect of project management, good risk management can often result in significant improvements in the chance of a project succeeding. What is risk as it relates to a project? PMI defines a project **risk** as an uncertainty that can have a *negative or positive* effect on meeting project objectives. Key outputs of project risk management planning include a risk management plan, a probability/impact matrix, a risk register, and risk-related contractual agreements.

Risk Management Plans

A risk management plan documents the procedures for managing risk *throughout the life of a project*. Project teams should hold several planning meetings early in the project's life cycle to help develop the risk management plan. The project team should review project documents as well as corporate risk management policies, risk categories, lessons learned from past projects, and templates for creating a risk management plan. It is also important to review the risk tolerances of various stakeholders. For example, if the project sponsor is risk-averse, the project might require a different approach to risk management than if the project sponsor were a risk seeker.

A risk management plan summarizes how risk management will be performed on a particular project. Like other specific knowledge area plans, it becomes a subset of the project management plan. The general topics that a risk management plan should address include the methodology for risk management, roles and responsibilities, budget and schedule estimates for risk-related activities, risk categories, probability and impact matrices, and risk documentation. The level of detail included in the risk management plan will vary with the needs of the project.

In addition to a risk management plan, many projects also include contingency plans, fallback plans, and contingency reserves.

- **Contingency plans** are predefined actions that the project team will take if an identified risk event occurs. For example, if the project team knows that the new version of a product they need might not be available in time, they might have a contingency plan to use the existing, older version of the product.
- **Fallback plans** are developed for risks that have a high impact on meeting project objectives, and are put into effect if attempts to reduce the risk are not effective. For example, a new college graduate might have a main plan and several contingency plans on where to live after graduation, but if none of those plans work out, a fallback plan might be to live at home for a while. Sometimes the terms *contingency plan* and *fallback plan* are used interchangeably, and some people view fallback plans as contingency plans of last resort.
- **Contingency reserves** or **contingency allowances** are funds held by the project sponsor that can be used to mitigate cost or schedule overruns if unknown risks occur. For example, if a project appears to be off course because the staff is not experienced with a new technology and the team had not identified that as a risk, the project sponsor might provide additional funds from contingency reserves to hire an outside consultant to train and advise the project staff in using the new technology. All of these contingency plans, fallback plans, and contingency reserves show the importance of taking a proactive approach to managing project risks.

Figure 5-12 provides a humorous example of preparing for risks that might cause schedule delays by purchasing extra wide computer monitors to display the long schedules.

FIGURE 5-12 Special monitor to help manage schedule delays

Sample Risk Management Plan

Kristin knew that it was important to plan efficiently for the risk management of the Just-In-Time Training project. There were several negative and positive risks associated with this project. Kristin asked Ron Ryan, the project manager of the Phase I project, to assist her in drafting the first version of the risk management plan. She also received input from the project steering committee, and as her team and suppliers were identified, they would work together to update the plan as needed. Figure 5-13 shows the initial risk management plan.

Risk Management Plan
September 3, 2009

Project Name: Just-In-Time Training Project

1. Methodology

The project team will review data available from the Phase I project and past training programs within Global Construction to assist in risk management planning. They will also review information related to external projects similar to this one. The team will use several tools and techniques, including brainstorming, surveys, and risk-related checklists to assist in risk management.

2. Roles and Responsibilities

The project manager will be responsible for leading the team and other stakeholders in performing risk-related activities. As detailed tasks and deliverables are determined, the project manager will delegate those tasks as appropriate.

3. Budget and Schedule Estimates

As specific risk-related tasks and deliverables are determined, budget and schedule information will be provided.

4. Risk Categories

General categories and subcategories for risk on this project include business risks (suppliers and cash flow), technical risks (course content, hardware, software, and network), organizational risks (executive support, user/employee support, supplier support, and team support), and project management risks (estimates, communications, and resources).

5. Risk Communications and Impact

Risk probability and impact will initially be estimated as high, medium, or low based on expert advice. If more advanced scoring is needed, the project team will determine an appropriate approach.

6. Risk Documentation

All risk-related information will be summarized in a risk register. Detailed documentation will be available in a secure area on the project Web site.

FIGURE 5-13   Sample risk management plan

Probability/Impact Matrices

It is important to evaluate risks to determine which ones need the most attention. **Risk events** refer to specific, uncertain events that may occur to the detriment or enhancement of the project. For example, negative risk events might include the performance failure of a product produced as part of a project, delays in completing work as scheduled, increases in estimated costs, supply shortages, litigation against the company, and strikes. Examples of positive risk events include completing work sooner than planned or at an unexpectedly reduced cost, collaborating with suppliers to produce better products, and obtaining good publicity from the project.

There are two important dimensions of risk events: probability of the risk event occurring and the impact or consequence if the risk does occur. People often describe a risk event probability or impact as being high, medium, or low. For example, a meteorologist might predict that there is a high probability of severe rain showers on a certain day. If that happens to be your wedding day and you are planning a large outdoor wedding, the impact or consequences of severe showers would also be high.

A project manager can chart the probability and impact of risk events on a probability/impact matrix or chart. One side (axis) of a probability/impact matrix or chart lists the relative *probability* of a risk event occurring, and the other side (axis) of the chart shows the relative *impact* of the risk event occurring. To use this approach, project stakeholders identify and list the risk events related to their projects. They then label each risk event as being high, medium, or low in terms of its probability of occurrence and level of impact. The project manager then summarizes the results in a probability/impact matrix. Project teams should initially focus on risk events that fall in the high sections of the probability/impact matrix and develop strategies for minimizing negative risk events and maximizing positive ones.

Sample Probability/Impact Matrix

Kristin Maur worked with several project stakeholders early in the project to begin identifying several negative and positive risk events related to the Just-In-Time Training project. She held a brainstorming session in which over 100 risk events were identified. To differentiate between the two, she asked participants to identify negative risk events and then positive ones. After people identified a risk event and wrote it down on a sticky note, Kristin asked them to mark each one as having a high, medium, or low probability of occurrence and impact. Kristin had posted on the whiteboard large probability/impact matrices—one for negative risk events and another for positive risk events. Everyone put their sticky notes in the appropriate sections of the appropriate matrix. They then examined the results to combine and reword risk events to improve collaboration and avoid duplicates.

Figure 5-14 shows part of the resulting probability/impact matrix. For example, risks 1 and 4 are listed as high in both categories of probability and impact. Risk 6 is high in the probability category but low in the impact category. Risk 9 is high in the probability category and medium in the impact category. Risk 12 is low in the probability category but high in the impact category. The team then discussed in detail how they planned to respond to risks in the medium and high categories, Risks 1, 4, and 9, bolded in Figure 5-14, and documented the results in the risk register, as described in the following section.

Risk Registers

A **risk register** is a document that contains results of various risk management processes, often displayed in a table or spreadsheet format. It is a tool for documenting potential risk events and related information. The risk register often includes the following main headings:

- *An identification number for each risk event:* The project team might want to sort or quickly search for specific risk events, so they need to identify each risk with some type of unique descriptor, such as an identification number.
- *A rank for each risk event:* The rank can be indicated as high, medium, or low, or it can be a number, with 1 being the highest-ranked risk. The project team would have to determine these rankings.
- *The name of the risk event:* For example, defective product, poor survey results, reduced consulting costs, or good publicity.

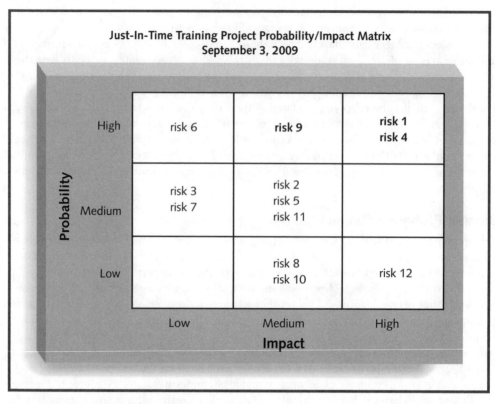

FIGURE 5-14   Sample probability/impact matrix

- A *description of the risk event:* Because the name of a risk event is often abbreviated, it helps to provide a detailed description in the risk register. For example, reduced consulting costs might be expanded in the description to say that the organization might be able to negotiate lower-than-average costs for a particular consultant because the consultant enjoys working for the company in that particular location.
- *The category under which the risk event falls:* For example, a defective product might fall under the broader category of technology.
- *The root cause of the risk event:* It is important to find the **root cause** of a problem—the real or underlying reason a problem occurs. By finding the root cause, you can deal with it directly rather than dealing with the symptoms of the problem. You can help identify the root cause of problems by creating a cause-and-effect or fishbone diagram (see Chapter 7), or continually asking why until you find a root cause. For example, the root cause of a defective product, like a defective computer, might be a defective hard drive. Instead of purchasing a brand-new computer or wasting time on other potential causes of the defect, knowing that you need to replace the hard drive provides valuable information that you can act on to fix the problem.

- *Triggers for each risk event:* **Triggers** are indicators or symptoms of actual risk events. For example, a clicking noise or increasing number of bad sectors would be triggers of a bad hard drive. Documenting potential risk triggers also helps the project team identify more potential risk events.
- *Potential responses to each risk event:* There can be one or more potential responses to each risk event.
- *The risk owner, or person who will own or take responsibility for the risk event:* One person should be responsible for monitoring each risk event.
- *The probability of the risk event occurring:* The chance of the risk event becoming a reality is rated as high, medium, or low.
- *The impact to the project if the risk event occurs:* The impact to project success if the risk event actually occurs can be rated as high, medium, or low.
- *The status of the risk event:* Did the risk event occur? Was the response strategy completed? Is the risk event no longer relevant to the project? For example, a clause may have been written into a contract to address the risk event of a defective product so that the supplier would have to replace the item at no additional cost.

Sample Risk Register

Kristin began developing a risk register after she and the other stakeholders had prepared the probability/impact matrix. Figure 5-15 shows the format of the risk register and one of the entries. Note that the risk event identification (ID) number is shown in the first column, followed by the rank of the risk event. The risk events are sorted by rank order. As information is added, deleted, or changed, the risk register will be updated on the project Web site.

Risk-Related Contractual Agreements

Many projects, including the Just-In-Time Training project, involve outside suppliers. Work done by outside suppliers or sellers should be well documented in **contracts**, which are mutually binding agreements that obligate the seller to provide the specified products or services, and obligate the buyer to pay for them. Project managers should include clauses in contracts to help manage project risks. For example, sellers can agree to be responsible for certain negative risks and incur the costs themselves if they occur. Or there can be incentive or penalty clauses in contracts based on seller performance to encourage positive risks and discourage negative risks. Project teams can also use certain types of contracts, such as fixed-price contracts, to reduce their risk of incurring higher costs than expected. Competition for supplying goods and services can also help reduce negative risks and enhance positive risks on projects.

**Risk Register
September 3, 2009**

Project Name: Just-In-Time Training Project

ID No.	Rank	Risk	Description	Category	Root Cause	Triggers	Potential Responses	Risk Owner	Probability	Impact	Status
R15	1										
R21	2										
R7	3										

To understand the risk register more fully, imagine that the following data is entered for the first risk in the register.

- ID No.: R15
- Rank: 1
- Risk: Poor survey response.
- Description: Many people dislike surveys and avoid filling them out, or if they do, they don't offer good or honest feedback.
- Category: Organizational/user support risk
- Root cause: People don't want to take the time and think their inputs aren't important.
- Triggers: Low survey response rate the first few days; incomplete surveys.
- Potential Responses: Make sure senior management emphasizes the importance of this project and the survey for designing good courses. Have the functional managers personally mention the survey to their people and stress its importance. Offer a reward to the department with the most responses. Ensure that the survey instructions say it will take 10 minutes or less to complete. Extend the deadline for survey responses.
- Risk owner: Mike Sundby, project champion
- Probability: Medium
- Impact: High
- Status: PM will set up a meeting within a week with a project steering committee to decide which response strategies to implement if the survey response is low.

FIGURE 5-15   Sample risk register

Sample Risk-Related Contractual Agreements

Kristin's team had not yet prepared any contractual documents for the Just-In-Time Training project, but they did have access to several other contracts that Global Construction had used in the past. Kristin had come from the supplier management area of the company, so she had personal experience working with suppliers and contracts. She also knew several people who could advise her on writing risk-related contractual agreements. Figure 5-16 provides a list of a few risk-related contractual agreements that Kristin's team would consider for this project. Kristin received these guidelines from the project team's representative from the contracting department. These agreements can take the form of contracts or clauses within contracts that can help prevent negative risk events and promote positive ones related to the project. Kristin also knew that the company's legal professionals would have to review all contracts because they were legally binding.

Guidelines for Risk-Related Contractual Agreements
January 10, 2009

The following guidelines are provided for your consideration as you develop contracts between Global Construction (the buyer) and its suppliers (the seller). Be sure to work with a member of the contracting department to write your specific contracts. All contracts must be reviewed and signed by the legal department, as well.

- Contract termination clauses: These clauses list circumstances under which the buyer and/or seller can terminate a contract and how final payment will be settled. All the contracts must include a termination clause.

- Incentive clauses: These clauses provide incentives for the seller to provide goods or services at certain times, of certain quality, and so on. Incentive clauses can include extra payments or profit sharing, if appropriate.

- Penalty clauses: These clauses specify penalties that will be applied when the seller does not provide goods or services as specified in the contract. For example, if a product is delivered late, the seller might be required to pay a certain dollar amount for each day the product is late.

- Fixed-price contracts: To minimize the negative risk of paying more than planned for specific goods or services, Global Construction should try to negotiate for fixed-priced contracts, which specify that the seller agrees to a fixed price and bears the risk if it costs more to provide the goods or services than originally assumed.

- Competitive contracts: In many situations, Global Construction can use competition to help reduce risks. In addition to reviewing bids from several sellers, a good strategy may be to award two small contracts and then award the following larger contract to the seller that performs the best on the first job.

FIGURE 5-16   Sample guidelines for risk-related contractual agreements

The example in the following What Went Right? passage shows another contractual approach for managing positive risk on a large project. By having suppliers visibly compete against each other, the buyers reduced their risks and benefited from competition.

The Petronis Twin Towers in Malaysia are famous landmarks in Kuala Lumpur. They were the tallest buildings constructed at the time, and the first large construction project to use GPS (Global Positioning System). Over 7000 people were working on the site during the peak of construction. The project management team decided to use competition to help keep the project on time and on budget. The Japanese firm Hazama Corporation led the construction of Tower 1, and the Korean firm Samsung Engineering Co. led the construction of Tower 2. Because the towers were constructed simultaneously, everyone could see the progress of the two competitors as the 88-story towers rose into the sky. "Construction of the towers was fast paced, thanks in part to the decision to grant two contracts, one for each tower, to two separate contractors. This naturally created a competitive environment, to the benefit of the building."[3]

As you can see, risk management planning addresses procurement-related topics, such as preparing risk-related contractual agreements. The following section addresses planning tasks directly related to project procurement management.

PROJECT PROCUREMENT MANAGEMENT PLANNING TASKS

Project procurement management includes acquiring or procuring goods and services for a project from outside the organization. As the business world continues to become more competitive and global, more and more projects include procurement. Many project managers realize the advantages of buying goods and services required for their projects, especially as sellers with better goods and services continue to become increasingly available. They also realize that they can find qualified sellers throughout the world. Remember that project managers strive to do what is best for the project and the organization, and that often means acquiring goods and services from the outside. Good procurement management often provides a win-win situation for both buyers and sellers.

Key outputs produced by project procurement management planning include make-or-buy analyses, procurement management plans, requests for proposal or quote, contract statements of work, and supplier evaluation matrices.

MEDIA SNAPSHOT

Information technology has made a tremendous impact on how organizations and individuals select sellers. A major use of the Internet is advertising. The Interactive Advertising Bureau (IAB) and PricewaterhouseCoopers reported that U.S. Internet advertising revenues reached a new record of $4.9 billion for the first quarter of 2007. "The continued growth of online ad revenues clearly illustrates marketers' increased comfort with

continued

the extraordinary vitality and accountability of this medium," said IAB President and CEO Randall Rothenberg. "It reaches consumers with an unprecedented level of efficiency andmeasurability that provides marketers with actionable data. And the ever-changing landscape of new platforms and technologies that enrich interactive advertising guarantees that this growth trend will continue."[4]

Many individuals have benefitted from ad revenues. For example, on September 28, 2007, The View television show included a story about Ashley Qualls, the 17-year-old founder of *www.whateverlife.com*, who has made over a million dollars in ad money by providing over 3,000 free MySpace designs. The site attracts more than 7 million individuals and 60 million page views a month, topping popular sites like AmericanIdol.com, Oprah.com, and CBS.com.

Make-or-Buy Analyses

With a make-or-buy decision, an organization decides if it would benefit more by making a product or performing a service itself, or by buying the product or service from a supplier. If there is no need to buy products or services from outside the organization, the organization can avoid the costs involved in managing procurement management processes. **Make-or-buy analysis** involves estimating the internal costs of providing a product or service, and comparing that estimate to the cost of outsourcing.

Many organizations also use a lease-or-buy analysis to decide if they should purchase or lease items for a particular project. For example, suppose you need a piece of equipment for a project that has a purchase price of $12,000. Assume it also has a daily operational cost of $400. Suppose you can lease the same piece of equipment for $800 per day, including the operational costs. You can set up an equation that shows the amount of time it will take for the purchase cost to equal the lease cost. In this way, you can determine when it makes sense financially to buy rather than lease the equipment. In the equation that follows, d = the number of days you need the piece of equipment.

$$\$12,000 + \$400d = \$800d$$

Subtracting $400d from both sides, you get:

$$\$12,000 = \$400d$$

Dividing both sides by $400, you get:

$$d = 30,$$

which means that the purchase cost equals the lease cost in 30 days. Therefore, if you need the equipment for less than 30 days, it would be more economical to lease it. If you need the equipment for more than 30 days, you should purchase it. Note that this simple example assumes there is no disposal value for the purchased item and does not include any tax considerations.

Figure 5-17 graphically shows the costs each day to lease or buy the equipment in the preceding example. Notice that the lines cross at Day 30, showing that the costs are the same to lease or buy the equipment that day. Before Day 30, the lease line is lower than the buy line, meaning it is less expensive to lease the item if it is needed for less than 30 days. After Day 30, the buy line is lower, meaning it is less expensive to buy the item after Day 30.

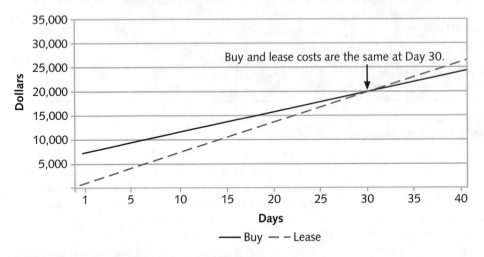

FIGURE 5-17   Comparing the cost of leasing versus buying

Sample Make-or-Buy Analysis

Kristin and her team needed to make several make-or-buy decisions for the Just-In-Time Training project. They knew that they wanted to outsource most of the development and delivery for much of the new training, but because internal expertise existed, it might make sense to do some of the work in-house.

For example, based on information collected in the Phase I project, it was suggested that Global Construction could probably identify internal people to conduct some of the face-to-face training or provide online advice for several courses. Internal resources would be much less expensive than external contractors. In particular, one of the requirements for the Just-In-Time Training project was to provide instructor-led basic project management training and facilitation for online materials. To train 100 employees, there would be five, two-day instructor-led classes with 20 participants in each class in the first year. There would also be 500 hours of online facilitation.

One specific suggestion was to have current employees conduct the basic project management training—the "make" option—instead of having an outside firm provide the training—the "buy" option. There were a couple of project management professionals (PMPs) in the training department with experience in teaching face-to-face and online courses. They had taken college courses in basic project management and knew of excellent books with online materials. They also knew of several companies that conducted their own in-house courses for basic project management training and then brought in an outside expert, often a qualified college professor, who would conduct advanced courses.

They found that college professors or other independent consultants provided high-quality training for much less than most training firms.

Figure 5-18 summarizes the make-or-buy analysis for the basic project management training. In this case, Kristin's team recommended doing the training in-house; for much of the other training, however, they did not have internal experts or training materials available.

Make-or-Buy Analysis
September 1, 2009

Project Name: Just-In-Time Training Project
Background: Global Construction wants to train 100 employees and will consider having the employees sent to an outside course (Buy option) or provide the education using internal employees (Make option). Assuming 20 participants/class and 2 days average course length, 10 total days of training will be needed. Assume 500 hours of online facilitation will be needed as well (5 hours per participant).
Decision Being Analyzed: Project management training
Option 1: (Make) Use in-house instructors for the instructor-led basic project management training and facilitation for online materials (includes purchasing course materials)
Estimated cost per hour for in-house trainer (excludes student time): $60
Estimated training hours: 80 (10 total days of training x 8 hours per day)
Subtotal: $4,800 (80 hours x $60 per hour)
Materials cost: $7,500 ($75/participant/course, 100 participants total)
Estimated cost per hour for online facilitation (excludes participant time): $60
Estimated hours: 500
Subtotal: $30,000 (500 hours $\times$ $60 per hour)
Materials cost: $7,500 ($75/participant/course, 100 participants)
    Total: $49,800 ($4,800 + $7,500 + $30,000 + $7,500)
Option 2: (Buy) Outsource instructor-led basic project management training and facilitation for online materials (includes purchasing course materials)
Estimated cost for class per participant = (Estimated Cost x Number of Days) = $500 $\times$ 2 days = $1,000
Cost of instructor-led classes ($1,000 $\times$ 100 participants)
Subtotal: $100,000
Estimated cost per hour for online facilitation (excludes student time): $100
Estimated hours: 500
Subtotal: $50,000 (500 hours $\times$ $100 per hour)
Total $150,000 ($100,000 + $50,000)
Cost Difference: $150,000 - $49,800 = $100,200
Recommendation: Because we have qualified internal staff and can purchase suitable materials, we recommend Option 1, in which we conduct the basic project management training in-house. Global Construction could save even more money by having employees take the courses after hours or on weekends. Employee time is not included in these estimates.

FIGURE 5-18   Sample make-or-buy analysis

Procurement Management Plans

A procurement management plan is a document that describes how the procurement processes will be managed, from developing documentation for making outside purchases or acquisitions to contract closure. Like other project plans, the contents of the procurement management plan varies with project needs. Topics that can be included in a procurement management plan are as follows:

- Guidelines on types of contracts to be used in different situations
- Standard procurement documents or templates to be used, if applicable
- Guidelines for creating contract work breakdown structures, statements of work, and other procurement documents
- Roles and responsibilities of the project team and related departments, such as the purchasing or legal department
- Guidelines on using independent estimates for evaluating sellers' cost proposals
- Suggestions on managing multiple providers
- Processes for coordinating procurement decisions, such as make-or-buy decisions, with other project areas
- Constraints and assumptions related to purchases and acquisitions
- Lead times for purchases and acquisitions
- Risk-mitigation strategies for purchases and acquisitions, such as insurance contracts and bonds
- Guidelines for identifying prequalified sellers and organizational lists of preferred sellers
- Procurement metrics to assist in evaluating sellers and managing contracts

Types of Contracts

Contract type is a key consideration in a procurement management plan. Different types of contracts can be used in different situations. Three broad categories of contracts are fixed price, or lump sum; cost reimbursable; and time and material. A single contract can actually include all three of these categories, if it makes sense for that particular procurement. For example, you could have a contract with a seller that includes purchasing specific products for a fixed price or lump sum, some services that are provided on a cost-reimbursable basis, and other services that are provided on a time-and-material basis. It is important to understand and decide which approaches to use to meet particular project needs.

- **Fixed-price** or **lump-sum contracts** involve a fixed total price for a well-defined product or service. The buyer incurs little risk or uncertainty in this situation because the price is predetermined. Sellers often pad their estimates somewhat to reduce their risk, while keeping in mind that their price must still be competitive. For example, using a two-week, fixed-price contract, Global Construction could hire a consultant to develop a survey to determine requirements for its new supplier management training courses under the Just-In-Time Training project. Fixed-price contracts generally have well-defined deliverables and deadlines, and may include incentives for meeting or exceeding selected project objectives. For example, the contract could include an incentive fee that would be paid for early delivery of the survey. A firm-fixed price (FFP) contract has the least amount of risk for the buyer, followed by a fixed-price incentive (FPI) contract.

- **Cost-reimbursable contracts** involve payment to the seller for direct and indirect actual costs. For example, the salaries for people working directly on a project and materials purchased for a specific project are direct costs, whereas the cost of providing a work space for those workers, office furniture, electricity, a cafeteria, and so on, are indirect costs. Indirect costs are often calculated as a percentage of direct costs. Cost-reimbursable contracts often include fees such as a profit percentage, and they can also include incentives for meeting or exceeding selected project objectives. For example, many contracts to build homes are cost-reimbursable contracts. The buyer might expect the home to cost a certain amount, but the total cost could vary if any of the costs of individual goods or services increase or decrease. The buyer reimburses the contractor for costs incurred, and pays a fee or profit percentage as well. Buyers absorb more of the risk with cost-reimbursable contracts than they do with fixed-price contracts. For example, if the cost of wood doubles, the buyer would have to absorb the additional cost.

- **Time-and-material contracts** are a hybrid of both fixed-price and cost-reimbursable contracts. For example, an independent consultant might have a contract with a company based on a fee of $100 per hour for his or her services plus a fixed price of $10,000 for providing specific materials for the project. The materials fee might also be based on approved receipts for purchasing items, with a ceiling of $10,000. The consultant would send an invoice to the company each week or month, listing the materials fee, the number of hours worked, and a description of the work produced. This type of contract is often used for services that are needed when the work cannot be clearly specified and total costs cannot be estimated in a contract. Many consultants prefer time-and-material contracts.

Unit pricing can also be used in various types of contracts to require the buyer to pay the supplier a predetermined amount per unit of service. The total value of the contract is a function of the quantities needed to complete the work. For example, many companies use unit price contracts for purchasing computer hardware. If the company purchases only one unit, the cost is $1,000. If it purchases 10 units, the cost is $10,000 if there were no volume discounts involved, but this type of pricing often does involve volume discounts. For example, if the company purchases between 5 and 50 units, the contracted cost is $900 per unit. If it purchases over 50 units, the cost reduces to $800 per unit. This flexible pricing strategy is often advantageous to both the buyer and the seller.

Sample Procurement Management Plan

Figure 5-19 displays a section of a procurement management plan for the Just-In-Time Training project.

```
┌─────────────────────────────────────────────────────────────────────┐
│                    Procurement Management Plan                        │
│                       September 17, 2009                              │
│                                                                       │
│  Project Name: Just-In-Time Training Project                          │
│  Guidelines on types of contracts: To reduce Global Construction's    │
│  risk, contracts for the Just-In-Time Training project should be      │
│  fixed price as often as possible. When goods or services cannot be   │
│  well defined, cost-reimbursable or time-and-material contracts may   │
│  be used. The representative from the contracting department          │
│  assigned to this project will work with the project manager to       │
│  determine the appropriate contract type for each contract developed. │
│                                                                       │
│  Standard procurement documents or templates: Global                  │
│  Construction's intranet site includes many sample documents and      │
│  templates for project procurement. The project team will review      │
│  these documents and templates and use them as often as possible.     │
│                                                                       │
│  Guidelines for creating procurement documents: Global                │
│  Construction's intranet site provides guidelines for creating many   │
│  procurement documents. The Just-In-Time Training project team        │
│  should review our current work breakdown structure and scope         │
│  statement to provide the basis for contract work breakdown           │
│  structures and statements of work.                                   │
│                                                                       │
│  Roles and responsibilities: The project manager is the main          │
│  contact for all procurement matters directly related to the          │
│  Just-In-Time Training project. The representative from the           │
│  contracting department assigned to this project will coordinate      │
│  with other staff in the contracting and legal departments, as        │
│  needed. Etc.                                                         │
│                                                                       │
└─────────────────────────────────────────────────────────────────────┘
```

FIGURE 5-19   Sample procurement management plan

Requests for Proposal or Quote

When organizations decide to procure goods or services, they often create documents to describe what they plan to procure and how potential sellers should respond. Two common examples of procurement documents include a Request for Proposal (RFP) and a Request for Quote (RFQ).

- A **Request for Proposal (RFP)** is a document used to solicit proposals from prospective suppliers. A **proposal** is a document in which sellers describe what they will do to meet the requirements of a buyer. It can be expensive and time-consuming to prepare a good RFP or proposal for a large contract, such as building a new bridge or designing a complex information system. For smaller contracts, it would take less time and money. For example, there are several different ways to meet many of Global Construction's training needs. Kristin and her team can write and issue an RFP that outlines training needs so that suppliers can respond with their unique proposals describing how they would meet those needs.

- A **Request for Quote (RFQ)** is a document used to solicit quotes or bids from prospective suppliers. A **bid** (also called a quote) is a document prepared by sellers providing pricing for standard items that have been clearly defined by the buyer. For example, if Kristin's team decided to use a specific book for training courses, they could ask for bids from different sellers for those books. Creating and responding to RFQs is usually much quicker than the same process for RFPs. Selections are often made based on the lowest bid.

RFPs and RFQs can be issued in several ways. The organization might contact one or several preferred sellers directly and send the RFP or RFQ only to them. To reach more sellers, the organization might post the information on its Web site, or advertise on other sites or in newspapers. Project managers must carefully consider which approaches are most appropriate in various situations.

Topics addressed in an RFP usually include the following:

- Purpose of the RFP
- Background information, describing the organization issuing the RFP and the project itself
- Basic requirements for the products and/or services being proposed
- Hardware and software environment (for technology-related proposals)
- RFP process, describing how sellers should prepare and submit their proposals
- Statement of work and schedule information
- Appendices providing more detailed information, as appropriate

A simple RFP might be three- to five-pages long, whereas an RFP for a larger, more complicated procurement might be hundreds of pages long.

Sample Requests for Proposal or Quote

Kristin knew that the project would require several RFPs and RFQs, but it was still very early in the project. Because procurement was not her area of expertise, Kristin asked the project steering committee for advice. They suggested that Kristin's team work with the contracting department to issue an RFP for expert advise to help make major procurement decisions related to the project. The RFP would be for a fixed-price contract to hire an expert to help develop a list of qualified sellers for developing the courses for the Just-In-Time Training project. Figure 5-20 shows the RFP. Lucy, the project sponsor and training director for Global Construction, suggested that they send the RFP to several preferred vendors. They estimated that the work required to develop this qualified-sellers list should take no more than a couple weeks and cost no more than $5,000.

Request for Proposal
August 1, 2009

Project Name: Just-In-Time Training Project
RFP Name: Qualified-Sellers List for Just-In-Time Training Project
Purpose of RFP
Global Construction wants to improve training in supplier management, negotiating skills, project management, and software for its employees. In the fast-paced, ever-changing construction market, effectively training employees across a globally dispersed company with different populations is a challenge. By redesigning our current training, Global Construction can reduce training costs and improve productivity. In addition to providing traditional instructor-led courses on-site, we want to allow our employees to learn about specific topics on a just-in-time basis by having quick access to materials and expert advice. The purpose of this RFP is to hire experts to help us find qualified sellers to develop and deliver these new training courses.

Background Information
Global Construction employs 10,000 full-time employees in 10 different countries and 15 U.S. states. We want to increase the productivity of our employees, especially in the sales, purchasing, engineering, and information technology departments. The Just-In-Time Training project, a one-year project, began on July 2, 2009. A key part of this project is working with outside firms to develop and provide just-in-time training in supplier management, negotiating skills, project management, and software applications. See Appendix A for detailed information on the project and specific training needs.

Basic Requirements
The basic requirements for this work include the following:
1. Develop a list of qualified sellers to develop and provide the training as described in Appendix A.
2. Provide a summary description and detailed evaluation of each seller. Provide company brochures, Web sites, annual reports, and other appropriate information.
3. Work with Global Construction to develop an evaluation system to assess each seller.
4. Provide an objective assessment of each seller using this evaluation system.
5. Develop a list of the top five sellers for each course.
6. Provide recommendations for developing partnerships/relationships with each of the top five sellers.
7. Complete the above work no later than September 9, 2009.

RFP Process
Prospective sellers will send written proposals to Global Construction no later than August 10, 2009. To prepare your proposal, use the outline in Appendix B, and examine Appendix C for our evaluation criteria. We expect to award the contract no later than August 20, 2009.

FIGURE 5-20 Sample RFP

> **Statement of Work and Schedule Information**
> See Appendix C for a statement of work. The work must be completed no later than September 9, 2009.
> **Appendices**
> Appendix A: Just-In-Time Training Project Documents
> Appendix B: Proposal Outline
> Appendix C: Evaluation Criteria
> Appendix D: Statement of Work

FIGURE 5-20   Sample RFP (continued)

Contract Statements of Work

A **contract statement of work (SOW)** is a description of the work that is to be purchased. As shown in Figure 5-20, the SOW should be included with the RFP to clarify the work that needs to be performed. The contract SOW is a type of scope statement that describes the work in sufficient detail to allow prospective suppliers to both determine if they are capable of providing the goods and services required and to determine an appropriate price for the work. A contract SOW should be clear, concise, and as complete as possible. It should describe all services required and include performance information, such as the location and timing of the work. It is important to use appropriate words in a contract SOW—for example, *must* instead of *may*. *Must* implies that something has to be done; *may* implies that there is a choice involved. The contract SOW should specify the products and services required for the project, use industry terms, and refer to industry standards.

Sample Contract Statement of Work

Figure 5-21 shows the contract statement of work for the qualified-sellers list described in the RFP.

Supplier Evaluation Matrices

It is highly recommended that buyers use formal supplier evaluation procedures to help select sellers. In addition to reviewing their proposals or quotes, buyers should also review sellers' past performance, talk to recent customers, interview their management team, and request sample products or demos, if applicable. After doing a thorough evaluation, many organizations summarize evaluations using a supplier evaluation matrix—a type of weighted scoring model. Recall from Chapter 2 that a weighted scoring model provides a systematic process for selection based on numerous criteria. For example, suppliers are often evaluated on criteria related to cost, quality, technology, past performance, and management.

Contract Statement of Work
August 1, 2009

Project Name: Just-in-Time Training Project
Contract Name: Qualified-Sellers List
Scope of Work:
1. Develop a list of qualified sellers to develop and provide the training as described in Appendix A.
2. Provide a summary description and detailed evaluation of each seller. Provide company brochures, Web sites, annual reports, and other appropriate information.
3. Work with Global Construction to develop an evaluation system to assess each seller.
4. Provide an objective assessment of each seller using this evaluation system.
5. Develop a list of the top five sellers for each course.
6. Provide recommendations for developing partnerships/relationships with each of the top five sellers.
7. Complete the above work no later than September 9, 2009.
Location of Work:
The seller can perform the work at any location. The seller must physically meet with representatives from Global Construction in our corporate office at least twice during the term of the contract.
Period of Performance:
Work is expected to start on or around August 20, 2009, and end no later than September 9, 2009. The seller will prepare a detailed schedule for all work required, including dates for deliverables and meetings. After meeting with representatives from Global Construction to review and update the schedule, the seller will agree to the schedule for this work.
Deliverables Schedule:
The seller will prepare a detailed schedule for all of the work required, including dates for all deliverables and meetings. After meeting with representatives from Global Construction to review and update the schedule, the seller will agree to the schedule for this work.
Applicable Standards:
The seller will use standard software to produce the required documentation for this project. Draft and final documents will be sent via e-mail.
Acceptance Criteria:
The seller will work closely with the project manager, Kristin Maur, to clarify expectations and avoid problems in providing acceptable work. Kristin will provide written acceptance/non-acceptance of all deliverables.
Special Requirements:
The seller's staff assigned to work on this contract must have appropriate education and experience. Resumes of proposed staff will be provided as part of the proposal. The seller will work with Global Construction to make all travel arrangements and minimize travel costs.

FIGURE 5-21   Sample contract statement of work

Sample Supplier Evaluation Matrix

Kristin knew her team would have to evaluate suppliers for various goods and services as part of the Just-In-Time Training project. Kristin and her team reviewed Global Construction's previously used supplier evaluation matrices, and then prepared a simple matrix to evaluate the supplier for the qualified-sellers list, as shown in Figure 5-22. This figure was created using the weighted scoring model template from the companion Web site, and it shows results based on three proposals. In this example, Proposal 2 has the highest weighted score, so that supplier would be selected.

Just-In-Time Training Project Supplier Evaluation Matrix
September 9, 2009

Criteria	Weight	Proposal 1	Proposal 2	Proposal 3
Past performance	30%	70	90	70
Cost	25%	80	75	70
Educational background	25%	70	75	70
Management approach	20%	85	80	70
Weighted Project Scores	**100%**	**75.5**	**80.5**	70

FIGURE 5-22 Sample supplier evaluation matrix

CASE WRAP-UP

Kristin was pleased with the progress on planning tasks for the Just-In-Time Training project. Several members of her project team and the project steering committee had complimented Kristin on her ability to get key stakeholders involved. They also liked the way she admitted her own areas of weakness and sought out expert advice. Kristin was grateful for the steering committee's suggestion to hire an outside firm early in the project to help find qualified suppliers for the training courses. Everyone felt confident that the project team had a handle on risk management. Kristin felt ready to tackle the challenges she would face in leading her team during project execution.

Chapter Summary

Successful project managers know how important it is to develop, refine, and follow plans to meet project goals. This chapter summarizes the planning tasks and outputs for quality, human resource, communications, risk, and procurement management.

Planning outputs related to quality management include a quality management plan, a project dashboard, quality metrics descriptions, and a quality checklist. Samples of these documents are provided for the Just-In-Time Training project.

Planning outputs related to human resource management include creating a project organizational chart, responsibility assignment matrix, resource histogram, and staffing management plan. Samples of these documents are provided for the Just-In-Time Training project.

Planning outputs related to communications management include developing a communications management plan and project Web site. Samples of these documents are provided for the Just-In-Time Training project.

Planning outputs related to risk management include developing a risk management plan, a probability/impact matrix, a risk register, and risk-related contractual agreements. Samples of these documents are provided for the Just-In-Time Training project.

Planning outputs related to procurement management include performing a make-or-buy analysis and preparing a procurement management plan, requests for proposal/quote, a contract statement of work, and a supplier evaluation matrix. Samples of these documents are provided for the Just-In-Time Training project.

Quick Quiz

1. _____ is defined as the degree to which a set of inherent characteristics fulfill requirements.

   a. Fitness for use

   b. Conformance to requirements

   c. Metrics

   d. Quality

2. _____ allow organizations to measure their performance in certain areas—such as failure rates, availability, and reliability—and compare them over time or with other organizations.

   a. Ratings

   b. Metrics

   c. Quality-control charts

   d. Checklists

3. A RACI chart is a type of _____ .

   a. project organizational chart

   b. resource histogram

   c. responsibility assignment matrix

   d. project dashboard

4. A _____ describes when and how people will be added to and taken off of a project.

   a. project organizational chart

   b. resource histogram

   c. responsibility assignment matrix

   d. staffing management plan

5. Topics such as who will receive project information and who will produce it, suggested methods or guidelines for conveying the information, frequency of communication, and escalation procedures for resolving issues should be described in a _____ .

   a. communications management plan

   b. staffing management plan

   c. team contract

   d. scope statement

6. Suppose you are a member of Kristin's team and you are having difficulties communicating with one of the supplier management experts who is providing important content for a class you are developing. What strategy might you use to help improve communications?

   a. put all communications in writing

   b. put all communications on your project Web site

   c. use several different methods to communicate with this person

   d. ask Kristin to find a better person to provide the technical content

7. What two dimensions should you use when evaluating project risks?

   a. probability and impact

   b. cost and schedule

   c. negative and positive

   d. source and responsibility

8. A _____ is a document that contains results of various risk management processes, often displayed in a table or spreadsheet format.

   a. risk event

   b. trigger

   c. risk register

   d. risk management plan

9. You can purchase an item you need for a project for $10,000 and it has daily operating costs of $500, or you can lease the item for $700 per day. On which day will the purchase cost be the same as the lease cost?

   a. day 5

   b. day 10

   c. day 50

   d. day 100

10. You want to have the least risk possible in setting up a contract to purchase goods and services from an outside firm. As the buyer, what type of contract should you use?

    a. fixed price

    b. unit price

    c. cost reimbursable

    d. time and materials

Quick Quiz Answers

1. D; 2. B; 3. C; 4. D; 5. A; 6. C; 7. A; 8. C; 9. C; 10. A

Discussion Questions

1. What is the main purpose of a quality management plan? What are two metrics besides those provided in this chapter that Kristin and her team could use on the Just-In-Time Training project? Besides ensuring that classrooms are ready for training, where else might they use a checklist on the project?

2. What is the main purpose of a staffing management plan? What tool should you use to graphically show total staffing needs for a project? What tool should you use to clarify roles and responsibilities for tasks?

3. Why is it so difficult to ensure good communication on projects? What strategies can any project team use to improve communications?

4. Why is risk management often neglected on projects? Why is it important to take the time to identify and rank risks throughout the project's life?

5. What is the difference between an RFP and an RFQ? Give an example of the appropriate use of each.

Exercises

1. Find an example of a large project that took more than a year to complete. You can ask people at your college, university, or work about a recent project, such as a major fund raising campaign, information systems installation, or building project. You can also find information about projects online such as the Big Dig in Boston (*www.masspike.com/bigdig*), the Patronas Twin Towers in Malaysia and many other building projects (*www.greatbuildings.com*), etc. Describe some of the tasks performed in planning the quality, human resource, communications, risk, and procurement aspects of the project. Write a one-page paper or prepare a short presentation summarizing your findings.

2. Search the Internet for "project dashboard." Find at least three different charts or examples that can be used on a project dashboard. Document your findings in a two-page paper or short presentation, including screen shots of the charts you find and your assessment of their value.

3. Your company is planning to launch an important project starting January 1, which will last one year. You estimate that you will need one half-time project manager; two full-time business analysts for the first six months; two full-time marketing analysts for the whole year; four full-time business interns for the months of June, July, and August; and one full-time salesperson for the last three months. Use spreadsheet software such as Microsoft Excel to create a stacked-column chart showing a resource histogram for this project, similar to the one shown in Figure 5-8. Be sure to include a legend to label the types of resources needed, and use appropriate titles and axis labels. You can use the resource histogram template on the companion Web site to make this exercise easier.

4. List three negative risk events and three positive risk events for the Just-In-Time Training project. Briefly describe each risk, and then rate each one as high, medium, or low in terms of probability and impact. Plot the results on a probability/impact matrix. Also, prepare an entry for one of the risks for the risk register.

5. Assume the source selection criteria for evaluating proposals for a project is as follows:

   - Management approach 15%
   - Technical approach 15%
   - Past performance 20%
   - Price 20%
   - Interview results and samples 30%

   Use Figure 5-22 as a guide and the weighted scoring model template from the companion Web site to calculate the total weighted scores for three proposals. Enter scores for Proposal 1 as 80, 90, 70, 90, and 80, respectively. Enter scores for Proposal 2 as 90, 50, 95, 80, and 95. Enter scores for Proposal 3 as 60, 90, 90, 80, and 65. Add a paragraph summarizing the results and your recommendation on the spreadsheet. Print your results on one page.

Team Projects

1. Your organization initiated a project to raise money for an important charity. Assume that there are 1,000 people in your organization. Also, assume that you have six months to raise as much money as possible, with a goal of $100,000. Create a checklist to use in soliciting sponsors for the fundraiser, a responsibility assignment matrix for various stakeholders, a project Web site (just the home page), a probability/impact matrix with six potential negative risks, and a request for quote for obtaining items your team will need. Be creative in your responses. Remember that this project is entirely run by volunteers.

2. You are part of a team in charge of a project to help people in your company (500 people) lose weight. This project is part of a competition, and the top "losers" will be featured in a popular television show. Assume that you have six months to complete the project and a budget of $10,000. Develop metrics for the project, a project organizational chart, a communications management plan, and a risk register with at least three entries for the project.

3. Using the information you developed in Team Project 1 or 2, role-play a meeting to review one of these planning documents with key stakeholders. Determine who will play what role (project manager, team member from a certain department, senior managers, and so on). Be creative in displaying different personalities (a senior manager who questions the importance of the project to the organization, a team member who is very shy or obnoxious).

4. Develop a project dashboard for your team project, using Figure 5-3 as an example. Be sure to include at least eight different metrics. Document your results in a one-page paper or short presentation, showing the actual dashboard you created.

5. Perform the planning tasks (tasks 6-10, quality through procurement management) for the New Business Venture case study provided in Appendix C or for one of the cases on the companion Web site. If you are working on a real team project, perform the planning tasks for that project. Remember to be thorough in your planning so that your execution goes smoothly. Be sure to have your sponsor and other stakeholders provide inputs on your plans.

Companion Web Site

Visit the companion Web site for this text (*www.course.com/mis/pm2/schwalbe* or *http://login.course.com*) to access:

- Lecture notes
- Interactive quizzes and Jeopardy games
- Template files
- Sample documents
- Podcasts
- More ideas for team projects, including real projects and case studies
- Links to additional resources related to project management

Key Terms

bid — A document prepared by sellers providing pricing for standard items that have been clearly defined by the buyer.

blogs — Easy-to-use journals on the Web that allow users to write entries, create links, and upload pictures, while allowing readers to post comments to particular journal entries.

checklist — A list of items to be noted or consulted.

communications management plan — A document that guides project communications.

conformance to requirements — The process of ensuring that the project's processes and products meet written specifications.

contingency plans — The predefined actions that the project team will take if an identified risk event occurs.

contingency reserves or **contingency allowances** — The funds held by the project sponsor that can be used to mitigate cost or schedule overruns if unknown risks occur.

contracts — The mutually binding agreements that obligate the seller to provide the specified products or services, and obligate the buyer to pay for them.

contract statement of work (SOW) — A description of the work that is to be purchased.

cost-reimbursable contract — A contract that involves payment to the seller for direct and indirect actual costs.

fallback plans — The plans that are developed for risks that have a high impact on meeting project objectives, and are put into effect if attempts to reduce the risk are not effective.

fitness for use — The ability of a product to be used as it was intended.

fixed-price or **lump-sum contract** — A type of contract that involves a fixed price for a well-defined product or service.

make-or-buy analysis — The process of estimating the internal costs of providing a product or service and comparing that estimate to the cost of outsourcing.

metric — A standard of measurement.

project dashboard — A graphic screen summarizing key project metrics.

project organizational chart — A graphic representation of how authority and responsibility is distributed within the project.

proposal — A document in which sellers describe what they will do to meet the requirements of a buyer.

quality — The degree to which a set of inherent characteristics fulfill requirements.

RACI charts — A type of responsibility assignment matrix that shows Responsibility, Accountability, Consultation, and Informed roles for project stakeholders.

Request for Proposal (RFP) — A document used to solicit proposals from prospective suppliers.

Request for Quote (RFQ) — A document used to solicit quotes or bids from prospective suppliers.

resource histogram — A column chart that shows the number of resources required for or assigned to a project over time.

responsibility assignment matrix (RAM) — A matrix that maps the work of the project as described in the WBS to the people responsible for performing the work.

risk — An uncertainty that can have a negative or positive effect on meeting project objectives.

risk events — The specific, uncertain events that may occur to the detriment or enhancement of the project.

risk register — A document that contains results of various risk management processes, often displayed in a table or spreadsheet format.

root cause — The real or underlying reason a problem occurs.

staffing management plan — A plan that describes when and how people will be added to and taken off of a project.

time-and-material contract — A type of contract that is a hybrid of both a fixed-price and cost-reimbursable contract.

triggers — The indicators or symptoms of actual risk events.

End Notes

[1] Dragan Milosevic, Portland State University, "Delivering Projects: What the Winners Do," PMI Conference Proceedings (November 2001).

[2] Projectzone, "Humor," (*http://corporatedump.com/dilbertmanagers.html*) (2004).

[3] Cesar Pelli and Michael J. Crosbie, "Building Petronas Towers," *Architecture Week* (February 19, 2003).

[4] Interactive Advertising Bureau News, "Internet Advertising Revenues Soar Again, Near $5 Billion in Q1 '07" (June 6, 2007).

204

CHAPTER **6**

EXECUTING PROJECTS

LEARNING OBJECTIVES

After reading this chapter, you will be able to:

- List several tasks and outputs of project execution
- Discuss what is involved in directing and managing project execution as part of project integration management, including the importance of producing promised deliverables, implementing solutions to problems, evaluating work performance information, and requesting changes to a project
- Explain the importance of recommending corrective actions and updating project plans as part of quality assurance
- Describe the executing tasks performed as part of human resource management, summarize important concepts related to managing people, and explain what is involved in leveling resources, creating staffing updates, and developing team performance assessments
- Discuss important communications concepts, and describe the executing tasks performed as part of communications management to ensure good communications
- Explain the executing tasks performed as part of procurement management, and describe how to prepare procurement document packages and contracts

OPENING CASE

Kristin reviewed initial project plans with the steering committee for the Just-In-Time Training project. Committee members felt that everything was going well so far and that it was time to commit more resources to the project. At later steering committee meetings, Kristin brought up several challenges she was facing in executing the project plans. For example, Jamie, the supplier management expert assigned to her team half-time, was not working out. In addition, there were several conflicts between various stakeholders on how to perform certain tasks, and several people complained about a lack of communication about the project. The IT people supporting the project were overallocated, yet some of their tasks were on the critical path for the project. The prototype for the supplier management basics course was not as well received as the team had hoped, and Kristin was afraid that the seller might demand more money to make major changes to the course. Kristin would need to use her experience—especially her soft (interpersonal) skills—as well as advice from the project steering committee to deal with these and other challenges.

INTRODUCTION

Whereas project planning is considered to be the most unappreciated project management process group, project execution is the most noticed. Of course, good plans are important, but it is even more important to execute them well. In fact, the June 21, 1999, issue of *Fortune* summarized research showing that without a doubt, the main reason chief executive officers (CEOs) failed was poor execution. Failed CEOs simply did not get things done, were indecisive, and did not deliver on commitments. The same is true for project managers and all leaders. Stakeholders expect to see results from their projects through effective execution.

⊗ WHAT WENT WRONG?

"The results are not acceptable," stated President Bush four days after Hurricane Katrina caused major damage to New Orleans and surrounding areas. After Federal Emergency Management Agency (FEMA) officials returned in January 2005 from a tour of the tsunami devastation in Asia, New Orleans was the number one disaster they discussed. Officials had drawn up dozens of plans and conducted preparedness drills for years, but despite all the warnings, Hurricane Katrina overwhelmed government agencies, and many people suffered from slow response to their needs for emergency aid. The mayor of New Orleans, C. Ray Nagin, blasted the government for its lack of an immediate response. "I've talked directly with the president, I've talked to the head of the Homeland Security, I've talked to everybody under the sun, I've been out there."[1] People were disappointed with the poor execution of disaster relief efforts during the first few days, and officials took corrective actions to address the challenges caused by the hurricane.

On a lighter note, Figure 6-1 shows a cartoon related to poor execution by a sports team and a play on the word *execution.*

FIGURE 6-1 All for the team's execution?

Recall that, in general, the majority of a project's time and budget is spent on project execution. Many of the tasks and outputs created in the other process groups are fairly similar from project to project, but no two projects are ever executed in the exact same way. Why? Because projects involve uncertainty. No one can ever predict the challenges that project teams will face in trying to meet project goals. This chapter summarizes the main tasks involved in executing projects and discusses some challenges that Kristin faced in managing the execution of the Just-In-Time Training project.

Summary of Executing Tasks and Outputs

Figure 6-2 summarizes key outputs of project execution by knowledge area, based on the *PMBOK® Guide.* Notice that not every knowledge area is included, and requested changes are listed only under project integration management, although they are outputs of other knowledge areas as well. Although there are many planning tasks related to scope, time, cost, and risk management, these knowledge areas do not have tasks directly related to project execution. Changes to the triple constraint and risk management are addressed in the next chapter on project monitoring and control. This chapter focuses on tasks and outputs that project teams perform to execute projects, and provides specific examples for Global Construction's Just-In-Time Training project.

Knowledge area	Outputs
Project integration management	Deliverables, implemented solutions to problems, work performance information, requested changes
Project quality management	Recommended corrective actions, project plan updates
Project human resource management	Staffing updates, team performance assessment
Project communications management	Business process updates
Project procurement management	Procurement document packages and contracts

FIGURE 6-2 Executing process summary

EXECUTING TASKS FOR PROJECT INTEGRATION MANAGEMENT

As part of project integration management, the project manager must perform the task of directing and managing stakeholders to complete the project. Project managers can follow several important practices to help accomplish this challenging job:

- *Coordinate planning and execution:* As mentioned earlier, the main purpose of project planning is to guide execution. If the project manager and team did a good job planning, the plans will be easier to execute. As things change, team members need to update the plans to keep everyone working on the same page.
- *Develop and use soft skills:* Several studies of project managers suggest that soft skills (for example, strong leadership, effective team building, strong communication, motivation, negotiation, conflict management, and problem solving) are crucial to the success of project managers, especially during project execution. Project managers must lead by example in demonstrating the importance of creating good project plans and then following them in project execution. Project managers often create plans for things they need to do themselves, such as meeting with key stakeholders, reviewing important information, and so on. If project managers follow through on their own plans, their team members are more likely to do the same.
- *Provide a supportive organizational culture:* Good project execution requires a supportive organizational culture. For example, organizational procedures can help or hinder project execution. If an organization has useful guidelines and templates for project management that everyone in the organization follows, it will be easier for project managers and their teams to plan and do their work. If the organization uses the project plans as the basis for performing and monitoring progress during execution, the culture will promote the relationship between good planning and execution. Even if the organizational culture is not supportive, project managers can create a supportive culture within their own project and work on improving the culture in other parts of the organization.

- *Break the rules when needed:* Even with a supportive organizational culture, project managers might sometimes find it necessary to break the rules to produce project results in a timely manner. When project managers break the rules, politics will play a role in the results. For example, if a particular project requires use of nonstandard software, the project manager must use his or her political skills to convince concerned stakeholders of the need to break the rules.
- *Capitalize on product, business, and application area knowledge:* The application area of the project directly affects project execution because the products of the project are produced during project execution. For example, if a project involves constructing a new building, the project manager and other stakeholders would need to use their expertise in architecture, engineering, and construction to produce the product successfully. Project managers should use their expertise to guide their team and make important decisions.
- *Use project execution tools and techniques:* For example, following a project management methodology and using a project management information system can help project execution go more smoothly. The project management methodology should include guidelines on how to communicate project status, handle conflicts, work with suppliers and other stakeholders, and perform other important tasks.

Deliverables

Most project sponsors would say that the most important output of any project is its deliverables. Recall that deliverables are products or services produced or provided as part of a project. They include product and process-related items. For the Just-In-Time Training project at Global Construction, key product-related deliverables include the training materials and courses (instructor-led, Web-based, and CD-ROM). Process-related deliverables related to developing and delivering those training materials and courses include researching existing training and meeting with potential partners.

Sample Deliverables

Because the Just-In-Time Training project is fictitious, it is impossible to show the actual training materials, courses, and other deliverables produced during execution. Because you are probably reading this book as part of a course and have taken other courses in both an instructor-led or online fashion, you have some feel for what training materials and courses are like. Recall that several of the training courses for this project must be available on a just-in-time basis (that is, they must be available whenever the employee wants to learn), so deliverables must be created to provide effective Web-based and/or CD-ROM instruction. Note the word *effective*. The main objective of this training is to provide employees with the knowledge and skills they need to do their jobs when they need it. Just because training is available around the clock does not mean that it is effective. The section on quality later in this chapter describes the importance of ensuring quality during project execution.

Implemented Solutions to Problems

Of course, all project teams face numerous problems. Some surface early during project initiation or planning, but some do not occur until project execution, when many things are happening at once. Many problems can be avoided by doing a good job of initiating, planning, or monitoring and controlling the project, but other problems cannot be avoided. Some common problems encountered during project execution include the following:

1. The project sponsor and/or other senior managers are not very supportive of the project.
2. Project stakeholders, such as people who would use the products and services the project is attempting to create, are not sufficiently involved in project decision-making.
3. The project manager is inexperienced in managing people, working in a particular organization, or understanding the application area of the project.
4. The project objectives/scope are unclear.
5. Estimates for time and cost goals are unreliable or unrealistic.
6. Business needs/technology changes have impacted the project.
7. People working on the project are incompetent or unmotivated.
8. There are poor conflict-management procedures.
9. Communications are poor.
10. Suppliers are not delivering as promised.

The first five problems should have been addressed during project initiation or planning (and were addressed in previous chapters), but they can also cause difficulties during execution. Addressing business and technology changes are discussed in the next chapter on monitoring and controlling. The last four problems are discussed in this chapter and presented in the context of the Just-In-Time Training project.

Sample Implemented Solutions to Problems

Kristin Maur had been working hard to direct and manage project execution, but she encountered several problems. The following sections discuss the problems of incompetent or unmotivated people working on the project and poor conflict-management procedures. Later sections discuss strategies for improving communications and supplier delivery.

Issues with Competence and Motivation

Jamie, the project team member assigned to work half-time from the supplier management department, was not contributing much to the project. Jamie's main role was to provide expertise in developing the supplier management courses. She was well qualified for this assignment, having over 10 years' experience with Global Construction managing major accounts with suppliers. (Recall that supplier management was the most important training topic for the project.) Kristin knew that Jamie was very good at negotiating with and managing suppliers, but Jamie felt that she was assigned to the project primarily because she was available, having recently finished another large project. Although Jamie was assigned to work on this project from its start, she was on vacation for most of the first month and seemed uninterested in the project when she was around. Kristin tried her best to motivate her, but she could see that Jamie was simply not the right person for the project. (See a later section in this chapter on motivation.) Kristin talked to Jamie directly, and she admitted that she would much rather deal directly with suppliers than work on this training project. Just two months into the project, Kristin used her experience and contacts within the company to find a suitable replacement. She worked through the project steering committee and other managers to quickly approve the personnel change.

Poor Conflict Management

Most large projects are high-stake endeavors that are highly visible within organizations. They require tremendous effort from team members, are expensive, require significant resources, and can have an extensive impact on the way work is done in an organization. When the stakes are high, conflict is never far away, and even small projects with low budgets have conflicts—it is a natural part of work and life in general. Project managers should lead their teams in developing norms for dealing with various types of conflicts that might arise. For example, team members should know that disrespectful behavior toward any project stakeholder is inappropriate, and that team members are expected to try to work out small conflicts themselves before elevating them to higher levels. The team contract, created during project planning, should address team conduct and conflict management.

Blake and Mouton (1964) delineated five basic modes for handling conflicts. Each strategy can be considered as being high, medium, or low on two dimensions: importance of the task or goal, and importance of the relationship between the people having the conflict.

1. *Confrontation*: When using the **confrontation mode**, project managers directly face a conflict using a problem-solving approach that allows affected parties to work through their disagreements. This approach is also called the problem-solving mode. It is best used when *both the task and the relationship are of high importance*. For example, Kristin confronted Jamie when she was not working well on the project. They discussed the problem and decided it was best for both parties for Jamie to leave the project team. They also discussed who could take her place. This mode reflects a win/win approach.

2. *Compromise*: With the **compromise mode**, project managers use a give-and-take approach to resolve conflicts, bargaining and searching for solutions that will bring some degree of satisfaction to all the parties in a dispute. This give-and-take approach works best when both the task and the relationship are of medium importance. For example, the IT person responsible for creating and sending out the surveys for Kristin's project might be swamped with work. Kristin might either agree to pay several hundred dollars for overtime to get the task completed on time or provide a few days extension for the task at no additional cost. This mode reflects a lose/lose approach, since both parties are giving up something.

3. *Smoothing*: When using the **smoothing mode**, the project manager de-emphasizes or avoids areas of differences and emphasizes areas of agreement. This method is best used when the *relationship is of high importance and the task is of low importance*. For example, two members of the project steering committee might totally disagree on whether they should provide incentive bonuses to suppliers for achieving outstanding ratings on courses. Kristin could use the smoothing mode to ensure that the relationship between the steering committee members remains harmonious

by discussing with these team members the areas in which they agree and by downplaying the topic of bonuses during meetings.

4. *Forcing*: The **forcing mode** can be viewed as the win-lose approach to conflict resolution. People exert their viewpoints even though they contradict the viewpoints of others. This approach is appropriate when *the task is of high importance and the relationship is of low importance*. For example, if you are competing against another firm for a contract, it may be appropriate to use the forcing mode.

5. *Withdrawal*: When using the **withdrawal mode**, project managers retreat or withdraw from an actual or potential disagreement. This approach is the least desirable conflict-handling mode. It may be appropriate when *both the task and the relationship are of low importance*.

Effective project managers often use confrontation for conflict resolution instead of the other four modes. However, it is important to keep in mind that the term *confrontation* may be misleading. This mode focuses on a win-win problem-solving approach, in which all parties work together to find the best way to solve the conflict.

Project managers must also realize that not all conflict is bad. In fact, conflict can often be good. Conflict often produces important results, such as new ideas, better alternatives, and motivation to work harder and more collaboratively. Project team members might become stagnant or develop **groupthink**—conformance to the values or ethical standards of a group—if there are no conflicting viewpoints on various aspects of a project. Research suggests that task-related conflict, which is derived from differences over team objectives and how to achieve them, often improves team performance. Emotional conflict, however, which stems from personality clashes and misunderstandings, often depresses team performance. Project managers should create an environment that encourages and maintains the positive and productive aspects of conflict.

Work Performance Information

One of Kristin's main jobs during project execution was collecting, assessing, and communicating work performance information. Kristin used the "management by wandering around" (MBWA) approach, meaning she informally observed and talked to her project team members, suppliers, and other stakeholders as much as possible. She wanted to know firsthand how project activities were progressing, and she wanted to offer suggestions as often as possible. Of course, she also used more formal communications, such as status reports, the project dashboard (which summarized key project metrics, as described in Chapter 5), survey results, and course evaluations, to address work performance on the project.

Sample Work Performance Information

A common way to summarize work performance information is by using a milestone report. Recall that a milestone is a significant event on a project, such as completing a major deliverable or awarding a major contract. Figure 6-3 provides part of a milestone report for the Just-In-Time Training project. Notice that in addition to listing the milestones, the report lists the planned date for completion (in month/day format), the status, the person responsible for the milestone, and issues/comments. Project 2007 also includes a standard milestone report, as described in Appendix A. You can also create customized reports in Project 2007 to tailor the content and format of reports.

Just-In-Time Training Project Milestone Report

September 1, 2009

Milestone	Date	Status	Responsible	Issues/Comments
Researched existing training	8/13	Completed	Jamie (replaced by Abner)	Many basic courses available, but not much advanced/tailored training (Note: Replaced Jamie with better candidate for project after Jamie completed this task)
Supplier management training survey results reported to steering committee	8/24	Completed	Kristin	Great feedback; many people stressed the need to have instructor-led training and mentors for soft skills development
Meetings to determine potential partners completed	9/21	In progress	Kristin/Contracting	May need more time for meetings
Partnership agreements completed	9/28	Not started yet	Kristin/Contracting	May need more times to set up agreements
Developed executive course	11/9	Not started yet	TBD Supplier	
Developed introductory course	11/9	Not started yet	TBD Supplier	
Developed advanced course	11/23	Not started yet	TBD Supplier	
Held pilot course	11/23	Not started yet	TBD Supplier	
Pilot course results reported to steering committee	11/30	Not started yet	Kristin	

FIGURE 6-3 Sample milestone report for reporting work performance information

Requested Changes

Often, a number of requests for changes emerge during project execution. Recall that a process for handling changes should be defined during project planning as part of the project management plan. Chapter 7, which covers monitoring and controlling projects, provides detailed information on handling changes. It is important during project execution to formally and informally request appropriate changes. Project managers, team members, suppliers, and other stakeholders can make change requests, so it is important to have a good process in place for handling them.

Sample Requested Changes

Successful project teams use well-defined processes and standard forms for requesting project changes. Some changes are requested using other established change processes. For example, when Kristin requested that Jamie be replaced with Abner as the project team member from the supplier management department, she used Global Construction's personnel transfer process. Jamie's department head and the human resources department handled necessary paperwork for the reassignment. For other change requests—especially those that may impact achieving scope, time, or cost goals of the project—a formal change request form should be submitted through the appropriate channels. Figure 6-4 provides a sample of a completed change request form for the Just-In-Time Training project. It is important to have a good justification for the requested change and address the benefits of incurring any additional costs. In this case, if the additional $550 is not provided, the entire project will be delayed.

Change Request

September 22, 2009

Project Name: Just-In-Time Training Project
Date Request Submitted: September 22, 2009
Title of Change Request: Additional funds for supplier management course survey
Change Order Number: A200-17
Submitted by: Kristin Maur

Change Category: __Scope __Schedule **X** Cost __Technology __Other
Description of change requested:
To avoid a schedule slip and have appropriate internal resources available, we are requesting the approval of paid overtime for creating and distributing the survey for the supplier management course.
Events that made this change necessary or desirable:
The IT person assigned to our project has several other important projects on hand. If these survey tasks are delayed, the entire project will be delayed.
Justification for the change/why it is needed/desired to continue/complete the project:
We must send out and analyze the survey in a timely manner because we need the information to develop the first supplier management course and select an appropriate supplier.
Impact of the proposed change on:
Scope: None
Schedule: None
Cost: $550
Staffing: One IT person will work 10 hours of paid overtime over a period of several weeks.
Risk: Low. This person suggested the paid overtime and has successfully worked overtime in the past.
Other: None
Suggested implementation if the change request is approved: Include the overtime pay in the normal paycheck.
Required approvals:

Name/Title	Date	Approve/Reject
Evan George/Affected Employee		
Stella Jacobs/Employee's Supervisor		
Julia Portman, VP of IT		

FIGURE 6-4 Sample change request

EXECUTING TASKS FOR PROJECT QUALITY MANAGEMENT

It is one thing to develop a plan for ensuring quality on a project; it is another to ensure delivery of quality products and services. The main quality management task required during execution is quality assurance. **Quality assurance** includes all the activities related to satisfying the relevant quality standards for a project. For example, it was important for the Just-In-Time Training project that the course materials included content that would meet participants' needs. Kristin made sure that the people developing those materials reviewed results of the needs assessment, were experts in the field, and reviewed the content with Global Construction, Inc. managers in those areas (supplier management, negotiating skills, project management, and software applications). Another goal of quality assurance is continual quality improvement. Many companies understand the importance of quality assurance and have entire departments dedicated to this discipline. These companies have detailed processes in place to make sure that their products and services conform to various quality requirements. They also know they must produce products and services at competitive prices. To be successful in today's competitive business environment, successful companies develop their own best practices and evaluate other organizations' best practices to continuously improve the way they do business. See Chapter 8 for more information on and examples of best practices in project management.

Top management and project managers can impact the quality of projects most significantly by implementing quality assurance. Key outputs of quality assurance include recommended corrective actions and project plan updates.

Recommended Corrective Actions

Before learning about recommended corrective actions that Kristin and her team took, it is important to understand how you know they are needed. The previous section addressed resolving problems. Obviously, corrective actions are developed to resolve problems. It is also important, however, for organizations to use other techniques to identify areas in which they would benefit from taking actions to improve quality. Several quality improvement techniques include benchmarking, quality audits, and cause-and-effect diagrams.

- **Benchmarking** generates ideas for quality improvements by comparing specific project practices or product characteristics to those of other projects or products within or outside of the organization itself. For example, one reason that Global Construction initiated the Just-In-Time Training project was because it discovered that its cost of training per employee was higher than that of similar firms. The amount of money that organizations spend on training is a benchmark. As another example, many organizations have overall course ratings using a Likert scale, with 1 being the lowest rating and 5 being the highest. A benchmark for a good rating might be an average rating of 3.5 or higher. If training participants rated the prototype supplier management course lower than 3.5 on average, then Kristin's team would need to take corrective actions to improve the quality of the course.

- A **quality audit** is a structured review of specific quality management activities that helps identify lessons learned, which could improve performance on current or future projects. In-house auditors or third parties with expertise in specific areas can perform quality audits, which can be either scheduled or random. Recall that several of the main goals of the Just-In-Time Training project were to reduce training costs at Global Construction, provide training when it was needed, and improve employee productivity. By establishing measurement techniques for monitoring these goals and performing an audit to see how well they are being met, Kristin's team can see how well they are doing in meeting specific goals. For example, they could send out a monthly survey asking employees if they are getting training when they need it and if it is helping improve their productivity. A quality audit could be done periodically to review the survey results. If there is a sudden decrease in ratings, Kristin's team would need to take corrective actions.

- **Cause-and-effect diagrams**—also called fishbone diagrams (because their structure resembles a fishbone) or Ishikawa diagrams (named after their founder)—can assist in ensuring and improving quality by finding the root causes of quality problems. Recall from Chapter 5 that a root cause is the real or underlying reason a problem occurs. Kristin and her team created several of these diagrams to find the root causes of quality problems, as described in the next section.

Sample Recommended Corrective Actions

After training participants rated the prototype supplier management course less than 3.5 on average, Kristin's team knew they had to recommend corrective actions. They first decided to analyze what the root cause of the problem really was. The prototype course was available in three formats: instructor-led, Web-based, and CD-ROM. The Web-based and CD-ROM courses were virtually identical, except participants in the Web-based course could also access interactive discussion boards and chat rooms as they accessed the course via the Internet. The evaluations for the instructor-led course were actually above average; however, the Web-based and CD-ROM courses were rated below average.

The student evaluation forms provided some open-ended feedback, so Kristin and her team decided to use that information plus other possible causes of the low ratings to prepare a cause-and-effect diagram, as shown in Figure 6-5. The main effect is the low course ratings, and potential causes are grouped into several main categories: content, interactivity, speed, and graphics/fonts. Potential subcategories are listed in each area, such as "too simple" and "not enough examples" under content. Kristin and her team contacted the participants in the prototype courses to get more specific information to help identify the root cause(s) of the low ratings. When they discovered that the majority of respondents rated the CD-ROM course poorly because it lacked interactivity, they discussed the option of supplementing the course with the Web-based interactivity features, such as the discussion board and chat room. Respondents were generally enthusiastic about the Web-based course, except for those who accessed it with a slow Internet connection. A simple solution would be to have them use the CD-ROM for most of the course and use the Internet for the discussion board and chat room. Because the other potential causes were not the main reasons for the low ratings, they were not addressed.

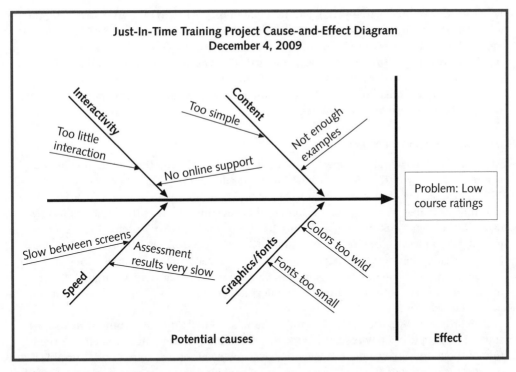

FIGURE 6-5   Sample cause-and-effect diagram

Kristin and her team recommended that the discussion board and chat room features of the Web-based course be integrated into the CD-ROM course. The supplier who developed both courses said it would be a very simple change and would not affect time or cost estimates.

EXECUTING TASKS FOR PROJECT HUMAN RESOURCE MANAGEMENT

Effective project human resource management is crucial to project execution. The two main tasks project managers perform include acquiring the project team and developing the project team. Key outputs include staffing updates and team performance assessment.

Before discussing these tasks and outputs, it is important to understand basic concepts related to dealing with people in a work setting. Key concepts include motivation, influence, and effectiveness.

Motivation

Psychologists, managers, coworkers, teachers, parents, and most people in general still struggle to understand what motivates people, or why they do what they do. **Intrinsic motivation** causes people to participate in an activity for their own enjoyment. For example, some people love to read, write, or play an instrument because it makes them feel good. **Extrinsic motivation** causes people to do something for a reward or to avoid a penalty. For example, some young children would prefer *not* to play an instrument, but do so to receive a reward or avoid a punishment. Why do some people require no external motivation whatsoever to produce high-quality work while others require significant external motivation to perform routine tasks? Why can't you get someone who is extremely productive at work to do simple tasks at home? Mankind will continue to try to answer these overarching questions, but a basic understanding of motivational theory will help anyone who has to work or live with other people.

Maslow's Hierarchy of Needs

Abraham Maslow, a highly respected psychologist who rejected the dehumanizing negativism of psychology in the 1950s, is best known for developing a hierarchy of needs. In the 1950s, proponents of Sigmund Freud's psychoanalytic theory were promoting the idea that human beings were not the masters of their destiny and that their actions were governed by unconscious processes dominated by primitive sexual urges. During the same period, behavioral psychologists saw human beings as controlled by the environment. Maslow argued that both schools of thought failed to recognize unique qualities of human behavior: love, self-esteem, belonging, self-expression, and creativity. He argued that these unique qualities enable people to make independent choices, which give them full control over their destiny.

Figure 6-6 shows the basic pyramid structure of **Maslow's hierarchy of needs**, which states that people's behaviors are guided or motivated by a sequence of needs. At the bottom of the hierarchy are physiological needs, such as air, water, and food. After physiological needs are satisfied, safety needs—such as shelter from bad weather, lack of physical or mental abuse, and a low-crime environment—guide behavior. After safety needs are satisfied, social needs—such as having friends, belonging to groups, and having a sense of community—come to the forefront, and so on up the hierarchy. Examples of esteem needs include personal achievement, recognition, and respect, whereas self-actualization needs include a sense of fulfillment and belief that one is working to his or her potential. The order of these needs in the pyramid is significant. Maslow suggests that each level of the hierarchy is a prerequisite for the level above. For example, it is not possible for people to consider self-actualization if they have not addressed basic needs concerning security and safety. People in an emergency situation, such as a flood or hurricane, cannot be concerned with personal growth but will be motivated solely by the requirements of personal survival. After a particular need is satisfied, however, it no longer serves as a potent motivator of behavior.

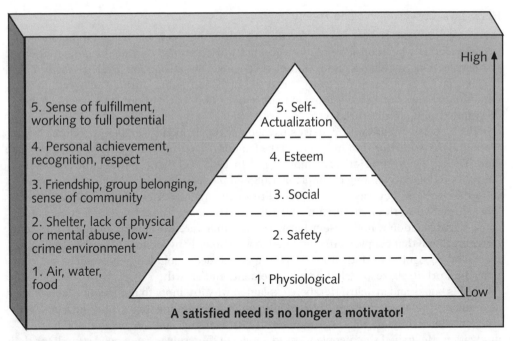

High ↑

5. Sense of fulfillment, working to full potential

5. Self-Actualization

4. Personal achievement, recognition, respect

4. Esteem

3. Friendship, group belonging, sense of community

3. Social

2. Shelter, lack of physical or mental abuse, low-crime environment

2. Safety

1. Air, water, food

1. Physiological

Low

A satisfied need is no longer a motivator!

FIGURE 6-6 Maslow's hierarchy of needs

The bottom four needs in Maslow's hierarchy—physiological, safety, social, and esteem needs—are referred to as deficiency needs, and the highest level, self-actualization, is considered a growth need. Only after meeting deficiency needs can individuals act on growth needs. Self-actualized people are problem-focused, have an appreciation for life, are concerned about personal growth, and can have peak experiences.

Most people working on corporate projects probably have their basic physiological and safety needs met. If someone has a sudden medical emergency or is laid off from work, however, physiological and safety needs move to the forefront. To motivate project team members, the project manager needs to understand each person's motivation, especially with regard to social, esteem, and self-actualization needs. For example, team members new to a company and city might be motivated by social needs. To address social needs, a project manager could organize gatherings and social events for new workers. If a project manager knew a team member was interested in pursing an advanced degree, he or she could offer suggestions on graduate programs, provide information on tuition reimbursement policies, and allow the team member some scheduling flexibility to balance work and school.

Maslow's hierarchy conveys a message of hope and growth. People can work to control their own destinies and naturally strive to achieve higher and higher needs. Some cultures disagree with Maslow's philosophy and have other beliefs on motivation. Recent brain research also suggests that there are physiological reasons for certain behaviors. In any case, successful project managers know that to provide appropriate motivation and maximize team performance, they must both meet project goals and understand team members' personal goals and needs.

Herzberg's Motivation-Hygiene Theory

Frederick Herzberg is best known for distinguishing between motivational factors and hygiene factors when considering motivation in work settings. He called factors that cause job satisfaction motivators, and factors that cause dissatisfaction hygiene factors. A hygiene factor is a basic necessity, such as air-conditioning during hot weather. Air-conditioning does not in itself provide team satisfaction, but without it you would have disgruntled staff on hot workdays.

Head of Case Western University's psychology department, Herzberg wrote the book *Work and the Nature of Man* in 1966 and the famous *Harvard Business Review* article "One More Time: How Do You Motivate Employees?" in 1968. Herzberg analyzed the factors that affected productivity among a sample of 1,685 employees. Popular beliefs at that time were that work output was most improved through larger salaries, more supervision, or a more attractive work environment. According to Herzberg, these hygiene factors would cause dissatisfaction if not present but would not motivate workers to do more if present. Herzberg found that people were motivated to work mainly by feelings of personal achievement and recognition. Motivators, Herzberg concluded, included achievement, recognition, the work itself, responsibility, advancement, and growth.

In his books and articles, Herzberg explained why attempts to use positive factors such as reducing time spent at work, implementing upward-spiraling wages, offering fringe benefits, providing human relations and sensitivity training, and so on did not instill motivation. He argued that people want to actualize themselves; they need stimuli for their growth and advancement needs in accordance with Maslow's hierarchy of needs. Factors such as achievement, recognition, responsibility, advancement, and growth produce job satisfaction and are work motivators.

McClelland's Acquired-Needs Theory

David McClelland proposed that an individual's specific needs are acquired or learned over time and shaped by life experiences. The main categories of acquired needs include achievement, affiliation, and power. Normally, one or two of these needs is dominant in individuals.

- *Achievement*: People with a high need for achievement (nAch) seek to excel and tend to avoid both low-risk and high-risk situations to improve their chances of achieving something worthwhile. Achievers need regular feedback and often prefer to work alone or with other high achievers. Managers should give high achievers challenging projects with achievable goals. Achievers should receive frequent performance feedback, and although money is not an important motivator to them, it is an effective form of feedback.
- *Affiliation*: People with a high need for affiliation (nAff) desire harmonious relationships with other people and need to feel accepted by others. They tend to conform to the norms of their work group and prefer work that involves significant personal interaction. Managers should try to create a cooperative work environment to meet the needs of people with a high need for affiliation.
- *Power*: People with a need for power (nPow) desire either personal power or institutional power. People who need personal power want to direct others and can be seen as bossy. People who need institutional, or social, power want to

organize others to further the goals of the organization. Management should provide those seeking institutional power with the opportunity to manage others, emphasizing the importance of meeting organizational goals.

The Thematic Apperception Test (TAT) is a tool to measure the individual needs of different people using McClelland's categories. The TAT presents subjects with a series of ambiguous pictures and asks them to develop a spontaneous story for each picture, assuming they will project their own needs into the story. Consult books or Web sites on this test for further information.

McGregor's Theory X and Theory Y

Douglas McGregor was one of the great popularizers of a human relations approach to management, and he is best known for developing Theory X and Theory Y. In his research, documented in his 1960 book *The Human Side of Enterprise,* McGregor found that although many managers spouted the right ideas, they actually followed a set of assumptions about worker motivation that he called Theory X (sometimes referred to as classical systems theory). People who believe in Theory X assume that workers dislike and avoid work if possible, so managers must use coercion, threats, and various control schemes to get workers to make adequate efforts to meet objectives. Theory X managers assume that the average worker wants to be directed and prefers to avoid responsibility, has little ambition, and wants security above all else. When research seemed to demonstrate that these assumptions were not valid, McGregor suggested a different series of assumptions about human behavior that he called Theory Y (sometimes referred to as human relations theory). Managers who believe in Theory Y assume that individuals do not inherently dislike work but consider it as natural as play or rest. The most significant rewards are the satisfaction of esteem and self-actualization needs, as described by Maslow. McGregor urged managers to motivate people based on these more valid Theory Y notions.

Thamhain and Wilemon's Influence Bases

Many people working on a project do not report directly to project managers, and project managers often do not have control over project staff that report to them. For example, people are free to change jobs. If they are given work assignments they do not like, many workers will simply quit or transfer to other departments or projects. H. J. Thamhain and D. L. Wilemon investigated the approaches project managers use to deal with workers and how those approaches relate to project success. They identified nine influence bases available to project managers:

1. *Authority:* The legitimate hierarchical right to issue orders
2. *Assignment:* The project manager's perceived ability to influence a worker's assignment to future projects
3. *Budget:* The project manager's perceived ability to authorize the use of discretionary funds
4. *Promotion:* The ability to improve a worker's position
5. *Money:* The ability to increase a worker's pay and benefits
6. *Penalty:* The project manager's perceived ability to dispense or cause punishment

7. *Work challenge:* The ability to assign work that capitalizes on a worker's enjoyment of doing a particular task, which taps an intrinsic motivational factor
8. *Expertise:* The project manager's perceived specialized knowledge that others deem important
9. *Friendship:* The ability to establish friendly personal relationships between the project manager and others

Top management grants authority to the project manager, but not necessarily the power to control personnel assignments, budgets, promotions, and penalties. Team members, however, may misperceive their project manager's sphere of influence and expect him to have the power, for example, to grant promotions and transfers. If project managers' power is limited, they can still influence workers by providing challenging work, and they can increase the power of their influence by using expertise and friendship.

Thamhain and Wilemon found that projects were more likely to fail when project managers relied too heavily on using *authority, money, or penalty* to influence people. When project managers used *work challenge and expertise* to influence people, projects were more likely to succeed. The effectiveness of work challenge in influencing people is consistent with Maslow's and Herzberg's research on motivation. The importance of expertise as a means of influencing people makes sense on projects that involve special knowledge. For example, people working on a project to build a spaceship would expect the project manager to have appropriate education and experience in that area. They would also be impressed if he or she had actually worked on other space projects or traveled into space.

Covey's Effectiveness Research

Stephen Covey, author of *The 7 Habits of Highly Effective People* and several other books, expanded on the work done by Maslow, Herzberg, and others to develop an approach for helping people and teams become more effective. Covey's first three habits of effective people—be proactive, begin with the end in mind, and put first things first—help people achieve a private victory by becoming independent. After achieving independence, people can then strive for interdependence by developing the next three habits—think win/win; seek first to understand, then to be understood; and synergize. (**Synergy** is the concept that the whole is equal to more than the sum of its parts.) Finally, everyone can work on Covey's seventh habit—sharpen the saw—to develop and renew their physical, spiritual, mental, and social/emotional selves.

Project managers can apply Covey's seven habits to improve effectiveness on projects, as follows:

1. *Be proactive:* Covey, like Maslow, believes that people have the ability to be proactive and choose their responses to different situations. Project managers must be proactive, anticipate, and plan for problems and inevitable changes on projects. They can also encourage team members to be proactive in their work.
2. *Begin with the end in mind:* Covey suggests that people focus on their values, what they really want to accomplish, and how they really want to be remembered in their lives. He suggests writing a mission statement to help achieve this habit. Many organizations and projects have mission statements that help them focus on their main purpose.

3. *Put first things first:* Covey developed a time-management system and matrix to help people prioritize their time. He suggests that most people need to spend more time doing things that are important but not urgent. Important but not urgent activities include planning, reading, and exercising. Project managers should focus on important and not urgent activities, such as developing various project plans, building relationships with major project stakeholders, and mentoring project team members. They also need to avoid focusing only on important and urgent activities—that is, putting out fires.

4. *Think win/win:* Covey presents several paradigms of interdependence, with "think win/win" being the best choice in most situations. When you use a win/win paradigm, parties in potential conflict work together to develop new solutions that make them all winners. Project managers should strive to use a win/win approach in making decisions, but sometimes, especially in competitive situations, they must use a win/lose paradigm.

5. *Seek first to understand, then to be understood:* **Empathic listening** is listening with the intent to understand by putting yourself in the shoes of the other person. You forget your personal interests and focus on truly understanding the other person and feeling what he or she is feeling. To really understand other people, you must learn to focus on others first. When you practice empathic listening, you can begin two-way communication. Making empathic listening a habit enables project managers to fully understand their stakeholders' needs and expectations.

6. *Synergize:* In projects, a project team can synergize by creating collaborative products that are much better than a collection of individual efforts. For example, engineers helped the crew of the *Apollo 13* return to Earth safely by working together to develop a solution to their potentially deadly technical problems. One person came up with an idea, which prompted another person to have an idea, and so on. The team devised a solution that no one person could have discovered. Covey also emphasizes the importance of valuing differences in others to achieve synergy. Synergy is essential to many complex projects; in fact, several major breakthroughs in technology, such as manned flight, drug development, and various computer technologies, occurred because of synergy.

7. *Sharpen the saw:* When you practice sharpening the saw, you take time to renew yourself physically, spiritually, mentally, and socially. The practice of self-renewal helps people avoid burnout. Project managers must make sure that they themselves and their project team have time to retrain, reenergize, and occasionally even relax to avoid burnout.

Several experts suggest that empathic listening is a powerful skill for project managers and their teams to possess. Understanding what motivates key stakeholders and customers can mean the difference between project success and project failure. After project managers and team members begin to practice empathic listening, they can communicate and work together to tackle problems more effectively.

Before you can practice empathic listening, you first have to get people to talk to you. In many cases, you must work on developing a rapport with other people before they will really open up to you. **Rapport** is a relationship of harmony, conformity, accord, or affinity. Without rapport, people cannot begin to communicate, or the strong person might dominate the weaker one. For example, if you meet someone for the first time and find that you cannot communicate, you need to focus on developing rapport.

One technique for establishing rapport is using a process called mirroring. **Mirroring** is the matching of certain behaviors of the other person. Although establishing rapport involves a number of complex human interactions, the simple technique of mirroring can sometimes help. You can mirror someone's voice tone and/or tempo, breathing, movements, or body postures. For example, when Kristin was negotiating with suppliers, she found that some of them were very abrupt, while she was fairly laid back. Kristin would use mirroring by matching the supplier's posture or voice tone to develop rapport and a strong negotiating position. In fact, mirroring was one of the skills emphasized in the negotiations course the Just-In-Time Training project team was developing.

☑ WHAT WENT RIGHT?

A young business consultant who worked in the IT department of a major aerospace firm met with a senior project manager and his core team. The project involved providing updated electronic kits for a major aircraft program. The company was losing money on the project because the upgrade kits were not being delivered on time. Most buyers had written severe late-penalty fees into their contracts, and other customers were threatening to take their business elsewhere. The project manager blamed it all on the IT department for not letting his staff access the information system directly to track the status of kit development and delivery. The tracking system was old and difficult to use. The business consultant was warned that this project manager was very difficult to work with. When the project manager entered the meeting room with three of his staff, all older men, he threw his books on the table and started yelling at the young consultant and her even younger assistant. Instead of backing down, the consultant mirrored the project manager's behavior and started yelling right back at him. He stood back, paused, and said, "You're the first person who's had the guts to stand up to me. I like that!" After that brief introduction, rapport was established, and everyone began communicating and working together as a team to solve the problem at hand.

You should, of course, take the message of the What Went Right? episode with a grain of salt. Few circumstances merit or benefit from yelling matches, but once in a while they cut through the tangle of human complexities. (The story is completely true; the author of this book, who very rarely yells at anyone, was the business consultant and had just completed a weeklong course on communications skills.)

You can see from the material covered in this chapter so far that many important topics related to motivation, influence, and effectiveness are relevant to project management. Projects are done by and for people, so it is important for project managers and team members to understand and practice key concepts related to these topics. Kristin must keep these topics in mind and use her knowledge and skills to successfully execute the project.

Acquiring the Project Team and Making Staffing Updates

There's a saying that the project manager who is the smartest person on the team has done a poor job of recruiting. After developing a staffing management plan during project planning, project managers must work with other managers in their organizations to assign personnel to their project or to acquire additional human resources needed to staff their project. Project managers with strong influencing and negotiating skills are often good at getting internal people to work on their project. However, the organization must ensure that people assigned to the project best fit the organization's requirements, and that these people are motivated to remain on the project.

Several organizations, publications, and Web sites address the need for good staff acquisition and retention. William C. Taylor, cofounder of *Fast Company* magazine and a public speaker, also believes that people today are more demanding and have higher expectations of their jobs than just earning a paycheck. His company's research has found that the top three reasons people leave their jobs (by choice) are because:

1. They feel they do not make a difference.
2. They do not get proper recognition.
3. They are not learning anything new or growing as a person.

 BEST PRACTICE

Best practices can also be applied to include the best places for people to work. For example, Fortune Magazine lists the "100 Best Companies to Work For" in the United States every year. Working Mothers Magazine lists the best companies in the U.S. for women based on benefits for working families. The Timesonline (*www.timesonline.co.uk*) provides the Sunday Times list of the 100 Best Companies to Work For, a key benchmark against which UK companies can judge their performance as employers. The Great Place to Work Institute, which produces Fortune's "100 Best Companies to Work For," uses the same selection methodology for more than 20 international lists, including "Best Companies to Work For" lists in all 15 countries of the European Union, Brazil, Korea, and a number of other countries throughout Latin America and Asia. Companies make these lists based on feedback from their best critics: their own employees. Quotes from employees often show why certain companies made the lists:

- "It is a friendly, courteous, caring hospital. We generally care about our co-workers and our patients. I can always get the help and support that I need to function in this hospital. This goes from the top all the way down to the cleaning people."
- "This is the best place I have ever worked. There's an open door policy. Every one is allowed to voice their opinion."
- "I get information about everything—profits, losses, problems. Relationships with people are easier here. It's more direct and open."[2]

Resource Loading and Leveling

Once people are assigned to projects, there are two techniques available to project managers that help them use project staff most effectively: resource loading and resource leveling. **Resource loading** refers to the amount of individual resources an existing schedule requires during specific time periods. Resource loading helps project managers develop a general understanding of the demands a project will make on the organization's resources, as well as on individual people's schedules. Project managers often use resource histograms, as described in Chapter 5, to depict period-by-period variations in resource loading. A histogram can be very helpful in determining staffing needs or in identifying staffing problems.

A resource histogram can also show when work is being overallocated to a certain person or group. **Overallocation** means more resources than are available are assigned to perform work at a given time. For example, Figure 6-7 provides a sample resource histogram created in Microsoft Project. It was actually one of the template files Microsoft used to provide with the software. This histogram illustrates how much one individual, Joe Franklin, is assigned to work on the project each week. The percentage numbers on the vertical axis represent the percentage of Joe's available time that is allocated for him to work on the project. The top horizontal axis represents time in weeks. Note that Joe Franklin is overallocated most of the time. For example, for most of March and April and part of May, Joe's work allocation is 300 percent of his available time. If Joe is normally available eight hours per day, this means he would have to work 24 hours a day to meet this staffing projection! Many people don't use the resource assignment features of project management software properly. See Appendix A for detailed information on using Project 2007.

Resource leveling is a technique for resolving resource conflicts by delaying tasks. It is a form of network analysis in which resource management concerns drive scheduling decisions (start and finish dates). The main purpose of resource leveling is to create a smoother distribution of resource usage. Project managers examine the network diagram for areas of slack or float, and to identify resource conflicts. For example, you can sometimes remove overallocations by delaying noncritical tasks, which does not result in an overall schedule delay. Other times you will need to delay the project completion date to reduce or remove overallocations. See Appendix A for information on using Project 2007 to level resources using both of these approaches. Overallocation is one type of resource conflict. If a certain resource is overallocated, the project manager can change the schedule to remove resource overallocation. If a certain resource is underallocated, the project manager can change the schedule to try to improve the use of the resource. Resource leveling, therefore, aims to minimize period-by-period variations in resource loading by shifting tasks within their slack allowances.

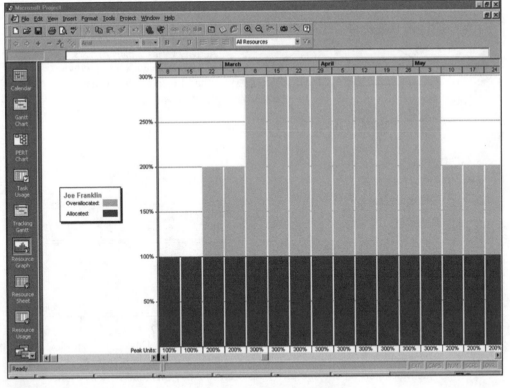

FIGURE 6-7 Sample histogram showing an overallocated individual

Figure 6-8 illustrates a simple example of resource leveling. The network diagram at the top of this figure shows that Activities A, B, and C can all start at the same time. Activity A has a duration of two days and will take two people to complete; Activity B has a duration of five days and will take four people to complete; and Activity C has a duration of three days and will take two people to complete. The histogram on the lower-left of this figure shows the resource usage if all activities start on day one. The histogram on the lower right of Figure 6-8 shows the resource usage if Activity C is delayed two days, its total slack allowance. Notice that the lower-right histogram is flat or leveled; that is, its pieces (activities) are arranged to take up the least space (lowering the highest number of workers needed). You may recognize this strategy from the computer game Tetris, in which you earn points for keeping the falling shapes as level as possible. The player with the most points (most level shape allocation) wins.

Resource leveling has several benefits:

1. When resources are used on a more constant basis, they require less management. For example, it is much easier to manage a part-time project member who is scheduled to work 20 hours per week on a project for the next three months than it is to manage the same person who is scheduled to work 10 hours one week, 40 the next, 5 the next, and so on.

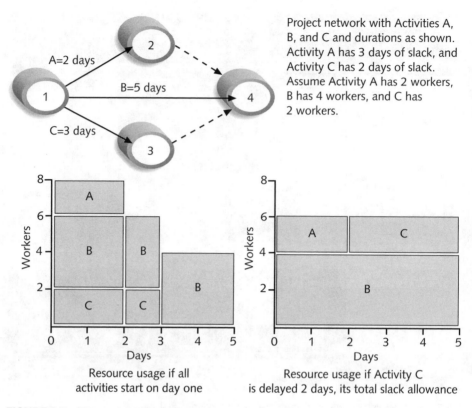

Project network with Activities A, B, and C and durations as shown. Activity A has 3 days of slack, and Activity C has 2 days of slack. Assume Activity A has 2 workers, B has 4 workers, and C has 2 workers.

Resource usage if all activities start on day one

Resource usage if Activity C is delayed 2 days, its total slack allowance

FIGURE 6-8   Resource leveling example

2. Resource leveling may enable project managers to use a just-in-time inventory type of policy for using subcontractors or other expensive resources. For example, a project manager might want to level resources related to work that must be done by particular subcontractors such as testing consultants. This leveling might allow the project to use four outside consultants full-time to do testing for four months instead of spreading the work out over more time or needing to use more than four people. The latter approach is usually more expensive.

3. Resource leveling results in fewer problems for project personnel and accounting departments. Increasing and decreasing labor levels and particular human resources often produce additional work and confusion. For example, if a person with expertise in a particular area is only assigned to a project two days a week and another person they need to work with is not assigned to the project those same days, they cannot work well together. The Accounting department might complain when subcontractors charge a higher rate for billing less than 20 hours a week on a project. The accountants will remind project managers to strive for getting the lowest rates possible.

4. Resource leveling often improves morale. People like to have some stability in their jobs. It is very stressful for people not to know from week to week or even day to day what projects they will be working on and with whom they will be working.

Sample Staffing Updates

Kristin worked with managers in the human resource department and other managers to staff the internal project team members for the Just-In-Time Training project. She also made staffing changes, such as replacing Jamie, the supplier management expert assigned to the team. Although Jamie had great qualifications, she was not a good fit for the project. Jamie needed a break after coming off of a big project, and she did not feel that she would personally enjoy working on the Just-In-Time Training project. Kristin updated the project staff by replacing Jamie with Abner. Kristin was also involved with other staffing updates as people joined and left the project team.

To keep everyone up to date on current project staffing assignments, Kristin provided a current team roster on the project Web site, including team member names, roles, and contact information. As suppliers were added to the project, she included supplier staff information as well. Figure 6-9 provides a sample of part of the team roster for the Just-In-Time Training project.

<table>
<tr><td colspan="6" align="center">**Team Roster**

September 1, 2009</td></tr>
<tr><th>Name</th><th>Role on Project</th><th>Position</th><th>E-Mail</th><th>Phone</th><th>Location</th></tr>
<tr><td>Mike Sundby</td><td>Project Champion</td><td>VP of HR</td><td>mike_sundby@ globalconstruction.com</td><td></td><td></td></tr>
<tr><td>Lucy Camarena</td><td>Project Sponsor</td><td>Training Director</td><td>lucy_camarena@ globalconstruction.com</td><td></td><td></td></tr>
<tr><td>Kristin Maur</td><td>Project Manager</td><td>Project Manager</td><td>kristin_maur@ globalconstruction.com</td><td></td><td></td></tr>
<tr><td>Mohamed Abdul</td><td>Team Member</td><td>Senior Programmer/Analyst</td><td>mohamed_abdul@ globalconstruction.com</td><td></td><td></td></tr>
<tr><td>Kim Johnson</td><td>Team Member</td><td>Curriculum Designer</td><td>kim_johnson@ globalconstruction.com</td><td></td><td></td></tr>
<tr><td>Abner Tomass</td><td>Team Member</td><td>Supplier Management Expert</td><td>abner_tomass@ globalconstruction.com</td><td></td><td></td></tr>
</table>

FIGURE 6-9 Sample team roster

Developing the Project Team and Assessing Team Performance

Even if a project manager has successfully recruited enough skilled people to work on a project, he or she must ensure that people can work together as a team to achieve project goals. Many failed projects have been staffed by highly talented individuals; however, it takes teamwork to complete projects successfully. The main goal of team development is to help people work together more effectively to improve project performance.

Dr. Bruce Tuckman published his four-stage model of team development in 1965 and modified it to include an additional stage in the 1970s. The **Tuckman model** describes five stages of team development:

1. *Forming* involves the introduction of team members, either at the initiation of the team or as new members are introduced. This stage is necessary, but little work is actually achieved.
2. *Storming* occurs as team members have different opinions as to how the team should operate. People test each other, and there is often conflict within the team.
3. *Norming* is achieved when team members have developed a common working method, and cooperation and collaboration replace the conflict and mistrust of the previous phase.
4. *Performing* occurs when the emphasis shifts to reaching the team goals rather than working on team process. Relationships are settled, and team members are likely to build loyalty toward each other. At this stage, the team is able to manage tasks that are more complex and cope with greater change. Note that not all teams are able to progress through the team development stages to reach the performance level.
5. *Adjourning* involves the breakup of the team after they successfully reach their goals and complete the work. Teams might also adjourn due to poor performance or project cancellation.

There is an extensive body of literature on team development. This section highlights a few important tools and techniques for team development, including training, team-building activities, and reward and recognition systems. Keep in mind that having teams focus on completing specific tasks is often the most effective way to help teams be productive.

Training

Project managers often recommend that people take specific training courses to improve individual and team development. For example, Kristin recommended that Mohamed, the IT member of her project team, take training courses in designing e-learning courses so that he could contribute even more to this project. Early in the project, she also organized a special team-building session for her internal project team. In addition to traditional, instructor-led training, many organizations provide e-learning opportunities for their employees so that they can learn specific skills at any time and any place, similar to several of the courses being developed for the Just-In-Time Training project. It is important to make sure that the timing and delivery methods for the training are appropriate for specific situations and individuals.

Team-Building Activities

Many organizations provide in-house team-building training activities, and many also use specialized services provided by external companies that specialize in this area. Two common approaches to team-building activities include using physical challenges and psychological preference indicator tools.

Sometimes, organizations have teams of people go through certain physically challenging activities to help them develop as a team. Military basic training or boot camps provide one example. Men and women who want to join the military must first make it through basic training, which often involves several strenuous physical activities such as rappelling off towers, running and marching in full military gear, going through obstacle courses, passing marksmanship training, and mastering survival training. Many non-military organizations use a similar approach by sending teams of people to special locations, where they work as a team to navigate white-water rapids, climb mountains or rocks, participate in ropes courses, and so on.

More often, organizations have teams participate in mental team-building activities in which they learn about themselves, about each other, and how to work as a group most effectively. It is important for people to understand and value each other's differences to work effectively as a team. Two common tools used in mental team building include the Myers-Briggs Type Indicator and the Wilson Learning Social Styles Profile. Effective teams include a variety of personalities. The main purpose of these tools is to help people understand each other and learn to adjust their personal communication styles to work well as a team.

The **Myers-Briggs Type Indicator (MBTI)** is a popular tool for determining personality preferences. During World War II, Isabel B. Myers and Katherine C. Briggs developed the first version of the MBTI based on psychologist Carl Jung's theory of psychological type. The four dimensions of psychological type in the MBTI are as follows:

1. *Extrovert/Introvert (E/I):* This first dimension determines if you are generally extroverted or introverted. The dimension also signifies whether people draw their energy from other people (extroverts) or from inside themselves (introverts). About 75 percent of people in the general population are extroverts.

2. *Sensation/Intuition (S/N):* This second dimension relates to the manner in which you gather information. Sensation (or Sensing) type people take in facts, details, and reality and describe themselves as practical. Intuitive type people are imaginative, ingenious, and attentive to hunches or intuition. They describe themselves as innovative and conceptual. About 75 percent of people in the general population have a preference for sensation.

3. *Thinking/Feeling (T/F):* This third dimension represents thinking judgment and feeling judgment. Thinking judgment is objective and logical, and feeling judgment is subjective and personal. The general population is generally split evenly between these two preferences.

4. *Judgment/Perception (J/P):* This fourth dimension concerns people's attitude toward structure. Judgment type people like closure and task completion. They tend to establish deadlines and take them seriously, expecting others to do the same. Perceiving types prefer to keep things open and flexible. They regard deadlines more as a signal to start rather than complete a project and do not feel that work must be done before play or rest begins. People are generally split evenly between these two preferences.

There are 16 MBTI categories based on combinations of the four dimensions. For example, one MBTI category is ESTJ, another is INFP, and another is ENTP. Project managers can often benefit from knowing their team members' MBTI profiles by adjusting their management styles for each individual. For example, if the project manager is a strong N and one of the team members is a strong S, the project manager should take the time to provide more concrete, detailed explanations when discussing that person's task assignments. Project managers might also want to make sure that they have a variety of personality types on their team. For example, if all team members are strong introverts, it might be difficult for them to work well with other stakeholders who are often extroverts.

Many organizations use Wilson Learning's Social Styles Profile in team-building activities. Psychologist David Merril, who helped develop the Social Skills Profile, categorizes four approximate behavioral profiles, or zones. People are perceived as behaving primarily in one of four zones, based on their assertiveness and responsiveness:

- "Drivers" are proactive and task oriented. They are firmly rooted in the present, and they strive for action. Adjectives to describe drivers include pushy, severe, tough, dominating, harsh, strong-willed, independent, practical, decisive, and efficient.
- "Expressives" are proactive and people oriented. They are future oriented and use their intuition to look for fresh perspectives on the world around them. Adjectives to describe expressives include manipulating, excitable, undisciplined, reacting, egotistical, ambitious, stimulating, wacky, enthusiastic, dramatic, and friendly.
- "Analyticals" are reactive and task oriented. They are past oriented and strong thinkers. Adjectives to describe analyticals include critical, indecisive, stuffy, picky, moralistic, industrious, persistent, serious, expecting, and orderly.
- "Amiables" are reactive and people oriented. Their time orientation varies depending on whom they are with at the time, and they strongly value relationships. Adjectives to describe amiables include conforming, unsure, ingratiating, dependent, awkward, supportive, respectful, willing, dependable, and agreeable.

Figure 6-10 shows these four social styles and how they relate to assertiveness and responsiveness. Note that the main determinants of the social style are levels of assertiveness—if you are more likely to tell people what to do or ask what should be done—and how you respond to tasks—by focusing on the task itself or on the people involved in performing the task. For example, a driver is assertive in telling other people what to do and focuses on completing tasks. An amiable prefers to ask others what to do and focuses on pleasing people versus completing tasks.

Knowing the social styles of project stakeholders can help project managers understand why certain people may have problems working together. For example, drivers are often very impatient working with amiables, and analyticals often have difficulties understanding expressives. Project managers can use their facilitation skills to help all types of people communicate better with each other and focus on meeting project goals.

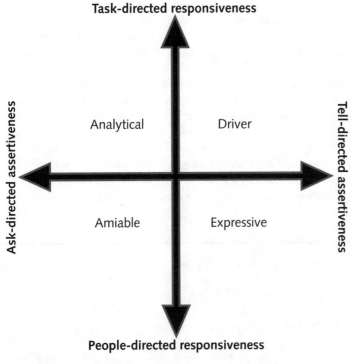

Task-directed responsiveness

Analytical   Driver

Ask-directed assertiveness   Tell-directed assertiveness

Amiable   Expressive

People-directed responsiveness

FIGURE 6-10   Social styles of Wilson Learning

Reward and Recognition Systems

Another important tool for promoting team development is the use of team-based reward and recognition systems. If management rewards teamwork, it promotes or reinforces people to work more effectively in teams. Some organizations offer bonuses, trips, or other rewards to workers who meet or exceed company or project goals. In a project setting, project managers can recognize and reward people who willingly work overtime to meet an aggressive schedule objective or go out of their way to help a teammate. If teamwork is the essential goal, project managers should not reward people who work overtime just to get extra pay or because of their own poor work or planning. They should, however, recognize individuals who volunteer to put in additional time to meet a deadline or show other exemplary behavior.

Project managers must continually assess their team's performance. When they identify weaknesses in individuals or in the entire team, it's their job to find the best way to develop their people and improve performance.

Sample Team Performance Assessment

Project managers assess team performance in several different ways. As mentioned earlier, Kristin believed in management by wandering around, and she liked to have many short, informal discussions with various stakeholders, especially her project team members. She also observed them working alone and as a team, and assessed the quality of deliverables they produced. Kristin and other project managers at Global Construction also filled out performance appraisals for each team member once a year or when a project was completed. These performance appraisals can be addressed in the team contract during project planning or discussed in early team meetings.

Kristin also felt that it was important for people to assess their own performance and the performance of their teammates. She talked to each team member individually and the team as a group about this assessment because she knew that some people felt uncomfortable evaluating themselves or other people. She stressed that she had successfully used this approach in the past, and she would keep the information confidential. Her main goal was to help everyone work well together on the project. Figure 6-11 is a sample of an informal questionnaire that Kristin periodically asked her project team members to fill out to assist in performance assessment. Kristin would discuss each person's assessment and take corrective actions as needed.

Team Performance Assessment

August 1, 2009

Project Name: Just-In-Time Training Project
Individual Name: _____   **Project Manager:** Kristin Maur
Team Member Name: _____
Date: _____

1. Using a scale of 0-100, assess how you think **the project team** is performing: _____
2. Explain the rationale behind the above score.

3. Using a scale of 0-100, assess how you think **you** are performing on this project: _____
4. Explain the rationale behind the above score. What are your roles and responsibilities, and how well have you performed them?

5. Briefly assess each team member's performance. If you had to give each person a score between 0-100, what would it be?

6. To compare individual contributions, if you had 100 points to allocate to your team, how would you allocate them?

7. What suggestions do you have for improving team performance?

FIGURE 6-11 Sample team performance assessment

EXECUTING TASKS FOR PROJECT COMMUNICATIONS MANAGEMENT

Good communications management is also crucial to project execution. Information distribution is the main communications management task performed during project execution. The main output of this task is updating business processes.

Important Project Communications Concepts

Some project managers say that 90 percent of their job is communicating. Therefore, it is important to address important concepts related to improving project communications. Key concepts include formal and informal communications, nonverbal communications, using the appropriate communications medium, understanding individual and group communication needs, and the impact of team size on project communications.

Formal and Informal Communications

It is not enough for project team members to submit formal status reports to their project managers and other stakeholders and assume that everyone who needs to know that information will read the reports. In fact, many people may prefer to have a two-way conversation about project information rather than reading detailed reports, e-mails, or Web pages to try to find pertinent information. These people may want to know the people working on their projects and develop a trusting relationship with them, and so they use informal discussions about the project to develop these relationships. Therefore, project managers must be good at nurturing relationships through good communication. Many experts believe that the difference between good project managers and excellent project managers is their ability to nurture relationships and use empathic listening skills, as described earlier.

Nonverbal Communications

People make or break projects, and people like to interact with each other to get a true feeling for how a project is going. Research poses the theory that in a face-to-face interaction, 58 percent of communication is through body language, 35 percent through how the words are said, and a mere 7 percent through the content or words that are spoken. The author of this information (see *Silent Messages* by Albert Mehrabian, 1980) was careful to note that these percentages were specific findings for a specific set of variables. Even if the actual percentages are different in verbal project communications today, it is safe to say that it is important to pay attention to more than just the actual words someone is saying. Nonverbal communications, such as a person's tone of voice and body language, are often more important than the words being used.

Using the Appropriate Communications Medium

Figure 6-12 provides guidelines from Practical Communications, Inc., a communications consulting firm, about how well different types of media—such as hard copy, phone calls, voice mail, e-mail, meetings, and Web sites—are suited to different communication needs. For example, if you were trying to assess commitment of project stakeholders, a meeting would be the most appropriate medium to use. A phone call would be adequate, but the other media would not be appropriate. Project managers must assess the needs of the organization, the project, and individuals in determining which communication medium to use, and when.

Additional media not included in this table include the use of Web logs or blogs, instant messaging, Webcasts, and live or delayed video. Global Construction was just starting to use several of these newer media.

KEY: 1 = EXCELLENT   2 = ADEQUATE   3 = INAPPROPRIATE

HOW WELL MEDIUM IS SUITED TO:	Hard Copy	Phone Call	Voice Mail	E-Mail	Meeting	Web Site
Assessing commitment	3	2	3	3	1	3
Building consensus	3	2	3	3	1	3
Mediating a conflict	3	2	3	3	1	3
Resolving a misunderstanding	3	1	3	3	2	3
Addressing negative behavior	3	2	3	2	1	3
Expressing support/appreciation	1	2	2	1	2	3
Encouraging creative thinking	2	3	3	1	3	3
Making an ironic statement	3	2	2	3	1	3
Conveying a reference document	1	3	3	3	3	2
Reinforcing one's authority	1	2	3	3	1	1
Providing a permanent record	1	3	3	1	3	3
Maintaining confidentiality	2	1	2	3	1	3
Conveying simple information	3	1	1	1	2	3
Asking an informational question	3	1	1	1	3	3
Making a simple request	3	1	1	1	3	3
Giving complex instructions	3	3	2	2	1	2
Addressing many people	2	3 or 1*	2	2	3	1

Galati, Tess. *Email Composition and Communication (EmC2)*. Practical Communications, Inc. (*www.praccom.com*) (2001).

*Depends on system functionality

FIGURE 6-12   Media choice table

MEDIA SNAPSHOT

Although most projects do not use live video as a medium for sending project information, the technology is becoming more available and less expensive. You can reach many people at once using live video, and viewers can see and hear important information.

For example, Microsoft had been experimenting with its new conferencing product, Livemeeting. Anoop Gupta, a vice president of Microsoft's real-time collaboration group, says that one in every five face-to-face meetings can be replaced with Web conferencing tools, and Microsoft estimates that it will save $70 million in reduced travel for organizations worldwide in one year alone.[3] Web-based meeting tools can also help the environment. For example, in May 2007, WebEx, the leading provider of on-demand web collaboration applications, kicked off the WebEx Experience Online Forum. They say they saved over one million pounds of carbon dioxide by not requiring the more than 650 attendees to travel to participate in sessions.[4]

However, any live communication broadcast can also backfire, especially if millions of people are watching. In fact, one event, Janet Jackson's "wardrobe malfunction" during the 2004 Super Bowl in the United States, had a major impact on the entire broadcasting industry, causing television and radio stations to use several second delays to prevent offensive video or audio from reaching the airwaves. Reuters reported on September 22, 2004, that the Federal Communications Commission had officially voted to fine each of the 20 stations owned by the CBS television network $27,500 for violating indecency rules. The fine was the maximum allowed by law at the time, and Congress is considering legislation to increase the fine to as much as $500,000 per incident.[5]

Understanding Individual and Group Communication Needs

Many top managers think they can remediate project delays simply by adding people to a project. Unfortunately, this approach often causes setbacks because of the increased complexity of communications. In his popular book *The Mythical Man-Month,* Frederick Brooks illustrates this concept very clearly. People are not interchangeable parts. You cannot assume that a task originally scheduled to take two months of one person's time can be done in one month by two people. A popular analogy is that you cannot take nine women and produce a baby in one month!

In addition to understanding that people are not interchangeable, it is also important to understand individuals' personal preferences for communications. People have different personality traits, which often affect their communication preferences. For example, if you want to praise a project team member for doing a good job, an introvert might be more comfortable receiving that praise in private, whereas an extrovert might like everyone to hear about his or her good work. An intuitive person might want to understand how something fits into the big picture, whereas a sensing person might prefer to have more focused, step-by-step details. A strong thinker might want to know the logic behind information, whereas a feeling person might want to know how the information affects him or her personally, as well as other people. Someone who is a judging person might be very driven to meet deadlines with few reminders, whereas a perceiving person might need more assistance in developing and following plans.

Geographic location and cultural backgrounds also add to the complexity of project communications. For example, if project stakeholders are in different countries, it is often difficult or impossible to schedule times for two-way communication during normal working hours. Language barriers can also cause communication problems—for example, the same word may have very different meanings in different languages. Times, dates, and other units of measure are also interpreted differently. People from some cultures also prefer to communicate in ways that may be uncomfortable to others. For example, managers in some countries still do not allow workers of lower ranks or women to give formal presentations.

The Impact of Team Size on Project Communications

Another important aspect of information distribution is the number of people involved in a project. As the number of people involved increases, the complexity of communications increases because there are more communications channels, or pathways, through which people can communicate. The number of communications channels in relation to the number of people involved can be calculated as follows:

$$\text{number of communications channels} = \frac{n(n-1)}{2}$$

where n is the number of people involved.

For example, two people have one communications channel: $(2(2-1))/2 = 1$. Three people have three channels: $(3(3-1))/2 = 3$. Four people have six channels, five people have 10, and so on. You can see that as the number of people communicating increases, the number of communications channels increases rapidly. The lesson is a simple one: If you want to enhance communications, you must consider the interactions among different project team members and stakeholders. It is often helpful to form several smaller teams within a large project team to help improve project communications.

As you can see, information distribution involves more than creating and sending status reports or holding periodic meetings. Many good project managers know their personal strengths and weaknesses in this area and surround themselves with people who complement their skills. It is good practice to share the responsibility for project communications management with the entire project team.

Information Distribution and Updating Business Processes

Getting project information to the right people at the right time and in a useful format is just as important as developing the information in the first place. The communications management plan prepared during project planning serves as a good starting point for information distribution. During execution, project teams must address important considerations for information distribution, as described previously. The main output of information distribution is updating business processes through improved communications.

Sample Updates to Business Processes

Organizations have many different organizational process assets to help them improve business processes. Examples of these assets include various policies and procedures, guidelines, information systems, financial systems, management systems, lessons learned, and historical documents that help people understand, follow, and improve business processes.

As part of the Just-In-Time Training project, Kristin's team followed several existing business processes and provided new information to update some of them. For example, they used several communications media already well established at Global Construction, such as e-mail and project Web sites. Kristin's team also used several new technologies to enhance project communications and processes. Examples of these updated business processes include the following:

- Kristin and her team used instant messaging on a regular basis both within their team and with suppliers. Several of the people working on the project were in various parts of the world, so they found it very useful to use instant messaging.
- Several suppliers used Webcasts to communicate information in a more dynamic way without incurring travel expenses. The Webcasts included visuals, such as PowerPoint slides, along with audio and animation to point to and write in key information. There were several other interactive features available in the Webcasts, such as polling the audience and letting other people add their audio input.
- The Web-based courses that suppliers were developing for the project included discussion threads and an "Ask the Expert" feature, in which learners could ask specific questions of the instructor or experts within the company on various topics related to the course. The questions and their answers were automatically added to a database that future learners could access.
- Kristin kept her own personal project blog to document important events and lessons she was learning while managing the project. She had used blogs for personal communications in the past, such as documenting her last trip to Europe, but she had never used one in a work setting before. She found it very useful for personal reflection and knew it would help her write her final lessons-learned document for the project.

The project steering committee—pleased and fascinated with the success of these new communications media—asked Kristin to prepare guidelines on using them that employees could access on the corporate intranet after the project was completed. Kristin was glad to do so.

EXECUTING TASKS FOR PROJECT PROCUREMENT MANAGEMENT

Many projects include work performed by outside sources. The main executing tasks performed as part of project procurement include requesting seller responses and selecting sellers. Key outputs include procurement document packages, contracts, and contract management plans.

Requesting Seller Responses, Qualified Sellers Lists, and Procurement Document Packages

After planning for contracting, the next procurement management process involves choosing suppliers (sellers), sending appropriate documentation to potential sellers, and obtaining proposals or bids. Prospective sellers do most of the work in this process by preparing their proposals and bids, normally at no cost to the buyer. The buying organization is responsible for deciding how to approach sellers and providing required procurement document packages. A procurement document package generally includes a summary letter, a request for proposal or quote, and a contract statement of work, as described in Chapter 5.

Organizations can use several different methods to approach and select qualified sellers or suppliers:

- *Approaching a preferred supplier:* Sometimes, a specific supplier might be the number-one choice for the buyer. In this case, the buyer gives procurement information to just that company. If the preferred supplier responds favorably, the organizations proceed to work together. Many organizations have formed good working relationships with certain suppliers, so they want to continue working with them.
- *Approaching several qualified suppliers:* In many cases, several suppliers could meet an organization's procurement needs. The buying organization can send procurement information to those potential sellers and then evaluate the results. If it does not get the desired response, the buyer can either expand its list of potential sellers until it gets the desired response or revise its procurement plans.
- *Advertising to many potential suppliers:* In many cases, several suppliers may be qualified to provide the goods and services, and the buyer may not know who they are in advance. Advertising the procurement (on a Web site, in a trade journal, or by other means) and receiving proposals and bids from multiple sources often takes advantage of the competitive business environment. Increased globalization and virtual project teams have increased tremendously as organizations find suitable sellers around the globe. As a result of pursuing a competitive bidding strategy, the buyer can receive better goods and services than expected at a lower price.

Sample Qualified Seller List

The Just-In-Time Training project required goods and services from several different suppliers. Recall that the project involved training in four different areas: supplier management, negotiating skills, project management, and software application. The training also had to be provided in various delivery formats—instructor-led, Web-based, and CD-ROM. Kristin and her team used their knowledge of current training suppliers and researched additional ones. They were not sure if they should have different suppliers for each course or have a different supplier based on each delivery method.

As described in Chapter 5, because Global Construction was new to the concept of just-in-time training, the company decided to hire a consulting firm that both specialized in just-in-time training and worked with all types of training suppliers. The consulting firm then developed a qualified sellers list containing 30 potential sellers, as provided in Figure 6-13. In addition to the list, the firm also provided a report with information on each seller, such as relevant products and services, backgrounds of senior management, and current customers. It also provided recommendations for developing partnerships with each seller. See Chapter 5 for the RFP and contract statement of work for this procurement.

Qualified Sellers List **September 9, 2009**			
Project Name: Just-In-Time Training Project			
Seller Name/ Web Site	**Areas of Expertise**	**Full-Time Staff**	**Reputation**
Company A *www.coA.com*	Construction industry, supplier management, project management	40	One of few training firms that specializes in training for the construction industry
Company B *www.coB.com*	E-learning, custom course development	100	Has many partnerships with other companies, reasonable prices
Company C *www.coC.com*	Project management, negotiating skills	10	Small firm but well respected; does instructor-led and e-learning
Etc.			

FIGURE 6-13   Sample qualified sellers list

Selecting Sellers and Writing Contracts

After buyers receive proposals or bids, they can select a supplier or decide to cancel the procurement. Selecting suppliers or sellers, often called source selection, involves evaluating proposals or bids from sellers, choosing the best one, negotiating the contract, and awarding the contract. Several stakeholders in the procurement process should be involved in selecting the best suppliers for the project. Often, teams of people are responsible for evaluating various sections of the proposals. There might be a technical team, a management team, and a cost team to focus on each of those major areas. Often, buyers develop a **short list** of the top three to five suppliers to reduce the work involved in selecting a source. Reviewers often follow a more detailed proposal evaluation process for sellers who make the short list, often checking their references, requesting special presentations, or having them provide sample products. Recall from Chapter 5 that a weighted scoring model is often used to help select sellers.

It is customary to conduct contract negotiations during the source selection process. Sellers on the short list are often asked to prepare a best and final offer (BAFO). Expert negotiators often conduct these negotiations, especially for contracts involving large amounts of money. In addition, senior managers from both buying and selling organizations often meet before making final decisions. The final output of the seller selection process is a contract. It is also appropriate on some projects to prepare a contract management plan to describe details about how the contract will be managed.

Sample Contract

As mentioned in Chapter 5, a contract is a mutually binding agreement that obligates the seller to provide the specified products or services, and obligates the buyer to pay for them. Chapter 5 also described the different types of contracts and provided sample clauses that can be included to address risks. The Just-In-Time Training project would include contracts with several different suppliers. Some might be short, fixed-price contracts, such as one for the consulting firm to develop a list of qualified sellers. Others might be much longer and involve fixed-price, cost-reimbursable, and unit-pricing aspects, such as a contract to develop and deliver several training courses in different formats.

Figure 6-14 provides a sample of part of a contract or service agreement, as some contracts are called, that could be used to produce a qualified sellers list. Note the reference to exhibit A, the statement of work. (A sample was provided in Chapter 5 and sent out to prospective sellers as part of the procurement package.) This document should be modified based on the selected seller's proposal. There is also a reference to a schedule for the work, which the seller also prepared as part of the proposal. It is good practice to include a detailed statement of work and schedule as part of the contract to clarify exactly what work the seller will perform and when.

```
┌─────────────────────────────────────────────────────────────────────┐
│                                                                       │
│                        Global Construction, Inc.                      │
│                           Service Agreement                           │
│                            August 10, 2009                            │
│                                                                       │
│   Title of Work: Qualified Sellers List and Report                    │
│                                                                       │
│   This is an Agreement made as of August 10, 2009 by ABC Training     │
│   Consultants, 2255 River Road, Boston, MA (the "Seller"), and Global │
│   Construction, Inc., 5000 Industrial Drive, Minneapolis, MN          │
│   (the "Buyer").                                                      │
│                                                                       │
│   THE SELLER AND THE BUYER AGREE THAT:                                │
│                                                                       │
│     1. The Work: The Seller will create the Work as set forth in      │
│        Exhibit A hereto. The Buyer will provide the Seller with the   │
│        format and specifications in which each element of the Work is │
│        to be submitted. The Seller agrees to conform to such format   │
│        and specifications.                                            │
│                                                                       │
│     2. Delivery of the Work: The Seller agrees to deliver to the      │
│        Buyer the Work in form and content acceptable to the Buyer on  │
│        or before the dates outlined in Exhibit B of this Agreement,   │
│        time being of the essence to the Buyer.                        │
│                                                                       │
│     3. Right to Terminate: If the Seller materially departs from the  │
│        agreed-upon schedule or if the Work is not satisfactory to the │
│        Buyer (based on reviews of drafts, market conditions, and/or   │
│        other criteria as determined by the Buyer), the Buyer may at   │
│        its option:                                                    │
│        A. Allow the Seller to finish, correct, or improve the Work by │
│           a date specified by the Buyer;                              │
│        B. Terminate this Agreement by giving written notice to the    │
│           Seller.                                                     │
│                                                                       │
│     4. Payments: The Buyer will pay the Seller a fixed price of       │
│        $5,000 upon accepted completion of the Work.                   │
│                                                                       │
│     5. Exhibit: The following Exhibit is hereby incorporated by       │
│        reference into this Agreement:                                 │
│        Exhibit A:  Statement of Work                                  │
│        Exhibit B:  Schedule                                           │
│                                                                       │
│   IN WITNESS WHEREOF, THE PARTIES HERETO HAVE EXECUTED THIS Agreement  │
│   as a sealed instrument as of the date first above written.          │
│                                                                       │
│      Global Construction, Inc.           ABC Training Consultants     │
│   By:  _____          _____      │
│   Date: _____         _____      │
│                                                                       │
└─────────────────────────────────────────────────────────────────────┘
```

FIGURE 6-14 Sample contract

CLOSING CASE

Kristin did her best to lead the team in executing the Just-In-Time Training project. Like most project managers, however, she faced several challenges. It was hard for Kristin to confront Jamie, a key project team member, about her poor performance. Kristin knew that it was best to address problems head on and come up with the best possible solution. Kristin and her team also had to determine how to address poor ratings for the prototype supplier management course. She was proud of the way they worked together to find the root cause of problems and take corrective actions. Understanding important quality, motivation, and communications concepts and using several tools and techniques helped ensure successful project execution.

Chapter Summary

Good execution is crucial to project success. Without it, the products, services, and results planned from the project cannot materialize. This chapter summarizes the executing tasks and key outputs for project integration, quality, human resource, communications, and procurement management.

Executing outputs related to integration management include deliverables, implemented solutions to problems, work performance information, and requested changes. Samples of these outputs are provided for the Just-In-Time Training project.

Executing outputs related to quality management include recommended corrective actions and project plan updates. Samples of these outputs are provided for the Just-In-Time Training project.

Executing outputs related to human resource management include staffing updates and team performance assessment. Samples of these outputs are provided for the Just-In-Time Training project. Project managers must also apply concepts related to motivation, influence, effectiveness, resource loading, and resource leveling to lead people during project execution.

Executing outputs related to communications management consist of business process updates. Samples of these outputs are provided for the Just-In-Time Training project. Project managers must apply important concepts related to communications, such as formal and informal communications, nonverbal communications, the appropriate communications medium, individual and group communication needs, and the impact of team size on project communications.

Executing outputs related to procurement management include procurement document packages and contracts. Samples of these outputs are provided for the Just-In-Time Training project.

Quick Quiz

1. *Fortune* magazine summarized research showing that the main reason CEOs failed was due to _____ .

   a. poor planning

   b. poor execution

   c. global competition

   d. low stock prices

2. Which of the following is not an example of a soft skill?

   a. leadership

   b. motivation

   c. team building

   d. financial analysis

3. Most project sponsors would say that the most important output of any project is _____ .

   a. a satisfied customer/sponsor

   b. good financial results

   c. its deliverables

   d. good plans

4. Which conflict handling mode do successful project managers use most often?

   a. confrontation

   b. compromise

   c. smoothing

   d. forcing

5. _____ includes all of the activities related to satisfying the relevant quality standards for a project.

   a. Quality assurance

   b. Quality control

   c. Customer satisfaction

   d. ISO certification

6. _____ diagrams can assist in ensuring and improving quality by finding the root causes of quality problems.

   a. Pareto

   b. Mind map

   c. Fishbone or Ishikawa

   d. Social styles

7. Which of the following statements is false?

   a. The highest need in Maslow's pyramid is called self-actualization.

   b. Most people today prefer managers who follow Theory X versus Theory Y.

   c. Herzberg distinguished between motivating and hygiene factors.

   d. Projects are more likely to succeed when project managers influence team members by using work challenge and expertise.

8. Some project managers like to assess team performance by using a technique known as MBWA, which stands for _____ .

   a. management by wondering aloud

   b. management by wandering around

   c. measuring by work areas

   d. measuring by watching alertly

9. If a project team goes from three people to six, how many more communications channels are there?

   a. 3

   b. 6

   c. 9

   d. 12

10. A procurement document package generally includes all of the following except
   _____ .

   a. a short list

   b. a summary letter

   c. a request for proposal or quote

   d. a contract statement of work

Quick Quiz Answers

1. B; 2. D; 3. C; 4. A; 5. A; 6. C; 7. B; 8. B; 9. D; 10. A

Discussion Questions

1. Describe practices that should be followed in directing and managing project execution. Why are deliverables such an important output of project execution? What are some of the typical problems that project teams face during project execution?

2. What is quality assurance, and how does it affect project execution? What are some examples of recommended corrective actions that Kristin made during project execution? Do you agree with her decisions? Why or why not?

3. Why is human resource management so important during project execution? How does Maslow's hierarchy of needs affect motivation? What are some examples of motivators and hygiene factors, according to Herzberg? What are the three main categories in McClelland's acquired-needs theory? What is the difference between Theory X and Theory Y? What are the five steps in Tuckman's team-building model? What are the advantages of resource leveling?

4. Why is communications management so important during project execution? What is the difference between formal and informal communications? Why are nonverbal communications so important? Why do communications become more complicated when team size increases?

5. What is involved in requesting seller responses and selecting sellers? How do project teams develop a list of qualified sellers? What are some of the main topics addressed in a contract or service agreement?

Exercises

1. Find an example of a large project that took more than a year to complete, such as a major construction project. You can ask people at your college, university, or work about a recent project, such as a major fund raising campaign, information systems installation, or building project. You can also find information about projects online such as the Big Dig in Boston (www.masspike.com/bigdig), the Patronas Twin Towers in Malaysia and many other building projects (www.greatbuildings.com), etc. Describe some of the tasks performed to execute the integration, quality, human resource, communications, and procurement aspects of the project. Write a one-page paper or prepare a short presentation summarizing your findings.

2. Assume that you are working on a one-year project that involves about 20 team members and many different stakeholders working across the globe. Even though your team created a communications management plan and you have all types of communication technologies available, everyone knows that communications is a problem. Using Figure 6-5 as a guide, create a cause and effect diagram to identify potential root causes of the communications problems. You can use the cause and effect diagram template or create the diagram by hand or using other software. Be creative in your response.

3. Take the Myers-Briggs Type Indicator (MBTI) test and research information on this tool. There are several Web sites that have different versions of the test available free, such as *www.humanmetrics.com*, *www.personalitytype.com*, and *www.keirsey.com*. Write a two-page paper describing your MBTI type and what you think about this test as a team-building tool.

4. Review the following scenarios, and then write a paragraph for each one describing what media you think would be most appropriate to use, and why. See Figure 6-12 for suggestions.

   a. Many of the technical staff on the project come in between 9:30 and 10:00 a.m., while the business users always come in before 9:00 a.m. The business users have been making comments. The project manager wants the technical staff to come in by 9:00 a.m., although many of them leave late.

   b. Your company is bidding on a project for the entertainment industry. You know that you need new ideas on how to put together the proposal and communicate your approach in a way that will impress the customer.

   c. Your business has been growing successfully, but you are becoming inundated with phone calls and e-mails asking similar types of questions.

   d. You need to make a general announcement to a large group of people and want to make sure they get the information.

5. Develop your own scenarios for when it would be appropriate to use each of the five conflict-handling modes discussed in this chapter (confrontation, compromise, smoothing, forcing, and withdrawal). Document your ideas in a one- to two-page paper.

Team Projects

1. Your organization initiated a project to raise money for an important charity. Assume that there are 1,000 people in your organization. Also, assume that you have six months to raise as much money as possible, with a goal of $100,000. List three problems that could arise while executing the project. Describe each problem in detail, and then develop realistic approaches to solving them in a two- to three-page paper or a 15-minute presentation. Be creative in your responses, and reference ideas discussed in this chapter. Remember that this project is run solely by volunteers.

2. You are part of a team in charge of a project to help people in your company (500 people) lose weight. This project is part of a competition, and the top "losers" will be featured in a popular television show. Assume that you have six months to complete the project and a budget of $10,000. You are halfway though the project, and morale is very low. People are also complaining about a lack of communication and support on the project. Although many people have been participating and have lost weight, many have plateaued or started gaining weight back. Identify four strategies you can implement to improve morale and communications, referencing some of the theories discussed in this chapter. Document your responses in a two- to three-page paper or a 15-minute presentation.

3. Using the information you developed in Team Project 1 or 2, role-play a meeting to brainstorm and develop strategies for solving problems with key stakeholders. Determine who will play what role (project manager, team member from a certain department, senior managers, and so on). Be creative in displaying different personalities (a senior manager who questions the importance of the project to the organization, a team member who is very shy or obnoxious).

4. Perform the executing tasks for the New Business Venture case study provided in Appendix C or for one of the cases on the companion Web site. (Note: Your instructor might select just a few of these tasks as they can be very time-consuming.) If you are working on a real team project, perform the applicable executing tasks for that project. Remember to address common problems, focus on deliverables, and practice good soft skills.

5. As you are executing your team project, document the top three problems you have experienced and how you are dealing with them. Document your results in a one- to two-page paper or short presentation.

Companion Web Site

Visit the companion Web site for this text (*www.course.com/mis/pm2/schwalbe* or *http://login.course.com*) to access:

- Lecture notes
- Interactive quizzes and Jeopardy games
- Template files
- Sample documents
- Podcasts
- More ideas for team projects, including real projects and case studies
- Links to additional resources related to project management

Key Terms

benchmarking — The process of generating ideas for quality improvements by comparing specific project practices or product characteristics to those of other projects or products within or outside of the performing organization.

cause-and-effect diagrams — Also called fishbone or Ishikawa diagrams, these diagrams can assist in ensuring and improving quality by finding the root causes of quality problems.

compromise mode — The conflict-handling mode that uses a give-and-take approach to resolve conflicts.

confrontation mode — The conflict-handling mode that involves directly facing a conflict using a problem-solving approach that allows affected parties to work through their disagreements.

empathic listening — The process of listening with the intent to understand by putting yourself in the shoes of the other person.

extrinsic motivation — A motivation that causes people to do something for a reward or to avoid a penalty.

forcing mode — The conflict-handling mode that involves exerting one's viewpoint at the potential expense of another viewpoint.

groupthink — The conformance to the values or ethical standards of a group.

intrinsic motivation — A motivation that causes people to participate in an activity for their own enjoyment.

Maslow's hierarchy of needs — A hierarchy that states that people's behaviors are guided or motivated by a sequence of needs (physiological, safety, social, esteem, and self-actualization).

mirroring — The matching of certain behaviors of the other person.

Myers-Briggs Type Indicator (MBTI) — A popular tool for determining personality preferences.

overallocation — When more resources than are available are assigned to perform work at a given time.

quality assurance — The activities related to satisfying the relevant quality standards for a project.

quality audit — A structured review of specific quality management activities that helps identify lessons learned, which could improve performance on current or future projects.

rapport — A relationship of harmony, conformity, accord, or affinity.

resource leveling — A technique for resolving resource conflicts by delaying tasks.

resource loading — The amount of individual resources an existing schedule requires during specific time periods.

short list — A list of the top three to five suppliers created to reduce the work involved in selecting a source.

smoothing mode — The conflict-handling mode that de-emphasizes or avoids areas of differences and emphasizes areas of agreement.

synergy — The concept that the whole is equal to more than the sum of its parts.

Tuckman model — A model that describes five stages of team development (forming, storming, norming, performing, and adjourning).

withdrawal mode — The conflict-handling mode that involves retreating or withdrawing from an actual or potential disagreement.

End Notes

1 Shadi Rahimi, "Bush Embarks on Tour to Survey Damage," *The New York Times* (September 2, 2005).

2 Great Place to Work Institute, Best Companies Lists, (*www.greatplacetowork.com*) (June 2005).

3 Steve Lohr, "Ambitious Package to Raise Productivity (and Microsoft's Profit)," *The New York Times* (August 16, 2004).

4 Colin Smith, "WebEx Experience Online Forum Saves Over 1 Million Pounds of Carbon Dioxide Emissions in First Week," (*www.webex.com*) (May 22, 2007).

5 Reuters, "TV Stations Fined for Janet Jackson Breast Flash," *http://www.reuters.com/* (September 22, 2004).

251

CHAPTER 7

MONITORING AND CONTROLLING PROJECTS

LEARNING OBJECTIVES

After reading this chapter, you will be able to:

- List several tasks and outputs of project monitoring and controlling, and describe outputs common to all knowledge areas
- Discuss performing integration change control as part of project integration management and how to use earned value management
- Explain the importance of scope verification, scope control, and accepting deliverables
- Describe the schedule control process and schedule performance measurement tools, such as tracking Gantt charts
- Discuss tools and techniques to assist in cost control
- List the Seven Basic Tools of Quality, and provide examples of how they assist in quality control
- Explain the monitoring and controlling work done as part of project human resource management to help manage project teams and stakeholders
- Summarize methods for performance reporting and managing stakeholders as part of project communications management
- Describe the risk monitoring and controlling process
- Explain how to monitor and control projects through good contract administration

Kristin worked closely with the project steering committee to monitor and control the Just-In-Time Training project. She knew that they were keeping a watchful eye on this project to ensure that it met its objectives and also addressed changing business needs. For example, since the project started, Global Construction had won several major construction projects and increased hiring by 10%. Therefore, there were more people than ever who needed the training the Just-In-Time Training project would provide. At their weekly meetings, Kristin, her team, and suppliers provided performance information and discussed changes that were required. The steering committee decided to have major suppliers report their progress directly to them as often as needed. They knew from past projects that to get the best results, it was important to develop a close relationship with suppliers and to monitor them as closely as internal employees. They also hoped to continue their partnerships with several suppliers to expand the training into other areas after this project was completed.

INTRODUCTION

Monitoring and controlling involves regularly measuring progress to ensure that the project is meeting its objectives and addressing current business needs. The project manager and other staff monitor progress against plans and take corrective action when necessary. This chapter summarizes the main tasks involved in monitoring and controlling projects, and provides examples of key outputs from this process group for the Just-In-Time Training project.

SUMMARY OF MONITORING AND CONTROLLING OUTPUTS

Figure 7-1 summarizes key outputs of project monitoring and controlling by knowledge area, based on the *PMBOK® Guide*. Notice that every knowledge area is included. Also note that the table includes the category "All," which lists several outputs common to all the knowledge areas. Recall from Chapter 6 that these items (requested changes, recommended corrective actions, and updates to applicable plans and processes) can also be outputs of project execution, so examples of them are not repeated in this chapter.

Knowledge area	Outputs
All	Requested changes, recommended corrective actions, updates to applicable plans and processes
Project integration management	Forecasts, approved change requests, corrective actions, preventive actions, defect repair, rejected change requests, validated defect repair, deliverables

FIGURE 7-1 Summary of project monitoring and controlling outputs

Knowledge area	Outputs
Project scope management	Accepted deliverables
Project time management	Performance measurements, forecasted completion time
Project cost management	Performance measurements, forecasted completion cost
Project quality management	Quality-control measurements
Project human resource management	Outputs under "All" category
Project communications management	Performance reports, resolved issues
Project risk management	Risk register updates
Project procurement management	Contract documentation

FIGURE 7-1 Summary of project monitoring and controlling outputs (continued)

MONITORING AND CONTROLLING TASKS FOR PROJECT INTEGRATION MANAGEMENT

The main monitoring and controlling tasks performed as part of project integration management include monitoring and controlling project work and performing integrated change control. These are crucial tasks that must be done well to ensure project success.

Monitoring and Controlling Project Work

Project changes are inevitable, so it is important to develop and follow a process to monitor and control them. Monitoring and controlling project work includes collecting, measuring, and disseminating performance information. It also involves assessing measurements and analyzing trends to determine what process improvements can be made. The project team should continuously monitor project performance to assess the overall health of the project and identify areas that require special attention.

The project management plan, work performance information, performance reports, and change requests are all important inputs for monitoring and controlling project work. Key tools and techniques for performing this process include using a project management methodology, a project management information system, and expert judgment, as described earlier in this text. Another powerful technique is earned value management, which helps forecast future project performance.

Forecasting with Earned Value Management

Earned value management (EVM) is a project performance measurement technique that integrates scope, time, and cost data. Given a baseline, project managers and their teams can determine how well the project is meeting scope, time, and cost goals by entering actual information and then comparing it to the baseline. As defined in Chapter 4, a baseline is a starting point, a measurement, or an observation that is documented so that it can be used for future comparison.

In earned value management, a baseline includes the following:

- Scope (WBS tasks)

- Time (start and finish estimates for each task)
- Cost information (cost estimates for each task)

Actual information includes whether or not a WBS was completed or approximately how much of the work was completed; when the work actually started and ended; and how much it actually cost to do the completed work. Some project teams do not define work using a WBS or have cost estimates for each task. Some project teams do not periodically enter actuals for scope, time, and cost information. If you do not have a good baseline or actual information, you cannot use earned value management.

In the past, earned value management was primarily used on large government projects. Today, however, more and more companies are realizing the value of using this tool to help control projects. Most project management software products, including Microsoft Project 2007, provide tables and reports for entering and viewing earned value information. See the *Guide to Using Microsoft Project 2007* in Appendix A for detailed instructions on using this software for earned value management.

Earned value management involves calculating three values for each activity or summary activity from a project's WBS.

1. The **planned value (PV)** is that portion of the approved total cost estimate planned to be spent on an activity during a given period. The cost baseline for the Just-In-Time Training project included $5,000 to be spent on course development for supplier management training. If the activity involved delivering a detailed course outline to be finished in one week for $5,000, then the planned value (PV) for that activity that week would be $5,000.

2. The **actual cost (AC)** is the total direct and indirect costs incurred in accomplishing work on an activity during a given period. For example, suppose it actually took one week and cost $6,000 to create the detailed course outline because the hourly rate for the person doing the work was higher than planned. The actual cost (AC) for the activity would therefore be $6,000.

3. The **earned value (EV)** is an estimate of the value of the physical work actually completed. It is based on the original planned costs for the activity and the rate at which the team is completing work on the activity to date. The **rate of performance (RP)** is the percentage of actual work completed divided by the percentage of work planned to have been completed at any given time. For example, suppose an activity is only half completed by the end of the week, when it should have been totally completed. The rate of performance for that activity that week would be 50%. In this example, the activity to develop a detailed course outline was totally completed at the end of the week, so the RP was 100%. Because the PV was $5,000, the EV would also be $5,000.

Figure 7-2 summarizes the general formulas used in earned value management. Note that the formulas for variances and indexes start with EV, the earned value. Variances are calculated by subtracting the actual cost or planned value from EV, and indexes are calculated by dividing EV by the actual cost or planned value. You can use the indexes to forecast what it will cost (the Estimate at Completion or EAC) and when the project will finish, the Estimated Time to Complete.

Term	Formula
Earned Value (EV)	EV = PV to date × RP
Rate of Performance (RP)	RP = Actual work completed/percentage of work planned to have been completed
Cost Variance (CV)	CV = EV − AC
Schedule Variance (SV)	SV = EV − PV
Cost Performance Index (CPI)	CPI = EV/AC
Schedule Performance Index (SPI)	SPI = EV/PV
Estimate at Completion (EAC)	EAC = Budget at Completion (BAC)/CPI
Estimated Time to Complete	Original time estimate/SPI

FIGURE 7-2   Earned value formulas

NOTE

In general, *negative numbers for cost and schedule variance indicate problems in those areas.* Negative numbers mean the project is costing more than planned or taking longer than planned. Likewise, *CPI and SPI less than one or less than 100% indicate problems.*

Note that you can use earned value management at either a detailed or a summary level. In other words, you can use a detailed WBS and its associated time and cost data (using level four, five, or whatever is the most detailed), or you can apply earned value at a higher WBS level, such as level two or three.

Figure 7-3 summarizes the earned value information and also computes the cost and schedule variance and the cost and schedule performance indexes for the Just-In-Time Training project task for course development for supplier management training discussed earlier.

Term or Calculation	Amount
Earned Value (EV)	$5,000
Planned Value (PV)	$5,000
Actual Cost (AC)	$6,000
Cost Variance (CV)	−$1,000
Schedule Variance (SV)	0
Cost Performance Index (CPI)	83.33%
Schedule Performance Index (SPI)	100%

FIGURE 7-3   Earned value calculations for one activity after one week

The earned value calculations in Figure 7-3 are carried out as follows:

$$EV = \$5,000 \times 100\% = \$5,000$$
$$CV = \$5,000 - \$6,000 = -\$1,000$$
$$SV = \$5,000 - \$5,000 = 0$$
$$CPI = \$5,000/\$6,000 = 83.33\%$$
$$SPI = \$5,000/\$5,000 = 100\%$$

Earned value calculations for all project activities (or summary level activities) are required to estimate the earned value for the entire project. Some activities may be over budget or behind schedule, whereas others may be under budget and ahead of schedule. By adding all of the earned values for all project activities, you can determine how the project as a whole is performing and forecast both when it will be completed and how much it will cost at completion.

The **budget at completion (BAC)**, or the approved total budget for the project, can be divided by the cost performance index to calculate the **estimate at completion (EAC)**, which is a forecast of how much the project will cost upon completion. Likewise, the approved time estimate for the project can be divided by the schedule performance index to calculate when the project will be completed. Earned value, therefore, provides an excellent way to monitor project performance and provide forecasts based on performance to date.

Sample Forecast Using an Earned Value Chart

You can graph earned value information to track project performance and to forecast when a project will be completed and for how much. Figure 7-4 shows an earned value chart for a project that has larger and simpler variances than the Just-In-Time Training project to make the chart easier to read. The budget at completion is $1.2 million for this one-year project. The BAC point on the chart, therefore, is at 12 months and $1.2 million. Based on data for months one through six, an earned value chart was created. In this example, the planned value is $100,000 for each month, so the cumulative planned value at month 6 is $600,000. The earned value is $150,000 each month, with the cumulative earned value at month 6 of $900,000. The actual cost is $200,000 each month, with the cumulative actual cost at month 6 of $1,200,000.

NOTE

The detailed numbers used to create an earned value chart for the Just-In-Time Training project are provided in the Excel file named JIT-earned-value on the companion Web site.

You can also forecast when the project will be completed and what its final cost will be based on this information.

$$CPI = EV/AC = \$900,000/\$1,200,000 = .75$$
$$SPI = EV/PV = \$900,000/\$600,000 = 1.5$$
$$EAC = BAC/CPI = \$1,200,000/.75 = \$1,600,000$$
$$\text{New time estimate} = \text{Original time estimate} / SPI$$
$$= 12 \text{ months}/1.5 = 8 \text{ months}$$

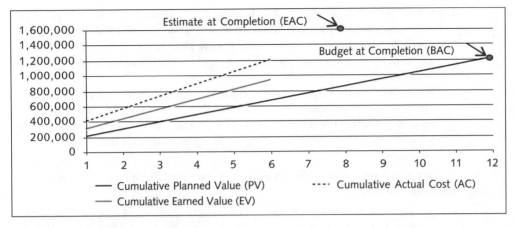

FIGURE 7-4 Sample earned value chart

Notice that the EAC point is provided on the chart in Figure 7-4 at 8 months and at the cost of $1,600,000. Viewing earned value information in chart form helps you visualize how the project has been performing and forecasts both the end date and the total cost. For example, you can see the planned performance by looking at the planned value line. If the project goes exactly as planned, it will finish in 12 months and cost $1,200,000, as represented by the BAC point. Notice in the example that the actual cost line is always above the earned value line. When the actual cost line is above the earned value line, costs are more than planned. The planned value line in this example is always below the earned value line. This relationship means that the project has been ahead of schedule the first six months. The forecasted completion date, therefore, is earlier than planned while the forecasted total cost is higher than planned.

If there are serious cost and schedule performance problems, management may decide to terminate projects or take other corrective action. The estimate at completion (EAC) is an important input to budget decisions, especially if total funds are limited. Earned value management is an important technique because when used effectively, it helps in evaluating progress and making sound management decisions.

Integrated Change Control

Integrated change control involves identifying, evaluating, and managing changes throughout the project's life cycle. The three main objectives of integrated change control are as follows:

1. *Influencing the factors that cause changes to ensure that changes are beneficial*: Changes can often be good for a project, so it is important to let everyone know that and focus on promoting changes that are beneficial. For example, changes that improve quality, reduce costs, save time, or improve stakeholder relationships are beneficial.

2. *Determining that a change has occurred*: To determine that a change has occurred, project managers must know the status of key project areas at all times. In addition, they must communicate significant changes to senior management and key stakeholders, who normally do not like surprises—especially unpleasant ones.

3. *Managing actual changes as they occur*: Managing change is a key role of project managers and their teams. It is important that project managers exercise discipline in managing the project to help control the number of changes that occur. Managers should focus on achieving project goals rather than putting out fires.

The project management plan provides the baseline for identifying and controlling project changes as follows:

- A section of the plan describes the work to be performed on a project, including key deliverables for the project and quality requirements.
- The schedule section of the plan lists the planned dates for completing key deliverables.
- The budget section provides the planned cost for these deliverables.

The project team must focus on delivering the work as planned. If the project team or someone else causes significant changes during project execution, project managers must formally revise the project management plan and have it approved by the project sponsor.

MONITORING AND CONTROLLING TASKS FOR PROJECT SCOPE MANAGEMENT

The main monitoring and controlling tasks performed as part of project scope management are scope verification and scope control. Key outputs are deliverables that are accepted by the customer. It is difficult to create a good project scope statement and WBS. It is often even more difficult to verify the project scope and minimize scope changes. Some project teams know from the start that the scope is very unclear and that they must work closely with the project customer to design and produce various deliverables. The project team must develop a process for scope verification that meets unique project needs. Careful procedures must be developed to ensure that customers are getting what they want and that the project team has enough time and money to produce the desired products and services.

Even when the project scope is fairly well defined, many projects suffer from scope creep, as discussed in Chapter 3. There are many horror stories about projects failing due to scope creep. Even for fairly simple projects, people have a tendency to want more. How many people do you know, for example, who said they wanted a simple wedding or a basic new house constructed, only to end up with many more extras than they initially planned? In contrast, some projects also suffer from *not* delivering the minimum scope due to time or cost issues. A couple may have planned to go on a luxurious honeymoon until they saw how much the wedding cost, or a new homeowner may have settled for an unfinished basement in order to move in on time. These scenarios are similar to those faced by a project manager who must constantly cope with the triple constraint of balancing scope, time, and cost.

Scope Verification

Scope verification involves formal acceptance of the completed project scope by the project customer or designated stakeholders. This acceptance is often achieved through customer inspection and then sign-off on key deliverables. To receive formal acceptance of the project scope, the project team must develop clear documentation of the project's products and procedures, which the appropriate stakeholders can then evaluate for completion and their satisfaction with the results. For example, part of the scope of Kristin's project was to develop a survey to help assess training needs. As part of scope verification, the project steering committee would need to approve the survey before it could be sent out. Scope planning documents, such as the WBS dictionary for that task (see Figure 4-10) would define the scope verification required.

The project scope statement, WBS dictionary, project scope management plan, and deliverables are the main inputs for scope verification. The main tool for performing scope verification is inspection. The customer inspects the work after it is delivered to decide if it is acceptable.

Sample of Accepted and Unaccepted Deliverables

The Just-In-Time Training project included many deliverables. Kristin, the project sponsor, the project steering committee, and other stakeholders—including employees taking the training courses—were all involved in verifying that deliverables were acceptable. Kristin worked closely with her project team and suppliers to make sure that deliverables were being developed correctly along the way. She knew that working closely with key stakeholders and reviewing progress was often the best way to ensure that final deliverables would be acceptable. Kristin knew from experience that foregoing draft reviews and delaying consultation with stakeholders until the final deliverable was ready often resulted in disaster.

Because Global Construction often worked with suppliers on projects, they had a formal process for verifying deliverables produced by suppliers. The project manager was responsible for signing off on their acceptance, as was the project sponsor. Figure 7-5 provides a sample deliverable acceptance form. In this example, Kristin and Lucy, the project sponsor, document the fact that they do not accept the deliverable and provide feedback on what must be done to make it acceptable. Kristin did talk to the supplier about the changes required before accepting this particular deliverable—the course materials for the introductory supplier management course—but the supplier still did not deliver what was expected. The deliverable acceptance form provides formal documentation to ensure that deliverables meet project needs. In this case, because the particular deliverable was part of a contract, the supplier would not be paid until the deliverable was accepted.

Deliverable Acceptance Form

November 12, 2009

Project Name:	Just-In-Time Training Project
Deliverable Name:	Course materials for introductory supplier management course
Project Manager:	Kristin Maur
Project Sponsor:	Lucy Camarena

(We), the undersigned, acknowledge and accept delivery of the work completed for this deliverable on behalf of our organization. My (Our) signature(s) attest(s) to my (our) agreement that this deliverable has been completed. No further work should be done on this deliverable. If the deliverable is not acceptable, reasons are stated and corrective actions are described.

Name	Title	Signature	Date

1.   Was this deliverable completed to your satisfaction?   Yes ___   No _X_

2.   Please provide the main reasons for your satisfaction or dissatisfaction with this deliverable.

As stated in the contract statement of work, the course materials are not completed until all constructive

feedback from the prototype course has been incorporated or the supplier has provided strong rationale as

to why the feedback should not be incorporated. We requested that a new section be added to the course to

cover issues related to working with suppliers in virtual settings. The final materials delivered did not

include this new section or discuss why it was not added. We believe it was an oversight that can be

corrected with a minimal amount of additional work.

3.   If the deliverable is not acceptable, describe in detail what additional work must be done to complete it.

The supplier will add a new section to the course on working with suppliers in a virtual setting. This section should take about 30 minutes of class time in a face-to-face or e-learning setting. This new section will follow the format and review process used for other topics in the course. We request delivery of the draft of this new section within one week and the final delivery within two weeks.

Contact's signature for resubmission of deliverable if found unacceptable: ____*Kristin Maur*____

FIGURE 7-5   Sample deliverable acceptance form

Scope Control

You cannot control the scope of a project unless you have first clearly defined the scope and set a scope verification process in place. You also need to develop a process for soliciting and monitoring changes to project scope. Stakeholders should be encouraged to suggest beneficial changes and discouraged from suggesting unnecessary changes.

BEST PRACTICE

An example of successfully controlling scope comes from Northwest Airlines. The company developed a new reservation system in the late 1990s that took several years and millions of dollars to develop. They knew that users would request changes and enhancements to the system, so they built in a special function key for submitting change requests. They also allocated resources for specifically handling change requests by assigning three full-time programmers to work exclusively on them. Users made over 11,000 enhancement requests the first year the system was in use, which was much more than the three programmers could handle. The managers who sponsored the four main software applications had to prioritize the software enhancement requests and decide as a group what changes to approve. Given the time they had, the three programmers then implemented as many items as they could, in priority order. Although they only implemented 38% of the requested enhancements, these were the most important, and users were very satisfied with the system and process.

Another example of scope control is a practice some parents follow when their children get married. The parents provide a fixed budget for the wedding and honeymoon and let the young couple decide how to spend it. If the couple minimizes and controls the scope of the wedding, they can have extra money to pay off other debts or save for a down payment on a home. If they suffer from scope creep, they may not have any money for a honeymoon or become further in debt. This practice can be adapted to most business projects by providing incentives for workers to deliver the work as planned within time and budget constraints.

MONITORING AND CONTROLLING TASKS FOR PROJECT TIME MANAGEMENT

The main monitoring and controlling task performed as part of project time management is schedule control. Project managers often cite delivering projects on time (schedule control) as one of their biggest challenges, because schedule problems often cause more conflict than other issues. During project initiation, priorities and procedures are often most important, but as the project proceeds, especially during the middle and latter stages of a project, schedule issues become the predominant source of conflict.

Perhaps part of the reason schedule problems are so common is that time is easily and simply measured. After a project schedule is set, anyone can quickly estimate schedule performance by subtracting the original time estimate from the time actually expended. People often compare planned and actual project-completion times without taking into account the approved project changes. Time is also the variable with the least amount of flexibility. Time passes no matter what happens on a project.

Individual work styles and cultural differences may also cause schedule conflicts. For example, one dimension of the Myers-Briggs team-building tool that was described in Chapter 6 (Judgment/Perception, or J/P) deals with peoples' attitudes toward structure and deadlines. Some people (J's) prefer detailed schedules and focus on task completion. Others (P's) prefer to keep things open and flexible. Different cultures and even entire countries have different attitudes about schedules. For example, some countries close businesses for several hours every afternoon to have siestas. Others observe religious or secular holidays during which little work is accomplished. Cultures may also have different perceptions of work ethic—some may value hard work and strict schedules, whereas others may value the ability to remain relaxed and flexible.

MEDIA SNAPSHOT

Planning and scheduling varied greatly for the 2002 Olympic Winter Games in Salt Lake City (see the Media Snapshot of Chapter 4) and the 2004 Olympic Summer Games in Athens, Greece. Many articles were written before the opening ceremonies of the Athens Games predicting that the facilities would not be ready in time. "With just 162 days to go to the opening of the Athens Olympics, the Greek capital is still not ready for the expected onslaught....By now 22 of the 30 Olympic projects were supposed to be finished. This week the Athens Olympic Committee proudly announced 19 venues would be finished by the end of next month. That's a long way off target."[1]

However, many people were pleasantly surprised by the amazing opening ceremonies, beautiful new buildings, and state-of-the-art security and transportation systems in Athens. For example, traffic flow, considered a major pre-Games hurdle, was superb. One spectator at the Games commented on the prediction that the facilities would not be ready in time, "Athens proved them all wrong....It has never looked better."[2] There were, however, several last-minute changes and many extra hours worked in the last few months before the games began. Costs exceeded $12 billion—*more than double the original budget.*[3] Many project managers and team members would have been more comfortable if the original plans had been followed, but Greek workers take pride in putting in major efforts near a deadline. The Greeks even made fun of critics by having construction workers pretend to still be working as the ceremonies began.

The goal of schedule control is to know the status of the schedule, influence the factors that cause schedule changes, determine whether the schedule has changed, and manage changes when they occur. A key output of schedule control is performance measurements.

Sample Schedule Performance Measurements

Earned value management, as described earlier, is a key tool for measuring schedule performance. Given the earned value and planned value, you can see how well the project team is meeting schedule goals and forecast when the project will be completed based on past schedule performance. Additional ways to measure schedule performance include:

- *Indicators:* Many senior managers like to focus on high-level color indicators of performance, such as green (on target), yellow (fair), and red (poor). They will oversee projects or tasks with red or yellow indicators much more closely than those with green indicators. Project management software offers color indicators as well as numerous reports to show schedule performance information. For example, Microsoft Project 2007 includes activity reports to show "should have started tasks" and "slipping tasks" to quickly identify problem areas. See the *Guide to Using Microsoft Project 2007* in Appendix A for more information.

- *Milestone completion:* Experienced managers and buyers know that it is not enough to merely review indicators; they like to see the planned and actual completion dates of project milestones *and* the physical evidence that the work was actually completed. (See Chapter 4 for information on milestones.) For example, people having a house built often check on the physical progress to make sure work is completed on schedule. Even though the contractor reports that key milestones are being completed, the buyer wants to see and review the work in person.

- *Worker morale and discipline:* Reviewing morale and work behavior is also a good way to measure schedule performance. If project team members are always working extra hours, the schedule might not be realistic. The project manager might need to negotiate a new schedule or request more resources. On the other hand, if workers are coming in late and leaving early while still producing quality work on time, the schedule might not be challenging enough. Project managers must empower team members to be responsible for completing work on time, yet they often have to use discipline to keep things on track and do what is in the best interest of the organization. (See Chapter 6 for information on motivating workers.)

- *Performance review meetings and tracking Gantt charts:* Another way to control project schedules is by holding periodic performance review meetings with the project sponsor or appropriate stakeholders. The project steering committee for the Just-In-Time Training project held weekly meetings to make sure the project was meeting schedule and other goals. Project managers often illustrate progress with a **tracking Gantt chart**—a Gantt chart that compares planned and actual project schedule information. Many project managers believe that tracking Gantt charts are an excellent tool for tracking project schedule performance and reporting that information to stakeholders. Figure 7-6 provides a sample tracking Gantt chart that Kristin might use to measure schedule performance for a supplier. The tracking Gantt chart includes columns (hidden in Figure 7-6) labeled "Start" and "Finish" to represent actual start and finish dates for each task, as well as columns labeled "Baseline Start" and "Baseline Finish" to represent planned start and finish dates for each task. In this example, the project is completed, but several tasks missed their planned start and finish dates. See the *Guide to Using Microsoft Project 2007* in Appendix A for information on creating a tracking Gantt chart and other types of performance reports.

FIGURE 7-6 Sample schedule performance measurement using a tracking Gantt chart

To serve as a schedule performance measurement tool, a tracking Gantt chart uses a few additional symbols not found on a normal Gantt chart:

- Notice that the tracking Gantt chart in Figure 7-6 often shows two horizontal bars for tasks. The top horizontal bar represents the planned or baseline duration for each task. The bar below it represents the actual duration. Subtasks 1.2 and 1.3 illustrate this type of display. If the top and bottom bars are the same length and start and end on the same date, the actual schedule was the same as the planned schedule for that task. This scheduling occurred for Subtask 1.1, in which the task started and ended as planned on March 4. If the bars do not start and end on the same date, the actual schedule differed from the planned or baseline schedule. If the top horizontal bar is shorter than the bottom one, the task took longer than planned, as you can see for Subtask 1.2. If the top horizontal bar is longer than the bottom one, the task took less time than planned. A striped horizontal bar, illustrated by the bolded tasks named Main Tasks 1 and 2, represents the planned duration for those summary tasks. Recall from Chapter 4 that summary tasks are tasks that are decomposed into smaller tasks. The black bar adjoining the striped horizontal bar shows the progress for summary tasks. For example, Main Task 2 clearly shows that the actual duration took longer than what was planned.
- A white diamond on the tracking Gantt chart represents a slipped milestone. A **slipped milestone** refers to a milestone activity that was actually completed later than originally planned. For example, the last task provides an example of a slipped milestone because the final report and presentation were completed later than planned.
- Percentages to the right of the horizontal bars display the percentage of work completed for each task. For example, 100% indicates that the task is finished, whereas 50% indicates that the task is still in progress and is 50% completed.

- In the columns to the left of the tracking Gantt chart, you can display baseline and actual start and finish dates. See Appendix A for more information on tracking Gantt charts.

☑ WHAT WENT RIGHT?

Canadian Imperial Bank of Commerce (CIBC) provides an excellent example of successfully controlling the schedule for a large information technology project in the banking industry. CIBC transformed 20,000 workstations in 1,200 different financial branches in just one year. It created a Web-based tool to enable large, geographically dispersed teams to access information simultaneously. Each of the 1,200 sites had 75 milestones to track, including the baseline, latest plan, and actual finish dates, resulting in 90,000 data points. According to Jack Newhouse, the company's director of application support, CIBC's Web-based tracking tool "was a critical component to success....Accurate, timely data was an invaluable management tool."[4]

Project sponsors hate surprises, so the project manager must be clear and honest in communicating project status. By no means should project managers create the illusion that the project is going fine when, in fact, serious problems have emerged. When conflicts arise that could affect the project schedule, the project manager must alert the project sponsor and other stakeholders and work with them to resolve the conflicts. Recall from Chapter 5 that the communications management plan should describe escalation procedures for resolving issues.

MONITORING AND CONTROLLING TASKS FOR PROJECT COST MANAGEMENT

The main monitoring and controlling task performed as part of project cost management is cost control. Cost control includes monitoring cost performance, ensuring that only appropriate project changes are included in a revised cost baseline, and informing project stakeholders of authorized changes to the project that will affect costs. The cost baseline, performance reports, change requests, and project funding requirements are inputs to the cost-control process. Outputs of cost control include project management plan updates, documentation of corrective actions, revised estimates for project completion, requested changes, and updates to organizational process assets, such as lessons-learned documents.

Several tools and techniques assist in project cost control:

- *Project management software:* Software packages, such as Microsoft Project 2007, have many cost-management features to help you enter budgeted costs, set a baseline, enter actuals, calculate variances, and run various cost reports.
- *Change-control system:* Projects should have a change-control system that defines procedures for changing the cost baseline. This cost-control change system is part of the integrated change-control system described earlier in this

chapter. Because many projects do not progress exactly as planned, new or revised cost estimates are often required, as are estimates to evaluate alternative courses of action.

- *Performance review meetings:* These meetings can be a powerful aid for controlling project costs, just as they are for controlling schedules. People often perform better when they know they must report on their progress and are held accountable for their performance.
- *Earned value:* Another very important tool for cost control is earned value management, as described earlier.

Some projects leaders who encounter major problems, especially quality problems, blame those problems on poor cost control, as described in the "What Went Wrong?" passage.

⊗ WHAT WENT WRONG?

Many people have heard about the problems with Boston's Big Dig project. Newspapers and Web sites showed the many leaks in the eight- to 10-lane underground expressway that took over 14 years and $14 billion to build. Did the project overseers cut corners to save time and money?

Representative Stephen F. Lynch believes the answer to that question is yes, and that at some point, pressure to get the project done distracted Bechtel/Parsons Brinckerhoff from getting the project done right. "Under the pressure and scrutiny of a lot of people, they went back to look at areas where they could reduce cost in areas of material and time," said Lynch, a South Boston Democrat, in the aftermath of the Big Dig congressional hearing he brought to Boston on April 22, 2005. Pressure to finally speed up the costly, long-running project may explain why the new Artery tunnel is plagued by leaks. "As a casual observer, I am forced to conclude that the focus on the cost overrun and the schedule distracted attention from quality control issues on the Central Artery project," declared George J. Tamaro in written testimony to the Congressional Committee on Government Reform.[5]

MONITORING AND CONTROLLING TASKS FOR PROJECT QUALITY MANAGEMENT

The main project quality management task for monitoring and controlling is quality control. Key outputs include quality-control measurements, validated defect repair, and validated deliverables. Although one of the main goals of quality control is to ensure and improve quality, the main outcomes of this process are acceptance decisions, rework, and process adjustments.

- Acceptance decisions determine if the products or services produced as part of the project will be accepted or rejected. If they are accepted, they are considered to be validated deliverables. If project stakeholders reject some of the products or services produced as part of the project, there must be rework.

- Rework is action taken to bring rejected items into compliance with product requirements or specifications or other stakeholder expectations. Rework can be very expensive, so the project manager who excels at quality planning and quality assurance can reduce the need for rework.
- Process adjustments correct or prevent further quality problems. Based on the implementation of quality-control measurements, process adjustments often result in updates to the quality baseline, organizational process assets, and the project management plan.

Sample Quality-Control Measurements

Many different tools and techniques for performing quality control and developing control measurements are available. Some of these tools and techniques are also used for quality planning and assurance. The following seven tools are known as the Seven Basic Tools of Quality:

1. *Cause-and-effect diagram*: As described in Chapter 6, cause-and-effect diagrams help you find the root cause of quality problems. Figure 6-5, repeated in this chapter as Figure 7-7, provides a sample cause-and-effect diagram that can be used to find the root cause of low course ratings for the Just-In-Time Training project.

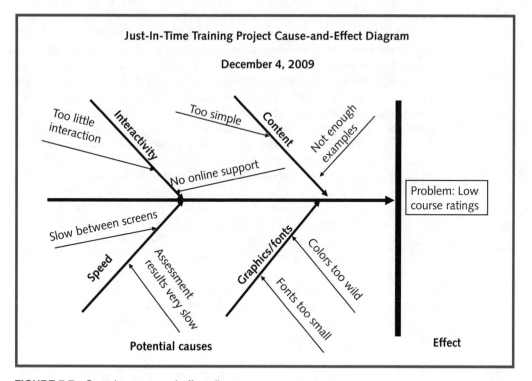

FIGURE 7-7   Sample cause-and-effect diagram

2. *Control chart:* A **control chart** is a graphic display of data that illustrates the results of a process over time. Control charts allow you to determine whether a process is in control or out of control. When a process is in control, any variations in the results of the process are created by random events. Processes that are in control do not need to be adjusted. When a process is out of control, variations in the results of the process are caused by nonrandom events. When a process is out of control, you need to identify the causes of those nonrandom events and adjust the process to correct or eliminate them. Figure 7-8 provides an example of a control chart for a process that manufactures 12-inch rulers. Assume that these are wooden rulers created by machines on an assembly line. Each point on the chart represents a length measurement for a ruler that comes off the assembly line. The scale on the vertical axis goes from 11.90 to 12.10. These numbers represent the lower and upper specification limits for the ruler. In this case, this would mean that the customer for the rulers has specified that all rulers purchased must be between 11.90 and 12.10 inches long, or 12 inches plus or minus 0.10 inches. The lower and upper control limits on the control chart are 11.91 and 12.09 inches, respectively. This means the manufacturing process is designed to produce rulers between 11.91 and 12.09 inches long. Looking for and analyzing patterns in process data is an important part of quality control. You can use control charts and the seven run rule to look for patterns in data. The seven run rule states that if seven data points in a row are all below the mean, above the mean, increasing, or decreasing, then the process needs to be examined for nonrandom problems. In Figure 7-8, data points that violate the seven run rule are starred. The first starred point has seven data points in a row that are all below the mean. The second one has seven data points in a row that are all decreasing. Note that you include the first point in a series of points that are all increasing or decreasing. In the ruler-manufacturing process, these data points may indicate that a calibration device may need adjustment. For example, the machine that cuts the wood for the rulers might need to be adjusted, or the blade on the machine might need to be replaced.

3. *Run charts:* A run chart displays the history and pattern of variation of a process over time. It is a line chart that shows data points plotted in the order in which they occur. You can use run charts to perform trend analysis to forecast future outcomes based on historical results. For example, trend analysis can help you analyze how many defects have been identified over time to determine if there are trends. Figure 7-9 shows a sample run chart, charting the number of defects each month for three different types of defects. Notice that you can easily see the patterns of Defect 1 continuing to increase over time, Defect 2 decreasing the first several months and then holding steady, and Defect 3 fluctuating each month.

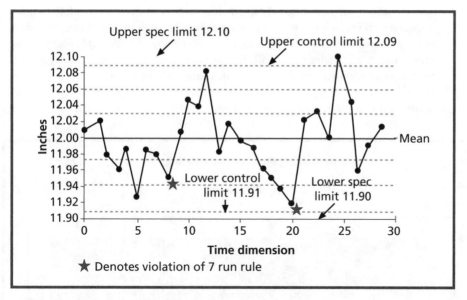

FIGURE 7-8 Sample control chart

FIGURE 7-9 Sample run chart

4. *Scatter diagram:* A **scatter diagram** helps show if there is a relationship between two variables. The closer data points are to a diagonal line, the more closely the two variables are related. Figure 7-10 provides a sample scatter diagram that the Just-In-Time Training project team might create to compare training participants' course evaluation ratings with their ages to see if there is a relationship. They might find that younger workers prefer the Web-based courses, for example, and make decisions based on that finding.

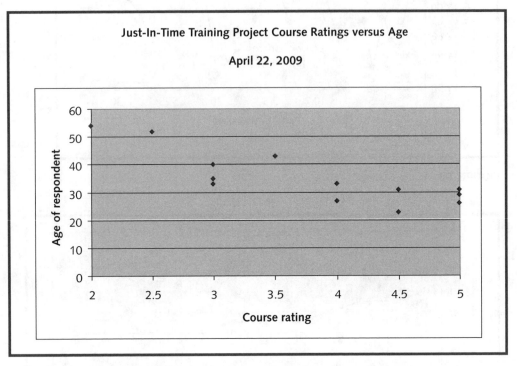

FIGURE 7-10 Sample scatter diagram

5. *Histograms:* A **histogram** is a bar graph of a distribution of variables. Each bar represents an attribute or a characteristic of a problem or situation, and the height of the bar represents its frequency. Chapter 5 provides a sample resource histogram, showing the number of people required for a project over time. The Just-In-Time Training project team created a histogram to show how many total complaints they received each month related to the project. Figure 7-11 shows the sample histogram.

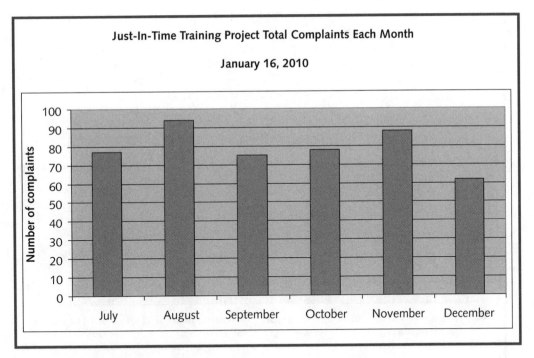

Just-In-Time Training Project Total Complaints Each Month

January 16, 2010

FIGURE 7-11   Sample histogram

6. *Pareto charts:* A **Pareto chart** is a histogram that can help you identify and pri-oritize problem areas. The variables described by the histogram are ordered by frequency of occurrence in a column chart, and a line chart is added to show cumulative percentage on the right of the chart. (You can use the template file to help create this and other charts.) Pareto charts help you identify the vital few contributors that account for most quality problems in a system. Pareto analysis is sometimes referred to as the 80/20 rule, meaning that 80% of problems are often due to 20% of the causes. Figure 7-12 is a sample Pareto chart that the Just-In-Time Training project team developed. They used it to help improve the quality of the information they provided about training courses on the corporate intranet. It shows the number of times people com-plained about the information on the intranet by category of complaint. Notice that the first two complaints account for a large percentage of the prob-lems, so the team should focus on improving those areas to improve quality.

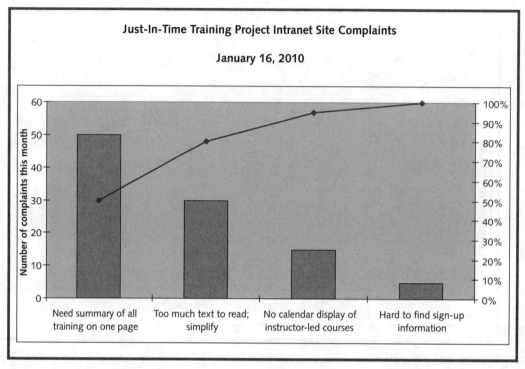

Just-In-Time Training Project Intranet Site Complaints

January 16, 2010

FIGURE 7-12   Sample Pareto chart

7. *Flowcharts:* **Flowcharts** are graphic displays of the logic and flow of processes that help you analyze how problems occur and how processes can be improved. They show activities (using the square symbol), decision points (using the diamond symbol), and the order of how information is processed (using arrow symbols). Figure 7-13 provides a simple example of a flowchart that shows the process Kristin's team used for accepting or rejecting deliverables.

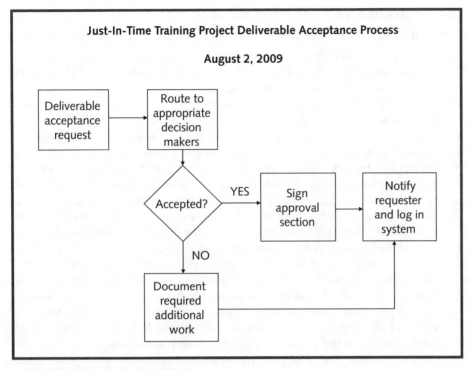

FIGURE 7-13   Sample flowchart

MONITORING AND CONTROLLING TASKS FOR PROJECT HUMAN RESOURCE MANAGEMENT

The main human resource management task performed as part of monitoring and controlling a project is managing the project team, which, of course, is no small task. After assessing team performance and related information, the project manager must decide if changes to the project should be requested, if corrective or preventive actions should be recommended, or if updates need to be made to the project management plan or organizational process assets. Project managers must use their soft skills to find the best way to motivate and manage each team member. Chapter 6 described many of these soft skills. The following sections describe tools and techniques to help manage project teams and offer general advice on managing teams.

Tools and Techniques for Managing Project Teams

Several tools and techniques are available to assist in managing project teams:

- *Observation and conversation:* It is hard to assess how your team members are performing or how they are feeling about their work if you seldom see or discuss these issues. Many project managers, like Kristin, like to physically see and hear their team members at work. Informal or formal conversations about how a project is going can provide crucial information. For virtual workers, project managers can still observe and discuss work and personal issues via e-mail, telephone, or other communications media.

- *Project performance appraisals:* Just as general managers provide performance appraisals for their workers, so can project managers. The need for and type of project performance appraisals varies depending on the length of the project, the complexity of the project, organizational policies, contract requirements, and related communications. Even if a project manager does not provide official project performance appraisals for team members, it is still important to provide timely performance feedback. If a team member hands in sloppy or late work, the project manager should determine the reason for this behavior and take appropriate action. Perhaps the team member had a death in the family and could not concentrate. Perhaps the team member was planning to leave the project. The reasons for the behavior would have a strong impact on the action the project manager would take.

- *Conflict management:* Few projects are completed without any conflict. Some types of conflict are actually desirable on projects, but many are not. As described in Chapter 6, there are several ways to handle conflicts. It's important for project managers to understand strategies for handling conflicts and to proactively manage them.

- *Issue logs:* Many project managers keep an issue log (described in the next section) to document, monitor, and track issues that need to be resolved for effective work to take place. Issues could include situations in which people disagree, situations that need more clarification or investigation, or general concerns that need to be addressed. It is important to acknowledge issues that can hurt team performance and take action to resolve them. The project manager should assign someone to resolve each issue and assign a target date for resolution.

General Advice on Managing Teams

Effective project managers must be good team leaders. Suggestions for ensuring that teams are productive include the following:

- Be patient and kind with your team. Assume the best about people; do not assume that your team members are lazy and careless.
- Fix the problem instead of blaming people. Help people work out problems by focusing on behaviors.
- Establish regular, effective meetings. Focus on meeting project objectives and producing positive results.

- Allow time for teams to go through the basic team-building stages of forming, storming, norming, performing, and adjourning, as described in Chapter 6. Do not expect teams to work at the highest performance level from the start; moreover, not all teams will even reach the performing level.
- Limit the size of work teams to three to seven members to enhance communications.
- Plan some social activities to help project team members and other stakeholders become acquainted. Make the social events fun and not mandatory.
- Stress team identity. Create traditions that team members enjoy.
- Nurture team members and encourage them to help each other. Identify and provide training that will help individuals and the team as a whole become more effective.
- Acknowledge individual and group accomplishments.
- Take the additional actions necessary to work with virtual team members. If possible, have a face-to-face or phone meeting at the start of a virtual project or when introducing a virtual team member. Screen people carefully to make sure they can work effectively in a virtual environment. Clarify how virtual team members will communicate.

MONITORING AND CONTROLLING TASKS FOR PROJECT COMMUNICATIONS MANAGEMENT

The main communications management tasks performed as part of monitoring and controlling include performance reporting and managing stakeholders. Key outputs include performance reports, forecasts, and resolved issues.

Performance Reporting

Performance reporting keeps stakeholders informed about how resources are being used to achieve project objectives. Work performance information and measurements, forecasted completion dates, quality-control measurements, the project management plan, approved change requests, and deliverables are all important inputs to performance reporting. Two key outputs of performance reporting are performance reports and forecasts. Performance reports are normally provided as status reports or progress reports. Many people use the two terms interchangeably, but some people distinguish between them as follows:

- **Status reports** describe where the project stands at a specific point in time. Recall the importance of the triple constraint. Status reports address where the project stands in terms of meeting scope, time, and cost goals. Is work being accomplished as planned? How long did it take to do certain tasks? How much money has been spent to date? Status reports can take various formats depending on the stakeholders' needs.
- **Progress reports** describe what the project team has accomplished during a certain period. In many projects, each team member prepares a weekly or monthly progress report. Team leaders often create consolidated progress reports based on the information received from team members.

- **Forecasts** predict future project status and progress based on past information and trends. How long will it take to finish the project based on how things are going? How much more money will be needed to complete the project? Project managers can also use earned value management, as described earlier in this chapter, to answer these questions by estimating the budget at completion and the projected completion date based on how the project is progressing.

Stakeholders often review project performance information at status review meetings, such as the ones Kristin has with the project steering committee. Status review meetings are a good way to highlight important information, empower people to be accountable for their work, and have face-to-face discussions about key project issues. Many project managers also hold periodic status review meetings with their own team members to exchange important project information and motivate people to make progress on their parts of the project. Likewise, many senior managers, who are often part of a review board or oversight committee, hold status review meetings. At these meetings, several program and project managers must report overall status information to keep everyone abreast of important events and to learn from each other as well.

Unlike the managers found in Dilbert cartoons (Figure 7-14), most senior managers do want to review pertinent information at status review meetings and discuss problems, issues, and forecasts.

DILBERT: © Scott Adams/Dist. by United Feature Syndicate, Inc.

FIGURE 7-14 The shortest performance review meeting ever

Sample Performance Report

Figure 7-15 provides a sample report that Kristin gave at a performance review meeting with the Just-In-Time Training project steering committee. Notice that the report references an earned value chart, similar to the one shown in Figure 7-4. Also notice the use of numbers that are of key interest to senior managers, such as the number of people trained to date and registered for courses. Also note the issues and suggestions and the project changes sections of the report. Performance review meetings should focus on addressing these items to ensure that projects succeed.

Progress Report

February 1, 2010

Project Name: Just-In-Time Training Project

Reporting Period: January 1 – February 1, 2010

Work completed this reporting period:
Held first negotiating skills course (instructor-led) with 20 participants
Held first supplier management executive course (instructor-led) with 17 participants
Held second supplier management introductory course (instructor-led) with 20 participants
Had 32 people begin the Web-based introductory supplier management course
Continued developing other Web-based courses
Prepared evaluations of all courses held to date

Work to complete next reporting period:
Hold first advanced supplier management course
Hold fist project management course
Hold first software applications course

What's going well and why:
Participation in all courses is good. Every instructor-led course was full, except the supplier management executive course. All of the courses were advertised well, and we had more than enough people sign-up for the classes. We put several people on the list for later courses after courses were filled in the registration system.
The average course ratings were above 3.8 on a 5.0 scale. Comments were generally very positive.
More people than expected started the first Web-based course. Development of new Web-based courses is going well.

What's not going well and why:
We did not fill the supplier management executive course, as planned. Three people could not attend at the last minute, and it was too late to get a replacement. We will work on a policy to help prevent this problem in the future for all instructor-led classes.
We were surprised that so many people started the Web-based introductory supplier management course. We can handle the numbers, but we could have done a better job at forecasting demand.

Suggestions/Issues:
Develop a policy to handle people not being able to attend instructor-led courses at the last minute.
Try to do a better job at forecasting demand for Web-based courses.

Project changes:
No major changes to report. The earned value chart in Attachment 1 shows planned value, actual cost, and earned value information to date. We are very close to our plans, running slightly ahead of schedule and a bit overbudget.

FIGURE 7-15   Sample performance report

Managing Stakeholders

Project managers must understand and work with various stakeholders while monitoring and controlling projects. In particular, they need to address how they will identify and resolve issues. An important tool that many project teams use is an issue log. An **issue** is a matter under question or dispute that could impede project success. An **issue log** is a tool used to document and monitor the resolution of project issues. It's important to resolve issues as soon as possible so that the project can proceed as planned.

Sample Issue Log

Figure 7-16 shows part of an early issue log that Kristin and her team used to help document and manage the resolution of issues on their project. The issue log includes columns for the issue number, the issue description, the impact of the issue on the project, the date the issue was reported, who reported the issue, who the issue resolution was assigned to, the priority of the issue (High, Medium, or Low), the due date to report back on the issue, the status of the issue, and comments related to the issue. Project managers can tailor the format of issue logs as needed. The project management software that Kristin's team used for the Just-In-Time Training project included an online issue log that could be sorted and filtered various ways. For example, Kristin always sorted issues by priority so that she could focus on high priorities. She also sorted them by who reported the issue and who was assigned to each issue to make sure that the appropriate people were making progress.

Issue Log

August 20, 2009

Project Name: Just-In-Time Training Project

Issue #	Issue Description	Impact on Project	Date Reported	Reported By	Assigned To	Priority (H/M/L)	Due Date	Status	Comments
1	Key project team member is not working out	Can severely hurt project because Jamie is our supplier management expert	Aug 2	Kristin	Kristin	H	Sep 2	Open	Working with Jamie and appropriate managers to find a replacement
2	IT staff that is performing survey is overallocated	Delaying the survey will delay the entire project because it is a critical task	Sep 26	Mohammed	Kristin	H	Aug 5	Closed	Paid overtime was approved
3	Julia Portman, VP of IT and steering committee member, now has conflicts with our weekly meeting time	Julia is a key member of the steering committee, and we need her at meetings	Oct 2	Julia	Steering committee	H	Oct 9	Open	Everyone will check calendars to find a new meeting time

FIGURE 7-16 Sample issue log

MONITORING AND CONTROLLING TASKS FOR PROJECT RISK MANAGEMENT

Monitoring and controlling risks involves executing the risk management processes to respond to risk events. Recall from Chapter 5 that a risk event is a specific, uncertain event that may occur to the detriment or enhancement of the project. Executing the risk management processes means ensuring that risk awareness is an ongoing activity performed by the entire project team throughout the project. Project risk management does not stop with the initial risk analysis. Identified risk events may not materialize, or their probabilities of occurrence or impact may diminish or increase. Similarly, new risk events are normally identified as the project progresses. Newly identified risk events need to go through the same process of analysis and control as those identified during the initial risk assessment. A redistribution of resources devoted to risk management may be necessary because of relative changes in risk exposure.

Carrying out individual risk management plans involves monitoring risks based on defined milestones and making decisions regarding risks and their response strategies. It might be necessary to alter a strategy if it becomes ineffective, implement planned contingency activities, or eliminate a risk event from the list of potential risks. Project teams sometimes use **workarounds**—unplanned responses to risk events—when they do not have contingency plans in place.

Risk reassessment, risk audits, variance and trend analysis, technical performance measurements, reserve analysis, and status meetings or periodic risk reviews are all tools and techniques for performing risk monitoring and control. Outputs of this process include the following:

- Requested changes
- Recommended corrective and preventive actions
- Updates to the risk register, project management plan, or organizational process assets, such as lessons learned information that might help future projects

Sample Risk Register Updates

Recall from Chapter 5 that the number one risk event in the risk register for the Just-In-Time Training project at that time was a poor survey response. Because the project was now halfway completed, the risk register would have to change significantly. New risks would be identified and potential responses would change based on the current situation. Status of all risks would also be updated.

For example, halfway through the project, senior management informed Kristin that the company, Global Construction, Inc., was growing faster than expected, and they thought the number of people needing training would be higher than expected. This information resulted in the identification of several new risks related to the difficulty of accommodating this growth in trainees. For example, although the Web-based courses were the most popular and adding participants to them would be less expensive than adding to any other type of course, there was a risk that the discussion board would become unmanageable. People might waste time reading through hundreds of messages or just ignore this part of the course altogether. Kristin and her team, including suppliers for the Web-based courses, would need to develop potential responses to this risk and take action if it did occur.

Another risk related to employee growth might be the need to offer more instructor-led classes, which would result in increased costs to the project. As you can see, the risk register must be constantly updated as part of project monitoring and control.

MONITORING AND CONTROLLING TASKS FOR PROJECT PROCUREMENT MANAGEMENT

The main procurement management task performed to monitor and control projects is administering the contract. Administering the contract, or contract administration, ensures that the seller's performance meets contractual requirements. The contractual relationship is a legal relationship and, as such, is subject to state and federal contract laws. It is very important that appropriate legal and contracting professionals be involved in writing and administering contracts.

Several tools and techniques can help in contract administration:

- Formal contract change-control system
- Buyer-conducted performance reviews
- Inspections and audits
- Performance reporting
- Payment systems
- Claims administration
- Records management
- Information technology to support contract administration

A key output of contract administration is contract documentation. Contract documentation would include the contract itself along with requested unapproved contract changes and approved change requests. It is very important to document all changes to the contract and communicate those changes to all affected stakeholders. For example, if a supplier developing a course for the Just-In-Time Training project agreed to add a topic to the course at no extra cost, that agreement must be added to the contract to make it legal. Likewise, if Global Construction decided to add more than the agreed on number of instructor-led courses, it would need to update that information in the contract as well. Updates are often made by having both parties—the buyer and the seller—sign an addendum to the contract.

Project team members must be aware of the potential legal problems of their not understanding a contract. Changes must be handled properly for items under contract. Without understanding the provisions of the contract, a project manager might not realize that she is authorizing the contractor to do additional work at additional cost. Therefore, change control is an important part of the contract administration process.

It is critical that project managers and team members watch for constructive change orders. **Constructive change orders** are oral or written acts or omissions by someone with actual or apparent authority that can be construed to have the same effect as a written change order. For example, if a member of Kristin's project team has met with a supplier or contractor on a weekly basis for three months to provide guidelines for performing work, he can be viewed as an apparent authority. If he tells the contractor to redo part of a report that has already been delivered and accepted by the project manager, that action can be viewed as a constructive change order and the contractor can legally bill the buyer for the additional work. Likewise, if this apparent authority tells the contractor to skip parts of a critical review meeting in the interests of time, it would not be the contractor's fault if he missed important information.

Suggestions for Administering Contracts

The following suggestions help ensure adequate change control and good contract administration:

- Changes to any part of the project need to be reviewed, approved, and documented by the same people in the same way that the original part of the plan was approved.
- Evaluation of any change should include an impact analysis. How will the change affect the scope, time, cost, and quality of the goods or services being provided? There must also be a baseline against which to compare and analyze changes.
- Changes must be documented in writing. Project team members should document all important meetings and telephone calls.
- Project managers and their teams must stay closely involved with suppliers to make sure that their deliverables meet business needs and work in the organization's environment. Do not assume that work will run smoothly because you hired a reputable supplier. The buying organization needs to provide expertise as well.
- Have backup plans in case the procurement does not produce the desired results.

Chapter Summary

Monitoring and controlling involves regularly measuring progress to ensure that the project is meeting its objectives and addressing current business needs. The project manager and other staff monitor progress against plans and take corrective action when necessary. This chapter summarizes the monitoring and controlling tasks and key outputs for all nine knowledge areas.

Every knowledge area includes tasks and outputs to help monitor and control projects. Outputs common to all knowledge areas include requested changes, recommended corrective actions, and updates to applicable plans and processes.

Monitoring and controlling outputs related to integration management also include forecasts. Earned value management is a project performance measurement technique that integrates scope, time, and cost data. You can use it to forecast when a project will be completed and how much it will cost given past performance data.

Monitoring and controlling tasks related to scope management include scope verification and scope change control, and its unique output includes accepted deliverables. A sample form for verifying acceptance of deliverables is provided for the Just-In-Time Training project.

Monitoring and controlling outputs related to time, cost, and quality management include schedule control, cost control, and quality control. Unique outputs include performance measurements, forecasted completion, and quality-control measurements. Sample outputs are provided for the Just-In-Time Training project.

Monitoring and controlling outputs related to communications management include performance reports, forecasts, and resolved issues. Sample outputs are provided for the Just-In-Time Training project.

Monitoring and controlling outputs related to risk management include updating the risk register. Sample updates are provided for the Just-In-Time Training project.

Monitoring and controlling outputs related to procurement management include contract documentation. Suggestions are provided for administering contracts.

Quick Quiz

1. Which knowledge areas include tasks related to monitoring and controlling?

    a. project scope, time, cost, and quality management

    b. project integration, scope, time, cost, and quality management

    c. project human resource, communications, risk, and procurement management

    d. all nine knowledge areas

2. _____ is a project performance measurement technique that integrates scope, time, and cost data.

    a. Integrated change control

    b. Flowcharting

    c. Earned value management

    d. Forecasting

3. _____ involves formal acceptance of the completed project scope by the stakeholders.

   a. Scope creep

   b. Scope verification

   c. Deliverable acceptance

   d. Customer sign-off

4. _____ issues cause the most conflict over the life of projects.

   a. Change control

   b. Scope creep

   c. Cost

   d. Schedule

5. A _____ chart is a histogram that can help you identify and prioritize problem areas.

   a. Pareto

   b. control

   c. run

   d. scatter

6. When a process is out of control, variations in the results of the process are caused by _____ events.

   a. random

   b. nonrandom

   c. planned

   d. unplanned

7. Which of the following is not a tool or technique for managing project teams?

   a. observation and conversation

   b. issue logs

   c. performance appraisals

   d. control charts

8. _____ predict future project status and progress based on past information and trends.

   a. Forecasts

   b. Status reports

   c. Progress reports

   d. Histograms

9. _____ are unplanned responses to risk events.

    a. Contingencies

    b. Reserves

    c. Workarounds

    d. Overallocations

10. _____ change orders are oral or written acts or omissions by someone with actual or apparent authority that can be construed to have the same effect as a written change order.

    a. Constructive

    b. Contract

    c. Procurement

    d. Controlled

Quick Quiz Answers

1. D; 2. C; 3. B; 4. D; 5. A; 6. B; 7. D; 8. A; 9. C; 10. A

Discussion Questions

1. What is involved in monitoring and controlling projects? What outputs of monitoring and controlling are common to all knowledge areas?

2. Explain how earned value management helps you monitor project performance and forecast future cost and schedule information. What do you need to do to use earned value management?

3. What are the three main objectives of integrated change control?

4. What is the difference between scope verification and scope control? Why are both important to project success?

5. What are some of the tools and techniques for performing time, cost, and quality control? What are the Seven Basic Tools of Quality?

6. What are some of the tools and techniques for managing project teams? Summarize some of the advice typically given for managing teams. Which items do you think are most important?

7. Why is it important to keep the risk register up to date?

8. Why is it important to document contract changes? Why should project teams be watchful for constructive change orders?

Exercises

1. Find an example of a large project that took more than one year to complete, such as a major construction project. You can ask people at your college, university, or work about a recent project, such as a major fund raising campaign, information systems installation, or building project. You can also find information about projects online such as the Big Dig in Boston (*www.masspike.com/bigdig*), the Patronas Twin Towers in Malaysia and many other building projects (*www.greatbuildings.com*), etc. Describe some of the tasks performed to monitor and control the project. Write a one-page paper or prepare a short presentation summarizing your findings.

2. Given the following information for a one-year project, answer the following questions. Assume you have actual and earned value data at the end of the second month. Recall that PV is the planned value, EV is the earned value, AC is the actual cost, and BAC is the budget at completion.

   PV = $23,000

   EV = $20,000

   AC = $25,000

   BAC = $120,000

   a. What is the cost variance, schedule variance, cost performance index (CPI), and schedule performance index (SPI) for the project?

   b. How is the project progressing? Is it ahead of schedule or behind schedule? Is it under budget or over budget?

   c. Use the CPI to calculate the estimate at completion (EAC) for this project. Is the project performing better or worse than planned?

   d. Use the SPI to estimate how long it will take to finish this project.

   e. Sketch the earned value chart for this project, using Figure 7-4 as a guide. Assume the data for month 1 is half of the values given for PV, EV, and AC at the end of month 2.

3. Follow the steps for using Microsoft Project 2007 provided in the *Guide to Using Microsoft Project 2007* in Appendix A, pages A.60–A.68. Open the data files as directed and then establish a baseline plan, create a tracking Gantt chart, and implement earned value management using this software. The data files are also provided on the companion site.

4. Assume you are working on a project to improve customer service. Create a Pareto chart based on the information in the following table. Use the Pareto chart template from the companion Web site or sketch the chart by hand so that your resulting chart looks similar to Figure 7-12.

Customer complaints	Frequency/week
Customer is on hold too long	90
Customer gets transferred to wrong area or cut off	20
Service rep cannot answer customer's questions	120
Service rep does not follow through as promised	40

5. If you purchased the Fissure simulation software bundled with this text, follow the detailed instructions on the companion Web site to run the Fissure simulation software. Summarize information from each of your workweek reports and print out the final earned value chart as well as any other information you think is valuable. Write a two- to three-page single-spaced report summarizing what you learned by using this simulation software.

Team Projects

1. Your organization initiated a project to raise money for an important charity. Assume that there are 1,000 people in your organization. Also, assume that you have six months to raise as much money as possible, with a goal of $100,000. List three problems that could arise while monitoring and controlling the project. Describe each problem in detail, and then develop realistic approaches to solving them in a two- to three-page paper or a 15-minute presentation. Be creative in your responses, and use at least one quality-control tool in your analysis. Remember that this project is run solely by volunteers.

2. You are part of a team in charge of a project to help people in your company (500 people) lose weight. This project is part of a competition, and the top "losers" will be featured in a popular television show. Assume that you have six months to complete the project and a budget of $10,000. You are halfway though the project, and morale is very low. People are also complaining about a lack of communication and support on the project. Although many people have been participating and have lost weight, many have plateaued or started gaining weight back. Create an issue log to document these and related issues. Also create a new entry for the risk register for this project. Document your responses in a two- to three-page paper or a 15-minute presentation.

3. Using the information you developed in Team Project 1 or 2, role-play a meeting to brainstorm and develop strategies for solving problems with key stakeholders. Determine who will play what role (project manager, team member from a certain department, senior managers, and so on). Be creative in displaying different personalities (a senior manager who questions the importance of the project to the organization, a team member who is very shy or obnoxious).

4. Brainstorm two different quality related problems that you are aware of at your college or organization. Then review the charts found in the section of this chapter on the seven basic tools of quality and create two charts to help analyze the quality problems. Prepare a one- to two-page paper or short presentation describing the problems and how the charts help to visualize them.

5. Perform the monitoring and controlling tasks for the New Business Venture case study provided in Appendix C or for one of the cases on the companion Web site. If you are working on a real team project, create relevant monitoring and controlling documents, such as a performance report and issue log using the templates and samples in this chapter as guides. Present your results to the class.

Companion Web Sites

Visit the companion Web site for this text (*www.course.com/mis/pm2/schwalbe* or *http://login. course.com*) to access:

- Lecture notes
- Interactive quizzes and Jeopardy game
- Template files
- Sample documents
- Podcasts
- More ideas for team projects, including real projects and case studies
- Links to additional resources related to project management

Key Terms

actual cost (AC) — The total direct and indirect costs incurred in accomplishing work on an activity during a given period.

budget at completion (BAC) — The approved total budget for the project.

constructive change orders — Oral or written acts or omissions by someone with actual or apparent authority that can be construed to have the same effect as a written change order.

control chart — A graphic display of data that illustrates the results of a process over time.

earned value (EV) — An estimate of the value of the physical work actually completed.

earned value management (EVM) — A project performance measurement technique that integrates scope, time, and cost data.

estimate at completion (EAC) — A forecast of how much the project will cost upon completion.

flowcharts — The graphic displays of the logic and flow of processes that help you analyze how problems occur and how processes can be improved.

forecasts — The reports that predict future project status and progress based on past information and trends.

histogram — A bar graph of a distribution of variables.

integrated change control — The process of identifying, evaluating, and managing changes throughout the project's life cycle.

issue — A matter under question or dispute that could impede project success.

issue log — A tool used to document and monitor the resolution of project issues.

Pareto chart — A histogram that can help you identify and prioritize problem areas.

planned value (PV) — That portion of the approved total cost estimate planned to be spent on an activity during a given period.

progress reports — The reports that describe what the project team has accomplished during a certain period.

rate of performance (RP) — The percentage of actual work completed divided by the percentage of work planned to have been completed at any given time.

scatter diagram — A diagram that helps show if there is a relationship between two variables.

scope verification — The formal acceptance of the completed project scope by the customer or designated stakeholders.

slipped milestone — A milestone activity that was actually completed later than originally planned.

status reports — The reports that describe where the project stands at a specific point in time.

tracking Gantt chart — A Gantt chart that compares planned and actual project schedule information.

workarounds — The unplanned responses to risk events.

End Notes

[1] Fran Kelly, "The World Today—Olympic Planning Schedule behind Time," *ABC Online* (March 4, 2004).

[2] Jay Weiner and Rachel Blount, "Olympics Are Safe but Crowds Are Sparse," *Minneapolis Star Tribune* (August 22, 2004), A9.

[3] Reuters, "Olympics Bill Reportedly Passes $12 Billion," *MSNBC.com* (August 25, 2004).

[4] Tom Chauduri and David Schlotzhauer, "So Many Projects, So Little Time," *PM Network* (October 2003), 58.

[5] Joan Vennochi, "Time, Money, and the Big Dig," *Boston Globe* (April 26, 2005).

CLOSING PROJECTS AND BEST PRACTICES

LEARNING OBJECTIVES

After reading this chapter, you will be able to:

- List several tasks and outputs of project closing
- Discuss the process of closing a project performed as part of project integration management, explain the importance of a project close-out meeting and knowledge transfer, and describe the contents of a customer acceptance/project completion form, final project report, and lessons-learned report
- Explain the process of contract closure performed as part of project procurement management, and describe the contents of a written notice of a closed contract
- List several best practices used in project management
- Discuss how improving project management maturity can improve project performance
- Read final advice about project management

OPENING CASE

The Just-In-Time Training project was almost finished. Twenty instructor-led courses had been conducted over the past year, and a majority of Global Construction's employees took at least one Just-In Time course, most using the Web-based delivery option. Some senior managers were surprised at how quickly workers took to the Web-based courses and were also pleased that many employees took the courses on their own time. Participants liked the interactive feedback and started networking more internally to improve productivity and collaboration. Employees provided excellent feedback on the new approach to training and suggested several new topics to be added to the list of training subjects. The project steering committee was looking forward to Kristin's final report and presentation on the project.

INTRODUCTION

Closing projects involves gaining stakeholder and customer acceptance of the final products and services, and bringing the project to an orderly end. It includes verifying that all of the deliverables are complete, and often includes a final presentation and report. For both projects that are completed and those that are canceled before completion, it is important to formally close the project and reflect on what can be learned to improve future projects. As philosopher George Santayana said, "Those who cannot remember the past are condemned to repeat it."

It is also important to plan for and execute a smooth transition of the project into the normal operations of the company. Most projects produce results that are integrated into the existing organizational structure. For example, Global Construction's Just-In-Time Training project will require staff to coordinate future training after the project is completed. Recall from Chapter 3 that the life-cycle cost estimate for the project included $400,000 each year for three years, or 40 percent of the total project cost, for work to be done after the project was completed. Before ending the project, Kristin and her team created a transition plan as part of the final report to integrate the new training into the firm's standard operations.

SUMMARY OF CLOSING OUTPUTS

Figure 8-1 summarizes key outputs of project closing by knowledge area, based on the *PMBOK® Guide*. Notice that the first output listed is procedures for administrative and contract closure. Every project should have procedures to guide closure. Samples of closing procedures and other outputs produced in closing the Just-In-Time Training project are provided in this chapter.

Knowledge area	Outputs
Project integration management	Administrative and contract closure procedures Final products, services, or results Updates to organizational process assets
Project procurement management	Closed contracts Updates to organizational process assets

FIGURE 8-1   Summary of project closing outputs

CLOSING TASKS FOR PROJECT INTEGRATION MANAGEMENT

The last task in project integration management is closing the project. To close a project, you must finalize all activities and transfer the completed or canceled work to the appropriate people. The main outputs of closing projects are as follows:

- *Administrative closure procedures:* It is important for project teams and other stakeholders to develop and follow a step-by-step process for closing projects. In particular, administrative closure procedures should define the approval process for all project deliverables and how records will be retained. Chapter 7 provided a sample deliverable acceptance form used by Global Construction. The company also used a customer acceptance/project completion form to formally close the entire project, which will be shown later in this chapter.

- *Contract closure procedures:* Many projects involve contracts, which are legally binding agreements. Contract closure procedures describe the methodology for making sure that the contract has been completed, including both delivery of goods and services, and payment for them.

- *Final products, services, or results:* Project sponsors are usually most interested in making sure that final products, services, or results are delivered on schedule and within budget. A final project report and presentation are also commonly used during project closing. A sample table of contents from the Just-In-Time Training project's final report is provided in the next section, as well as part of the transition plan produced as part of the final report. The section of the final report summarizing project results should also address how well the project met key project metrics. It is important for project teams to set aside time to prepare a good final report and presentation, as these items often receive high visibility.

- *Updates to organizational process assets:* Recall from Chapter 6 that organizational process assets help people understand, follow, and improve business processes. Examples of organizational process assets include policies and procedures, guidelines, information systems, financial systems, management systems, lessons learned, and historical information. During project closing, the project team should update appropriate process assets, especially lessons learned. At the end of the Just-In-Time Training project, Kristin's team prepared a lessons-learned report, which will serve as a tremendous asset for future projects.

In closing the Just-In-Time Training project, Kristin and her team prepared a customer acceptance/project completion form, a final report and presentation, a transition plan (provided as part of the final report), and a lessons-learned report. They also held a project close-out meeting to help transfer knowledge to other people in the organization. Kristin also organized a project closure luncheon for the project team right after the final project presentation. She used the luncheon to celebrate a job well done.

Sample Customer Acceptance/Project Completion Form

As part of project closing, Global Construction had the project sponsor complete a customer acceptance/project completion form. Even if the project had been terminated, the sponsor would still have completed the form to signify the end of the project. Figure 8-2 shows the form that was filled out for the Just-In-Time Training project. Note that this form refers to completion of the entire project, not just a specific deliverable. It should be completed and signed by the project sponsor.

Customer Acceptance/Project Completion Form
June 30, 2010

Project Name: <u>Just-In-Time Training Project</u>
Project Manager: <u>Kristin Maur</u>

I (We), the undersigned, acknowledge and accept delivery of the work completed for this project on behalf of our organization. My (Our) signature(s) attest(s) to my (our) agreement that this project has been completed. No further work should be done on this project.

Name	Title	Signature	Date
Lucy Camerena	Training Director	Lucy Camarena	June 30, 2010

1. Was this project completed to your satisfaction?   **X** Yes ___   No ___

2. Please provide the main reasons for your satisfaction or dissatisfaction with this project.
The project met and exceeded my expectations. In my 15 years with this company, I have never seen workers so interested in training courses. Kristin effectively coordinated all of the people who worked on this project. We worked with a number of new suppliers, and everything went very smoothly.

3. Please provide suggestions on how our organization could improve its project delivery capability in the future.
One suggestion would be to try to improve our estimating and forecasting abilities. The project costs were slightly over budget, even with some reserve built in. The schedule buffer prevented the project from finishing late. We also need to improve the way we forecast the number of people who want to take courses. The demand for the Web-based courses was much higher than expected. Even though that was a pleasant surprise, it was still poor forecasting and caused extra work for project and support staff.

Thank you for your inputs.

FIGURE 8-2 Sample customer acceptance/project completion form

Sample Final Report

Figure 8-3 is the table of contents for the final project report for the Just-In-Time Training project (the cover page of the report included the project title, date, and team member names). Notice that the report includes a transition plan and a plan to analyze the benefits of the training each year. Also notice that the final report includes attachments for all the project management and product-related documents. Kristin knew the importance of providing complete final documentation on projects and that the project steering committee would expect a comprehensive final report on such an important project. The project team produced a hard copy of the final documentation for the project sponsor and each steering committee member, and placed an electronic copy on the corporate intranet with the other project archives. Kristin also led the team in giving a final project presentation, which summarized key information in the final project report.

Final Project Report
June 20, 2010

Project Name: Just-In-Time Training Project

1. Project Objectives
2. Summary of Project Results
3. Original and Actual Schedule
4. Original and Actual Budget
5. Project Assessment
6. Transition Plan
7. Training Benefits Plan

Attachments:

A. Key Project Management Documentation
   - Business case
   - Project charter
   - Project management plan
   - Performance reports

B. Product-Related Documentation

   - Survey and results
   - Summary of user inputs
   - Report on research of existing training
   - Partnership agreements
   - Course materials
   - Intranet site training information
   - Summary of course evaluations

FIGURE 8-3 Sample table of contents for a final project report

Sample Transition Plan

As mentioned earlier, the life-cycle cost estimate for Global Construction's Just-In-Time Training project included $400,000 each year for three years for work to be done after the project was completed. The transition plan included information related to what work had to be done, by whom, and when. When developing a transition plan, the project team should work with managers in affected operating departments, and the contents of the plan should be tailored to fit the support needs of the project. Figure 8-4 provides part of the transition plan for the Just-In-Time Training project.

Transition Plan

June 20, 2010

Project Name: Just-In-Time Training Project

Introduction

The main goal of this project was to develop a new training program at Global Construction to provide just-in-time training to employees on key topics, including supplier management, negotiating skills, project management, and software applications. New courses were developed and offered in instructor-led, CD-ROM, and Web-based formats. These courses will continue to be offered at Global Construction for the next several years. This transition plan describes the work required to support these courses.

Assumptions

- Support for the just-in-time training will be handled by staff in affected operational departments, including the training, IT, HR, and contract departments.
- Funding for the required support is budgeted at $400,000 per year for three years. These funds will be used to pay staff in the operational departments supporting this project, experts providing information for courses, and suppliers providing training materials and courses.
- New course topics will be developed under a new project and are not part of this transition plan.

Organization

The Training Director, Lucy Camarena, will lead all efforts to support the Just-In-Time Training courses. Staff from the training, IT, HR, and contract departments will provide support as required. See the organizational chart provided in Attachment 1.

Work Required

The main work required to support the training developed from this project includes:

- Maintaining related information on the intranet site
- Handling course registration
- Determining the number of courses offered each year and when they will be offered
- Providing classrooms for the instructor-led training
- Coordinating with suppliers for all training courses
- Planning and managing the internal experts who provide some of the training and expert support for the courses
- Collecting course evaluation information and suggestions for changing the content or format of courses
- Reporting information to senior management on a monthly basis

See Attachment 2 for detailed information on the work required.

Schedule

See Attachment 3 for a draft schedule of work to be performed in the next year. The training director is responsible for scheduling and managing the work required to support the just-in-time training.

FIGURE 8-4 Sample transition plan

Sample Lessons-Learned Report

Instead of asking each member of the Just-In-Time Training project team and the project managers from the major supplier organizations to write individual lessons-learned reports, Kristin decided to use a technique she had read about in an article in which key stakeholders held a sticky-note party to document lessons learned. Instead of writing lessons learned in a traditional way, key stakeholders met, wrote down all of the lessons they had learned on sticky notes, and then posted them to the wall. It was an enjoyable way for everyone to get together and share what they had learned from the project. After they finished, Kristin summarized the inputs in a list that everyone could access on the project Web site. She also used the corporate template to prepare a short lessons-learned report for inclusion in the final documentation for the project, as shown in Figure 8-5. Notice the question-and-answer format of the report, which is part of the lessons-learned template used for all projects done at Global Construction, Inc. Also notice that the lessons-learned report was finished 10 days before the project ended.

Lessons-Learned Report

June 20, 2010

Project Name:	The Just-In-Time Training Project of Global Construction Inc.
Project Sponsor:	Lucy Camarena
Project Manager:	Kristin Maur
Project Dates:	July 1, 2009–June 30, 2010
Final Budget:	$1,072,000

1. Did the project meet scope, time, and cost goals?

We did meet scope and time goals, but we had to request an additional $72,000, which the sponsor approved. We actually exceeded scope goals by having more people take training courses than planned, primarily the Web-based courses.

2. What was the success criteria listed in the project scope statement?

The following statement outlined the project scope and success criteria:
"Our sponsor has stated that the project will be a success if the new training courses are all available within one year, if the average course evaluations are at least 3.0 on a 1-5 scale, and if the company recoups the cost of the project in reduced training costs within two years after project completion."

3. Reflect on whether or not you met the project success criteria.

All of the new training courses were offered within a year, and the course evaluations averaged 3.4 on a 5.0 scale. We do not know if the cost of the project will be recouped within two years after completion, but the number of people who took the Web-based training courses far exceeded our expectations. Because the Web-based training is more cost-effective than the instructor-led training, we are confident that the costs will be recouped in less than two years.

FIGURE 8-5 Project lessons-learned report

4. What were the main lessons your team learned from this project?

The main lessons we learned include the following:

- Having good communication was instrumental to project success. We had a separate item in the WBS for stakeholder communications, which was very important. Moving from traditional to primarily Web-based training was a big change for Global Construction, so the strong communication was crucial. The intranet-site information was excellent, thanks to support from the IT department. It was also very effective to have different departments create project description posters to hang in their work areas. They showed creativity and team spirit.
- Teamwork and supplier partnerships were essential. It was extremely helpful to take time to develop and follow a team contract for the project team and to focus on developing good partnerships with suppliers.
- Good planning paid off in terms of when plans were executed. We spent a fair amount of time developing a good project charter, scope statement, WBS, schedules, and so on. Everyone worked together to develop these planning documents, and there was strong buy-in. We kept the plans up to date and made key project information available for everyone on a secure Web site.
- Creativity and innovation are infectious: After departments had so much fun making their posters in their work areas, people picked up on the idea of being creative and innovative throughout the project. Everyone realized that training and learning could be enjoyable.
- The project steering committee was very effective, and it was extremely helpful to meet regularly with the committee. Having committee members from departments throughout the company was very important and helped promote the training created as part of this project.

5. Describe one example of what went right on this project.

We were skeptical about hiring an outside consultant to help us develop a short list of potential suppliers for the training courses, but it was well worth the money. We gained a good deal of useful information very quickly, and the consultant made excellent recommendations and helped us develop partnerships that benefited us as well as our suppliers.

6. Describe one example of what went wrong on this project.

The senior supplier management specialist assigned to the team at the beginning of the project was not a good fit. The project manager should have had more involvement in selecting project team members.

7. What will you do differently on the next project based on your experience working on this project?

For future training projects, it would be helpful to line up experts and mentors further in advance. We underestimated the number of people who would take the Web-based courses, and participants liked the interactive features, such as getting expert advice and having a list of people willing to mentor them on various topics. We were scrambling to recruit people, and then had to figure out how to organize them in an effective manner.

FIGURE 8-5 Project lessons-learned report (continued)

Project Close-Out Meeting and Knowledge Transfer

It is good practice to hold a close-out meeting as a project nears completion or termination. At this meeting, like the kick-off meeting, you should invite key project stakeholders. The project champion should start off the meeting, and the project manager and his/her team should review information like the following:

- The scope, time, and cost goals and outcomes
- The success criteria and results in achieving them
- Main changes that occurred during the project and how they were addressed
- The main lessons learned on the project
- A summary of the transition plan

The project team should also ask for comments and questions from stakeholders. It's important to get other perspectives on how things went. If there are still any issues that need to be addressed, the project manager should follow through on them to successfully close them out.

It is also important to take time to transfer knowledge learned while working on the project. In particular, people who will take over products or results produced as part of the project would need to spend time with project team members so they understand what is involved in detail. In this example, people from the training, IT, HR, and contract departments would gain from knowledge transfer from the Just-In-Time Training project.

Of course, these people could read the final report, transition plan, and lessons learned, but most people also want face-to-face interaction to really benefit from knowledge transfer. For example, since Kristin would move on to another project after completing this one, she should sit down with the person from the training department who would handle many of the management tasks involved in planning and implementing future training courses. She should offer to mentor this person and be available as needed to answer questions. Likewise, the IT person who developed the intranet materials related to the project should also sit down with whoever will take over that work and share his/her expertise as well. If it makes sense to provide further documentation, the person who knows the most about the work should take the time to write it.

Many organizations are working hard to improve the knowledge transfer process, since employee knowledge or human capital is one of their key assets. It is crucial, therefore to make project knowledge transfer a priority, especially if the benefits of a project are not achieved immediately. For example, one of the success criteria for the Just-In-Time Training project was to recoup the cost of the project in reduced training costs within two years after project completion. The business case stated that the goal was to reduce training costs per employee by 10 percent each year or about $100 per employee per year. Kristin should work with the people taking over the training to ensure that they measure training costs and work to achieve this goal.

CLOSING TASKS FOR PROJECT PROCUREMENT MANAGEMENT

The final process in project procurement management is closing the contract, or contract closure. **Contract closure** involves completion and settlement of contracts, and resolution of any open items. The project team should determine if all work required in each contract was completed correctly and satisfactorily. The team should also update records to reflect final results and archive information for future use.

Two tools to assist in contract closure are procurement audits and a records management system. **Procurement audits** are often performed during contract closure to identify lessons learned in the entire procurement process. Organizations should strive to improve all their business processes, including procurement management. A **records management system** provides the ability to easily organize, find, and archive documents, such as those related to procurement. It is often an automated system, or at least partially automated, because there can be a large amount of information related to project procurement.

Outputs from contract closure include updates to organizational process assets and closed contracts. Just as with administrative closure, updating organizational process assets includes documentation, historical information, and lessons learned. To close contracts, the buying organization often provides the seller with formal written notice that the contract has been completed. Buyers might also consider the final payment to the seller as the contract closeout. The contract itself should include requirements for formal acceptance and closure.

Sample Written Notice of a Closed Contract

Figure 8-6 provides an example of a formal letter that Global Construction sent to one of its sellers, ABC Training Consultants, to formally close out their contract. The contract, a service agreement in this case, included a clause that stated that written notice would be provided to formally close the contract. The seller in this particular example also requested that the buyer provide a short performance assessment as part of the closure letter. (See Chapter 6 to review the service agreement and Chapter 5 for the contract statement of work. Recall that the work had to be completed by September 9, 2009, for this contract.)

300

Chapter 8

Global Construction, Inc., Contract Closure Notice

September 16, 2009

As described in our service agreement (SA390-7), this letter provides formal notice that the work you were contracted to perform for Global Construction has been completed. ABC Training developed a qualified-sellers list containing 30 potential sellers and a report with one page of key information on each seller. Payment is being processed based on the invoice provided by ABC Training.

Kristin Maur, the project manager, has provided the following performance assessment for the work provided:

"We were very pleased with the work of ABC Training. Members of the firm were professional, knowledgeable, and easy to work with. Global Construction depended on ABC Training to develop a qualified sellers list for this important project, and we were extremely happy with the results. On a scale of 1 to 10, you earned a 10!"

Lawrence Scheller

By: Lawrence Scheller, Contract Specialist, Global Construction, Inc.

Date: September 16, 2009

FIGURE 8-6 Sample contract closure notice

⊗ WHAT WENT WRONG?

Many organizations continue to struggle with project management. If you cannot manage projects well, you cannot manage programs or portfolios well either. People continue to try to understand the challenges of managing projects and question why there seem to have been few improvements in this important practice.

When George Stephenson built a railway from Liverpool to Manchester in the 1820s, it was completed behind schedule and 45 percent over budget. In 2005, the reconstruction of Wembley Stadium, the home of English soccer, was threatened when the Australian developer of the site said it faced huge losses on the GBP 750 million (1.4 billion U.S. dollars) project. The cost of steel doubled in 2004, and labor costs were exceeding estimates as they worked to complete the stadium in time for the May 2006 FA Cup final.

One suggested reason why problems prevail is that project initiation gets separated from execution. Many projects are done by outside firms, and bidders competing for the work often make overly optimistic assumptions about costs and revenues. A study published in 2005 in the *Journal of the American Planning Association* examined 210 large rail and road projects in 14 different countries and found that forecasts of future passengers were wildly optimistic. For rail projects, the forecasts, on average, were 106 percent higher than the actual number of passengers, and one in eight forecasts were off by over 400 percent. For road projects, the miscalculations were more accurate, but were still optimistic by over 20 percent in more than half the cases. The article's authors—led by Bent Flyvbjerg, a professor at Denmark's Aalborg University—claim that the forecasts on similar projects are no more accurate now than they were 30 years ago.[1]

To prevent problems and improve project management, many people are attempting to discover and use best practices, such as developing more realistic estimates and forecasts. This text described how Global Construction used several good practices in managing its Just-In-Time Training project. What exactly are good or best practices? The following sections describe PMI's view of best practices from its Organizational Project Management Maturity Model (OPM3, where the M3 stands for MMM for Management Maturity Model) publication, research results from Interthink Consulting's organizational project management baseline studies, information on best practices from the Ultimate Business Library, results from Andy Crowe's research on "alpha project managers" or the top two percent of project managers, as well as a summary of best practices described in this text.

Figure 8-7 shows Dilbert's view of best practices and how he put them to use to buy everyone T-shirts.

DILBERT: © Scott Adams/Dist. by United Feature Syndicate, Inc.

FIGURE 8-7   Dilbert's view of best practices

Organizational Project Management Maturity Model (OPM3) Best Practices

The Project Management Institute (PMI) Standards Development Program published the Organizational Project Management Maturity Model (OPM3) in December 2003 to address the need to bridge the gap between organizational strategy and successful projects. (Maturity models are described in more detail later in this chapter.) OPM3 defines **organizational project management** as "the systematic management of projects, programs, and portfolios in alignment with the achievement of strategic goals."[2] OPM3 is a standard developed to provide a way for organizations to measure their organizational project management maturity against a comprehensive set of best practices. A **best practice** is "an optimal way recognized by industry to achieve a stated goal or objective."[3] OPM3 lists 586 best practices, which PMI says are achieved through developing and consistently demonstrating their supporting capabilities, as observed through measurable outcomes. **Capabilities** are incremental steps that lead to best practices, and **outcomes** are the results of applying capabilities. A **key performance indicator (KPI)** is a criterion used to determine whether the outcome associated with a capability exists, or the degree to which it exists.

OPM3 provides the following example to illustrate a best practice, capability, outcome, and key performance indicator:

- *Best practice:* Establish internal project management communities
- *Capability (one of four for this best practice):* Facilitate project management activities
- *Outcome:* Local initiatives, meaning the organization develops pockets of consensus around areas of special interest
- *Key performance indicator:* Community addresses local issues[4]

Best practices are organized into three levels: project, program, and portfolio. Within each of those categories, best practices are categorized by four stages of process improvement: standardize, measure, control, and improve. For example, the list that follows contains names and descriptions of several best practices listed in OPM3:

- Project best practices:
  - *Project initiation process standardization*—Project initiation process standards are established.
  - *Project plan development process measurement*—Project plan development process measures are established, assembled, and analyzed.
  - *Project scope planning process control*—Project scope planning process controls are established and executed to control the stability of the process.
  - *Project scope definition process improvement*—Project scope definition process problem areas are assessed, process improvement recommendations are collected, and process improvements are implemented.
- Program best practices:
  - *Program activity definition process standardization*—Program activity definition process standards are established.
  - *Program activity sequencing process measurement*—Program activity sequencing process measures are established, assembled, and analyzed.
  - *Program activity duration estimating process control*—Program activity duration estimating process controls are established and executed to control the stability of the process.
  - *Program schedule development process improvement*—Program schedule development process problem areas are assessed, process improvement recommendations are collected, and process improvements are implemented.
- Portfolio best practices:
  - *Portfolio resource planning process standardization*—Portfolio resource planning process standards are established.
  - *Portfolio cost estimating process measurement*—Portfolio cost estimating process measures are established, assembled, and analyzed.

- *Portfolio cost budgeting process control*—Portfolio cost budgeting process controls are established and executed to control the stability of the process.
- *Portfolio risk management planning process improvement*—Portfolio risk management planning process problem areas are assessed, process improvement recommendations are collected, and process improvements are implemented.

Ultimate Business Library Best Practices

In 2003, the Ultimate Business Library published a book called *Best Practice: Ideas and Insights from the World's Foremost Business Thinkers*. This book includes articles by well-known business leaders such as Warren Bennis (author of over 30 books on leadership, including *On Becoming a Leader*), Daniel Goleman (author of *Emotional Intelligence* and other works), and Thomas Stewart (editor of the *Harvard Business Review* and author of *Intellectual Capital: The New Wealth of Organizations*).

In the book's introduction, Rosabeth Moss Kanter, a professor at Harvard Business School and a well-known author and consultant, says that visionary leaders know "the best practice secret: Stretching to learn from the best of the best in any sector can make a big vision more likely to succeed."[5] Kanter also emphasizes the need to have measurable standards for best practices. Organizations can measure performance against their own past; against peers; and, even better, against potential. Kanter suggests that organizations need to continue to reach for higher standards. She suggests the following exercise regimen for business leaders who want to intelligently adapt best practices to help their own organizations:

1. Reach high. Stretch. Raise standards and aspirations. Find the best of the best and then use it as inspiration for reaching full potential.
2. Help everyone in your organization become a professional. Empower people to manage themselves through benchmarks and standards based on best practice exchange.
3. Look everywhere. Go far afield. Think of the whole world as your laboratory for learning.[6]

In addition, Robert Butrick, author of *The Project Workout,* wrote an article on best practices in project management for the Ultimate Business Library book. He suggests that organizations need to follow these basic principles of project management:

- Make sure your projects are driven by your strategy. Be able to demonstrate how each project you undertake fits your business strategy, and screen out unwanted projects as soon as possible.
- Use a staged approach. You can rarely plan a project in its entirety. Use progressive steps or stages to project planning, and use the same generic stages for all types of projects. Have gate reviews before starting each stage to revalidate a project and before committing more resources and funding for the project. Place high emphasis on the early stages of a project to reduce risks and decrease time to market.
- Engage your stakeholders. Ignoring stakeholders often leads to project failure. Be sure to engage stakeholders at all stages of a project, and encourage teamwork and commitment at all times.

- Ensure success by planning for it. To help projects succeed, the balance of power often needs to be tipped toward the project and away from line management.
- Monitor against the plan. Everyone working on projects must have guidance, training, and support in creating plans and making project-related decisions. Organizations must develop and follow control techniques for managing risks, issues, scope changes, schedule, costs, and project reviews. Monitoring and forecasting against a plan ensure that everyone is on the same page and prevent unwanted surprises.
- Manage the project control cycle. Monitoring should focus more on the future than on the past. Project managers must continuously check that the project plan is still fit for the purpose of the project and likely to deliver the business benefits on time. Project changes must be managed to ensure that only those enabling project benefits to be realized are accepted. Avoid the dangers of scope creep, and let stakeholders know that project benefits drive the scope.
- Formally close the project: Every project should be closed to make sure that all work ceases, that lessons are learned, and that remaining resources are released for other purposes.

 BEST PRACTICE

Another view of best practices includes best places for people to work. For example, *Fortune* magazine lists the "100 Best Companies to Work For" in the United States every year, with Google earning the number one spot in 2007. *Working Mother* magazine lists the best companies in the United States for women based on benefits for working families. The *Times Online* (*www.timesonline.co.uk*) provides the *Sunday Times* list of the "100 Best Companies to Work For," a key benchmark against which UK companies can judge their performance as employers. The Great Place to Work Institute, which produces *Fortune's* "100 Best Companies to Work For," uses the same selection methodology for over 20 international lists, including "Best Companies to Work for" lists in all 15 countries of the European Union, Brazil, Korea, and a number of other countries throughout Latin America and Asia. Companies make these lists based on feedback from their best critics: their own employees. Quotes from employees often show why certain companies made the lists:

- "It is a friendly, courteous, caring hospital. We generally care about our co-workers and our patients. I can always get the help and support that I need to function in this hospital. This goes from the top all the way down to the cleaning people."
- "This is the best place I have ever worked. There's an open door policy. Every one is allowed to voice their opinion."
- "I get information about everything—profits, losses, problems. Relationships with people are easier here. It's more direct and open."[7]

305

Best Practices of Alpha Project Managers

Andy Crowe, founder and CEO of Velociteach, wrote a book in 2006 called "Alpha Project Managers: What the Top 2% Know That Everyone Else Does Not." As the title suggests, an alpha project manager is defined as one who falls in the top two percent of project managers in terms of performance. Project managers were rated by their customers, senior managers, and team members based on their performance in the following areas:

- Setting expectations
- Communicating efficiently and effectively
- Managing issues
- Identifying and managing risks
- Leading the project team
- Meeting the scope, quality, time, and budget baselines for the project
- Managing the procurement process
- Managing changes to the project
- Balancing competing stakeholder needs
- Delivering a product, service, or result that met expectations

For this study, Crowe surveyed 860 project managers who had all been clients/students at Velociteach. Although this was not a scientific study, the aggregate results provide interesting information that can help define best practices for project managers. The 860 project managers, their senior managers, customers, and project team members all answered numerous survey questions. The general format of the questions was as follows: Mark the degree with which you agree with the following statement: Strongly disagree (0%), Somewhat disagree (20%), Neutral (50%), Somewhat agree (75%), Strongly agree (100%). For some questions, the scale was based on the degree of importance, with 100% being the most important.

The 18 people identified as alpha project managers varied most from the other project managers in the following ways:

- *They enjoy their work more than their counterparts.* When asked to mark the degree to which they agreed with the statement: "On the whole, I generally love my job," the alpha average response was 67% while the non-alpha average was only 32%. They also view their jobs more as a career and took 19% more job-related training than the non-alphas (45.1 hours vs. 38.0 hours in the past three years).
- *They believe they have more authority than their counterparts.* When asked to mark the degree to which they agreed with the statement: "I have adequate authority to manage the projects for which I am responsible," the alpha average response was 89% while the non-alpha average was only 47%. It is interesting to note that from senior management's point of view, the alphas and non-alphas had about the same level of organizational authority at about 87%.
- *They believe they can have a personal impact on project success.* When asked to mark the degree to which they agreed with the statement: "What is the importance of your role on your current project," the alpha average response was 96% while the non-alpha average was only 70%. It is interesting to note that the senior managers' response to this question was very close to the project managers for both groups.

- *They are more efficient and effective communicators*. When project managers' customers, senior managers, and team members were asked, "How would you rank this project manager's overall responsiveness to your project-related requests?" (from very ineffective to very effective) the alphas' stakeholders' average response was 88% while the non-alpha average was only 49%. It is also interesting to note that alpha project managers send *fewer* e-mails per day and spend *less* time in meetings than the non-alphas. They know how to prioritize work and focus on what is most important. When the alphas were probed in interviews to understand more about their communication best practices, key traits emerged:

  - *They talk to stakeholders very early in the project and tailor communication to meet their needs.*
  - *They create a communication schedule and stick to it.*
  - *They communicate their messages quickly in a clear and concise manner.*
  - *They create an open communication channel and talk with stakeholders regularly about the topic of communication itself.*
  - *They know that on many projects, communication is the only deliverable stakeholders will receive until the product or service is completed.*
- *They allocate about twice as much time toward project planning.* Alpha project managers spend more time in every process group than their counterparts except for execution, as follows:
  - *Initiating:* 2% vs. 1%
  - *Planning:* 21% vs. 11%
  - *Executing:* 69% vs. 82%
  - *Controlling:* 5% vs. 4%
  - *Closing:* 3% vs. 2%
- *They think it is important for the project manager to be a hands-on manager and a domain expert.* When asked to "Rank the importance of the project manager being a domain expert as a contributor to overall project success," the average alpha response was 94% vs. 68% for the non-alphas.
- *They can get consensus and handle conflicts.* When senior managers and customers were asked "How would you rate this project manager's ability to identify, understand, and satisfy your individual goals for the project," the average alpha response was 92% vs. 64%. When asked a similar question about conflict resolution, the alpha average was 61% vs. 46%.
- *They are managing more strategic projects and understand strategic goals.* When asked "Is your primary project considered highly strategic to your organization," the average alpha response was 60% vs. 41%. When asked, "Can you state your organization's top (three) strategic goals," the average alpha response was 60% vs. 23%.

The results of this study can be interpreted in several ways, especially if you analyze the interview responses, as Crowe does in his book. Some of the areas where alpha project managers are different from non-alpha project managers are based on their attitudes and beliefs, such as enjoying their work, believing they have authority, and believing they can have a personal impact on a project. Most of the other areas, however, are based on best practices which can be learned, such as being a good communicator, spending more time on project planning, being a hands-on project manager and a domain expert, being able to get consensus and handle conflict, and understanding and supporting strategic goals.

Summary of Best Practices Mentioned in This Text

As you can see, understanding and applying best practices can help improve the management of projects, programs, portfolios, and entire companies. Several best practices were described throughout this text. Following is a brief summary of some of them:

- Determine how project, program, and portfolio management will work best in your own organization.
- Involve key stakeholders—including shareholders, customers, and employees—in making major decisions.
- Develop and follow a formal project selection process to ensure projects support business needs.
- Lay the groundwork for projects before they officially start.
- Separate projects by phases, such as a study phase project, when it makes sense to do so.
- Designate a project champion to provide high-level support and participate in key meetings.
- Assign a project manager from operations to lead projects that affect operations.
- Form a steering committee with key managers from various departments for projects that will cause major organizational change.
- Provide mentoring and training for project managers and other stakeholders.
- Document action items at meetings, and set the next meeting time.
- Document meeting minutes, focusing on key decisions and action items, and send them out quickly.
- Use more than one approach for creating cost estimates.
- Use formal supplier evaluation procedures to help select sellers.
- Include a detailed statement of work and schedule in contracts.
- Develop and follow a formal change-control process.
- Work with suppliers to ensure that deliverables are produced properly.
- Follow a deliverable acceptance process to verify project scope.
- Be clear and honest in communicating project status information, and share the responsibility for project communications with the entire project team.
- Formally close projects and share lessons learned.

PROJECT MANAGEMENT MATURITY

In addition to following best practices, organizations can improve project management performance by using **maturity models**, which are frameworks for helping organizations improve their processes and systems. Maturity models describe an evolutionary path of increasingly organized and systematically more mature processes. Many maturity models have four to six levels, with the first level describing characteristics of the least organized or mature organizations, and the highest level describing the characteristics of the most organized and mature organizations.

Capability Maturity Model Integration

A popular maturity model is in continuous development at the Software Engineering Institute at Carnegie Mellon University. The Software Engineering Institute (SEI) is a federally funded research and development center established in 1984 by the U.S. Department of Defense with a broad mandate to address the transition of software engineering technology. The Capability Maturity Model Integration (CMMI) is "a process improvement approach that provides organizations with the essential elements of effective processes. It can be used to guide process improvement across a project, a division, or an entire organization. CMMI helps integrate traditionally separate organizational functions, set process improvement goals and priorities, provide guidance for quality processes, and provide a point of reference for appraising current processes."[8] Many companies that want to work in the government market have realized that they will not get many opportunities even to bid on projects unless they have a CMMI Level 3.

The capability levels of the CMMI, numbered zero through five, are:

0. *Incomplete*: At this level, a process is either not performed or partially performed. No generic goals exist for this level, and one or more of the specific goals of the process area are not satisfied.

1. *Performed*: A performed process satisfies the specific goals of the process area and supports and enables the work needed to produce work products. Although this capability level can result in improvements, those improvements can be lost over time if they are not institutionalized.

2. *Managed*: At this level, a process has the basic infrastructure in place to support it. The process is planned and executed based on policies and employs skilled people who have adequate resources to produce controlled outputs. The process discipline reflected by this level ensures that existing practices are retained during times of stress.

3. *Defined*: At this maturity level, a process is rigorously defined and the standards, process descriptions, and procedures for a project are tailored from the organization's set of standard processes to suit that particular project.

4. *Quantitatively Managed*: At this level, a process is controlled using statistical and other quantitative techniques. The organization establishes quantitative objectives for quality and process performance that are used as criteria in managing the process.

5. *Optimizing*: An optimizing process is improved based on an understanding of the common causes of variation inherent in the process. The focus is on continually improving the range of process performance through incremental and innovative improvements.[9]

Project Management Maturity Models

In the late 1990s, several organizations began developing project management maturity models based on the Capability Maturity Model (CMM), an earlier version of CMMI. Just as organizations realized the need to improve their software development processes and systems, they also realized the need to enhance their project management processes and systems for all types of projects. A few of these maturity models include:

1. PMI's OPM3, as mentioned earlier, which includes four process improvement stages or levels:
    1. Standardize
    2. Measure
    3. Control
    4. Continuously improve
2. The International Institute for Learning, Inc. uses Kerzner's model, with five levels of project management maturity:
    1. Common language
    2. Common processes
    3. Singular methodology
    4. Benchmarking
    5. Continuous improvement
3. ESI International's ProjectFRAMEWORK™ is a five-level model:
    1. Ad-hoc
    2. Consistent
    3. Integrated
    4. Comprehensive
    5. Optimizing
4. Berkeley's Project Management Process Maturity $(PM)^2$ model includes these five levels:
    1. Ad-hoc: No project management processes or practices are consistently available, and data is not consistently collected or analyzed
    2. Planned: Project management processes, problem areas, and data are informally defined, identified, collected
    3. Managed: Formal project planning and control systems and data are managed
    4. Integrated: Program management is used, and project management data and processes are integrated and quantitatively analyzed, measured, and stored
    5. Sustained: Project management processes are continuously improved and are fully understood, and data is optimized and sustained

Figure 8-8 provides an illustration of the Berkeley model. Each project management maturity model shows a progression from the least mature to most mature level, although the number and title of levels vary somewhat.

Research on Project Management Maturity

Regardless of the project management maturity model followed, the goal is clear: organizations want to improve their ability to manage projects. Many organizations are assessing where they stand in terms of project management maturity, just as they did for

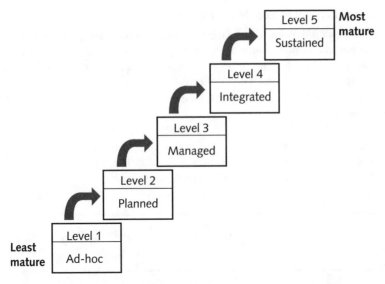

FIGURE 8-8 Berkeley Project Management Process Maturity Model

software development maturity with the CMMI maturity model. Organizations are recognizing that they must make a commitment to the discipline of project management to improve project quality and organizational performance.

Ibbs' The Value of Project Management Research

Several studies have proven the value of improving project management maturity to organizations. William Ibbs, a Professor at the University of California at Berkeley, led a research study published in 2002 called "The Value of Project Management." After assessing project management maturity using Berkeley's model and reviewing data from 52 companies in the U.S., the researchers made the following conclusions:

- *Companies with more mature project management practices have better project performance.* They deliver projects on time and on budget more often. Less mature companies often miss their schedule targets by 40 percent and their cost targets by 20 percent.
- *Project management maturity is strongly correlated with more predictable project schedule and cost performance.* More mature companies have a schedule performance index (SPI) variation of 0.08 and a cost performance index (CPI) variation of 0.11. Less mature companies have indexes of 0.16 for SPI and CPI. For a $10 million project, this translates into a $1.6 million cost variation.
- *High project management maturity results in lower direct costs of project management.* Companies with a high maturity level spend 6–7 percent of total project costs on project management. Companies with low maturity spent about 11 percent.[10]

Interthink Consulting's Organizational Project Management Study

Interthink Consulting Incorporated developed the Organizational Project Management (OPM) Baseline Study, which provides a comprehensive overview of project management practices in organizations and industries worldwide, with over 600 participants. Based on the 2004 study, there were definite relationships between maturity and project delivery. The study provides detailed results in several areas, such as maturity level, meeting budgets, schedules, customer satisfaction, and project goal attainment.

Figure 8-9 provides a graph from Interthink's 2004 OPM Baseline Study that compares project management process maturity with project goal attainment. Note that maturity is broken down into several categories, such as program initiation, project initiation, and project tracking. (See detailed study results from *www.interthink.ca*.)

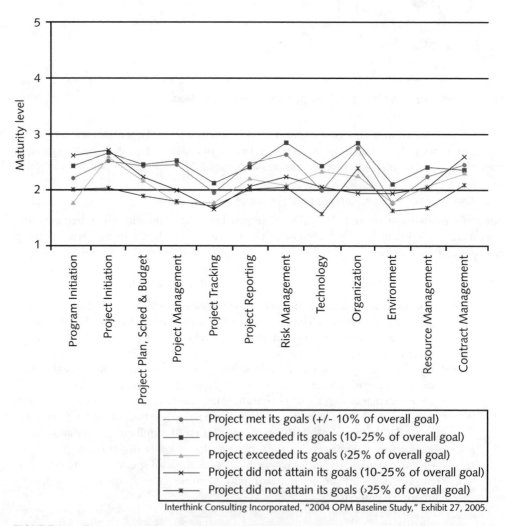

Interthink Consulting Incorporated, "2004 OPM Baseline Study," Exhibit 27, 2005.

FIGURE 8-9   Process maturity and project goal attainment

"For projects that met their goals or exceeded them by a factor of 10% to 25% there is a slight but clear increase in overall maturity through the majority of the process capability areas. For the organizational capability areas, the increase in maturity is most clear in the areas of Risk Management and Organization. For projects that failed to exceed their goals, the indicated maturity in the majority of the process capability areas are relatively lower."[11]

PriceWaterhouse Coopers' Study on Boosting Business Performance

As mentioned in Chapter 1, PriceWaterhouse Coopers surveyed 200 companies from 30 different countries about their project management maturity and found that *over half of all projects fail*. They also found that only 2.5% of corporations consistently meet their targets for scope, time, and cost goals for all types of projects. The survey's main objective, however, was to investigate whether a higher maturity level would provide a higher project performance level. The following conclusions were made by the survey authors:

- *A higher maturity level for an organization enhances overall project performance, not in just one project, but in the overall portfolio of projects.*
- *Most organizations are not satisfied with their current maturity level.* The total average for survey participants was 2.5 on a 5.0 scale, meaning the organizations use informal processes that are not yet institutionalized. This low maturity level contributes to the high project failure rate.
- *Project failures are often a consequence of organizational aspects over which project managers have little influence.* The top reasons cited for project failure included bad estimates, missed deadlines, scope changes, change in environment, insufficient resources, and change in strategy. Poor quality of deliverables and not adequately defining stakeholders were the least prevalent reasons for project failure.
- *Organizational structure has a big impact on overall project performance.* The higher the alignment between structure and business requirements, the higher the overall project performance. The optimal structure should be based on industry, location, and business objectives. The highest performing companies in terms of project results had a projectized or strong matrix structure, giving project managers the most authority and control over resources.
- *Staff development and professional certification enhance overall project performance.* However, more than 60% of the companies surveyed do not regularly offer a development program to their project managers. Investments in project management certification do pay off, and the organizational benefits exceed the risks.
- *A systematic approach to change management is fundamental for superior project performance.* The majority of the best performing and most mature organizations always or frequently apply change management to their projects.

- *Staffing projects with a majority of internal resources as opposed to external resources is a better guarantee of success.* External resources add value when employed in moderation. The highest performance was achieved by using 25% external resources and 75% internal resources.
- *The extent to which project management software is used is correlated to maturity levels.* The lower the maturity level, the more difficulties the organization will have in implementing software. Processes must be established for the software to provide benefits.[12]

☑ WHAT WENT RIGHT?

"Three years ago the board of Siemens launched a worldwide initiative to improve its project management. The German electronics group had worked out that half its turnover came from project-like work, and it calculated that if it could complete all of these projects on time and to budget, it would add EURO3 billion ($3.7 billion U.S. dollars) to its bottom line over three years. A key element of the scheme was the introduction of project managers to the company's sales teams to try and temper their more extravagant promises, a move that requires a careful balance between reining them in and killing the deal.

"Some companies have gone so far as to become more like project co-ordinators than producers of goods or services. The 'business-as-usual' bits of their operations have been outsourced, leaving them free to design and orchestrate new ideas. Nike, for instance, does not make shoes any more; it manages footwear projects. Coca-Cola, which hands most of the bottling and marketing of its drinks to others, is little more than a collection of projects, run by people it calls 'orchestrators.' Germany's BMW treats each new car 'platform,' which is the basis of new vehicle ranges, as a separate project. Meanwhile Capital One, a fast-growing American financial-services group, has a special team to handle its M&A 'projects.' For all these firms, project management has become an important competitive tool. Some of them call it a core competence. Good project management can certainly make a difference. BP's fortunes were transformed when it converted its exploration division, BPX, into a portfolio of projects, each of them more or less free from head-office control—a structure which the company describes as an 'asset federation.' Asset/project managers can no longer rely on head office for support. They are required to build their own self-sufficient teams."[13]

FINAL ADVICE ON PROJECT MANAGEMENT

Now that you have read this text and discussed project management with others, I hope that you have matured to see project management as a valuable skill for you as an individual and for all types of organizations. The number of projects and their complexity will continue to increase, so it is important to understand, apply, and improve the state of project management.

The knowledge and experience I have gained working on and managing projects continues to help me in my career and my personal life. I was fortunate to step into a project management role very early in my career as a U.S. Air Force officer. My first real job at the age of 22 was as a project manager, and we followed a very disciplined approach to project, program, and portfolio management. I have held several job titles at several organizations since then—systems analyst, senior engineer, technical specialist, information technology management consultant, independent consultant, college professor, and now author. All of these jobs included working on or managing projects. As a wife and mother of three, I can also attest to the fact that project management skills help in planning and executing personal activities (weddings, birthday parties, vacations, moves, fundraisers, and so on) and in dealing with the joys and challenges of everyday life. When people ask me how I can do so much, I have to say that using good project management definitely helps!

CASE WRAP-UP

Kristin Maur stood in front of the project steering committee. She invited her whole team to give the final presentation as a team effort. Of course they had several challenges along the way, but overall, the project was a success. All the new training courses were offered within a year, and the course evaluations averaged 3.4 on a 5.0 scale, which exceeded the committee's goal of 3.0. More people took training courses than planned, primarily the Web-based courses. Because the Web-based training was more cost-effective than the instructor-led training, the team was confident that the costs of the Just-In-Time Training project would be recouped in less than two years, as projected. Kristin watched each team member summarize key project results, and she sensed the pride that everyone felt in a job well done. She also felt good knowing that she helped her team members get assigned to even more challenging projects, and she was ready to start her next project as well.

Chapter Summary

Closing projects involves gaining stakeholder and customer acceptance of the final products and services, and bringing the project to an orderly end. It includes verifying that all of the deliverables are complete. This chapter summarizes the closing tasks and key outputs for project integration and procurement management.

Closing outputs related to integration management include administrative and contract closure procedures; final products, services, or results; and updates to organizational process assets. Sample closing documents for the Just-In-Time Training project include a final project report, lessons-learned report, and customer acceptance/project completion form. It is also good practice to hold a close-out meeting and address knowledge transfer as a project ends.

Closing outputs related to procurement management include closed contracts and updates to organizational process assets. A sample written contract closure notice is provided for the Just-In-Time Training project.

Many organizations study and apply best practices to improve their ability to manage projects, programs, and portfolios. PMI developed the Organizational Project Management Maturity Model (OPM3) to help organizations assess and improve their organizational project management maturity. OPM3 lists 586 best practices organized by project, program, and portfolio management. The Ultimate Business Library published *Best Practices*, which provides advice on best practices to follow for managing projects and organizations in general. Andy Crowe did a study to help understand best practices of alpha project managers, or the top 2%. This text also describes several best practices in managing projects, programs, and portfolios.

Several organizations are also using project management maturity models to help improve their project management processes and systems. Several studies, including those by Ibbs, Interthink Consulting, and PriceWaterhouse Coopers, show the benefits of improving project management maturity.

Project management is a valuable skill for individuals and organizations. As the number of projects and their complexity continue to increase, it is important to understand, apply, and improve the state of project management.

Quick Quiz

1. Which knowledge areas include tasks related to closing?
   a. project scope, time, cost, and quality management
   b. project integration, scope, time, cost, and quality management
   c. project integration and procurement management
   d. all nine knowledge areas

2. Which of the following statements is false?
   a. Even though many projects are canceled before completion, it is still important to formally close any project.
   b. Closing includes verifying that all of the deliverables are complete.
   c. Closing often includes a final presentation and report.
   d. Closing does not include developing a transition plan.

3. Providing a list of project documentation, project closure documents, and historical information produced by the project in a useful format is part of _____ .

    a. updating organizational process assets

    b. administrative and contract closure procedures

    c. contract closure procedures

    d. lessons learned

4. Answering questions such as, "What will you do differently on the next project based on your experience working on this project?" is part of a _____ .

    a. lessons-learned report

    b. customer acceptance/project completion form

    c. written notice of contract closure

    d. transition plan

5. Contract closure involves completion and settlement of contracts and resolution of _____ .

    a. payments

    b. any open items

    c. performance issues

    d. legal matters

6. The _____ should include requirements for formal acceptance and closure of contracts.

    a. project management plan

    b. procurement management plan

    c. contract itself

    d. contract management plan

7. A _____ is an optimal way recognized by industry to achieve a stated goal or objective.

    a. benchmark

    b. key performance indicator

    c. capability

    d. best practice

8. The Project Management Institute published the _____ in December 2003 to address the need to bridge the gap between organizational strategy and successful projects.

    a. Organizational Project Management Maturity Model (OPM3)

    b. Best Practices Report

    c. Alpha Project Managers Guide

    d. Project Management Process Maturity (PM)^2 model

9. Organizations can measure performance against their own past; against peers; and, even better, against _____ .

    a. profits

    b. potential

    c. revenues

    d. the future

10. Which of the following is not a benefit of having a high project management maturity level?

    a. lower turnover rates

    b. better project performance

    c. lower direct cost of project management

    d. more predictable cost and schedule performance

Quick Quiz Answers

1. C; 2. D; 3. A; 4. A; 5. B; 6. C; 7. D; 8. A; 9. B; 10. A

Discussion Questions

1. What is involved in closing projects? Why should all projects be formally closed?

2. What are the main closing outputs created as part of integration management? Why is it important to create a final project report, presentation, and lessons-learned report?

3. What are the main closing outputs created as part of procurement management?

4. Why should organizations identify and use best practices? What are the main categories of best practices developed as part of OPM3? What are some of the things that alpha project managers do differently from other project managers? What are some of the best practices mentioned in Ultimate Business Library's *Best Practice*? What additional best practices were suggested in this text?

5. What is a project management maturity model? What is CMMI? What benefits have studies shown from increasing project management maturity levels in organizations?

6. Do you believe that developing and applying project management skills can help most individuals and organizations? Justify your response.

Exercises

1. Find an example of a large project that took more than a year to complete, such as a major construction project. You can ask people at your college, university, or work about a recent project, such as a major fund raising campaign, information systems installation, or building project. You can also find information about projects online such as the Big Dig in Boston (*www.masspike. com/bigdig*), the Patronas Twin Towers in Malaysia and many other building projects (*www. greatbuildings.com*), etc. Describe some of the tasks performed to close the project. Write a one-page paper or prepare a short presentation summarizing your findings.

2. Using the lessons-learned template on the companion Web site, write a lessons-learned report for a project you worked on. If you cannot think of one, interview someone who recently completed a project and write a lessons-learned report on that project.

3. Review the project management best practices presented in this chapter or describe several used in an organization you are familiar with. Select any two of them and write a one- to two-page paper describing how each practice could help improve project management. Develop examples of how they could be applied to real project situations.

4. Read information from one of the references used in the section of this chapter on project management maturity models. Summarize your findings in a one- to two-page paper.

Team Projects

1. Your organization is about to complete a project to raise money for an important charity. Assume that there are 1,000 people in your organization. Also, assume that you had six months to raise as much money as possible, with a goal of $100,000. With just one week to go, you have raised $92,000. You did experience several problems with the project, which you described in Chapter 7. Using that information and information you prepared in other chapters related to this project, prepare a two- to three-page paper or 15-minute final presentation for the project. Be creative in your responses.

2. You are part of a team in charge of a project to help people in your company (500 people) lose weight. This project is part of a competition, and the top "losers" will be featured in a popular television show. Assume that you had six months to complete the project and a budget of $10,000. The project will end in one week, so you and your team are busy closing out the project. Prepare a lessons-learned report for the project, using information from your responses to this exercise in previous chapters as well as your creativity to determine what the final outcome was for the project.

3. Using the information you developed in Team Project 1 or 2, role-play the final project meeting, at which you present the final project presentation to key stakeholders. Determine who will play what role (project manager, team member from a certain department, senior managers, and so on). Be creative in displaying different personalities (a senior manager who questions the importance of the project to the organization, a team member who is very shy or obnoxious).

4. Perform the closing tasks for the New Business Venture case study provided in Appendix C or for one of the cases on the companion Web site. If you are working on a real team project, create relevant closing documents, such as a final project report and lessons-learned report, using the templates and samples in this chapter as guides. Present your results to the class.

5. Research two or three different project management maturity models in more detail, such as those described in this chapter. Several include a sample or free assessment you can take to determine your organization's maturity level. Summarize the results as well as other information about the maturity models in a two- to three-page paper or short presentation.

Companion Web Site

Visit the companion Web site for this text (*www.course.com/mis/pm2/schwalbe* or *http://login. course.com*) to access:

- Lecture notes
- Interactive quizzes and Jeopardy games
- Template files
- Sample documents

- Podcasts
- More ideas for team projects, including real projects and case studies
- Links to additional resources related to project management

Key Terms

best practice — An optimal way recognized by industry to achieve a stated goal or objective.[14]

capabilities — The incremental steps that lead to best practices.

contract closure — The completion and settlement of contracts, and resolution of any open items.

key performance indicator (KPI) — A criterion used to determine whether the outcome associated with a capability exists, or the degree to which it exists.

maturity model — A framework for helping organizations improve their processes and systems.

organizational project management — The systematic management of projects, programs, and portfolios in alignment with the achievement of strategic goals.[15]

outcomes — The results of applying capabilities.

procurement audits — Reviews often performed during contract closure to identify lessons learned in the entire procurement process.

records management system — A tool that provides the ability to easily organize, find, and archive documents.

End Notes

[1] Mary Evans, "Overdue and Over Budget, Over and Over Again," *Economist.com* (June 9, 2005).

[2] Project Management Institute, Inc., Organizational Project Management Maturity Model (OPM3) Knowledge Foundation (2003), p. xiii.

[3] Ibid., p. 13.

[4] Ibid., p. 15.

[5] Ultimate Business Library, *Best Practice: Ideas and Insights from the World's Foremost Business Thinkers.* Cambridge, MA: Perseus Publishing (2003), p. 1.

[6] Ibid., p. 8.

[7] Great Place to Work Institute, Best Companies Lists (*www.greatplacetowork.com*) (June 2005).

[8] Software Engineering Institute, "What is CMMI," Carnegie Mellon (*http://www.sei.cmu.edu/cmmi/general/general.html*) (January 2007).

[9] CMMI Product Team, "CMMI® for Development, Version 1.2," CMU/SEI-2006-TR-008ESC-TR-2006-008 (August 2006).

[10] William Ibbs, and Justin Reginato, "Quantifying the Value of Project Management," Project Management Institute (2002).

[11] Mark E. Mullaly, "2004 Organizational Project Management Baseline Study Results Overview," (*http://www.interthink.ca/*) (2005).

[12] PriceWaterhouseCoopers, "Boosting Business Performance through Programme and Project Management," (*www.pwc.com/extweb/pwcpublications.nsf/docid/1ccdd87f4daa410c852571290051976f*) (June 2004).

[13] Evans, "Overdue and Over Budget."

[14] Project Management Institute, Inc., Organizational Project Management Maturity Model (OPM3) Knowledge Foundation (2003), p. xiii.

[15] Ibid., p. 13.

APPENDIX **A**

GUIDE TO USING MICROSOFT PROJECT 2007

INTRODUCTION

This appendix provides a concise guide to using Microsoft Office Project Professional 2007 (often referred to as Project 2007) to assist in performing project management functions. The Office Project 2007 family includes several different products:

- Project Standard 2007, a non-Web-based, stand-alone program for individuals who manage projects independently, similar to earlier versions of Project Standard.
- Project Professional 2007, which is basically Project Standard 2007 plus Project Web Access and allows you to connect to Project Server 2007, if available. (Note: This text includes a 60-day trial of Project Professional 2007. This guide does not include information on connecting to Project Server 2007.)
- The Microsoft Office Enterprise Project Management (EPM) Solution, which combines Project Server 2007, Project Professional 2007, Project Web Access, Project Portfolio Server 2007, and Project Portfolio Web Access to form a business solution for organizations, departments, and teams. As its name suggests, this version is designed for use across an enterprise and provides project portfolio management capabilities. Organizations should develop and apply many standards, templates, codes, and procedures before using the enterprise version of Project 2007 to make the best use of its capabilities.

Each version of Project 2007 can help users manage different aspects of all nine project management knowledge areas. (Consult Microsoft's Web site for more details on all of the versions of Project 2007.) Most users, however, focus on using Project 2007 to assist with scope, time, cost, human resource, and communications management. This guide uses these project management knowledge areas as the context for learning how to use Project 2007. The basic order of steps in this appendix follows best practices in project management. That is, you should first determine the scope of a project, then the time, and then the resource and cost information. You can then set a baseline and enter actuals to track and communicate performance information.

Hundreds of project management software products are available today, but Microsoft Project is the clear market leader among midrange applications. Before you can use Project 2007 or any project management software effectively, you must understand the fundamental concepts of project management, such as creating work breakdown structures, linking tasks, entering duration estimates, and so on. See the Suggested Readings on the companion Web site (www.course.com/mis/pm2/schwalbe) for recommendations on other resources to help you gain an even deeper understanding of Project 2007.

New Features of Project 2007

Because there have been several previous versions of Microsoft Project, it is useful to understand some of the new capabilities of Project 2007, especially if you are working with people who are upgrading from a previous version. Several new or improved features are available in Project 2007, such as the following:

- The Review Tasks Drivers feature lets you show prerequisites and resource constraints that drive the start date of the selected task. Simply click these drivers to link to relevant information.
- The Visual Change Highlights feature allows you to determine the impact of each change you make on all other dependent tasks.
- The Multiple Level Undo feature allows you to reverse the most recent series of changes: undo and redo changes to views, data, and options. This function also lets you undo actions or sets of actions from macros or third-party applications.
- You can now apply predefined financial fields, such as cost codes, and improve mapping to the financial fields tracked in your organization's project accounting systems.
- The Budget Tracking feature lets you define a budget at a high level so you can allocate funds and track costs against the budget.
- The Cost Resources feature, which also supports integration of Project 2007 with accounting systems, allows you to assign planned and actual costs to a task, not just work or materials.
- You can now use Microsoft Excel and Office Visio Professional to produce charts, graphs, and diagrams based on Project 2007 data by means of the Visual Reports feature. For example, you can now create earned value charts using Visual Reports.
- You can now define and share custom report templates with other Project 2007 users. These reports include a data cube for drill downs and pivot tables.

- The Background Cell Highlighting feature lets you shade cells, similar to Excel, to add emphasis to cells.
- Enhancements to the Calendar Interface and the addition of 3-D Gantt bars allow you to create even more visually effective reports.

Backward Compatibility

Project 2007 can open files created in previous versions of Project, such as Project 98, 2000, 2002, or 2003. Any features that do not map to prior file formats will be discarded when a project is saved in the older file format. Project 2007 also saves to file formats including XML (extensible markup language), CSV (comma-separated values), text (tab-delimited), Excel workbook, Excel PivotTable, Web page, Project 2003, and Project 2002. Project 2007 no longer supports OLEDB.

Before You Begin

This appendix assumes you are using Project 2007 with Windows XP or Vista and are familiar with other Windows-based applications. This text includes a trial CD of Project Professional 2007 that is good for 60 days from the time it is first used. You can also download a free trial from Microsoft's Web site, and you can launch the trial application for a total of 25 times before having to enter the Product Key and Activating the product. Additionally, students and faculty can purchase software at deep discounts from several sources, including *www.journeyed.com*. Check your work by reviewing the many screen shots included in the steps, or by using the solution files that are available for download from the companion Web site for this text or from your instructor. Instructions for using previous editions of Project and their solution files are also available on the companion Web site for this text.

You need to be running Windows XP or Vista to use Project 2007. If you have any technical difficulties, contact Course Technology's Support Services at *www.course.com/support*.

This appendix uses a fictitious information technology project—the Project Tracking Database project—to illustrate how to use the software. The goal of this project is to create a database to keep track of all the projects a company is working on. Each section of the appendix includes hands-on activities for you to perform. To complete the hands-on activities in the appendix, you will need to copy a set of files from the companion Web site for this text (*www.course.com/mis/pm2/schwalbe*) to your computer. You can also download the files from the author's Web site (*www.kathyschwalbe.com*) under Book FAQs. When you begin each set of steps, make sure you are using the correct file. Before you begin your work you should have the finance.mpp, resource.mpp, and kickoffmeeting.doc files.

In addition, you will create the following files from scratch as you work through the steps:

- scope.mpp
- time.mpp
- tracking.mpp
- baseline.mpp
- level.mpp

Now that you understand project management concepts and the basic project management terminology, you will learn how to start Project 2007, review the Help facility and a template file, and begin to plan the Project Tracking Database project.

OVERVIEW OF PROJECT 2007

The first step to mastering Project 2007 is to become familiar with the Help facility, online tutorials, major screen elements, views, and filters. This section describes each of these features.

Starting Project 2007 and Using the Getting Started and Project Guide Features

To start Project 2007:

1. *Open Project 2007.* Click the **Start** button on the taskbar, point to **All Programs**, point to **Microsoft Office**, and then click **Microsoft Office Project 2007**. If you are using Vista, click Microsoft Office instead of pointing to it. Alternatively, a shortcut or icon might be available on the desktop; in this case, double-click the icon to start the software.

2. *Maximize Project 2007.* If the Project 2007 window does not fill the entire screen as shown in Figure A-1, click the **Maximize** button in the upper-right corner of the window.

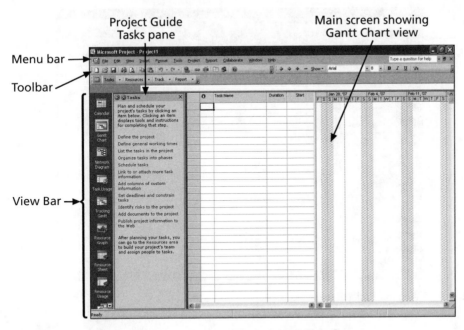

FIGURE A-1 Project Guide Tasks Pane and Project 2007 Main Screen

Project 2007 is now running and ready to use. Look at some of the elements of the Project 2007 screen. The default view is the Gantt Chart view, which shows tasks and other information in the Entry table as well as a calendar display. You can access other views by clicking each button in the View Bar on the left side of the screen. Notice that when Project 2007 starts, it opens a new file named Project1, as shown in the title bar. If you open a second file, the name will be Project2, and so on, until you save and rename the file.

When you start Project 2007, the Project Guide Tasks pane automatically opens, as shown in Figure A-1. The Project Guide helps you learn Project 2007 by providing instructions for completing various steps in building a Project 2007 file.

To use the Project Guide:

1. *Open the Project Guide*. Click the **Tasks** list arrow on the Project Guide toolbar, as shown in Figure A-2. Notice the various options listed. The Resources, Track, and Report buttons on the Project Guide toolbar list additional options. You will use some of these options later in this appendix.

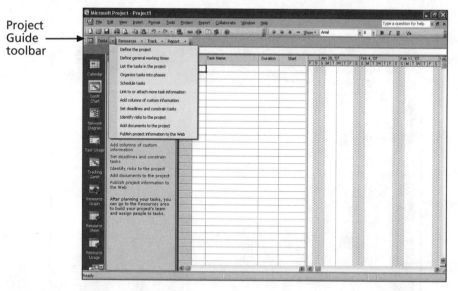

FIGURE A-2   Using the Project Guide

2. *Set the project start date.* Click the first option in the Tasks list, **Define the project**.

3. *Review the Project Guide instructions.* Review the information that displays in the pane on the left side of the screen. As you select different options in the Project Guide, the Task pane displays specific information related to that option. Notice that the default project start date is set at the current date. Click the **date** list arrow on the pop-up calendar to select a date. Select the last day of the month that displays.

4. *Close the Project Guide.* Click the **Close** button 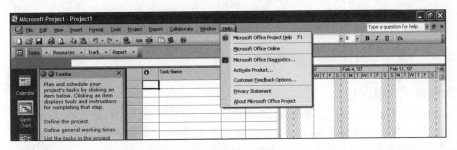 in the upper-right corner of the Project Guide window, and click Yes to exit the wizard.

In addition to using the Project Guide window, you can access other information to help you learn how to use Project 2007 under the Help menu. Figure A-3 shows the Help menu options available by clicking Help on the Menu bar or by pressing F1. Figure A-4 shows the detailed list of topics available from the first Help option, Microsoft Office Project Help.

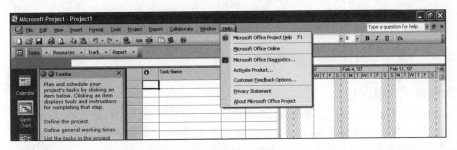

FIGURE A-3   Project 2007 Help Menu Options

Microsoft realizes that Project 2007 can take some time to learn and provides a number of resources on its Web site. Select Microsoft Office Online from the Project 2007 Help menu to go to Microsoft's Web site for Office products. Microsoft's Web site for Project 2007 (*www.microsoft.com/project*) provides files for users to download, case studies, articles, and other useful materials. Also see the Suggested Readings under Appendix A on the companion Web site for this text.

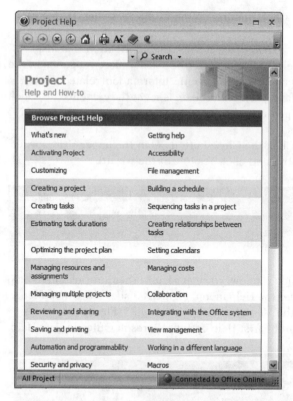

FIGURE A-4   Topics Under Microsoft Office Project Help

Main Screen Elements

The Project 2007 default main screen is called the Gantt Chart view. At the top of the main screen, the Menu bar and Standard toolbar are similar to those in *Windows 2003* programs. Project 2007 does *not* have the new ribbons found in other Office 2007 applications. The order and appearance of buttons on the Standard toolbar may vary, depending on the features you are using and how the Standard toolbar is customized. When you use a button, it automatically becomes visible on the toolbar it is associated with. You can display the Standard toolbar in one row or two, or you can set it to always show full menus so that all buttons are visible all the time. Additional toolbars in Project 2007 include the Formatting toolbar, the Custom Forms toolbar, and the Tracking toolbar, among others.

To customize the Standard toolbar:

1. *Open the Customize dialog box.* Click **Tools** on the Menu bar, point to **Customize**, and then click **Toolbars** to display the Customize dialog box. Click the **Options** tab.
2. *Show full menus.* Click the option to **Always show full menus**, as shown in Figure A-5, and then click the **Close** button to close the dialog box.

Check the toolbar options you prefer, such as always showing the full menus

FIGURE A-5   Customizing the Toolbar

3. *If needed, add the Zoom In and Zoom Out buttons to the toolbar.* Click the **Toolbar Options** button on the toolbar, and then click the **Zoom In** button 🔍. Click the **Toolbar Options** button again, and then click the **Zoom Out** button 🔍, as shown in Figure A-6.

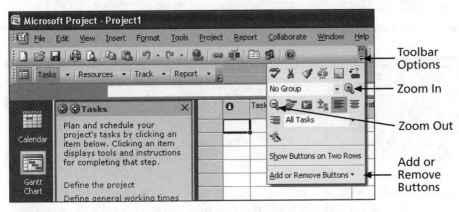

FIGURE A-6   Adding the Zoom In and Zoom Out Buttons to the Toolbar

TIP

You can select the Add or Remove Buttons option to add or remove several toolbar buttons at once.

Figure A-7 shows the main screen elements of Project 2007. Below the Standard toolbar is the Entry bar, which displays entries you make in the Entry table, located right below the Entry bar. The Gantt chart calendar display appears on the right of the split bar, which separates the Entry table and the Gantt chart. The column to the left of the Task Name column is the Indicators column. The Indicators column displays indicators or symbols related to items associated with each task, such as task notes or hyperlinks to other files.

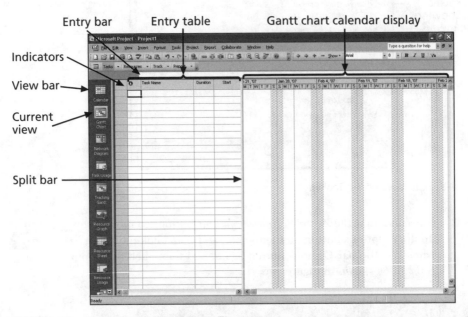

FIGURE A-7   Project 2007 Main Screen Elements

TIP

Many features in Project 2007 are similar to ones in other Windows programs. For example, to collapse or expand tasks, click the appropriate symbols to the left of the task name. To access shortcut items, right-click in either the Entry table area or the Gantt chart. Many of the Entry table operations in Project 2007 are very similar to operations in Excel. For example, to adjust a column width, click and drag or double-click between the column heading titles.

If you select another view and want to return to the Gantt Chart view, click the Gantt Chart button on the View Bar on the left of the screen, or select View from the Menu bar, and click Gantt Chart, as shown in Figure A-8. If the Entry table on the left appears to be different, select View from the Menu bar, point to Table: Entry, and then click Entry to return to the default Entry table view. If the View Bar does not display, select View Bar from the View menu.

Notice the split bar that separates the Entry table from the Gantt chart. When you move the mouse over the split bar, your cursor changes to the resize pointer. Clicking and dragging the split bar to the right reveals other task information in the Entry table, including the Duration, Start date, Finish date, Predecessors, and Resource Names columns.

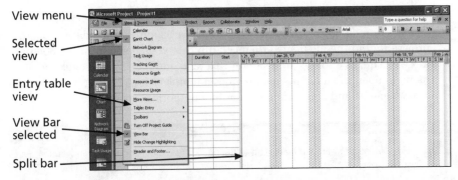

View menu —
Selected view —
Entry table view —
View Bar selected —
Split bar —

FIGURE A-8   Project 2007 View Menu Options

Next, you will open a template file to explore more screen elements. Project 2007 comes with several template files, and you can also access templates from Microsoft Office Online or other Web sites. To open template files on your computer, click File on the Menu bar, and then click New. In the New Project task pane, click the On computer option under Templates, as shown in Figure A-9.

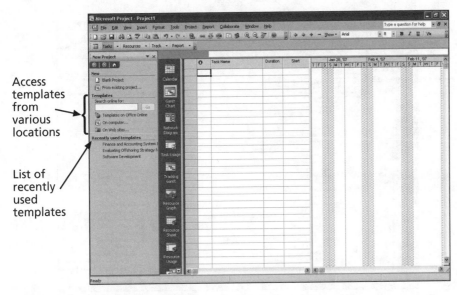

Access templates from various locations

List of recently used templates

FIGURE A-9   Opening a Template File

H E L P

To access template files on your computer, you must do a full or custom install of Project 2007.

To open a template file and adjust Project 2007 screen elements:

1. *Open a template file.* Click the **Open button** 📂 on the Standard toolbar, browse to find the file named **finance.mpp** that you copied from the companion Web site, or author's Web site for this text, and then double-click the filename to open the file. This file provides a template for a project to implement a new finance and accounting system in a corporate environment.

TIP

The finance.mpp file is identical to the template named "Finance and Accounting System Implementation" that comes with Project 2007, which you can also access from the Templates, On computer... option shown in Figure A-9.

2. *View the Note.* Move your mouse over the **Notes icon** 📝 in the Indicators column and read its contents. It is a good idea to provide a short note describing the purpose of project files. (You'll learn how to add notes in the Communications section of this guide.) Your screen should resemble Figure A-10.

Indicator column

Notes icon

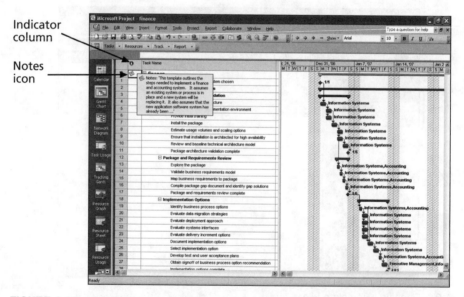

FIGURE A-10   The Finance.mpp File

3. *Adjust the timescale.* Click the **Zoom Out** button 🔍 on the toolbar *twice* to display the timescale in months and then weeks. If you cannot find the Zoom Out button, you can add it to the Standard toolbar by clicking the **Toolbar**

Options button, as described earlier. Notice that this project started on January 1, 2007, and ended in early April 2007. The first line in the Entry bar displays the filename, and the bar in the Gantt chart next to that line shows the timeline for the entire project.

4. *Select Outline Level 2 to display WBS level 1 tasks.* On the Standard toolbar, click the **Show** button's list arrow Show ▾, and then click **Outline Level 1**, as shown in Figure A-11. Notice that only the level 1 WBS items display in the Entry table after you select Outline Level 1, and the timescale shows months. The black bars on the Gantt chart represent the summary tasks. The entire project is normally referred to as WBS level zero, and the next highest level is called level 1. This view of the file also shows two milestone tasks in rows 1 and 137 indicating when a new Accounting and Finance system was chosen and when the project was completed. Recall that the black diamond symbol on a Gantt chart shows milestones.

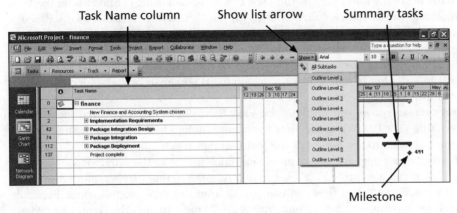

Task Name column   Show list arrow   Summary tasks

Milestone

FIGURE A-11 Viewing Summary Tasks Using the Show Button

5. *Adjust the Task Name column.* Move the cursor over the right-column gridline in the Task Name column heading until you see the resize pointer, and then double-click the **left mouse** button to resize the column width automatically.

6. *Move the split bar to reveal more Entry table columns.* Move the split bar to the right to reveal the Resource Names column. Your screen should resemble Figure A-12.

7. *Expand a task.* Click the **expand symbol** ➕ to the left of Task 112, Package Deployment, to see its subtasks. Click the **collapse symbol** ➖ to hide its subtasks.

Collapse
symbol

Expand
symbol

Move split
bar to
reveal
more
columns

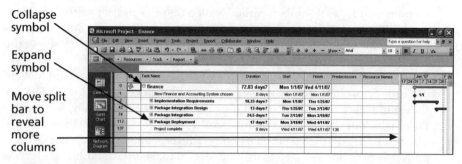

FIGURE A-12   Adjusting Screen Elements

Project 2007 Views

Project 2007 provides many ways to display project information. These displays are called views. To the left of the Entry table is the View Bar. Instead of using commands on the View menu to change views, you can click buttons on the View Bar. Several views discussed in the main text are on the default View Bar: Gantt Chart, Network Diagram, Tracking Gantt, and Resource Graph. Other views include Calendar, Task Usage, Resource Sheet, Resource Usage, and an option to display More Views. These different views allow you to examine project information in different ways, which helps you analyze and understand what is happening on your project.

To save screen space, you can hide the View Bar by selecting View from the Menu bar and deselecting View Bar. When the View Bar is not visible, a blue bar with the name of the current view appears to the far left of the main screen. When you right-click this blue bar, a shortcut menu appears, which gives you quick access to the other views.

The View menu also provides access to different tables that display information in a variety of ways. Some tables that you can access from the View menu include Schedule, Cost, Tracking, and Earned Value. Some Project 2007 views, such as the Gantt Chart view, present a broad look at the entire project, whereas others, such as the Form views, focus on specific pieces of information about each task. Three main categories of views are available:

- *Graphical*: A chart or graphical representation of data using bars, boxes, lines, and images.
- *Task Sheet or Table*: A spreadsheet-like representation of data in which each task appears as a new row and each piece of information about the task is represented by a column. Different tables are applied to a task sheet to display different kinds of information.
- *Form*: A specific view of information for one task. Forms are used to focus on the details of one task.

Table A-1 describes some of the predesigned views within each category that Project 2007 provides to help you display the project or task information that you need.

TABLE A-1 Common Project 2007 Views

Category of View	View Name	Description of View
Graphical	Gantt Chart	Standard format for displaying project schedule information that lists project tasks and their corresponding start and finish dates in a calendar format. Shows each task as a horizontal bar with the length and position corresponding to the timescale at the top of the Gantt chart.
	Network Diagram	Schematic display of the logical relationships or sequencing of project activities. Presents each task as a box with linking lines between tasks to show sequencing. Critical tasks appear in red.
Task Sheet or Table	Entry Table	Default table view showing columns for Task Name and Duration. By revealing more of the Entry table, you can enter start and end dates, predecessors, and resource names.
	Schedule Table	Displays columns for Task Name, Start, Finish, Late Start, Late Finish, Free Slack, and Total Slack.
	Cost Table	Displays columns for Task Name, Fixed Cost, Fixed Cost Accrual, Total Cost, Baseline, Variance, Actual, and Remaining.
	Tracking Table	Displays columns for Task Name, Actual Start, Actual Finish, % Complete, Physical % Complete, Actual Duration, Remaining Duration, Actual Cost, and Actual Work.
	Earned Value	Displays columns for Task Name, PV, EV, AC, SV, CV, EAC, BAC, and VAC. See the earned value section of this text for descriptions of these acronyms.
Form	Task Details Form	Displays detailed information about a single task in one window.
	Task Name Form	Displays columns for Task Name, Resources, and Predecessors for a single task.

Next, you will use the same file (finance.mpp) to access and explore some of the views available in Project 2007.

To access and explore different views:

1. *Show all subtasks.* Click the **Show** button ⌷Show ▾ on the toolbar, and then click **All Subtasks**. Click the Task Name for Task 0, finance.
2. *Explore the Network Diagram view.* Click the **Network Diagram** button 🔲 on the View Bar, and then click the **Zoom Out** button 🔍 on the toolbar *three times*. Your screen should resemble Figure A-13.

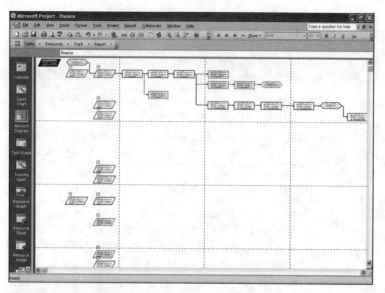

FIGURE A-13   Network Diagram View of Project 2007 Finance File

    3. *Explore the Calendar view.* Click the **Calendar** button 🔲 on the View Bar. Your screen should resemble Figure A-14.

FIGURE A-14   Calendar View of Project 2007 Finance File

    4. *Examine columns in the Entry table.* Click the **Gantt Chart** button 🔲 on the View Bar, and observe the information provided in each column of the Entry table.

5. *Examine the Table: Schedule view.* Click **View** on the Menu bar, move your mouse to **Table: Entry**, and then click **Schedule** in the cascading menu to the right. Notice that the columns to the left of the Gantt chart now display more detailed schedule information. Also notice that all of the text in the Task Name column is not visible. You can widen the column by moving the mouse to the right of the Task Name column and double-clicking the resize pointer ✛. You can also move the split bar to the right to reveal more columns.

6. *Right-click the Select All button to access different table views.* Move your mouse to the **Select All** button to the left of the Task Name column symbol, and then right-click with your mouse. A shortcut menu to different table views displays, as shown in Figure A-15. Experiment with other table views, then return to the Table: Entry view.

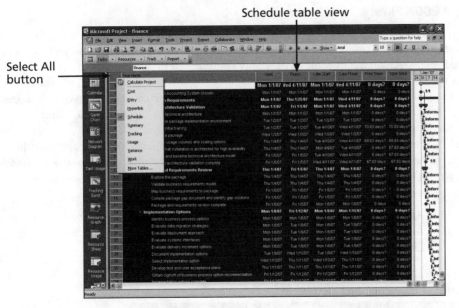

Schedule table view

Select All button

FIGURE A-15 Changing Table Views

7. *Explore the Reports feature.* Click **Report** on the Menu bar, and then click **Reports**. The Reports dialog box displays, as shown in Figure A-16.

8. *View the Project Summary report.* Double-click **Overview** from the Reports dialog box, and then double-click **Project Summary** in the Overview Reports dialog box. Notice that the insertion point now resembles a magnifying glass. Click inside the report to zoom in or zoom out. Click the **Close** button to close this report, and then experiment with viewing other reports. You will use several reports and other views throughout this appendix.

9. *Close the Reports feature.* Click **Close** to close the Reports dialog box and return to the Gantt Chart view.

FIGURE A-16 Reports Dialog Box

Project 2007 Filters

Project 2007 uses an underlying relational database to filter, sort, store, and display information. Filtering project information is very useful. For example, if a project includes hundreds of tasks, you might want to view only summary or milestone tasks to get an over-view of the project. To get this type of over-view of a project, select the Milestones or Summary Tasks filter from the Filter list. If you are concerned about the schedule, you can select a filter that shows only tasks on the critical path. Other filters include Completed Tasks, Late/Overbudget Tasks, and Date Range, which displays tasks based on dates you provide. As shown earlier, you can also click the Show button on the toolbar to display dif-ferent levels in the WBS quickly. For example, Outline Level 1 shows the highest-level items in the WBS, Outline Level 2 shows the next level of detail in the WBS, and so on.

To explore Project 2007 filters:

1. *Apply a filter to see only milestone tasks.* From the Table: Entry view in the finance.mpp file, click the **Toolbar Options** button ⁞ on the toolbar, and then click the **Filter** list arrow, as shown in Figure A-17.

Toolbar options

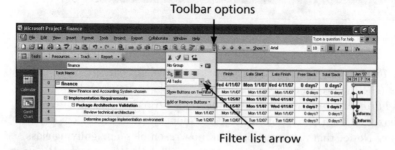

Filter list arrow

FIGURE A-17 Using a Filter

2. *Filter to show specific tasks.* Click **Milestones** in the list of filters, and move the split bar to the left to see all the milestones on the Gantt chart. Your screen

should resemble Figure A-18. The black diamond symbol represents a milestone, a significant event on a project.

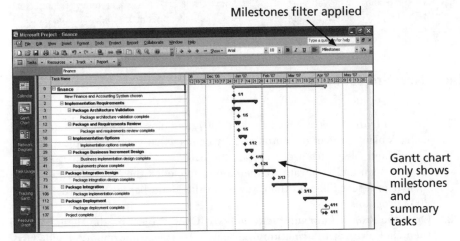

FIGURE A-18   Milestone Tasks Filter for Project 2007 Finance File

3. *Show summary tasks*. Select **All Tasks** from the Filter list box to reveal all the tasks in the WBS again. Click the **Filter** list arrow, scroll down until you see Summary Tasks, and then click **Summary Tasks**. Now only the summary tasks appear in the WBS. Experiment with other outline levels and filters.

4. *Close the file*. When you are finished reviewing the finance.mpp file, click **Close** from the File menu or click the **Close** button. A dialog box appears asking if you want to save changes. Click **No**.

5. *Exit Project 2007*. Select **Exit** from the File menu or click the **Close** button for Project 2007.

Now that you are familiar with the Project 2007 main screen elements, views, and filters, you will learn how to use Project 2007 to assist in project scope management by creating a new project file, developing a WBS, and setting a baseline.

PROJECT SCOPE MANAGEMENT

Project scope management involves defining the work to perform to carry out the project. To use Project 2007, you must first determine the scope of the project. To begin determining the project's scope, create a new file with the project name and start date. Develop a list of tasks that need to be done to carry out the project. This list of tasks becomes the work breakdown structure (WBS). If you intend to track actual project information against the initial plan, you must set a baseline. In this section, you will learn how to create a new project file, develop a WBS, and set a baseline to help plan and manage the Project Tracking Database project. To start, you will enter the scope-related information.

Creating a New Project File

To create a new project file:

1. *Create a blank project.* Open Project 2007, and close the Project Guide Tasks pane. A blank project file automatically opens when you start Project 2007. The default filenames are Project1, Project2, and so on. If Project 2007 is already open and you want to open a new file, click the **New** button on the toolbar or select File and then New from the Menu bar, as with other Office 2003 programs.

2. *Open the Project Information dialog box.* Click **Project** on the Menu bar, and then click **Project Information** to display the Project Information dialog box, as shown in Figure A-19. The Project Information dialog box enables you to set dates for the project, select the calendar to use, and view project statistics. The project start date will default to today's date.

Start date
text box →

FIGURE A-19   Project Information Dialog Box

3. *Enter the project start date.* In the Start date text box, enter **6/01/09**. Setting your project start date to 6/01/09 will ensure that your work matches the results that appear in this appendix. Leave the Finish date, Current date, and other information at the default settings. Click **OK**.

HELP

This appendix uses American date formats. For example, 6/01/09 represents June 1, 2009. Be sure to enter dates in this format for these steps. However, you can change the date format by selecting Tools from the Menu bar, clicking Options, and then selecting the View tab. In the Date Format box, click the date format you want to use.

4. *Enter project properties.* Click **File** on the Menu bar, and then click **Properties**.

TIP

Any command that you click in the expanded menu is added immediately to the personalized (short) version of the menu. If you stop using a command for a while, Project 2007 stops showing it on the short version of the menu.

5. *Enter project information.* Type **Project Tracking Database** in the Title text box, type **Terry Dunlay** in the Author text box, as shown in Figure A-20, and then click **OK**. You may have some default information entered in the Project Properties dialog box, such as your company's name. Keep this file open for the next set of steps.

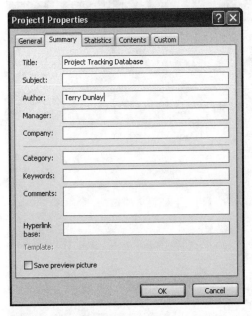

FIGURE A-20   Project Properties Dialog Box

Developing a Work Breakdown Structure

Before using Project 2007, you must develop a work breakdown structure (WBS) for your project. Developing a good WBS takes time, and it will make entering tasks into the Entry table easier if you develop the WBS first. It is also a good idea to establish milestones before entering tasks in Project 2007. You will use the information in Table A-2 to enter tasks for the Project Tracking Database project. Be aware that this example is much shorter and simpler than most WBSs.

To develop a WBS and enter milestones for the Project Tracking Database project:

1. *Enter task names.* Enter the 20 tasks in Table A-2 into the Task Name column in the order shown. Do not worry about durations or any other information at this time. Type the name of each task into the Task Name column of the Entry table, beginning with the first row. Press **Enter** or the **down arrow** key on your keyboard to move to the next row.

HELP

If you accidentally skip a task, highlight the task row and select **Insert** from the Menu bar, and then select **New Task** to insert a blank row. To edit a task entry, click the text for that task, click the Entry bar under the Formatting toolbar, and either type over the old text or edit the existing text.

TABLE A-2   Project Tracking Database Tasks

Order	Task Name
1	Initiating
2	Kickoff meeting
3	Develop project charter
4	Charter signed
5	Planning
6	Develop project plans
7	Review project plans
8	Project plans approved
9	Executing
10	Analysis
11	Design
12	Implementation
13	System implemented
14	Controlling
15	Report performance

TABLE A-2 Project Tracking Database Tasks (continued)

Order	Task Name
16	Control changes
17	Closing
18	Prepare final project report
19	Present final project
20	Project completed

TIP

Entering tasks into Project 2007 and editing the information is similar to entering and editing data in an Excel spreadsheet. Project 2007, like earlier versions, includes a feature called a SmartTag, which appears, for example, when you delete a row. The SmartTag clarifies whether you want to delete the entire task or only clear the contents of a cell.

2. *Move the split bar to reveal more columns*. If necessary, move the split bar to the right to reveal the entire Task Name and Duration columns.
3. *Adjust the Task Name column width as needed*. To make all the text display in the Task Name column, move the mouse over the right-column gridline in the Task Name column heading until you see the resize pointer ◆▶, and then click the **left mouse** button and drag the line to the right to make the column wider, or double-click to adjust the column width automatically.

This WBS separates tasks according to the project management process groups of initiating, planning, executing, controlling, and closing. These tasks will be the level 1 items in the WBS for this project. It is a good idea to include all of these process groups because there are important tasks that must be done under each of them. Recall that the WBS should include *all* of the work required for the project. In the Project Tracking Database WBS, the tasks will be purposefully left at a high WBS level (level 2). You will create these levels, or the WBS hierarchy, next when you create summary tasks. For a real project, you would usually break the WBS into even more levels to provide more details to describe all the work involved in the project. For example, analysis tasks for a database project might be broken down further to include preparing entity relationship diagrams for the database and developing guidelines for the user interface. Design tasks might be broken down to include preparing prototypes, incorporating user feedback, entering data, and testing the database. Implementation tasks might include more levels, such as installing new hardware or software, training the users, fully documenting the system, and so on.

Creating Summary Tasks

After entering the WBS tasks listed in Table A-2 into the Entry table, the next step is to show the WBS levels by creating summary tasks. The summary tasks in this example are Tasks 1 (initiating), 5 (planning), 9 (executing), 14 (controlling), and 17 (closing). You create summary tasks by highlighting and indenting their respective subtasks.

To create the summary tasks:

1. *Select lower level or subtasks.* Highlight **Tasks 2** through **4** by clicking the cell for Task 2 and dragging the mouse through the cells to Task 4.
2. *Indent subtasks.* Click the **Indent** button ➡ on the Formatting toolbar so your screen resembles Figure A-21. After the subtasks (Tasks 2 through 4) are indented, notice that Task 1 automatically becomes boldface, which indicates that it is a summary task. A collapse symbol ⊟ appears to the left of the new summary task name. Clicking the collapse symbol will collapse the summary task and hide the subtasks beneath it. When subtasks are hidden, an expand symbol ⊞ appears to the left of the summary task name. Clicking the expand symbol will expand the summary task. Also, notice that the symbol for the summary task on the Gantt chart has changed from a blue to a black line with arrows indicating the start and end dates.

Expand or collapse symbols by summary tasks   Indent   Summary task symbol

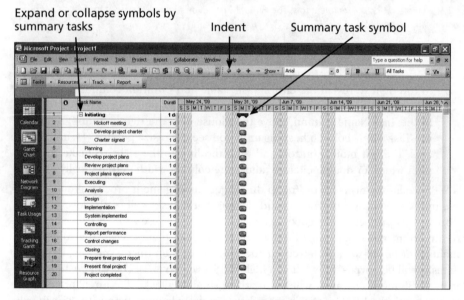

FIGURE A-21   Indenting Tasks to Create the WBS Hierarchy

3. *Create other summary tasks and subtasks.* Create subtasks and summary tasks for Tasks 5, 9, 14, and 17 by following the same steps. Indent **Tasks 6** through **8** to make Task 5 a summary task. Indent **Tasks 10** through **13** to make Task 9 a summary task. Indent **Tasks 15** through **16** to make Task 14 a summary task. Indent **Tasks 18** through **20** to make Task 17 a summary task. Widen the Task Name column to see all of your text, as needed.

Numbering Tasks

Depending on how Project 2007 is set up on your computer, you may or may not see numbers associated with tasks as you enter and indent them.

To display automatic numbering of tasks using the standard tabular numbering system for a WBS:

1. *Display the Options dialog box.* Click **Tools** on the Menu bar, and then click **Options**. The Options dialog box opens.
2. *Show outline numbers.* Click the **View** tab, if necessary. Check **Show** outline number in the "Outline options for Project1" section of the View tab. Click **OK** to close the dialog box. Figure A-22 shows the Options dialog box and resulting outline numbers applied to the WBS tasks.

Outline numbers show WBS hierarchy

Show outline number check box

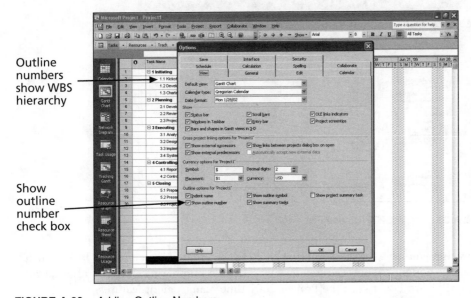

FIGURE A-22   Adding Outline Numbers

Saving Project Files With or Without a Baseline

An important part of project management is tracking performance against a baseline, or approved plan. Project 2007 does not prompt you to save a file with or without a baseline each time you save it, as some previous versions did. The default is to save without a baseline. It is important to wait until you are ready to save your file with a baseline because Project 2007 will show changes against a baseline. Since you are still developing your project file for the Project Tracking Database project, you want to save the file without a baseline. Later in this appendix, you will save the file with a baseline by selecting Tools, Tracking, and then Set Baseline. You will then enter actual information to compare planned and actual performance data.

To save a file without a baseline:

1. *Save your file.* Click **File** on the Menu bar and then click **Save**, or click the **Save** button 🖫 on the Standard toolbar.

2. *Enter a filename.* In the Save As dialog box, type **scope** in the File name text box. Browse to the location in which you want to save the file, and then click **Save**. Your Project 2007 file should look like Figure A-23. (You can adjust the timescale to show months by clicking Zoom In or Zoom Out.)

HELP

If you want to download the Project 2007 file scope.mpp to check your work or continue to the next section, a copy is available on the companion Web site for this text, the author's Web site, or from your instructor.

FIGURE A-23   Project 2007 Scope File

Now that you have finished entering all 20 tasks, created the summary tasks and subtasks, set the options to show the standard WBS tabular numbering system, and saved your file, you will learn how to use the Project 2007 time management features.

PROJECT TIME MANAGEMENT

Many people use Project 2007 for its time management features. The first step in using these features, after inputting the WBS for the project, is to enter durations for tasks or specific dates when tasks will occur. Inserting durations or specific dates will automatically update the Gantt chart. To use Project 2007 to adjust schedules automatically and to do critical path analysis, you must also enter task dependencies. After entering durations and task dependencies, you can view the network diagram and critical path information. This section describes how to use each of these time management features.

Entering Task Durations

When you enter a task, Project 2007 automatically assigns to it a default duration of one day, followed by a question mark. To change the default duration, type a task's estimated duration in the Duration column. If you are unsure of an estimate and want to review it again later, enter a question mark after it. For example, you could enter 5d? for a task with an estimated duration of five days that you want to review later. You can then use the Tasks With Estimated Durations filter to see quickly the tasks for which you need to review duration estimates.

To indicate the length of a task's duration, you must type both a number and an appropriate duration symbol. If you type only a number, Project 2007 automatically enters days as the duration unit. Duration unit symbols include:

- d = days (default)
- w = weeks
- m = minutes
- h = hours
- mo or mon = months
- ed = elapsed days
- ew = elapsed weeks

For example, to enter one week for a task duration, type 1w in the Duration column. (You can also type wk, wks, week, or weeks, instead of just w.) To enter two days for a task duration, type 2d in the Duration column. The default unit is days, so if you enter 2 for the duration, it will be entered as 2 days. You can also enter elapsed times in the Duration column. For example, 2ed means two elapsed days, and 2ew means two elapsed weeks. You would use an elapsed duration for a task like "Allow paint to dry." The paint will dry in exactly the same amount of time regardless of whether it is a workday, a weekend, or a holiday.

TIP

If the Duration column is not visible, drag the split bar to the right until the Duration column is in view.

Entering time estimates or durations might seem like a straightforward process. However, you must follow a few important procedures:

- As you saw in the previous section, when you enter a task in the Task Name column, 1 day? appears in the Duration column. The question mark means that you are unsure of the duration or want to go back to it. Be sure to enter the durations you want to appear.
- Do not enter durations for summary tasks. Summary task durations are calculated automatically based on the subtasks. If you enter a duration for a task and then make it a summary task, its duration will automatically change to match the durations of its subtasks. Project 2007 will not allow you to enter or change the

duration of a summary task. Think of it as entering durations for work packages, the lowest-level items in your WBS. The other items are really the WBS hierarchy. Let Project 2007 do the duration calculations for you.

- To mark a task as a milestone, enter 0 for the duration. You can also mark tasks that have a non-zero duration as milestones by checking the "Mark task as milestone" option in the Task Information dialog box on the Advanced tab. The milestone symbol for those tasks will appear at their start date. Double-click a task to access the Task Information dialog box.

- To enter recurring tasks, such as weekly meetings or monthly status reports, select Recurring Task from the Insert menu. Enter the task name, the duration, and when the task occurs. Project 2007 will automatically insert appropriate subtasks based on the length of the project and the number of tasks required for the recurring task. For example, if you enter a recurring task for monthly review meetings that occur on the first day of every month for a 12-month project, Project 2007 will enter a summary task for monthly review meetings and 12 subtasks—one meeting for each month.

- You can enter the exact start and finish dates for activities instead of entering durations. To enter start and finish dates, move the split bar to the right to reveal the Start and Finish columns. Enter start and finish dates only when those dates are certain. If you want task dates to adjust according to any other task dates, do not enter exact start and finish dates. Instead, enter a duration and then establish a dependency to related tasks. *The real scheduling power of Project 2007 comes from setting up dependencies or relationships among tasks, as described in the next section.*

- Project 2007 uses a default calendar with standard workdays and hours. Duration estimates will vary according to the calendar you use. For example, entering 5d in the standard calendar may result in more than five days on the Gantt chart if the time period includes Saturday or Sunday. You can change specific working and nonworking days, or the entire project calendar, by selecting Change Working Time from the Tools menu.

- You often need to adjust the timescale on the Gantt chart to see your project's schedule in different time frames, such as weeks, months, quarters, or years. You expand the timescale by clicking the Zoom Out button. The Zoom In button collapses the timescale. You can also change the format of the timescale by having three tiers instead of two or by formatting dates differently by double-clicking the timescale section of the Gantt chart.

Next, you will set task durations in the Project Tracking Database file (scope.mpp) that you created and saved in the previous section. If you did not create the file named scope.mpp, you can download it from the companion Web site for this text. You will create a new recurring task and enter its duration, and then you will enter other task durations. First, create a new recurring task called Status Reports above Task 15, Report performance.

To create a new recurring task:

1. *Insert a recurring task above Task 15, Report performance.* Open scope. mpp, if necessary, and then click **Report performance** (Task 15) in the Task Name column to select that task. Click **Insert** on the Menu bar, and then click **Recurring Task**. The Recurring Task Information dialog box opens.

2. *Enter task and duration information for the recurring task.* Type **Status Reports** as the task title in the Task Name text box. Type **1h** in the Duration text box. Select the **Weekly** radio button under Recurrence pattern. Make sure that 1 is entered in the **Recur every** list box. Select the **Wednesday** check box. In the Range of recurrence section, type **6/10/09** in the Start text box, click the **End by** radio button, and then type **10/28/09** in the End by text box. Click the **End by** list arrow to see the calendar, as shown in Figure A-24. You can use the calendar to enter the Start and End by dates. The new recurring task will appear above Task 15, Report performance, when you are finished.

TIP

You can also enter a number of occurrences instead of an End by for a recurring task. You might need to adjust the End by date after you enter all of your task durations and dependencies. Remember, the date on your computer determines the date listed as Today in the calendar.

FIGURE A-24   Recurring Task Information Dialog Box

3. *View the new summary task and its subtasks.* Click **OK**. Project 2007 inserts a new Status Reports subtask in the Task Name column. Expand the new subtask by clicking the **expand symbol** ⊞ to the left of Status Reports. To collapse the recurring task, click the **collapse symbol** ⊟.

4. *Adjust the Duration column width and Gantt chart timescale.* Notice the # signs that appear in the Duration column for the Status Reports task. Like Excel, Project 2007 uses these symbols to denote that the column width needs to be increased. Increase the Duration column's width by moving your mouse to the right of the Duration column heading until you see a resize pointer ✛. Double-click to adjust the column width and display the information. Click the **Zoom Out** 🔍 button on the toolbar twice to display the Gantt chart in months. Move your mouse over the Recurring Task symbol 🔄 in the Indicator column for row 15. Your screen should resemble Figure A-25. Notice that the recurring task appears on the appropriate dates on the Gantt chart.

FIGURE A-25 A Recurring Task

Use the information in Table A-3 to enter durations for the other tasks for the Project Tracking Database project. The Project 2007 row number is shown to the left of each task name in the table. Remember, you already entered a duration for the recurring task. Also, remember that you should *not* enter durations for summary tasks. Durations for summary tasks are automatically calculated to match the durations and dependencies of subtasks, as described further in the next section, Establishing Task Dependencies.

To enter task durations for the other tasks:

1. *Enter the duration for Task 2.* Click the **Duration** column for row 2, Kickoff meeting, type **2h**, and then press **Enter**.

2. *Enter the duration for Task 3.* In the **Duration** column for row 3, Develop project charter, type **10d**, then press **Enter**. You can also just type 10, since d or days is the default duration.

3. *Enter remaining task durations.* Continue to enter the durations using the information in Table A-3.

TABLE 1-3 Durations for Project Tracking Database Tasks

Task Number/Row	Task Name	Duration
2	Kickoff meeting	2h
3	Develop project charter	10d
4	Charter signed	0
6	Develop project management plans	3w
7	Review project management plans	4mo
8	Project management plans approved	0
10	Analysis	1mo
11	Design	2mo
12	Implementation	1mo
13	System implemented	0
37	Report performance	5mo
38	Control changes	5mo
40	Prepare final project report	2w
41	Present final project	1w
42	Project completed	0

4. Save your file and name it. Click **File** on the Menu bar, and then click **Save As**. Enter **time** as the filename, and then save the file to the desired location on your computer or network. Your file should resemble Figure A-26. Notice that all of the tasks still begin on June 1. This will change in the next section when we add task dependencies. Keep this file open for the next set of steps.

FIGURE A-26   Time File with Durations Entered

Establishing Task Dependencies

To use Project 2007 to adjust schedules automatically and to do critical path analysis, you *must* determine the dependencies or relationships among tasks. Project 2007 provides three methods for creating task dependencies: using the Link Tasks button, using the Predecessors column of the Entry table or the Predecessors tab in the Task Information dialog box, or clicking and dragging the Gantt chart symbols for tasks with dependencies.

To create dependencies using the Link Tasks button, highlight tasks that are related and then click the Link Tasks button 🔗 on the toolbar. For example, to create a finish-to-start dependency between Task 1 and Task 2, click any cell in row 1, drag down to row 2, and then click the Link Tasks button. The default type of link is finish-to-start. In the Project Tracking Database example, all the tasks use this default relationship. You will learn about other types of dependencies later in this appendix.

TIP

Selecting tasks is similar to selecting cells in Excel. To select adjacent tasks, click and drag the mouse. You can also click the first task, hold down the Shift key, and then click the last task. To select nonadjacent tasks, hold down the Control (Ctrl) key as you click tasks in order of their dependencies.

When you use the Predecessors column of the Entry table to create dependencies, you must manually enter the information. To create dependencies manually, type the task row number of the preceding task in the Predecessors column of the Entry table. For example, Task 3 in Table A-3 has Task 2 as a predecessor, which can be entered in the Predecessors column, meaning that Task 3 cannot start until Task 2 is finished. To see the Predecessors column of the Entry table, move the split bar to the right. You can also double-click on the task, click the Predecessors tab in the Task Information dialog box, and enter the predecessors there. (This is more work than just typing it in the Predecessor column.)

You can also create task dependencies by clicking the Gantt chart symbol for a task and then dragging to the Gantt chart symbol for a task that succeeds it. For example, you could click the Milestone symbol ◆ for Task 4, hold down the left mouse button, and drag to the Task Bar symbol for Task 6 to create a dependency, as shown in the Gantt chart in Figure A-27. Note the Finish-to-Start Link dialog box that appears when you use this method.

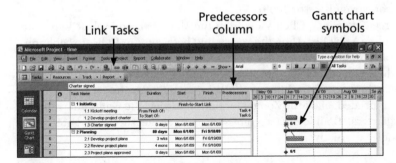

FIGURE A-27 Creating Task Dependencies

Next, you will use information from Figure A-28 to enter the predecessors for tasks as indicated. You will create some dependencies by manually typing the predecessors in the Predecessors column, some by using the Link Tasks button, some by using the Gantt chart symbols, and the remaining dependencies by using whichever method you prefer.

To link tasks or establish dependencies for the Project Tracking Database project:

1. *Display the Predecessors column in the Entry table.* Move the split bar to the right to reveal the full Predecessors column in the time.mpp file. Widen the Task Name or other columns, if needed.

2. *Highlight the cell where you want to enter a predecessor, and then type the task number for the preceding task.* Click the **Predecessors cell** for Task 3, type **2**, and press **Enter**. Notice that as you enter task dependencies, the Gantt chart changes to reflect the new schedule. Also notice that several cells become highlighted. In this case, the Duration and Finish cells for Task 1, and the Start and Finish cells for Task 3, are highlighted in light blue. *This is the new Visual Change Highlights feature of Project 2007.*

3. *Enter predecessors for Task 4.* Click the **Predecessors cell** for Task 4, type **3**, and press **Enter**.

4. *Establish dependencies using the Link Tasks button.* To link Tasks 10 through 13, click the task name for Task 10 in the Task Name column and drag down through Task 13. Then, click the **Link Tasks** button 🔗 on the toolbar. Alternately, you can click **Edit** on the Menu bar, and then click **Link Tasks**.

5. *Create a dependency using Gantt chart symbols.* Click the **Milestone** symbol ◆ for Task 4 on the Gantt chart, hold down the **left mouse** button, and drag to the **Task Bar** symbol for Task 6. (See Figure A-27 to see this step in progress.)

6. *Enter remaining dependencies.* Link the other tasks by either manually entering the predecessors into the Predecessors column, by using the Link Tasks button, or by clicking and dragging the Gantt chart symbols. Note the visual change highlighting feature that displays as you enter dependencies. You can

view the dependencies in Figure A-28. For example, Task 8 has Task 6 as a predecessor, Task 10 has Task 8 as a predecessor, Task 11 has 10, Task 12 has 11, Task 13 has 12, Task 40 has 13, Task 41 has 40, and Task 42 has 41 as a predecessor. If you have entered all data correctly, the project should end on 11/16/09, or November 16, 2009.

7. *Adjust screen elements*. Click **View** from the Menu bar, and select **View Bar** to collapse the View Bar. Drag the resize line between the Indicator column and the Task Name column to the left to remove the Indicator column. Click **View** on the Menu bar, point to **Toolbars**, and then click **Project Guide** to hide the Project Guide toolbar. When you finish, your screen should resemble Figure A-28. If needed, click the Zoom Out button to view the Gantt chart timescale in quarters. Double-check your screen to make sure you entered the dependencies correctly.

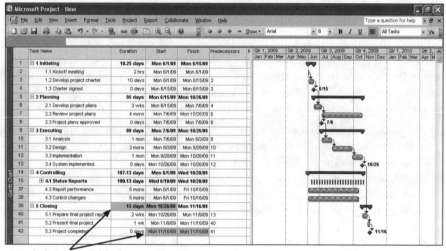

Visual change highlights

FIGURE A-28 Project Tracking Database File with Durations and Dependencies Entered

8. *Preview and save your file*. Click **File** on the Menu bar, and then select **Print Preview**, or click the **Print Preview** button on the Standard toolbar. When you are finished, close the Print Preview and save your file again by clicking the **Save** button on the Standard toolbar. If you desire, print your file by clicking the **Print** button on the Standard toolbar, or by selecting Print from the File menu. Keep the file open for the next set of steps.

Changing Task Dependency Types and Adding Lead or Lag Time

A task dependency or relationship describes how a task is related to the start or finish of another task. Project 2007 allows for four task dependencies: finish-to-start (FS), start-to-start (SS), finish-to-finish (FF), and start-to-finish (SF). By using these dependencies effectively, you can modify the critical path and shorten your project schedule. The most common type of dependency is finish-to-start (FS). All of the dependencies in the Project Tracking Database example are FS dependencies. However, sometimes you need to establish other types of dependencies. This section describes how to change task dependency types. It also explains how to add lead or lag times between tasks. You will shorten the duration of the Project Tracking Database project by adding lead time between some tasks.

To change a dependency type, open the Task Information dialog box for that task by double-clicking the task name. On the Predecessors tab of the Task Information dialog box, select a new dependency type from the Type column list arrow.

The Predecessors tab also allows you to add lead or lag time to a dependency. You can enter both lead and lag time using the Lag column on the Predecessors tab. Lead time reflects an overlap between tasks that have a dependency. For example, if Task B can start when its predecessor, Task A, is half-finished, you can specify a finish-to-start dependency with a lead time of 50% for the successor task. Enter lead times as negative numbers. In this example, enter –50% in the first cell of the Lag column. Adding lead times is also called fast tracking and is one way to compress a project's schedule.

Lag time is the opposite of lead time; it is a time gap or delay between tasks that have a dependency. If you need a two-day delay between the finish of Task C and the start of Task D, establish a finish-to-start dependency between Tasks C and D and specify a two-day lag time. Enter lag time as a positive value. In this example, type 2d in the Lag column.

In the Project Tracking Database example, notice that work on design tasks does not begin until all the work on the analysis tasks has been completed (see Rows 10 and 11), and work on implementation tasks does not begin until all the work on the design tasks has been completed (see Rows 11 and 12). In reality, it is rare to wait until all of the analysis work is complete before starting any design work, or to wait until all of the design work is finished before starting any implementation work. It is also a good idea to add some additional time, or a buffer, before crucial milestones, such as a system being implemented. To create a more realistic schedule, add lead times to the design and implementation tasks and lag time before the system implemented milestone.

To add lead and lag times:

1. *Open the Task Information dialog box for Task 11, Design.* In the Task Name column, double-click the text for Task 11, **Design**. The Task Information dialog box opens. Click the **Predecessors** tab.

2. *Enter lead time for Task 11.* Type **–10%** in the Lag column, as shown in Figure A-29. Click **OK**. You could also type a value such as –5d to indicate a five-day overlap. In the resulting Gantt chart, notice that the bar for this task has moved slightly to the left. Also, notice that the project completion date has moved from 11/16 to 11/12.

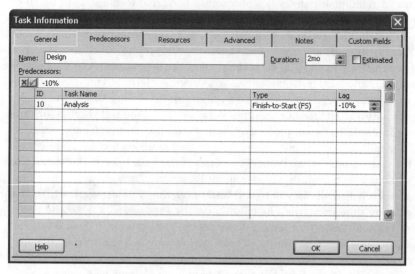

FIGURE A-29   Adding Lead or Lag Time to Task Dependencies

3. *Enter lead time for Task 12.* Double-click the text for Task 12, **Implementation**, type **–3d** in the Lag column, and click **OK**. Notice that the project now ends on 11/9.

4. *Enter lag time for Task 13.* Double-click the text for Task 13, **System Implemented**, type **5d** in the Lag column for this task, and click **OK**. Move the split bar to the right, if necessary, to reveal the Predecessors column. Also double-click the Zoom In button to see the Gantt chart bars more clearly. When you are finished, your screen should resemble Figure A-30. Notice the slight overlap in the taskbars for Tasks 10 and 11 and the short gap between the taskbars for Tasks 12 and 13. Also notice the changes in the Predecessors column for tasks 11, 12, and 13. Double-click the Zoom Out button to see all of the Gantt chart symbols and the main timeline in quarters. The project completion date should be 11/16.

Slight overlap due to lead time

Slight gap due to lag time

FIGURE A-30 Schedule for Project Tracking Database File with Lead and Lag Times

5. *Review the Task Drivers pane.* Project 2007 includes a new feature to help you clearly identify how tasks affect each other. Click Task 13, **System Implemented**, click **Project** on the Menu bar, and then click **Task Drivers**. The Task Drivers pane appears on the left, as shown in Figure A-31. The Task Drivers pane describes what other tasks or factors are affecting the start date for this task.

Task Drivers pane

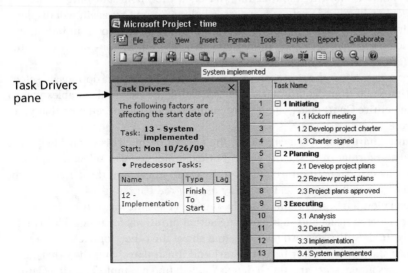

FIGURE A-31 Task Drivers Pane

6. *Save your file.* Click the **Close** button ☒ to close the Task Drivers pane. Click **File** on the Menu bar, and then click **Save**. Or, click the **Save** button 🖫 on the Standard toolbar. Keep this file open for the next set of steps.

TIP

You can enter or modify lead or lag times directly in the Predecessors column of the Entry table. Notice how the predecessors appear for Tasks 11, 12, and 13. For example, the Predecessors column for Task 11 shows 10FS-10%. This notation means that Task 11 has a finish-to-start (FS) dependency with Task 10 and a 10% lead. You can enter lead or lag times to task dependencies directly into the Predecessors column of the Entry table by using this same format: task row number, followed by type of dependency, followed by the amount of lead or lag.

Gantt Charts

Project 2007 shows a Gantt chart as the default view to the right of the Entry table. Gantt charts show the timescale for a project and all of its activities. In Project 2007, dependencies between tasks are shown on the Gantt chart by the arrows between tasks. Many Gantt charts, however, do not show any dependencies. Instead, as you might recall, network diagrams or PERT charts are used to show task dependencies. This section explains important information about Gantt charts and describes how to make critical path information more visible in the Gantt Chart view.

You must follow a few important procedures when working with Gantt charts:

- To adjust the timescale, click the Zoom Out button 🔍 or the Zoom In button 🔍. Clicking these buttons automatically makes the dates on the Gantt chart show more or less information. For example, if the timescale for the Gantt chart is showing months and you click the Zoom Out button, the timescale will adjust to show quarters. Clicking Zoom Out again will display the timescale in years. Similarly, each time you click the Zoom In button, the timescale changes to display more detailed time information—from years to quarters, quarters to months, and months to weeks.
- You can also adjust the timescale and access more formatting options by selecting Timescale from the Format menu. Adjusting the timescale enables you to see the entire Gantt chart on one screen and in the time increments that you desire.
- A Gantt Chart Wizard is available on the Format menu. This wizard helps you adjust the format of the Gantt chart. For example, you can select an option to display critical path information on the Gantt chart, and those items on the critical path will automatically display using a red bar.
- You can view a tracking Gantt chart by setting a baseline for your entire project or for selected tasks and then entering actual durations for tasks. The Tracking Gantt view displays two taskbars, one above the other, for each task. One taskbar shows planned or baseline start and finish dates, and the other taskbar shows actual start and finish dates. You will find a sample Tracking Gantt chart later in this appendix, after you enter actual information for the Project Tracking Database project.

Because you have already created task dependencies, you can now find the critical path for the Project Tracking Database project. You can view the critical tasks by changing the color of those items on the critical path in the Task Name column. You can also change the color of the bars on the Gantt chart. Tasks on the critical path will automatically be red in the Network Diagram view, as described in the following section.

To make the text for the critical path tasks appear in red in the Entry table and on the Gantt chart:

1. *Open the Text Styles dialog box*. Click **Format** on the Menu bar, and then click **Text Styles**. The Text Styles dialog box opens.
2. *Change the critical tasks color option to red*. Click the **Item to Change** list arrow, and then select **Critical Tasks**. Click the **Color** list arrow, and then select **Red**, as shown in Figure A-32. Click **OK** to accept the changes to the text styles.

FIGURE A-32   Text Styles Dialog Box Settings to Display Critical Tasks in Red

3. *Open the Gantt Chart Wizard*. Click **Format** on the Menu bar and then select **Gantt Chart Wizard**. Alternately, you can click the Gantt Chart Wizard button on the Formatting toolbar. The Gantt Chart Wizard opens. Click **Next**, and the next step of the wizard appears.
4. *Select the Critical Path option*. Click the **Critical path** radio button, as shown in Figure A-33. Notice that the sample Gantt chart in the Gantt Chart Wizard displays some bars in red, representing tasks on the critical path. Click **Finish** to proceed to the next step in the Gantt Chart Wizard.
5. *Format the Gantt chart*. Click **Format It**, and then click **Exit Wizard**. Critical taskbars on the Gantt chart will now be red. Your screen should resemble Figure A-34, with task information and bars for all the critical tasks displayed in red on your computer screen.
6. *Save your file without a baseline*. Click **File** on the Menu bar, and then click **Save**. Or, click the **Save** button on the Standard toolbar to save your file. Keep this file open for the next set of steps.

FIGURE A-33   Gantt Chart Wizard Showing Critical Path Format

Test and
Gantt chart
symbols for
critical tasks
should
display in
red on your
computer

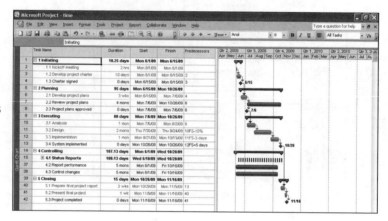

FIGURE A-34   Formatted Gantt Chart

Network Diagrams

The network diagrams in Project 2007 use the precedence diagramming method, with tasks displayed in rectangular boxes and relationships shown by lines connecting the boxes. In the Network Diagram view, tasks on the critical path are automatically shown in red.

To view the network diagram for the Project Tracking Database project:

1. *View the network diagram.* Click **View** on the Menu bar, and then click **View Bar**. Click the **Network Diagram** button 🖼 on the View Bar or select **Network Diagram** from the View menu.

2. *Adjust the Network Diagram view.* To see more tasks in the Network Diagram view, double-click the **Zoom Out** button 🔍. You can also use the scroll bars to see different parts of the network diagram. Figure A-35 shows several of the tasks in the Project Tracking Database network diagram. Note that milestone tasks, such as Charter signed, appear as pointed rectangular boxes,

while other tasks appear as rectangles. Tasks on the critical path automatically appear in red, while noncritical tasks appear in blue. Each task in the network diagram also shows information such as the start and finish dates, task ID, and duration. Move your mouse over the Charter signed box to see it in a larger view. A dashed line on a network diagram represents a page break. You often need to change some of the default settings for the Network Diagram view before printing it.

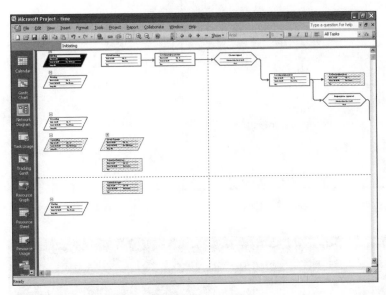

FIGURE A-35   Network Diagram View

3. *View the Help topic on rearranging network diagram boxes.* Click the **Microsoft Project Help** button ⊚ on the Standard toolbar or press **F1** to display the Project Help. Type **Network diagram layout** in the text box and then press **Enter**. Click the resulting Help topic called **Move Network Diagram boxes manually**. Note that you can change several layout options for the network diagram, hide fields, and manually position boxes. Close the Help window, and then close the Search Results window.

4. *View the Layout menu.* Click **Format** on the Menu bar and then click **Layout**. Review the various options for changing the Network diagram layout, as shown in Figure A-36, and then click **OK** to close the Layout dialog box.

5. *Return to Gantt Chart view.* Click the **Gantt Chart** button 🔳 on the View Bar to return to Gantt Chart view. Alternately, you can select **Gantt Chart** from the View menu on the Menu bar. Keep this file open for the next set of steps.

FIGURE A-36   Changing the Network Diagram Layout

Critical Path Analysis

The critical path is the path through the network diagram with the least amount of slack; it represents the shortest possible time to complete the project. If a task on the critical path takes longer than planned, the project schedule will slip unless time is reduced on a task later on the critical path. Sometimes you can shift resources between tasks to help keep a project on schedule. Project 2007 has several views and reports to help analyze critical path information.

Two particularly useful features are the Schedule table view and the Critical Tasks report. The Schedule table view shows the early and late start dates for each task, the early and late finish dates for each task, and the free and total slack for each task. This information shows how flexible the schedule is and helps in making schedule compression decisions. The Critical Tasks report lists only tasks that are on the critical path for the project. If meeting schedule deadlines is essential for a project, project managers will want to monitor tasks on the critical path closely.

To access the Schedule table view and view the Critical Tasks report for a file:

1. *View the Schedule table.* Right-click the **Select All** button to the left of the Task Name column heading and select **Schedule**. Alternatively, you can click **View** on the Menu bar, point to **Table: Entry**, and then click **Schedule**. The Schedule table replaces the Entry table to the left of the Gantt chart.

2. *Reveal all columns in the Schedule table.* Move the split bar to the right until you see the entire Schedule table. Your screen should resemble Figure A-37. This view shows the start and finish (meaning the early start and early finish) and late start and late finish dates for each task, as well as free and total slack. Right-click the **Select All** button and select **Entry** to return to the Entry table view.

Select All button

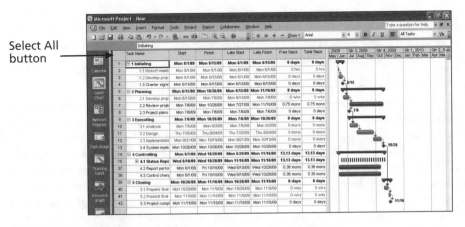

FIGURE A-37   Schedule Table View

3. *Open the Reports dialog box.* Click **Report** on the Menu bar, and then click **Reports**. Double-click **Overview** to open the Overview Reports dialog box. Your screen should resemble Figure A-38.

FIGURE A-38   Accessing the Critical Tasks Report

4. *Display the Critical Tasks report.* Double-click **Critical Tasks**. A Critical Tasks report as of today's date is displayed.

5. *Close the report and save your file.* When you are finished examining the Critical Tasks report, click **Close**. Click **Close** on the Reports dialog box. Click the **Save** button on the Standard toolbar to save your file. Close Project 2007 if you are not continuing to the next section.

HELP

If you want to download the Project 2007 file time.mpp to check your work or continue to the next section, a copy is available on the companion Web site for this text, the author's Web site, or from your instructor.

Now that you have entered task durations, established task dependencies, and reviewed the network diagram and critical path information, you are ready to explore some of the Project 2007 cost management features.

PROJECT COST MANAGEMENT

Many people do not use Project 2007 for cost management. Most organizations have more established cost management software products and procedures in place, and many people simply do not know how to use the cost features of Project 2007. However, the cost features of Project 2007 make it possible to integrate total project information more easily. This section offers brief instructions for entering fixed and variable cost estimates and actual cost and time information after establishing a baseline plan. It also explains how to use Project 2007 for earned value management. More details on these features are available in Project 2007 Help, online tutorials, or other texts.

TIP

To complete the steps in this section, you need to use the Project 2007 file resource.mpp mentioned earlier. You can download it from the companion Web site for this text or from the author's Web site under Book FAQs.

Fixed and Variable Cost Estimates

The first step to using the cost features of Project 2007 is entering cost-related information. You enter costs as fixed or variable based on per-use material costs, or variable based on the type and amount of resources used. Costs related to personnel are often a significant part of project costs. A new feature of Project 2007 is the addition of a "cost resource," which allows you to add a fixed cost to a task without making the cost dependent on the work performed.

Entering Fixed Costs in the Cost Table

The Cost table allows you to enter fixed costs related to each task. To access the Cost table, right-click the Select All button in the Entry table and select Cost or select Table: Cost from the View menu. Figure A-39 shows the resulting view for the Project Tracking Database project using time.mpp. You can also assign a per-use cost to a resource that represents materials or supplies and use it as a base for calculating the total materials or supplies cost of a task. See Project 2007 Help for details on this feature.

FIGURE A-39   Cost Table View

Entering Human Resource Costs

Human resources represent a major part of the costs on many projects. By defining and then assigning human resources and their related costs to tasks in Project 2007, you can calculate human resource costs, track how people are used, identify potential resource shortages that could force you to miss deadlines, and identify underutilized resources. It is often possible to shorten a project's schedule by reassigning underutilized resources. This section focuses on entering human resource costs and assigning resources to tasks. The following section describes other features of Project 2007 related to human resource management.

Several methods are available for entering resource information in Project 2007. One of the easiest is to enter basic resource information in the Resource Sheet. Access the Resource Sheet from the View Bar, or by selecting Resource Sheet from the View menu. The Resource Sheet allows you to enter the resource name, initials, resource group, maximum units, standard rate, overtime rate, cost/use, accrual method, base calendar, and code. Entering data into the Resource Sheet is similar to entering data into an Excel spreadsheet, and you can easily sort items by selecting Sort from the Project menu. In addition, you can use the Filter list on the Formatting toolbar to filter resources. Once you have established resources in the Resource Sheet, you can assign those resources to tasks in the Entry table with the list arrow that appears when you click a cell in the Resource Names column. The Resource Names column is the last column of the Entry table. You can also use other methods for assigning resources, as described below.

Next, you will use the Project 2007 file time.mpp, which you saved in the preceding section, to assign resources to tasks. (If you did not save your file, download it from the companion Web site or from the author's Web site.) Assume that there are four people working on the Project Tracking database project, and that the only costs for this project are for these human resources. Kathy is the project manager; John is the business analyst; Mary is the database analyst; and Chris is an intern or trainee.

To enter basic information about each person into the Resource Sheet:

1. *Display the Resource Sheet view*. Open your Project 2007 file time.mpp, if necessary. Click the **Resource Sheet** button 🖼 on the View Bar (you may need to scroll to see it), or click **View** on the Menu bar, and then click **Resource Sheet**.

2. *Enter resource information*. Enter the information from Table A-4 into the Resource Sheet. Type the information as shown and press the **Tab** key to move to the next field. Notice that you are putting abbreviated job titles in the Initials column: PM stands for project manager; BA, business analyst; DA, database analyst; and IN, intern. When you type the standard and overtime rates, you can just type 50, and Project 2007 will automatically enter $50.00/hr. The standard and overtime rates entered are based on hourly rates. You can also enter annual salaries by typing the annual salary number followed by /y for "per year." Leave the default values for the other columns in the Resource Sheet as they are. Your screen should resemble Figure A-40 when you are finished entering the resource data.

TABLE A-4 Project Tracking Database Resource Data

Resource Name	Initials	Group	Stand. Rate	Ovt. Rate
Kathy	PM	1	$50.00/h	$60.00/h
John	BA	1	$40.00/h	$50.00/h
Mary	DA	1	$40.00/h	$50.00/h
Chris	IN	1	$20.00/h	$25.00/h

FIGURE A-40   Resource Sheet View with Resource Data Entered

TIP

If you know that some people will be available for a project only part time, enter their percentage of availability in the Max Units column of the Resource Sheet. Project 2007 will then automatically assign those people based on their maximum units. For example, if someone can work only 25% of their time on a project throughout most of the project, enter 25% in the Max Units column for that person. When you enter that person as a resource for a task, his or her default number of hours will be 25% of a standard eight-hour workday, or two hours per day.

Adjusting Resource Costs

To make a resource cost adjustment, such as a raise, double-click the person's name in the Resource Name column, select the Costs tab in the Resource Information dialog box, and then enter the effective date and raise percentage. You can also adjust other resource cost information, such as standard and overtime rates.

To give the project manager a 10% raise starting 9/1/09:

1. *Open the Resource Information dialog box.* In Resource Sheet view, double-click **Kathy** in the Resource Name column. The Resource Information dialog box opens.

2. *Enter an effective date for a raise.* Select the **Costs** tab, and then select **tab A**, if needed. Type **9/1/09** in the second cell in the Effective Date column and press **Enter**. Alternately, click the **list arrow** in the second cell and use the calendar that appears to enter the effective date, September 1, 2009.

3. *Enter the raise percentage.* Type **10%** in the second cell for the Standard Rate column, and then press **Enter**. The Resource Information screen should resemble Figure A-41. Notice that Project 2007 calculated the 10% raise to be $55.00 per hour. Click **OK**.

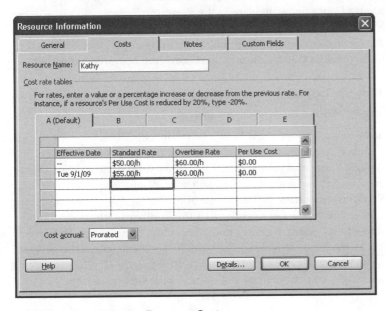

FIGURE A-41   Adjusting Resource Costs

Assigning Resources to Tasks

For Project 2007 to calculate resource costs, you must assign the appropriate resources to tasks in your WBS. There are several methods for assigning resources. The Resources column in the Entry table allows you to select a resource using a list. However, you can use this method to assign only one resource to a task full time, unless you know that you can enter a comma between each resource name. You can use other methods to assign resources, such as the Assign Resources button 🐼 on the Resource Management toolbar or the Resource Cost window, to ensure that Project 2007 captures resource assignments as you intend them. Next, you will use these three methods for assigning resources to the Project Tracking Database project.

Assigning Resources Using the Entry Table

To assign resources using the Entry table:

1. *Select the task to which you want to assign resources.* Click the **Gantt Chart** button on the View Bar. Click **View** on the Menu bar, and then point to **Table: Cost**, and then click **Entry.**, to return to the Entry table.
2. *Reveal the Resource Names column of the Entry table.* Move the split bar to the right to reveal the entire Resource Names column in the Entry table.
3. *Select a resource from the Resource Names column.* In the Resource Names column, click the cell associated with Task 2, **Kickoff meeting**. Click the cell's **list arrow**, and then click **Kathy** to assign her to Task 2. Notice that the resource choices are based on information that you entered in the Resource Sheet. If you had not entered any resources, you would not have a list arrow or any choices to select.
4. *Try to select another resource for Task 2.* Again, click the cell's **list arrow** in the Resource Names column for Task 2, click **John**, and then press **Enter**. Notice that only John's name appears in the Resource Names column. You can assign only one resource to a task using this method.
5. *Clear the resource assignment.* Right-click the **Resource Names** column for Task 2, and then select **Clear Contents** to remove the resource assignments.

Assigning Resources Using the Toolbar

To assign resources using the Resource Management toolbar:

1. *Select the task to which you want to assign resources.* Click the task name for Task 2, **Kickoff meeting**, in the second row of the Task Name column.
2. *Open the Assign Resources dialog box.* Click View on the menu bar, select Toolbars, and then click Resource Management to display that toolbar. Click the **Assign Resources** button 🐼 on the Resource Management toolbar. (If the Assign Resources button is not visible, click the **Toolbar Options** button on the Resource Management toolbar, and then click the **Assign Resources** button.) The Assign Resources dialog box, which lists the names of the people assigned to the project, is displayed, as shown in Figure A-42. This dialog box remains open while you move from task to task to assign resources.

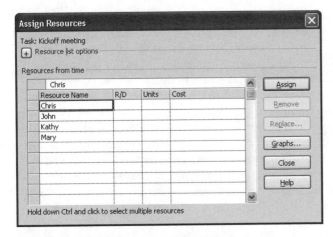

FIGURE A-42   Assign Resources Dialog Box

3. *Assign Kathy to Task 2.* Click **Kathy** in the Resource Name column of the Assign Resources dialog box, and then click **Assign**. Notice that the duration estimate for Task 2 remains at 2 hours, and Kathy's name appears on the Gantt chart by the bar for Task 2.

4. *Assign John to Task 2.* Click **John** in the Resource Name column of the Assign Resources dialog box, and then click **Assign**. The duration for Task 2 changes to 1 hour, *but you do not want this change to occur.* Click **Close** in the Assign Resources dialog box.

5. *Clear the resource assignments.* Right-click the **Resource Names** column for Task 2, and then select **Clear Contents** to remove the resource assignments.

6. *Reenter the duration for Task 2.* Type **2h** in the Duration column for Task 2 and press **Enter**.

TIP

Project 2007 includes a multiple-level undo feature, so you can click the Undo button on the standard toolbar several times to undo ↶ several steps in your file.

Assigning Resources Using the Split Window and Resource Cost View

Even though using the Assign Resources button seems simple, it is often better to use a split window and the Resource Cost view when assigning resources. When you assign resources using the split view, the durations of tasks will not automatically change when you assign more resources, and you have more control over how you enter information. Project 2007 Help offers more information on different options for resource assignment.

To assign both Kathy and John to attend the two-hour kickoff meeting:

1. *Split the window to reveal more information.* Click **Window** on the Menu bar, and then click **Split**. The Gantt Chart view is displayed at the top of the screen and a resource information table is displayed at the bottom of the screen.

2. *Open the Resource Cost window.* Right-click anywhere in the bottom window and select **Resource Cost**.

3. *Assign Kathy to Task 2.* Select Task 2, **Kickoff meeting** in the top window, and then click the first cell in the **Resource Name** column in the Resource Cost window. Click the cell's **list arrow** and select **Kathy**. Press **Enter**.

4. *Assign John to Task 2.* Click the cell's **list arrow** and select **John**. Press **Enter**.

5. *Enter the resource assignment and review the Gantt chart.* Click **OK** in the Resource Cost window. Your screen should resemble Figure A-43. Notice that the duration for Task 2 is still two hours, and both Kathy and John are assigned to that task 100%. You can also enter a different percentage under the Units column if resources will not work 100% of their available time on a task. Note that the default settings are tasks that are effort driven and that the Task type is Fixed Units. You will learn more about these settings later.

Effort driven check box

Task type

FIGURE A-43   Split Screen View for Entering Resource Information

6. *Open the Resource Schedule window.* Right-click anywhere in the lower window and select **Resource Schedule**. Notice that Kathy and John are assigned to Task 2 for two hours, as you intended. You can also enter resource information using the Resource Schedule option.

7. *Close the file and do not save it.* Close the file, but do not save the changes you made. Other resource information has been entered for you in the Project 2007 file named resource.mpp.

As you can see, you must be careful when assigning resources. Project 2007 assumes that the durations of tasks are not fixed, but are effort driven, and this assumption can create some problems when you are assigning resources. Figure A-44 shows the results of adding resources with different settings. The first four task entries assume the task, Design, is effort driven. When you assign one resource, John, to the Design task, the duration is one month. If you later assign two resources, John and Mary, to that same task without changing any settings, Project 2007 automatically adjusts the duration of that task to half its original duration, or 0.5 months. If you change the task type to be Fixed Duration and assign two resources, the duration remains at one month and each resource is assigned 50% to the task. If you change the type to Fixed Work and assign two resources, the duration is cut in half and the resources are assigned full time. The bottom part of Figure A-44 shows the results when a task is not effort driven or when you assign the Fixed Work task type. You must be very careful when entering resource information to make sure the task duration and work hours reflect what you want.

Fixed Work forces the Effort
Driven field to "yes"

Note the effects of type
on resource assignments

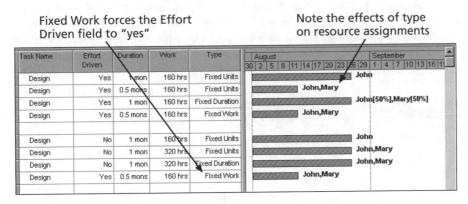

FIGURE A-44   Results of Adding Resources with Various Task Types

Viewing Project Cost Information

Once you enter resource information, Project 2007 automatically calculates resource costs for the project. There are several ways to view project cost information. You can view the Cost table to see cost information, or you can run various cost reports. Next, you will view cost information for the Project Tracking Database project.

To view cost information:

1. *Open resource.mpp.* Download **resource.mpp** from the companion Web site. Open the file.
2. *Open the Cost table.* Right-click the **Select All** button in the Entry table and click **Cost**, or click **View** on the Menu bar, point to **Table: Entry**, and then click

Cost. The Cost table displays cost information and the Gantt chart. Move the split bar to the right to reveal all of the columns. Your screen should resemble Figure A-45. Note that by assigning resources, costs have been automatically calculated for tasks. You could also enter fixed costs for tasks in the cost table, but there are no fixed costs associated with this project.

	Task Name	Fixed Cost	Fixed Cost Accrual	Total Cost	Baseline	Variance	Actual	Remaining
1	⊟ 1 Initiating	$0.00	Prorated	$2,710.00	$0.00	$2,710.00	$0.00	$2,710.00
2	1.1 Kickoff meeting	$0.00	Prorated	$190.00	$0.00	$190.00	$0.00	$190.00
3	1.2 Develop project charter	$0.00	Prorated	$2,520.00	$0.00	$2,520.00	$0.00	$2,520.00
4	1.3 Charter signed	$0.00	Prorated	$0.00	$0.00	$0.00	$0.00	$0.00
5	⊟ 2 Planning	$0.00	Prorated	$7,460.00	$0.00	$7,460.00	$0.00	$7,460.00
6	2.1 Develop project plans	$0.00	Prorated	$5,700.00	$0.00	$5,700.00	$0.00	$5,700.00
7	2.2 Review project plans	$0.00	Prorated	$1,760.00	$0.00	$1,760.00	$0.00	$1,760.00
8	2.3 Project plans approved	$0.00	Prorated	$0.00	$0.00	$0.00	$0.00	$0.00
9	⊟ 3 Executing	$0.00	Prorated	$30,400.00	$0.00	$30,400.00	$0.00	$30,400.00
10	3.1 Analysis	$0.00	Prorated	$7,920.00	$0.00	$7,920.00	$0.00	$7,920.00
11	3.2 Design	$0.00	Prorated	$12,000.00	$0.00	$12,000.00	$0.00	$12,000.00
12	3.3 Implementation	$0.00	Prorated	$10,480.00	$0.00	$10,480.00	$0.00	$10,480.00
13	3.4 System implemented	$0.00	Prorated	$0.00	$0.00	$0.00	$0.00	$0.00
14	⊟ 4 Controlling	$0.00	Prorated	$6,564.35	$0.00	$6,564.35	$0.00	$6,564.35
15	⊞ 4.1 Status Reports	$0.00	Prorated	$3,484.35	$0.00	$3,484.35	$0.00	$3,484.35
37	4.2 Report performance	$0.00	Prorated	$880.00	$0.00	$880.00	$0.00	$880.00
38	4.3 Control changes	$0.00	Prorated	$2,200.00	$0.00	$2,200.00	$0.00	$2,200.00
39	⊟ 5 Closing	$0.00	Prorated	$2,640.00	$0.00	$2,640.00	$0.00	$2,640.00
40	5.1 Prepare final project report	$0.00	Prorated	$2,200.00	$0.00	$2,200.00	$0.00	$2,200.00
41	5.2 Present final project	$0.00	Prorated	$440.00	$0.00	$440.00	$0.00	$440.00
42	5.3 Project completed	$0.00	Prorated	$0.00	$0.00	$0.00	$0.00	$0.00

FIGURE A-45   Cost Table for the Resource File

3. *Open the Cost Reports dialog box.* Click **Report** on the Menu bar, and then click **Reports**. Double-click **Costs** to display the Cost Reports dialog box.
4. *Set the time units for the report.* Click **Cash Flow**, if necessary, and then click **Edit**. The Crosstab Report dialog box is displayed. Click the **Column** list arrow and select **Months**, as shown in Figure A-46, to change the report's display from Weeks to Months. Click **OK**.

FIGURE A-46   Crosstab Report Dialog Box

5. *View the Cash Flow report.* Click **Select** in the Cost Reports dialog box. A Cash Flow report for the Project Tracking Database project appears, as shown in Figure A-47. Notice how it displays by WBS by month. Click **Close**.

	June	July	August	September	October	November	December	Total
Initiating								
Kickoff meeting	$190.00							$190.00
Develop project charter	$2,520.00							$2,520.00
Charter signed								
Planning								
Develop project plans	$4,465.00	$1,235.00						$5,700.00
Review project plans		$434.50	$462.00	$484.00	$379.50			$1,760.00
Project plans approved								
Executing								
Analysis		$7,821.00	$99.00					$7,920.00
Design		$525.00	$6,300.00	$5,175.00				$12,000.00
Implementation				$4,061.00	$6,419.00			$10,480.00
System implemented								
Controlling								
Status Reports	$522.00	$800.40	$730.80	$765.60	$965.55			$3,484.35
Report performance	$193.60	$202.40	$184.80	$193.60	$105.60			$880.00
Control changes	$484.00	$506.00	$462.00	$484.00	$264.00			$2,200.00
Closing								
Prepare final project report					$1,045.00	$1,155.00		$2,200.00
Present final project						$440.00		$440.00
Project completed								
Total	$8,374.60	$11,152.30	$8,238.60	$11,163.20	$8,878.65	$1,595.00		$49,774.35

FIGURE A-47   Cash Flow Report

6. *View the Project Summary report.* In the Reports dialog box, double-click **Overview**, and then double-click **Project Summary**. A Project Summary report for the Project Tracking Database project is displayed, listing information such as project baseline start and finish dates; actual start and finish dates; summaries of duration, work hours, and costs; as well as variance information. Since you have not yet saved the file as a baseline, much of this information is blank in the report. The Project Summary report provides a high-level overview of a project. Click **Close** to close the report after reviewing it. Click **Close** on the Reports dialog box. Keep this file open for the next set of steps.

TIP

You can edit many of the report formats in Project 2007. Instead of double-clicking the report, select the desired report, and then click **Edit**.

The total estimated cost for this project, based on the information entered, should be $49,774.35, as shown in the Cash Flow and Project Summary reports. In the next section, you will save this data as a baseline plan and enter actual information.

Baseline Plan, Actual Costs, and Actual Times

Once you complete the initial process of creating a plan—entering tasks, establishing dependencies, assigning costs, and so on—you are ready to set a baseline plan. By comparing the information in your baseline plan to an updated plan during the course of the project, you can identify and solve problems. After the project ends, you can use the baseline and actual information to plan similar, future projects more accurately. To use Project 2007 to help control projects, you must establish a baseline plan, enter actual costs, and enter actual durations.

Establishing a Baseline Plan

An important part of project management is setting a baseline plan. If you plan to compare actual information such as durations and costs, you must first save the Project 2007 file as a baseline. Select Tools from the Menu bar, point to Tracking, and then click Set Baseline. Before setting a baseline, you must complete the baseline plan by entering time, cost, and human resources information. Be careful not to set a baseline until you have completed the baseline plan. If you do save a baseline before completing the baseline plan, Project 2007 allows you to save up to 10 baselines. You can then clear unwanted baseline plans.

Even though you can clear a baseline plan or save multiple baselines, it is a good idea to save a separate, backup file of the original baseline for your project. Enter actuals and save that information in the main file, but always keep a backup baseline file without actuals. Keeping separate baseline and actual files will allow you to return to the original file in case you ever need to use it again.

To rename resource.mpp and then save it as a baseline plan in Project 2007:

1. *Save resource.mpp as a new file named baseline.mpp.* Click **File** on the Menu bar, and then click **Save As**. Type **baseline** as the filename, and then click **Save**.
2. *Open the Save Baseline dialog box.* Click **Tools** on the Menu bar, point to **Tracking**, and then click **Set Baseline**. The Set Baseline dialog box is displayed. Click the **Baseline** list arrow to reveal multiple baselines, as shown in Figure A-48.

FIGURE A-48   Set Baseline Dialog Box Showing Ability to Set Multiple Baselines

3. *Review the Set Baseline options, and save the entire project as a baseline.* If necessary, click the **Set baseline** radio button and the **Entire project** radio button. Use the default option of the first Set baseline name, Baseline. These options should be the default settings in Project 2007. Click **OK**.

TIP

There are several options in the Save Baseline dialog box, as shown in Figure A-48. You can save the file as an interim plan if you anticipate several versions of the plan. You can also select the entire project or selected tasks when saving a baseline or interim plan. As mentioned above, you can save up to 10 baselines with Project 2007.

Entering Actual Costs and Times

After you set the baseline plan, you can track information on each of the tasks as the project progresses. You can also adjust planned task information for tasks still in the future. The Tracking table displays tracking information, and the Tracking toolbar helps you enter this information. Figure A-49 describes each button on the Tracking toolbar. The 100% button and the Update as Scheduled button are the most commonly used buttons for entering actual information.

Button	Name	Description
-√ト-	Project Statistics	Provides summary information about the project baseline, the actual project start and finish dates, and overall project duration, costs, and work
→	Update as Scheduled	Updates the selected tasks to indicate that actual dates, costs, and work match the scheduled dates, costs, and work
→	Reschedule Work	Schedules the remaining duration for a task that is behind schedule so that it will continue from the status date
📊	Add Progress Line	Displays a progress line on the Gantt chart from a date that you select on the time scale
0%	0% Complete	Marks the selected tasks as 0% complete as of the status date (Actual date, work, and duration data is updated)
25%	25% Complete	Marks the selected tasks as 25% complete as of the status date (Actual date, work, and duration data is updated)
50%	50% Complete	Marks the selected tasks as 50% complete as of the status date (Actual date, work, and duration data is updated)
75%	75% Complete	Marks the selected tasks as 75% complete as of the status date (Actual date, work, and duration data is updated)
100%	100% Complete	Marks the selected tasks as 100% complete as of the status date (Actual date, work, and duration data is updated)
🗂	Update Tasks	Displays the Update Tasks dialog box for the selected tasks so that you can enter their percentages completed, actual durations, remaining durations, or actual start or finish dates
🖳	Set Reminder	Allows you to set a reminder for a specified time at the start or finish of a specific task
📇	Collaborate Toolbar	Turns the collaborate toolbar on and off

FIGURE A-49   Buttons on the Tracking Toolbar

To practice entering actual information, enter just a few changes to the baseline. Assume that Tasks 1 through 8 were completed as planned, but that Task 10 took longer than planned.

To enter actual information for tasks that were completed as planned:

1. *Display the Tracking toolbar*. Click **View** on the Menu bar, point to **Toolbars**, and then click **Tracking**. Move the toolbar as desired.
2. *Display the Tracking table*. Right-click the **Select All** button in the Entry table, and then click **Tracking** to see more information as you enter actual data. Widen the Task Name column to see all of the text, and then move the split bar to reveal all the columns in the Tracking table.

3. *Mark Tasks 1 though 8 as 100% complete.* Click the Task Name for Task 1, **Initiating**, and drag down through Task 8 to highlight the first eight tasks. Click the **100% Complete** button ![100%] on the Tracking toolbar. The columns with dates, durations, and cost information should now contain data instead of the default values, such as NA or 0. The % Comp column should display 100%. Adjust column widths if needed. Your screen should resemble Figure A-50.

Tracking toolbar

FIGURE A-50   Tracking Table Information

4. *Enter actual completion dates for Task 10.* Click the Task Name for Task 10, **Analysis**, and then click the **Update Tasks** button ![icon] on the far right side of the Tracking toolbar. The Update Tasks dialog box opens. For Task 10, enter the Actual Start date as **7/08/09** and the Actual Finish date as **8/13/09**, as shown in Figure A-51. Click **OK**. Notice how the information in the tracking sheet has changed.

FIGURE A-51   Update Tasks Dialog Box

5. *Display the Indicators column.* Click **Insert** on the Menu bar, and then click **Column**. The Column Definition dialog box opens. Click the **Field name** list arrow, select **Indicators**, and then click **OK**. The Indicators column is displayed, showing a check mark by completed tasks.

6. *Display a project summary task bar.* Click **Tools** on the Menu bar, and then click **Options**. The Options dialog box opens. Click the **Show project summary task** option in the lower right side of the dialog box, and then click **OK**. The name of the file is now displayed in Row 0.

7. *Review changes in the Gantt chart.* Move the split bar to the left to reveal more of the Gantt chart. Notice that the Gantt chart bars for completed tasks have changed. Gantt chart bars for completed tasks appear with a black line drawn through the middle. You can also see the project summary task bar as the first bar displayed.

TIP

You can hide the Indicators column by dragging the right border of the column heading to the left.

You can also view actual and baseline schedule information more clearly with the Tracking Gantt view. See the main text or use the Help facility for descriptions of the symbols on a Tracking Gantt chart.

To display the Tracking Gantt chart:

1. *View the Tracking Gantt chart.* Click **View** on the Menu bar, and then click **Tracking Gantt**. Alternatively, you can click the **Tracking Gantt** button 🔲 on the View Bar, if it is displayed. Use the horizontal scroll bar in the Gantt chart window, if necessary, to see symbols on the Tracking Gantt chart.

2. *Display Gantt chart information in months.* Double-click the **Zoom Out** 🔍 button to display information in months. Your screen should resemble Figure A-52. Notice that the delay in this one task on the critical path has caused the planned completion date for the entire project to slip. Because the Analysis task preceded others on the critical path, such as Design, Implementation, and so on, they were delayed in starting. A good project manager would take corrective action to make up for this lost time or renegotiate the completion date.

3. *Save your file as a new file named tracking.mpp.* Click **File** on the Menu bar, and then click **Save As**. Name the file **tracking**, and then click **Save**.

Notice the additional information available on the Tracking Gantt chart. Completed tasks have 100% by their symbols on the Tracking Gantt chart. Tasks that have not started yet display 0%. Tasks in progress, such as Task 9, show the percentage of the work completed (31% in this example). The project summary task bar indicates that the entire project is 32% complete. Also, note that the project completion date has moved to 11/26 since several tasks depended on the completion of Task 10, which took longer than planned. Recall from the main text that a white diamond represents a slipped milestone. Viewing the Tracking Gantt chart allows you to easily see your schedule progress against the baseline plan.

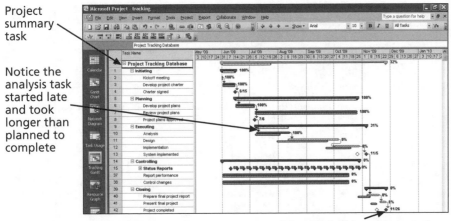

Project summary task

Notice the analysis task started late and took longer than planned to complete

This one delay could cause the project completion date to slip unless corrective action is taken

FIGURE A-52   Tracking Gantt Chart View

After you have entered some actuals, you can review earned value information for the initiating tasks of this project.

Earned Value Management

Earned value management is an important project management technique for measuring project performance. Because you have entered actual information for the initiating tasks in the Project Tracking Database project, you can now view earned value information in Project 2007. You can also view an earned value report using the new visual reports feature in Project 2007.

To view earned value information:

1. *View the Earned Value table.* Click **View** on the Menu bar, point to **Table: Entry,** and then select **More Tables.** The More Tables dialog box opens. Double-click **Earned Value.**

2. *Display all the Earned Value table columns.* Move the split bar to the right to reveal all of the columns, as shown in Figure A-53. Note that the Earned Value table includes columns for each earned value acronym, such as SV, CV, etc., as explained in this text. Also note that the EAC (Estimate at Completion) is higher than the BAC (Budget at Completion) starting with Task 9, where the task took longer than planned to complete. Task 9 shows a VAC (Variance at Completion) of ($2,772.00), meaning the project is projected to cost $2,772 more than planned at completion at that point in time. Remember that not all of the actual information has been entered yet. Also note that the date on your computer must be set later than the date of a completed task for the data to calculate properly.

	Task Name	BCWS	BCWP	ACWP	SV	CV	EAC	BAC	VAC
0	⊟ Project Tracking Database	$49,774.35	$18,090.00	$20,862.00	($31,684.35)	($2,772.00)	$52,546.35	$49,774.35	($7,627.11)
1	⊟ Initiating	$2,710.00	$2,710.00	$2,710.00	$0.00	$0.00	$2,710.00	$2,710.00	$0.00
2	Kickoff meeting	$190.00	$190.00	$190.00	$0.00	$0.00	$190.00	$190.00	$0.00
3	Develop project charter	$2,520.00	$2,520.00	$2,520.00	$0.00	$0.00	$2,520.00	$2,520.00	$0.00
4	Charter signed	$0.00	$0.00	$0.00	$0.00	$0.00	$0.00	$0.00	$0.00
5	⊟ Planning	$7,460.00	$7,460.00	$7,460.00	$0.00	$0.00	$7,460.00	$7,460.00	$0.00
6	Develop project plans	$5,700.00	$5,700.00	$5,700.00	$0.00	$0.00	$5,700.00	$5,700.00	$0.00
7	Review project plans	$1,760.00	$1,760.00	$1,760.00	$0.00	$0.00	$1,760.00	$1,760.00	$0.00
8	Project plans approved	$0.00	$0.00	$0.00	$0.00	$0.00	$0.00	$0.00	$0.00
9	⊟ Executing	$30,400.00	$7,920.00	$10,692.00	($22,480.00)	($2,772.00)	$33,172.00	$30,400.00	($10,640.00)
10	Analysis	$7,920.00	$7,920.00	$10,692.00	$0.00	($2,772.00)	$10,692.00	$7,920.00	($2,772.00)
11	Design	$12,000.00	$0.00	$0.00	($12,000.00)	$0.00	$12,000.00	$12,000.00	$0.00
12	Implementation	$10,480.00	$0.00	$0.00	($10,480.00)	$0.00	$10,480.00	$10,480.00	$0.00
13	System implemented	$0.00	$0.00	$0.00	$0.00	$0.00	$0.00	$0.00	$0.00
14	⊟ Controlling	$6,564.35	$0.00	$0.00	($6,564.35)	$0.00	$6,564.35	$6,564.35	$0.00
15	⊞ Status Reports	$3,484.35	$0.00	$0.00	($3,484.35)	$0.00	$3,484.35	$3,484.35	$0.00
37	Report performance	$880.00	$0.00	$0.00	($880.00)	$0.00	$880.00	$880.00	$0.00
38	Control changes	$2,200.00	$0.00	$0.00	($2,200.00)	$0.00	$2,200.00	$2,200.00	$0.00
39	⊟ Closing	$2,640.00	$0.00	$0.00	($2,640.00)	$0.00	$2,640.00	$2,640.00	$0.00
40	Prepare final project report	$2,200.00	$0.00	$0.00	($2,200.00)	$0.00	$2,200.00	$2,200.00	$0.00
41	Present final project	$440.00	$0.00	$0.00	($440.00)	$0.00	$440.00	$440.00	$0.00
42	Project completed	$0.00	$0.00	$0.00	$0.00	$0.00	$0.00	$0.00	$0.00

FIGURE A-53   Earned Value Table

HELP

The Earned Value table in Figure A-53 uses earned value terms from the first edition of the *PMBOK® Guide*, which was published in 1996. BCWS is the same as PV or planned value, BCWP is the same as EV or earned vale, and ACWP is the same as AC or actual cost. See the earned value section of this text for explanations of all the earned value terms.

3. *View the earned value chart*. Click **Report** on the Menu bar, and then click **Visual Reports** to open the Visual Reports dialog box. Click **Earned Value Over Time Report**, as shown in Figure A-54. Notice the sample of the selected report on the right side of the dialog box. If you have Excel, click **View** to see the resulting report as Project 2007 automatically creates Excel data and a chart based on your current file. Close Excel without saving the file, and then click the **Close** button of the Visual Reports dialog box.

4. *Save and close the file*. Click the **Save** button on the Standard toolbar, and then close the tracking.mpp file. You can also exit Project 2007 and take a break, if desired.

HELP

To take full advantage of the visual reports features, you must have .Net Framework 2.0, Excel 2007, and Visio 2007 installed on your computer. You may also need to adjust data, such as displaying weeks or months versus quarters, to get the reports to display as desired.

Visual Reports - Create Report

Select Template

Show report templates created in:

☑ Microsoft Office Excel   ☑ Microsoft Office Visio

| Task Summary | Resource Summary | Assignment Summary |
| All | Task Usage | Resource Usage | Assignment Usage |

- Baseline Cost Report
- Baseline Work Report
- Budget Cost Report
- Budget Work Report
- Cash Flow Report
- Earned Value Over Time Report
- Resource Cost Summary Report
- Resource Remaining Work Report
- Resource Work Availability Report
- Resource Work Summary Report

New Template...
Edit Template...
Manage Template...

Sample

Select level of usage data to include in the report: Weeks

☐ Include report templates from:

Modify...

Help   Save Data...   View   Close

FIGURE A-54 Visual Reports Dialog Box

HELP

If you want to download the Project 2007 files baseline.mpp and tracking.mpp to check your work or continue to the next section, a copy is available on the companion Web site, the author's Web site, or from your instructor.

Now that you have entered and analyzed various project cost information, you will examine some of the human resource management features of Project 2007.

PROJECT HUMAN RESOURCE MANAGEMENT

In the project cost management section, you learned how to enter resource information into Project 2007 and how to assign resources to tasks. Two other helpful human resource features include resource calendars and histograms. In addition, it is important to know how to use Project 2007 to assist in resource leveling.

Resource Calendars

When you created the Project Tracking Database file, you used the standard Project 2007 calendar. This calendar assumes that standard working hours are Monday through Friday, from 8:00 a.m. to 5:00 p.m., with an hour for lunch starting at noon. Rather than using this standard calendar, you can create a different calendar that takes into account each project's unique requirements. You can create a new calendar by using the Tasks pane or by changing the working time under the Tools menu.

To create a new base calendar:

1. *Open Project 2007, and open a new file.* After opening Project 2007, click the **New** button 🗋 on the Standard toolbar to open a new Project 2007 file. The Tasks pane opens on the left side of your screen.

2. *Use the Tasks pane to create a new calendar.* Click **Define general working times** in the Tasks pane. A calendar wizard appears, as shown in Figure A-55.

Calendar wizard ⟶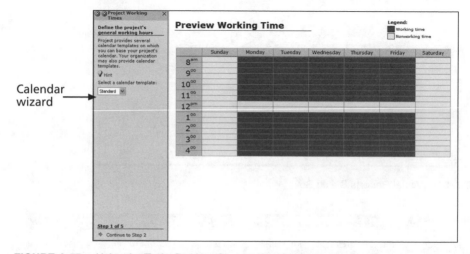

FIGURE A-55   Using the Tasks Pane to Change Working Time

HELP

If the Tasks pane does not appear on your screen, click **View** on the Menu bar, and then click **Turn On Project Guide** to see the Project Guide Task pane. Then click **Define general working times**.

3. *Make changes to the calendar using the wizard.* Click **Continue to Step 2** at the lower part of the Project Working Times pane, select the check box for **Saturday** to make it a working day, and then click the **I want to adjust the working hours shown for one or more days of the week** radio button. Scroll down to read the instructions for adjusting working hours, and make changes as desired. Click through the remaining steps to close the wizard.

4. *Create a new base calendar*. Click **Tools** on the Menu bar, and then click **Change Working Time**. The Change Working Time dialog box opens.

5. *Name the new base calendar*. In the Change Working Time dialog box, click **Create New Calendar**. The Create New Base Calendar dialog box opens. Click the **Create new base calendar** radio button, type **Mine** as the name of the new calendar in the **Name** text box, and then click **OK**. Click **OK** to close the Change Working Time dialog box.

You can use this new calendar for the whole project, or you can assign it to specific resources on the project.

To assign the new calendar to the whole project:

1. *Open the Project Information dialog box*. Click **Project** on the Menu bar, and then click **Project Information**. The Project Information dialog box opens.

2. *Select a new calendar*. Click the **Calendar** list arrow to display a list of available calendars. Select your new calendar named **Mine** from this list, and then click **OK**.

To assign a specific calendar to a specific resource:

1. *Assign a new calendar*. Click **View** on the Menu bar, and then click **Resource Sheet**. Type **Me** in the Resource Name column, press **Enter**, and then select the word **Me**.

2. *Select the calendar*. Click the **Base Calendar** cell for that resource name. If the Base Calendar column is not visible, click the horizontal scroll bar to view more columns. Click the **Base Calendar** list arrow to display the options, and then select **Mine,** if needed.

3. *Block off vacation time*. Double-click the resource name **Me** to display the Resource Information dialog box, and then click the **Change Working Time** button, located on the General tab in the Resource Information dialog box. You can block off vacation time for people by selecting the appropriate days on the calendar and marking them as nonworking days, as shown in Figure A-56. Click **OK** to accept your changes, and then click **OK** to close the Resource Information dialog box.

4. *Close the file without saving it*. Click **File** on the Menu bar, and then click **Close**. Click **No** when you are prompted to save the file.

FIGURE A-56   Blocking Off Vacation Time

Resource Histograms

A resource histogram is a type of chart that shows the number of resources assigned to a project over time. A histogram by individual shows whether a person is over- or underallocated during certain periods. To view histograms in Project 2007, select Resource Graph from the View Bar or select Resource Graph from the View menu. The Resource Graph helps you see which resources are overallocated, by how much, and when. It also shows you the percentage of capacity each resource is scheduled to work, so you can reallocate resources, if necessary, to meet the needs of the project.

To view resource histograms for the Project Tracking Database project:

1. *View the Resource Graph.* Open the **baseline.mpp** file, and open the View Bar, if necessary. Click the **Resource Graph** button [icon] on the View Bar. If you cannot see the Resource Graph button, you may need to click the up or down arrows on the View Bar. Alternatively, you can click **View** on the Menu bar, and then click **Resource Graph**. A histogram for Kathy appears, as shown in Figure A-57. The screen is divided into two sections: the left pane displays a person's name and the right pane displays a resource histogram for that person. You may need to click the right scroll bar to get the histogram to appear on your

screen. Notice that Kathy is overallocated slightly in the month of June, since the column for that month goes above the 100% line.

FIGURE A-57 Resource Histogram View

2. *Adjust the histogram's timescale.* Click **Zoom Out** or **Zoom In** , if necessary, to adjust the timescale for the histogram so that it appears in quarters and then months, as shown in Figure A-57.

3. *View the next resource's histogram.* Click the **right scroll arrow** at the bottom of the resource name pane on the left side of the screen. The resource histogram for the next person appears. View the resource histograms for all four people, and then go back to the first one for Kathy.

Notice that Kathy's histogram has a partially red bar in June 2007. This red portion of the bar means that she has been overallocated during that month. The percentages at the bottom of each bar show the percentage each resource is assigned to work. For example, Kathy is scheduled to work 107% of her available time in June, 62% of her available time in July, and so on. Project 2007 has two tools that enable you to see more details about resource overallocation: the Resource Usage view and the Resource Management toolbar.

To see more details about an overallocated resource using the Resource Usage view:

1. *Display the Resource Usage view.* Click the **Resource Usage** button from the View Bar or click **View** on the Menu bar, and then click **Resource Usage**.

2. *Adjust the information displayed.* On the right side of the screen, click the **right scroll arrow** to display the hours Kathy is assigned to work each day, starting on June 1, 2009. You may also need to click the scroll down arrow to see all of Kathy's hours. If you need to adjust the timescale to display weeks, click **Zoom Out** or **Zoom In**. When you are finished, your screen should resemble Figure A-58.

FIGURE A-58　Resource Usage View

3. *Examine overallocation information*. Notice in the Resource Usage View (Figure A-58) that Kathy's name appears in red, as does the value 5.57h in the column for Monday, June 1, 2009. Although Kathy is not scheduled to work more than eight hours on Monday, some of the tasks were entered as hours, and Project 2007 assumes those hours start as soon as possible, thus causing the scheduling conflict. You will remove the conflict using hour-by-hour leveling later in this section.

To learn more about an overallocated resource, you can also use the Resource Management toolbar for resource allocation.

To see more resource allocation information:

1. *View the Resource Management toolbar*. If the Resource Management toolbar is not already displayed, click **View** on the Menu bar, point to **Toolbars**, and then click **Resource Management**. The Resource Management toolbar displays below the Formatting toolbar.

2. *Select the Resource Allocation view*. Click the **Resource Allocation View** button, the first one on the left on the Resource Management toolbar. The Resource Allocation view appears, showing the Resource Usage view at the top of the screen and the Gantt Chart view at the bottom of the screen. Figure A-59 shows this view with Kathy's information highlighted.

HELP

If you are running Project 2007 Standard instead of Professional, you may have slightly different options on your screen.

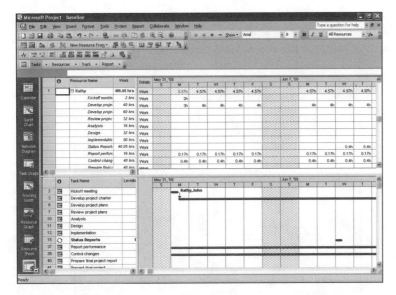

FIGURE A-59   Resource Allocation View

3. *Close the file, but do not save any changes*. Click **File** on the Menu bar, and then click **Close**. Click **No** when you are prompted to save changes.

The Resource Allocation view can help you identify the source of a resource overallocation. It is not obvious that Kathy has an overallocation the first day of the project because she is only assigned to work a total of 5.57 hours. The problem in this case is that she is assigned to several tasks that day that were entered with durations of hours, and Project 2007 assumes each of those tasks starts as soon as possible, thus resulting in the overallocation on an hourly basis. You could ignore this problem or fix it with resource leveling, as shown in the next section. By using the scroll bar, you can view information for other resources. If you scroll down to look at Mary's resource allocation information and scroll to the right to reveal August and September, you can see that overlapping the design and implementation tasks may have caused another overallocation problem. To fix the problem, you can have Mary work overtime, assign another resource to help, or reschedule the implementation task to reduce the overlap. You can also determine if resource leveling, as described in the next section, will help solve the problem.

Resource Leveling

Resource leveling is a technique for resolving resource conflicts by delaying tasks. Resource leveling also creates a smoother distribution of resource usage. You can find detailed information on resource leveling in the Help facility.

To use resource leveling:

1. *Reopen the baseline file*. Click **File** on the Menu bar, and then click the filename **baseline.mpp**, to open it. Notice by the last milestone on the Gantt chart that the project is projected to be completed on 11/16/09.

2. *Open the Resource Leveling dialog box*. Click **Tools** on the Menu bar, and then click **Level Resources**. The Resource Leveling dialog box opens, as shown in Figure A-60. Uncheck the **Level only within available slack** option, if necessary.

Uncheck **Level only within available slack**, if needed

FIGURE A-60   Resource Leveling Dialog Box

3. *Level the file and review the date changes*. Click the **Level Now** button. In this example, resource leveling moved the project completion date from 11/16 to 11/19, as shown on the Gantt chart milestone symbol for Task 42, Project completed. Also notice that Project 2007 automatically highlighted the cells that were affected by this change.

4. *View Kathy's Resource Graph again*. Click the **Resource Graph** button ☰ on the View Bar. If necessary, use the scroll bar in the resource histogram pane to display June 2009. Notice that Kathy is still overallocated in June 2009.

5. *Level using the Hour by Hour option*. Click **Tools** on the Menu bar, and then click **Level Resources**. Change the basis for leveling from Day by Day to **Hour by Hour**, click the **Level Now** button, keep the default option of Entire pool in the Level Now dialog box, and then click **OK**. Notice that Kathy's overallocation disappears. Double-click the right scroll arrow in the resource name pane to reveal information about Mary. Remember that the left pane displays different resources, and the right pane reveals the resource histogram over time. Mary's overallocations are also gone because of this resource leveling.

6. *View the Gantt chart again*. Click the **Gantt Chart** button ☷ on the View Bar and move the split bar to review the Gantt chart, if necessary. The project completion date has been moved back to 11/23 because of the resource leveling.

7. *View the Leveling Gantt chart*. Click **View** on the Menu bar, click **More Views**, and then double-click **Leveling Gantt**. Click the **Zoom Out** button ☌ to adjust the timescale to show months and weeks, and scroll to the right in the Gantt

chart to reach June 2009, as needed. Also reveal all of the contents in the Task Name column. Your screen should resemble Figure A-61. Notice that Project 2007 adds a green bar to the Gantt chart to show leveled tasks.

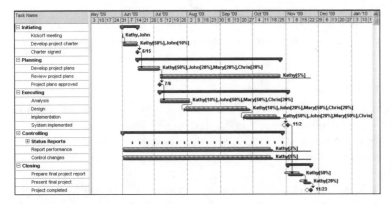

FIGURE A-61   Leveling Gantt Chart View

8. *Save the file as level.mpp.* Click **File** on the Menu bar, click **Save As**, type **level** as the filename, and then click **Save**. Close the file.

TIP

If you want to undo the leveling, immediately click the Undo button on the Standard toolbar. Alternatively, you can return to the Resource Leveling dialog box, and click the Clear Leveling button.

HELP

If you want to download the Project 2007 file level.mpp to check your work or continue to the next section, a copy is available on the companion Web site, the author's Web site, or from your instructor.

Consult the Project 2007 Help feature and use the keyword "level" for more information on resource leveling. Also, when setting options for this feature, be careful that the software adjusts resources only when it should. For example, the end date for the Project Tracking Database project was pushed back because you set the leveling options to allow the dates to slip. In this case, the project manager might prefer to ask her team to work a little overtime to remain on schedule.

Now that you have learned how to change resource calendars, view resource histograms, and level resources, you are ready to learn how to use Project 2007 to assist in project communications management.

PROJECT COMMUNICATIONS MANAGEMENT

Project 2007 can help you generate, collect, disseminate, store, and report project information. There are many different tables, views, reports, and formatting features to aid in project communications, as you have seen in the previous sections. This section highlights some common reports and views. It also describes how to use templates and insert hyperlinks from Project 2007 into other project documents, and how to use Project 2007 in a workgroup setting.

Common Reports and Views

To use Project 2007 to enhance project communications, it is important to know when to use the many different ways to collect, view, and display project information. Table A-5 provides a brief summary of Project 2007 features and their functions, which will help you understand when to use which feature. Examples of most of these features are provided as figures in this appendix.

You can see from Table A-5 that many different reports are available in Project 2007. The overview reports provide summary information that top management might want to see, such as a project summary or a report of milestone tasks. Current activities reports help project managers stay abreast of and control project activities. The reports of unstarted tasks and slipping tasks alert project managers to problem areas. Cost reports provide information related to the cash flow for the project, budget information, overbudget items, and earned value management.

Assignment reports help the entire project team by providing different views of who is doing what on a project. You can see who is overallocated by running the Overallocated Resources report or by viewing the two workload reports. You can also create custom reports based on any project information you have entered into Project 2007.

TABLE A-5 Functions of Project 2007 Features

Feature	Function
Gantt Chart view, Entry table	Enter basic task information
Network Diagram view	View task dependencies and critical path graphically
Schedule table	View schedule information in a tabular form
Cost table	Enter fixed costs or view cost information
Resource Sheet view	Enter resource information
Resource Information and Gantt Chart split view	Assign resources to tasks
Set Baseline	Save project baseline plan
Tracking toolbar	Enter actual information
Earned Value table	View earned value information
Resource Graph	View resource allocation

TABLE A-5 Functions of Project 2007 Features (continued)

Feature	Function
Resource Usage	View detailed resource usage
Resource Management	View resource usage and Gantt chart to find toolbar overallocation problems
Resource Leveling	Level resources
Overview Reports	View project summary, top-level tasks, critical tasks, milestones, working days
Current Activities Reports	View unstarted tasks, tasks starting soon, tasks in progress, completed tasks, should-have-started tasks, slipping tasks
Cost Reports	View cash flow, budget, overbudget tasks, overbudget resources, earned value
Assignment Reports	View who does what, who does what when, to-do list, overallocated resources
Workload Reports	View task usage, resource usage
Custom Reports	Allow customization of each type of report
Insert Hyperlink	Insert hyperlinks to other files or Web sites

Using Templates and Inserting Hyperlinks and Comments

This text provides examples of many templates that you can use to improve project communications. Because it is often difficult to create good project files, many organizations keep a repository of template or sample files. As shown earlier in this appendix, Project 2007 includes several template files, and you can also access several templates online. You must load the template files when installing Project 2007 or access templates via the Internet.

To access the Project 2007 templates:

1. *Open the New Project task pane.* Start Project 2007, if necessary, click **File** on the Menu bar, and then click **New** to display the New Project task pane, as shown in Figure A-62.

New Project
task pane

Templates
section

FIGURE A-62 Opening Templates

2. *Open the Templates dialog box.* Click the **On computer** link in the **Templates** section of the New Project task pane. The Templates dialog box is displayed. Click the **Project Templates** tab, as shown in Figure A-63. As you can see, many templates are available. You can also access additional templates from the **Templates on Office Online** link from the New Project task pane, from other Web sites, or from your own organization.

Access more
templates
online

FIGURE A-63 Project Templates On Computer

HELP

If you do not have any templates loaded on your computer, you will not see the files displayed in Figure A-63. You must load the template files when installing Project 2007.

3. *Open the Microsoft Office Templates Gallery*. Click the **Templates on Office Online** button on the lower left section of the Templates dialog box. The resulting screen should resemble Figure A-64. Experiment with searching for various template files.

Enter search information

FIGURE A-64   Microsoft Office Online Web Site

4. *Close your browser and the open Project file*. Click the **Close** button ✕ on your browser and then **close** the file in Project 2007.

Using templates can help you prepare your project files, but be careful to address the unique needs of your project and organization. For example, even though the Home Move template file can provide guidance in preparing a Project 2007 file for a specific home move project, you need to tailor the file for your particular situation and schedule. You can also create your own Project 2007 templates by saving your file as a template using the Save As option from the File menu. Simply change the Save As Type option to Template. Project 2007 then gives the file an .mpt extension (Microsoft Project Template) to identify the file as a template.

In addition to using templates for Project 2007 files, it is helpful to use templates for other project documents and insert hyperlinks to them from Project 2007. For example, your organization might have templates for meeting agendas, project charters, status reports, and project management plans. See the companion Web site for examples of other template files. Next, you will create hyperlinks to some template files created in other applications.

To insert a hyperlink within a Project 2007 file:

1. *Display the Entry table*. Open the **baseline.mpp** file. The Entry table and Gantt Chart view should display.
2. *Select the task in which you want to insert a hyperlink*. Click the Task Name for Task 2, **Kickoff meeting**.
3. *Open the Insert Hyperlink dialog box*. Click **Insert** on the Menu bar, and then click **Hyperlink**. Alternatively, you can right-click the task name and select

Hyperlink. The Insert Hyperlink dialog box opens, as shown in Figure A-65. You may have different folders visible based on your computer's directory structure.

FIGURE A-65 Insert Hyperlink Dialog Box

4. *Enter the filename of the hyperlink file*. Click the **Browse for File** button to browse for the kickoffmeeting.doc file you downloaded earlier. Double-click **kickoffmeeting.doc**, and then click **OK**.

5. *Reveal the Indicators column*. Click **Insert** on the Menu bar, and then click **Column**. Click the **Field Name** list arrow, select **Indicators**, and then click **OK**. A Hyperlink button appears in the Indicators column to the left of the Task Name for Task 2. Move your mouse over the hyperlink button until the mouse pointer changes to the Hand symbol to reveal the name of the hyperlinked file.

Clicking the Hyperlink button in the Indicators column or right-clicking, pointing to Hyperlink, and selecting Open will automatically open the hyperlinked file. Using hyperlinks is a good way to keep all project documents organized.

It is also a good idea to insert notes or comments into Project 2007 files to provide more information on specific tasks.

To insert a note for Task 4:

1. *Open the Task Information dialog box for Task 4*. Double-click the Task Name for Task 4, **Charter signed**. Click the **Notes** tab.

2. *Enter your note text*. Type **The charter was developed as a joint effort.** in the Notes text box, as shown in Figure A-66.

3. *See the resulting Notes icon*. Click **OK** to enter the note. The Notes icon appears in the Indicators column next to Task 4.

FIGURE A-66 Task Information Dialog Box Notes Tab

4. *Open the note.* Double-click the **Notes** icon in the Indicators column for Task 4 to view the note, and then click **OK**.

5. *Close the file without saving it.* Click **File** on the Menu bar, and then click **Close**. Click **No** when you are prompted to save the file.

Using the Copy Picture Feature

The Copy Picture feature is now under the Report menu in Project 2007. This feature helps you easily create and copy graphical images into other applications. After answering a few questions in the wizard, you can quickly display project data as a static picture in Office applications, including PowerPoint, Word, and Visio. You can access this wizard on the Analysis toolbar.

To use the Copy Picture feature:

1. *Prepare the file you want to copy.* Open **tracking.mpp**. Drag the split bar to the left so that only the entire Task Name column is showing. You should be able to see the entire Gantt chart on your screen.

2. *Open the Copy Picture dialog box.* Click **Report** on the Menu bar, and then click **Copy Picture** to display the Copy Picture dialog box, as shown in Figure A-67.

3. *Copy a Picture.* After reviewing and adjusting the settings in the Copy Picture dialog box (you can accept the defaults for now), click **OK**.

FIGURE A-67   Copy Picture Dialog Box

4. *Open the application where you want to copy the picture and paste it in.* Open PowerPoint, Word, or another application, if desired. Copy the picture of your Project 2007 file by pressing **Ctrl+V** or using another method to paste the picture. Figure A-68 shows the resulting picture in a PowerPoint file.

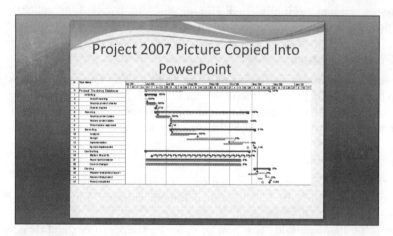

FIGURE A-68   Project 2007 Picture Copied into PowerPoint

5. *Close all open windows.* Click the Close button on any open windows. You do not need to save any of the open files.

As you can see, Project 2007 is a very powerful tool. If used properly, it can greatly help users successfully manage projects.

Discussion Questions

1. What are some new features of Project 2007 and how do they differ from previous versions of Microsoft Project?
2. How do you use Project 2007 to create a WBS hierarchy?
3. Summarize how you use Project 2007 to assist in time management. How do you enter durations, link tasks, and view critical path information?
4. How can Project 2007 assist you in project cost management? What table view would you use to enter fixed costs? How do you enter resources and assign them to tasks? How can you view earned value information?
5. Briefly describe how to change resource calendars, view resource histograms, and level resources.
6. Summarize ways to communicate information with Project 2007. How do you link to other files from within your Project 2007 file? How can you find and use templates? How can you copy pictures from Project 2007 into other applications?

EXERCISES

The more you practice using the features of Project 2007, the more quickly you will master the application and use it to manage projects. This section includes exercises based on three examples of information technology projects that could benefit from using Project 2007 to assist in project scope, time, cost, human resource, and communications management. It also includes an exercise you can use to apply Project 2007 on a real project. Simpler exercises that use Project 2007 are at the end of several chapters in this text. You can also recreate several screen shots in this text to practice your skills, or you can open and make changes to template files or the files that come with this text. You can find additional exercises on the companion Web site.

Exercise A-1: Web Site Development

A nonprofit organization would like you to lead a Web site development project. The organization has Internet access that includes space on a Web server, but no experience developing Web sites. In addition to creating its Web site, the organization would like you to train two people on its staff to do simple Web page updates. The Web site should include the following information, as a minimum: description of the organization (mission, history, and recent events), list of services, and contact information. The organization wants the Web site to include graphics (photographs and other images) and have an attractive, easy-to-use layout.

1. Project Scope Management

    Create a WBS for this project and enter the tasks in Project 2007. Create milestones and summary tasks. Assume that some of the project management tasks are similar to tasks from the Project Tracking Database project. Some of the specific analysis, design, and implementation tasks will be to:

    a. Collect information on the organization in hardcopy and digital form (brochures, reports, organization charts, photographs, and so on).
    b. Research Web sites of similar organizations.
    c. Collect detailed information about the customer's design preferences and access to space on a Web server.

d. Develop a template for the customer to review (background color for all pages, position of navigation buttons, layout of text and images, typography, including basic text font and display type, and so on).

e. Create a site map or hierarchy chart showing the flow of Web pages.

f. Digitize the photographs and find other images for the Web pages; digitize hardcopy text.

g. Create the individual Web pages for the site.

h. Test the pages and the site.

i. Implement the Web site on the customer's Web server.

j. Get customer feedback.

k. Incorporate changes.

l. Create training materials for the customer on how to update the Web pages.

m. Train the customer's staff on updating the Web pages.

2. Project Time Management

a. Enter realistic durations for each task, and then link the tasks as appropriate. Be sure that all tasks are linked (in some fashion) to the start and end of the project. Assume that you have four months to complete the entire project. (*Hint*: Use the Project Tracking Database as an example.)

b. Print the Gantt Chart view and Network Diagram view for the project.

c. Print the Schedule table to see key dates and slack times for each task.

3. Project Cost Management

a. Assume that you have three people working on the project, and each of them would charge $20 per hour. Enter this information in the Resource Sheet.

b. Estimate that each person will spend an average of about five hours per week for the four-month period. Assign resources to the tasks, and try to make the final cost in line with this estimate.

c. Print the budget report for your project.

4. Project Human Resource Management

a. Assume that one project team member will be unavailable (due to vacation) for two weeks in the middle of the project. Make adjustments to accommodate this vacation so that the schedule does not slip and the costs do not change. Document the changes from the original plan and the new plan.

b. Use the Resource Usage view to see each person's work each month. Print a copy of the Resource Usage view.

5. Project Communications Management

a. Print a Gantt chart for this project. Use a timescale that enables the chart to fit on one page. Then paste a copy of the Gantt chart in PowerPoint and print out the slide.

b. Print a "To-do List" report for each team member.

c. Create a "Who Does What Report" and print it out.

Exercise A-2: Software Training Program

ABC Company has 50,000 employees and wants to increase employee productivity by setting up an internal software applications training program. The training program will teach employees how to use Microsoft software programs such as Vista, Word 2007,

Excel 2007, PowerPoint 2007, Access 2007, and Project 2007. Courses will be offered in the evenings and on Saturdays and taught by qualified volunteer employees. Instructors will be paid $40 per hour. In the past, employees were sent to courses offered by local vendors during company time. In contrast, this internal training program should save the company money on training as well as make people more productive. The Human Resources department will manage the program, and any employee can take the courses. Employees will receive a certificate for completing courses, and a copy will be put in their personnel files. The company is not sure which vendor's off-the-shelf training materials to use. The company needs to set up a training classroom, survey employees on desired courses, find qualified volunteer instructors, and start offering courses. The company wants to offer the first courses within six months. One person from Human Resources is assigned full time to manage this project, and top management has pledged its support.

1. Project Scope Management

Create a WBS for this project and enter the tasks in Project 2007. Create milestones and summary tasks. Assume that some of the project management tasks you need to do are similar to tasks from the Project Tracking Database example. Some of the tasks specific to this project will be to:

a. Review off-the-shelf training materials from three major vendors and decide which materials to use.

b. Negotiate a contract with the selected vendor for its materials.

c. Develop communications information about this new training program. Disseminate the information via department meetings, e-mail, the company's intranet, and flyers to all employees.

d. Create a survey to determine the number and type of courses needed and employees' preferred times for taking courses.

e. Administer the survey.

f. Solicit qualified volunteers to teach the courses.

g. Review resumes, interview candidates for teaching the courses, and develop a list of preferred instructors.

h. Coordinate with the Facilities department to build two classrooms with 20 personal computers each, a teacher station, and an overhead projection system (assume that Facilities will manage this part of the project).

i. Schedule courses.

j. Develop a fair system for signing up for classes.

k. Develop a course evaluation form to assess the usefulness of each course and the instructor's teaching ability.

l. Offer classes.

2. Project Time Management

a. Enter realistic durations for each task and then link appropriate tasks. Be sure that all tasks are linked in some fashion to the start and end of the project. Use the Project Tracking Database as an example. Assume that you have six months to complete the entire project.

b. Print the Gantt Chart view and Network Diagram view for the project.

c. Print the Schedule table to see key dates and slack times for each task.

3. Project Cost Management
   a. Assume that you have four people from various departments available part time to support the full-time Human Resources person, Terry, on the project. Assume that Terry's hourly rate is $40. Two people from the Information Technology department will each spend up to 25% of their time supporting the project. Their hourly rate is $50. One person from the Marketing department is available 25% of the time at $40 per hour, and one person from Corporate is available 30% of the time at $35 per hour. Enter this information about time and hourly wages into the Resource Sheet. Assume that the cost to build the two classrooms will be $100,000, and enter it as a fixed cost.
   b. Using your best judgment, assign resources to the tasks.
   c. View the Resource Graphs for each person. If anyone is overallocated, make adjustments.
   d. Print the budget report for the project.
4. Project Human Resource Management
   a. Assume that the Marketing person will be unavailable for one week, two months into the project, and for another week, four months into the project. Make adjustments to accommodate this unavailability, so the schedule does not slip and costs do not change. Document the changes from the original plan and the new plan.
   b. Add to each resource a 5% raise that starts three months into the project. Print a new budget report.
   c. Use the Resource Usage view to see each person's work each month. Print a copy.
5. Project Communications Management
   a. Print a Gantt chart for this project. Use a timescale that enables the chart to fit on one page. Then copy a picture of the same Gantt chart in PowerPoint and print out the slide.
   b. Print a "To-do List" report for each team member.
   c. Review some of the other reports and print out one that you think would help in managing the project.

Exercise A-3: Project Tracking Database

Expand the Project Tracking Database example. Assume that XYZ Company wants to create a history of project information, and the Project Tracking Database example is the best format for this type of history. The company wants to track information on 20 past and current projects and wants the database to be able to handle 100 projects total. The company wants to track the following project information:

- Project name
- Sponsor name
- Sponsor department
- Type of project
- Project description
- Project manager
- Team members

- Date project was proposed
- Date project was approved or denied
- Initial cost estimate
- Initial time estimate
- Dates of milestones (for example, project approval, funding approval, project completion)
- Actual cost
- Actual time
- Location of project files

1. Project Scope Management

   Open scope.mpp and add more detail to Executing tasks, using the information in Table A-6.

TABLE A-6 Company XYZ Project Tracking Database Executing Tasks

Analysis Tasks	Design Tasks	Implementation Tasks
Collect list of 20 projects	Gather detailed requirements for desired outputs from the database	Enter project data
Gather information on projects	Create fully attributed, normalized data model	Test database
Define draft requirements	Create list of edit rules for fields, determine default values, develop queries, and determine formats for reports	Make adjustments, as needed
Create entity relationship diagram for database	Develop list of queries required for database	Conduct user testing
Create sample entry screen	Review design information with customer	Make adjustments based on user testing
Create sample report	Make adjustments to design based on customer feedback	Create online Help, user manual, and other documentation
Develop simple prototype of database	Create full table structure in database prototype	Train users on the system
Review prototype with customer	Create data input screens	
Make adjustments based on customer feedback	Write queries	
	Create reports	
	Create main screen	
	Review new prototype with customer	

2. Project Time Management
   a. Enter realistic durations for each task, and then link appropriate tasks. Make the additional tasks fit the time estimate: 20 days for analysis tasks, 30 days for design tasks, and 20 days for implementation tasks. Assume that all of the executing tasks have a total duration of 70 days. Do not overlap analysis, design, and implementation tasks.
   b. Print the Gantt Chart view and Network Diagram view for the project.
   c. Print the Schedule table to see key dates and slack times for each task.
3. Project Cost Management
   a. Use the resource and cost information provided in resource.mpp.
   b. Assign resources to the new tasks. Try to make the final cost about the same as that shown in the Project Tracking Database example: about $50,000.
   c. Print the budget report for the project.
4. Project Human Resources Management
   a. Two months after the project begins, give everyone on the team a 10% raise. Document the increase in costs that these raises cause.
   b. Use the Resource Usage view to see each person's work each month. Print a copy of the Resource Usage view.
5. Project Communications Management
   a. Print a Gantt chart for this project. Use a timescale that enables the chart to fit on one page. Then copy a picture of the Gantt chart in PowerPoint and print out the slide.
   b. Print a "Top-Level Tasks" report.
   c. Review some of the other reports and print out one that you think would help in managing the project.

Exercise A-4: Real Project Application

If you are doing a group project as part of your class or for a project at work, use Project 2007 to create a detailed file describing the work you plan to do. Enter a sufficient WBS, estimate task durations, link tasks, enter resources and costs, assign resources, and so on. Save your file as a baseline and track your progress. View earned value information when you are halfway through the project or course. Export the earned value information into Excel and create an earned value chart. Continue tracking your progress until the project or course is finished. Print your Gantt chart, Resource Sheet, Project Summary report, and relevant information. Write a two- to three-page report describing your experience. What did you learn about Project 2007 from this exercise? What did you learn about managing a project? How do you think Project 2007 helps in managing a project? You may also want to interview people who use Project 2007 for their experiences and suggestions.

APPENDIX

ADVICE FOR THE PROJECT MANAGEMENT PROFESSIONAL (PMP) EXAM AND RELATED CERTIFICATIONS

INTRODUCTION TO PROJECT MANAGEMENT CERTIFICATION PROGRAMS

This appendix provides information on project management certification programs and offers some advice for earning certifications. It briefly describes various certification programs and provides detailed information on PMI's PMP and CompTIA's Project+ certifications, the structure and content of these exams, suggestions on preparing for the exams, tips for taking the exams, sample questions, and information on related certifications.

WHAT IS PMP CERTIFICATION?

The Project Management Institute (PMI) offers certification as a Project Management Professional (PMP). As mentioned in Chapter 1, the number of people earning PMP certification grew rapidly in the past 10 years. There are PMPs in more than 120 countries throughout the world. Detailed information about PMP certification, the PMP Certification Handbook, and an online application is available from PMI's Web site (*www.pmi.org*) under Professional Development & Careers. The following information is quoted from PMI's Web site:

> The Project Management Institute (PMI®) is the world's leading association for the project management profession. It administers a globally recognized, rigorous, education, and/or professional experience and examination-based professional credentialing program that maintains an ISO 9001 certification in Quality Management Systems. To get the latest information, please visit the breaking news section.

> Earning a professional credential through PMI means that one has:

> - Demonstrated the appropriate education and/or professional experience;
> - Passed a rigorous examination;

- Agreed to abide by a professional code of conduct;
- Committed to maintaining their active credential through meeting continuing certification requirements.

> PMI professional credentials—available to members of the Institute and nonmembers alike—are widely recognized and accepted throughout the world as evidence of a proven level of education, knowledge and experience in project management.[1]

Many companies and organizations are recommending or even requiring PMP certification for their project managers. A February 2003 newsletter reported that Microsoft chose PMI's PMP Certification Program as the certification of choice for its Microsoft Services Operation. Microsoft chose the PMP certification because of its global recognition and proven record in professional development for project managers.[2] CertCities.com ranked the PMP as No. 4 in their 10 hottest certifications for 2006. It "made a strong showing this year, rising from its debut stop at No. 10 last year, thanks in part to even stronger buzz for this industry-neutral title within the IT community."[3]

Certification Magazine published its annual review of how certification affects salaries of information technology professionals. This industry-wide study uses real-world numbers to show how education and experience affect a person's bottom-line salary. During a down market, people might ask why they should seek additional technical certifications. According to Gary Gabelhouse of *Certification Magazine*, "Perhaps it is best expressed in two words: job security. In boom times, one constantly reviews the rate of growth in salary as a key personal-success measurement. However, in down times, job security is paramount."[4]

The October 2004 issue of *PM Network* included an article entitled "The Rise of PMP," which provided several examples of companies and countries that have made concerted efforts to increase their number of PMPs. Hewlett-Packard had only six registered PMPs in 1997, but by August 2004, it had more than 1,500 and was adding 500 per year. Although most PMPs are in the United States (51,498) and Canada (7,444), the PMP credential is growing in popularity in several countries, such as Japan (6,001), China (4,472), and India (2,281). Thomas Walenta, PMP, a senior project manager for IBM Germany, said, "The PMP credential lends portability to a career plan. It has significantly shaped careers in the IT industry, with global companies creating career models for project managers based on PMI certification requirements."[5]

PMI also offers certifications as a Certified Associate in Project Management (CAPM), a Program Management Professional (PgMPSM), and OPM3® ProductSuite. PMI developed the CAPM certification as a stepping-stone to PMP certification. Candidates for the CAPM certification must also meet specific education and experience requirements and pass an exam. As you can imagine, the requirements are not as rigorous as they are for the PMP exam. You might want to consider getting the CAPM, or just wait until you have enough experience to earn the more popular PMP certification. PMI reported only 1,828 active CAPMs by the end of December 2006 and 221,144 active PMPs.[6] As described on the following page, you need 4,500 hours of project experience or a minimum of three years if you have a bachelor's degree to qualify for PMP certification.

What Are the Requirements for Earning and Maintaining PMP Certification?

You can now apply to take the PMP exam online. You can also fill out the application forms and mail them in with a check, if desired. *Before* you apply to take the exam, you must meet the following four requirements:

1. Have experience working in the field of project management. When you apply to take the exam, you enter the role you played in leading and directing project tasks on one or several projects and how many hours you worked in each of the five project management process groups for each project. Roles include:

   - Project contributor
   - Supervisor
   - Manager
   - Project leader
   - Project manager
   - Educator
   - Consultant
   - Administrator
   - Other

   Note that you do not have to have experience as a project manager to take the PMP exam; any of these roles will suffice. PMP certification requires all applicants with a bachelor's degree to have a minimum of three years of unique, non-overlapping project management experience where at least 4,500 hours are spent leading and directing project tasks. Applicants without a bachelor's degree are required to have a minimum of five years of unique, non-overlapping project management experience where at least 7,500 hours were spent leading and directing project tasks. In both cases, the experience must be accrued within eight years of the date of application. You must fill out a simple form online (or by paper, if you choose not to apply online) listing the title of a project or projects you worked on; the start and end date for when you worked on the project(s); your role on the project; the number of hours you spent in leading and directing tasks related to the initiating, planning, executing, controlling, and closing processes; and a summary of the project tasks that you led and directed on the project. You must list some hours in each of the five process groups, but not for each project, if you worked on multiple projects. PMI staff will review your qualifications and let you know if you are qualified to take the PMP exam. *You cannot take the exam without this experience qualification.*

2. Document at least 35 contact hours of project management education. A contact hour is defined as one hour of participation in an educational activity. There is no time frame for this requirement. A university or college, a training company or independent consultant, a PMI chapter, a PMI Registered Education Provider (REP), a company-sponsored program, or a distance-learning company can provide the education. The hours must include content on project quality, scope, time, cost, human resources, communications, risk, procurement, and integration management. You must list the course title,

institution, date, and number of hours for each course. For example, if you took a "principles of management" course at a university 20 years ago, you could list that on the education form along with a one- or two-day PMP exam preparation class.

3. Agree to the PMP certificant and candidate agreement and release statement. This form certifies that application information is accurate and complete and that candidates will conduct themselves in accordance with the Code of Ethics and Professional Conduct, professional development requirements, and other PMI certification program policies and procedures. You can simply check a box saying you agree to this information when applying online. Note that PMI randomly audits 10–15 percent of applications, so be prepared to provide more detailed information as requested if audited, such as college transcripts, signatures of supervisors or managers to verify experience, etc.

4. Pay the appropriate exam fee. As of January 2007, the PMP certification fee was $405 for PMI members and $555 for non-members. The re-examination fee (if you don't pass the exam) is $275 for PMI members and $375 for non-members. The annual individual PMI membership fee is $129 (including the $10 application fee). Note that students, or anyone enrolled in a degree-granting program at an accredited, or globally equivalent, college or university, can join PMI at the student member rate of only $40 (including the $10 application fee). If you want to earn your PMP certification, it makes sense to join PMI, not only for the financial savings, but also for other benefits. Consult PMI's Web site for membership information.

The last step in earning PMP certification is passing the exam! After PMI sends you an eligibility letter to take the PMP exam, you can sign up to take it at several different testing sites. You must take the exam within one year of receiving your eligibility letter. The eligibility letter will include complete details for scheduling your exam. As of January 2007, the PMP exam consisted of 200 four-option multiple-choice questions, and 25 of those questions are considered pretest questions that do not affect your score. The pretest questions are randomly placed throughout the exam and are used to test the validity of future examination questions. Although you cannot use any study aids during the exam, you can bring a nonprogrammable calculator to assist in performing calculations required to answer some of the questions. You are also given two blank pieces of paper, so you can write down formulas or other information when you enter the exam room, but you cannot bring in any notes or other materials. The questions on each test are randomly selected from a large test bank, so each person taking the exam receives different questions. The exam is preceded by a 15-minute computer tutorial to familiarize you with the mechanics of taking the exam. Test takers have four hours to take this computerized exam, and a passing score is 60.5 percent, or at least 106 correct answers out of the 175 scored questions, as of January 2007. PMI reviews and revises the exam annually. *Be sure you consult PMI's Web site for any notices about changes to the PMP exam.* For example, the passing percentage was changed several times to achieve PMI's goal of having around 75 percent of people pass the exam. PMI uses the Modified Angoff Technique, a certification industry practice standard, to determine the passing score.

PMI offers a professional development program for maintaining the PMP certification. To maintain your PMP status, you must earn at least 60 Professional Development Units

within three years, pay a recertification fee every three years when you renew your certification ($60 as of January 2007), and agree to continue to adhere to PMI's Code of Eth-
ics and Professional Conduct. The Continuing Certification Requirements Handbook,
available from PMI's Web site, provides more details on maintaining your PMP status.

What Is the Structure and Content of the PMP Exam?

The PMP exam is based on information from the entire project management body of
knowledge as well as the area of professional responsibility. Essentially, the exam reviews
concepts and terminology in PMI's *PMBOK® Guide Third Edition*, and texts such as this
one will help to reinforce your understanding of key topics in project management. Table
B-1 shows the approximate breakdown of questions on the PMP exam by process group as
of January 2007. Candidates should review updated exam information on PMI's Web site to
make sure they are using the latest information. PMI also provides sample exam questions from their site as well. See a link to this site and other sites with free sample questions on the companion Web site.

TABLE B-1 Breakdown of Questions on the PMP Exam by Process Groups

Process Group	Percent of Questions on PMP Exam	Number of Questions on PMP Exam (out of 200)
Initiating	11	22
Planning	23	46
Executing	27	54
Monitoring and Controlling	21	42
Closing	9	18
Professional Responsibility	9	18

Study Figure 3-1 from Chapter 3 of this text to understand the relationships among
project management process groups, activities, and knowledge areas. Figure 3-1 briefly outlines which activities are performed during each of the project management process groups
and what is involved in each of the knowledge areas. It is also important to understand
what each of the project management activities includes. Several questions on the certification exam require an understanding of this framework for project management, and
many questions require an understanding of the various tools and techniques described in
the *PMBOK® Guide Third Edition* and this text.

The PMP exam includes three basic types of questions:

1. *Conceptual questions* test your understanding of key terms and concepts in
   project management. For example, you should know basic definitions such as
   what a project is, what project management is, and what key activities are
   included in project scope management.

2. *Application questions* test your ability to apply techniques to specific problems. For example, a question might provide information for constructing a network diagram and ask you to find the critical path or determine how much slack is available on another path. You might be given cost and schedule information and be asked to find the schedule or cost performance index by applying earned value formulas.

3. *Evaluative questions* provide situations or scenarios for you to analyze, and your response will indicate how you would handle them. For example, a project might have many problems. A question might ask what you would do in that situation, given the information provided. Remember that all questions are multiple-choice, so you must select the best answer from the options provided.

How Should You Prepare for the PMP Exam?

To prepare for the PMP exam, it is important to understand *your* learning and testing style, and to use whatever resources and study techniques work best for *you*. Below are some important questions to consider:

* *Are you a good test taker?* Some people are very good at studying and do well on multiple-choice exams, but others are not. If you have not taken a long multiple-choice test in a while, it may take you longer to prepare for the exam than others.

* *How confident do you need to be before taking the exam?* To pass the exam, you need to answer only 60.5 percent of the questions correctly. Your PMP certificate will not display your final score, so it does not matter if you get 61, 70, 80, 90, or even 100 percent correct.

* *How much information do you need to review before taking the exam?* The *PMBOK® Guide Third Edition* and this text should be enough content information, but many people want to review even more information before taking the PMP exam. Several companies sell books, sample tests, CD-ROMs, and audiotapes, or provide courses designed to help people pass the PMP exam. There's even a *PMP Certification for Dummies* book available with a CD-ROM of sample questions. In January 2007, performing a search using the keyword "PMP" at *www.amazon.com* resulted in 3,961 different books! Performing a search using the keywords "PMP exam" at *www.google.com* resulted in 547,000 hits. See the Suggested Readings section of the companion Web site for a list of suggested resources, many at no cost at all, such as *www.pmstudy.com* and *www.bestsamplequestions.com*.

* *How much time and money do you want to spend studying for the PMP exam?* Some people with little free time or money to spend on extra courses or materials would rather just take the PMP exam with little preparation; this will tell them what they need to study further if they don't pass on their first attempt. Even though there is a reexamination fee of $275 (for PMI members), this cost is generally less than what you would have to pay for most exam preparation courses. Spend the time and money you need to feel confident enough to pass the exam, but don't over-extend yourself.

- *Do you know PMI's language?* Even if you think you know about project management, studying the material in the *PMBOK® Guide Third Edition* before taking the exam will help you. Volunteer PMPs created the exam, and they often refer to information from the *PMBOK® Guide Third Edition* when writing questions. Many outstanding project managers might fail the exam if they don't use PMI's terminology or processes in their jobs.

- *Do you really understand the triple constraint of project management?* Many questions on the PMP exam are based on the scope, time, and cost knowledge areas. You should be familiar with project charters, WBSs, network diagrams, critical path analysis, cost estimates, earned value, and so on before you take the exam.

- *Do you want to meet other people in the field of project management as you study for your PMP exam?* Several chapters of PMI offer PMP exam review courses. These courses are often a good way to network with other local project managers or soon to be project managers. Many other organizations provide online and instructor-led courses in PMP preparation where you can also meet people in the field. Several organizations also provide their own in-house study groups as a means to network as well as pass the PMP exam.

- *Do you need extra support, peer pressure, or incentives to pass the PMP exam?* Having some support and positive peer pressure might help to ensure that you actually take and pass the exam in a timely manner. If you don't want to be part of a study group, even just telling a friend, colleague, or loved one that you have set a goal to pass the PMP exam by a certain date might provide motivation to actually do it. You could also reward yourself after you pass the exam.

- *How much are you willing to invest in getting PMP certification?* If you have the time and money, you could take one of the immersion courses several companies offer, like Cheetah Learning, Velociteach, Project Management Training Institute, or mScholar. These courses generally last four to five days and cost between two and three thousand dollars. The company offering the course will have you come to class with your qualification to take the PMP exam already completed, and you actually take the PMP exam on the fourth or fifth day of the class. If you don't pass, many training companies will let you take the class again at no additional cost. If you don't have any extra money to spend, you can find several free resources (see the companion Web site) and join or form your own study group, or just go take the exam and see how you do. However, try not to over study for the exam; if you know the material well and are passing practice exams, trust yourself and your skills. If you need to take it a second time to pass, just do so.

Ten Tips for Taking the PMP Exam

1. The PMP exam is computer based and begins with a short tutorial on how to use the testing software. The software makes it easy to mark questions you want to review later, so learning how to mark questions is helpful. Using this feature can give you a feel for how well you are doing on the test. It is a good

idea to go through every question somewhat quickly and mark those questions on which you want to spend more time. If you mark 79 questions or less (the total number you can miss to get 60.5 percent on all 200 questions), you should pass the exam. Remember that 25 of the questions are not scored, and you need 60.5 percent correct on the 175 scored questions.

2. The time allotted for the exam is four hours, and each multiple-choice question has four answer choices. You should have plenty of time to complete the exam. Use the first two to three hours to go through all of the questions. Do not spend too much time on any one question. As you work, mark each question that you would like to return to for further consideration. Then use the remaining time to check the questions you are not sure of. If you're a morning person, schedule your exam in the morning. If you work better after lunch, schedule an afternoon exam. Make sure you are alert and well rested when you go in to take the exam.

3. Some people believe it is better to change answers you were originally unsure of. If you think that a different answer is better, after reading the question again, then change your answer. Don't get hung up on any questions. Move on and focus on answering the questions you can answer correctly.

4. Do not try to read more into the questions than what is stated. There are no trick questions, but some may be poorly worded or just bad questions. Remember that they were written by volunteers and are part of a huge test bank. Most of the questions are relatively short, and there are only four options from which to choose the answer.

5. To increase your chances of getting the right answer, first eliminate obviously wrong options, and then choose among the remaining options. Take the time to read all of the options before selecting an answer. Remember you have to pick the *best* answer available.

6. Some questions require doing calculations such as earned value management. It is worthwhile to memorize the earned value formulas to make answering these questions easier. You may use a nonprogrammable calculator while taking the exam, so be sure to bring one to make performing calculations easier.

7. You should be given two pieces of blank paper to use during the exam. You might want to bring the paper yourself to make sure it is available. Before starting the test, you should write down important equations so that you do not have to rely on your memory. When you come to a question involving calculations, write the calculations down so you can check your work for errors. See Table B-2 for a summary of formulas you should know for the PMP exam.

8. Read all questions carefully. A few sections of the test require that you answer three to four questions about a scenario. These questions can be difficult; it can seem as if two of the choices could be correct, although you can choose only one. Read the directions for these types of questions several times to be sure you know exactly what you are supposed to do. Also, remember important concepts such as the importance of using a WBS, emphasizing teamwork, and practicing professional integrity. You might want to skip the longer or more difficult questions and answer the shorter or easier ones first.

9. If you do not know an answer and need to guess, be wary of choices that include words such as always, never, only, must, and completely. These extreme words usually indicate incorrect answers because there are many exceptions to rules.

10. After an hour or two, take a short break to clear your mind. You might want to bring a snack to have during your break. You might also consider bringing earplugs if you're easily distracted by noises in the room.

TABLE B-2   Formulas to Know for the PMP Exam

Time Related Formulas
Assume o = 6, m = 21, and p = 36 for the following examples, where o = optimistic, m = most likely, and p = pessimistic estimate
PERT weighted average = (o + 4m + p)/6 Example: PERT weighted average = (36 + 4(21) + 6)/6 = 21
PERT standard deviation = (p – o)/6 Example: PERT standard deviation = (36 – 6)/6 = 5
Range of outcomes using 1 std. dev. = 21 – 5 = 16 days and 21 + 5 = 26 days. Range of outcomes using 2 std. dev. = 21 – 10 = 11 days and 21 +10 – 31 days. Range of outcomes using 3 std. dev. = 21 – 15 = 6 days and 21 + 15 = 36 days. 1 std dev. = **68.3%** of the population 2 std dev. = **95.5%** of the population 3 std dev. = **99.7%** of the population
Cost/Earned Value Formulas
Earned Value = EV
Actual Cost = AC
Planned Value = PV
Cost Variance = CV = EV – AC
Schedule Variance = SV = EV – PV
Cost Performance Index = CPI = EV/AC
Schedule Performance Index = SPI = EV/PV
BAC = Budget At Completion or the planned total budget for the project EAC = Estimate At Completion = BAC/CPI
Estimated time at completion = estimated time/SPI
Estimate To Complete (ETC) = EAC – AC
Variance At Completion (VAC) = BAC – EAC Remember, a negative value for a variance or equivalently an index less than 100% means over budget/behind schedule.

Communications Formulas

Number of communications channels = $(n(n-1))/2$
Example: Assume n = 5, where n = number of people
Number of communications channels = $(5(5-1))/2 = (5*4)/2 = 10$

Procurement Formulas

Point of Total Assumption (PTA) = (Ceiling Price – Target Price)/Government Share + Target Cost

Make or Buy Analysis: Create a formula so the "make" option equals the "buy" or "lease" option, and then solve for the number of days.
Example: Assume you can purchase equipment for $3,000 and it costs $100/day to operate OR you can lease the equipment for $400/day. In how many days is the lease price equal to the purchase price? Set up an equation where the cost to lease or buy the item is equal to the cost to purchase or make the item.
1. Let d = the number of days you'll use the equipment: $400d = $3,000 + $100d
2. Then solve for d. Subtract $100d from both sides to get $300d = $3,000
3. Then divide each side by $300 to get d = 10
Therefore, if you need the equipment for more than 10 days, it would be cheaper to buy it.

Sample PMP Exam Questions

A few sample questions similar to those you will find on the PMP exam are provided on the following pages. You can check your answers at the end of this appendix. If you miss seven or less out of these 20 questions, you are probably ready to take the PMP exam. You can find additional sample questions and their answers on the companion Web site, as well as links to other free sample tests from various Web sites.

1. A document that formally recognizes the existence of a project is
   a _____ .
   a. Gantt chart
   b. WBS
   c. project charter
   d. scope statement
2. Decomposition is used in developing _____ .
   a. the management plan
   b. the communications plan
   c. the earned value
   d. the WBS
3. The critical path on a project represents _____ .
   a. the shortest path through a network diagram
   b. the longest path through a network diagram
   c. the most important tasks on a project
   d. the highest-risk tasks on a project

4. If the earned value (EV) for a project is $30,000, the actual cost (AC) is $33,000, and the planned value (PV) is $25,000, what is the cost variance?
   a. $3,000
   b. −$3,000
   c. $5,000
   d. −$5,000

5. If the earned value (EV) for a project is $30,000, the actual cost (AC) is $33,000, and the planned value (PV) is $25,000, how is the project performing?
   a. The project is over budget and ahead of schedule.
   b. The project is over budget and behind schedule.
   c. The project is under budget and ahead of schedule.
   d. The project is under budget and behind schedule.

6. What is the target goal for defects per million opportunities using Six Sigma?
   a. 1
   b. 3.4
   c. 34
   d. 100

7. Project human resource management does not include which of the following processes?
   a. acquiring the project team
   b. developing the project team
   c. managing the project team
   d. estimating activity resources

8. If a project team goes from three to five people, how many more communications channels are there?
   a. 7
   b. 6
   c. 5
   d. 4

9. Your project team has identified several risks related to your project. You decide to take actions to reduce the impact of a particular risk event by reducing the probability of its occurrence. What risk response strategy are you using?
   a. risk avoidance
   b. risk acceptance
   c. risk mitigation
   d. contingency planning

10. Which type of contract provides the least amount of risk for the buyer?
   a. firm fixed price
   b. fixed price incentive
   c. cost plus incentive fee
   d. cost plus fixed fee

11. Suppose you have a project with four tasks as follows:

- Task 1 can start immediately and has an estimated duration of 1.
- Task 2 can start after Task 1 is completed and has an estimated duration of 4.
- Task 3 can start after Task 2 is completed and has an estimated duration of 5.
- Task 4 can start after Task 1 is completed and must be completed when Task 3 is completed. Its estimated duration is 8.

What is the length of the critical path for this project?

a. 9
b. 10
c. 11
d. 12

12. In which of the following project management process groups are the most time and money typically spent?

a. initiating
b. planning
c. executing
d. controlling

13. Creating a probability/impact matrix is part of which risk management process?

a. risk management planning
b. risk identification
c. qualitative risk analysis
d. quantitative risk analysis

14. It is crucial that your project team finish your project on time. Your team is using a technique to account for limited resources. You have also added a project buffer before the end date and feeding buffers before each critical task. What technique are you using?

a. critical path analysis
b. PERT
c. critical chain scheduling
d. earned value management

15. One of your senior technical specialists informs you that a major design flaw exists in a systems development project you are managing. You are already testing the system and planned to roll it out to more than 5,000 users in a month. You know that changing the design now will cause several cost and schedule overruns. As project manager, what should you do first?

a. Issue a stop work order until you understand the extent of the flaw.
b. Notify your project sponsor immediately to see if there are additional funds available to work on this problem.
c. Notify your senior management and let them decide what to do.
d. Hold a meeting as soon as possible with key members of your project team to discuss possible solutions to the problem.

16. You are a member of a large government project. You know that the contract insists that all equipment be manufactured in the United States. You see a senior member of your team replacing a company etching on a piece of equipment that was made in a foreign country. You confront this person, and he says he is following the project manager's orders. What should you do?
    a. Nothing; the project manager made the decision.
    b. Immediately report the violation to the government.
    c. Update your resume and look for another job.
    d. Talk to the project manager about the situation, and then decide what to do.

17. Which of the following is not an output of the integrated change control process?
    a. project management plan updates
    b. approved corrective action
    c. forecasts
    d. deliverables

18. The ceiling price for a contract is $1.25 million, the target price is $1.1 million, the target cost is $1 million, and the government share is 75%. What is the point of total assumption?
    a. $1.2 million
    b. $1 million
    c. $1.1 million
    d. there is not enough information

19. Obtaining quotes, bids, offers, or proposals is part of which project procurement management process?
    a. plan purchases and acquisitions
    b. request seller responses
    c. select sellers
    d. contract administration

20. Your boss believes that all of your project team members avoid work as much as possible. He or she often uses threats and various control schemes to make sure people are doing their jobs. Which approach to managing people does your boss follow?
    a. Maslow's hierarchy of needs
    b. Theory X
    c. Theory Y
    d. Herzberg's motivation and hygiene factors

WHAT IS PROJECT+ CERTIFICATION?

The Computing Technology Industry Association (CompTIA) is the world's largest developer of vendor-neutral IT certification exams. By January 2007, more than 900,000 people worldwide have earned CompTIA certifications in topics such as PC service, networking, security, and Radio Frequency Identification (RFID). In April 2001, CompTIA started offering its IT Project+ certification, which was purchased from Prometric-Thomson Learning, and recognized as the Gartner Institute Certification Program. The certification was renamed Project+ in August 2004. According to CompTIA's manager of public relations, there are more than 9,000 people with CompTIA's Project+ certification as of January 2007. Detailed information about Project+ certification is available from CompTIA's Web site (*www.comptia.org*) under certification. The following information is quoted from a press release on their site:

> "Individuals managing any type of project for their company—whether or not it has an IT component to it—can benefit enormously from using the certification as a means of validating project management competency," said Lisa-Ann Barnes, president, IreeTec, Inc. and chair of the CompTIA Project+ advisory committee.

> Individuals passing the certification exam validate knowledge mastery equivalent to 2,000 hours of on-the-job practical experience. CompTIA Project+ can serve as a standalone certificate for individuals or as a stepping-stone toward the Project Management Institute PMP certification, which requires 4,500 hours of experience.[7]

What Are the Requirements for Earning and Maintaining Project+ Certification?

You can register to take the Project+ exam online from CompTIA's Web site. Testing sites include Thomson Prometric and Pearson VUE. Unlike the PMP exam, there are very few requirements you need to meet to take the Project+ exam. CompTIA does not require that you have any work experience or formal education in project management before you can take the Project+ exam, but they do recommend 2,000 hours of work experience. The main requirements include paying a fee and passing the exam. Important information is summarized below:

1. As of January 2007, the cost for taking the Project+ exam is $225 for non-members in the United States.
2. To pass this 90-minute, 80-question exam, you must score at least 63 percent.
3. You do not need to renew your Project+ certification.
4. Project+ certification is one of the prerequisites or equivalents to Novell's Certified Novell Engineer (CNE), Certified Novell Administrator (CNA), and Certified Novell Instructor (CNI) certifications. CompTIA's Project+ certification is also a Continuing Certification Requirement (CCR) to maintaining a Master CNE certification.
5. You can earn college credit with the Project+ certification. For example, CompTIA's Web site says that Capella University will provide six credit hours to someone with the Project+ certification. Many colleges and universities will grant credit based on your experience or other certifications. There is usually some fee involved, but it's often much less than the cost of taking the courses.

Additional Information on the Project+ Exam

Because there are no experience or education requirements for taking the Project+ exam, you might want to take it very early in your career. Once you have enough experience and education to take the PMP exam, you might want to earn and maintain PMP certification.

As stated above, the Project+ exam consists of 80 questions. Table B-3 shows the approximate breakdown of questions on the Project+ exam by four domain areas. Candidates should review updated exam information on CompTIA's Web site to make sure they are prepared for the exams. For example, CompTIA provides a detailed list of objectives you should understand before taking the Project+ exam. Studying information in this book will also help you prepare for the Project+ exam. You might also want to purchase an exam guide to get specific information and access to more sample questions.

TABLE B-3 Breakdown of Questions on the Project+ Exam by Domain Areas

Domain Area	Percent of Questions on Project+ Exam
Project Initiation and Scope Definition	20
Project Planning	30
Project Execution, Control, and, Coordination	43
Project Closure, Acceptance, and Support	7

Much of the advice for taking the PMP exam also applies to taking the Project+ exam. Many people find the questions to be similar on both exams, although the PMP exam is longer and more comprehensive. Below are some of the main differences between the content and types of questions you will find on the Project+ exam:

- The Project+ exam includes some scenarios and content specific to the information technology industry. For example, you should understand the various systems development life cycles and issues that often occur on information technology projects.
- You should understand the various roles of people on information technology projects, such as business analysts, database analysts, programmers, and so on.
- Although many of the questions are multiple-choice like the PMP exam questions, several questions involve choosing two or more correct answers. Several questions also involve matching or putting items in order, called drag-and-drop questions.
- The Project+ exam is not based on the *PMBOK® Guide Third Edition*, so you do not need to know the processes involved in the various knowledge areas. However, much of the terminology, concepts, tools, and techniques are the same on both exams.

Sample Project+ Exam Questions

A few sample questions similar to those you will find on the Project+ exam are provided below. CompTIA also provides sample questions on their Web site at *http://certification. comptia.org/resources/practice_test.aspx*. You can check your answers at the end of this appendix.

1. Two software developers on your project disagree on how to design an important part of a system. There are several technologies and methodologies they could use. What should be the primary driver in deciding how to proceed?
   a. following corporate standards
   b. following industry standards
   c. meeting business needs
   d. using the lowest-cost approach

2. Match the following items to their descriptions:

Stakeholder	a. Acts as a liaison between the business area and developers
Project manager	b. Writes software code
Business analyst	c. Person involved in or affected by project activities
Programmer	d. Responsible for managing project activities

3. For a project to be successful, the project manager should strive to understand and meet certain goals. What are the three main project goals to meet? Select three answers.
   a. scope or performance goals
   b. time goals
   c. political goals
   d. cost goals
   e. stock price goals

4. You have received an incomplete project scope definition. Put the following actions in order of how you should proceed to complete them.
   a. Incorporate additional changes to the scope definition document.
   b. Review the draft scope definition document with your project team.
   c. Get signatures on the completed scope definition document.
   d. Rewrite the draft scope definition document with your users and project team.

5. What term is used to describe the process of reaching agreement on a collective decision?
   a. collaboration
   b. cooperation
   c. coordination
   d. consensus

6. What is a variance?
   a. a buffer in a duration estimate
   b. a small amount of money set aside for contingencies
   c. a form of risk management
   d. a deviation from the project plan

7. Which of the following would be legitimate reasons for a vendor to request a delay in delivering a product? Select two answers.
   a. The vendor may have underestimated the amount of time required to produce and deliver the product.
   b. The project contact from the vendor's organization may be going on vacation.
   c. The vendor might be able to provide a better product by delivering the product late.
   d. The vendor might lose money by delivering the product late.

8. When should you involve stakeholders in the change control process on information technology projects?
   a. before a change is submitted
   b. after a change is submitted
   c. when a change is submitted
   d. throughout the life of a project

9. Which of the following techniques can be used to help manage requirements? Select three answers.
   a. prototyping
   b. use case modeling
   c. JAD
   d. worst case modeling

10. Match the following items to their descriptions:

Lessons learned	a. Leave a clear and complete history of a project
Project audits	b. Review project progress and results
Project archives	c. Document what went right or wrong on a project

WHAT OTHER EXAMS OR CERTIFICATIONS RELATED TO PROJECT MANAGEMENT ARE AVAILABLE?

In recent years, several organizations have been developing more certifications related to project management and information technology project management, in particular. Some involve taking exams while others require coursework or attendance at workshops. Below are brief descriptions of other existing exams or certifications related to project management:

- Microsoft provides certification as a Microsoft Office Specialist (MOS) to recognize proficiency in using its software products. In October 2006, Microsoft Learning launched a new Microsoft Office Project 2007 Certification program. You can become a Microsoft Certified Technology Specialist (MCTS) in either Managing Projects with Microsoft Office Project 2007 or Enterprise Project Management with Microsoft Office Project Server 2007. You can also earn a Microsoft Certified IT Professional (MCITP) in enterprise Project Management with Microsoft Office Project Server 2007. Its purpose is "to help advance project management as a profession and maximize value for its customer base of nearly 20 million Microsoft Office Project user licenses."[8] Microsoft is using the PMI's *PMBOK® Guide Third Edition* as a foundation for supporting specific Project 2007 competencies. See Microsoft's Web site (*www.microsoft.com*) for more details.

- The International Project Management Association (IPMA) offers a four-level certification program. The main requirements for each level are derived from typical activities, responsibilities, and requirements from practice. The IPMA four-level certification system, in descending order, includes the Certified Project Director, Certified Senior Project Manager, Certified Project Manager, and Certified Project Management Associate. More than 50,000 people worldwide had earned IPMA certifications, according to IPMA's Web site in January 2007. See *www.ipma.ch* for more details.

- Certified IT Project Manager (CITPM): In 1998, the Singapore Computer Society collaborated with the Infocomm Development Authority of Singapore to establish an Information Technology Project Management Certification Program. PMI signed a Memorandum of Understanding with the Singapore Computer Society to support and advance the global credentialing of project management and information technology expertise. In January 2007, the Singapore Computer Society's Web site listed three levels of the CITPM Certification: CITPM (Senior), CITPM, and CITPM (Associate). For more details consult their Web site (*www.scs.org.sg/about_certprog.php*).

- PMI's additional certifications. As mentioned earlier, PMI also offers certification as a Certified Associate in Project Management (CAPM), a Program Management Professional (PgMPSM), and OPM3® ProductSuite. Consult PMI's Web site for updated information on their certification programs.

- Many colleges, universities, and corporate training companies now provide their own certificate programs or entire degrees in project management. Typing "project management certificate" into *www.google.com* in January 2007 resulted in 81,400 hits. Some of the certificate courses apply toward bachelor's or advanced degrees, while many do not. Like any other educational program, it is important to research the quality of the program and find one that will meet your specific needs. The December 2006 issue of the Project Management Institute's PMI Today included a supplement that said they had identified over 284 project management degree programs at 235 institutions worldwide. See the author's Web site for a summary of more than 120 U.S. graduate programs created as part of a class project in 2006 (*www.kathyschwalbe.com*, under Project Management Info). Also see sites like *www.gradschools.com* to find more information on graduate programs in project management throughout the world.

DISCUSSION QUESTIONS

1. What is PMP certification, and why do you think the number of people earning it has grown so much in the past 10 years?

2. What do you need to do before you can take the PMP exam? What is the exam itself like? What do you need to do to maintain PMP certification? What do you need to do to take the Project+ exam? How does the Project+ exam differ from the PMP exam? Do you need to renew Project+ certification?

3. What is the difference between conceptual, application, and evaluative questions? Which project management process groups have the most questions on the PMP exam? What are the four domain areas tested on the Project+ exam?

4. Which tips for taking the PMP exam do you think would be most helpful for you?

5. If you plan to take the Project+ or PMP exam soon, what should you do to prepare?

6. Briefly describe project management certification programs other than the PMP or Project+ certifications.

EXERCISES

1. Go to PMI's Web site and review the information about taking the PMP exam. Write a two-page paper summarizing what you found.

2. Go to CompTIA's Web site and review the information about taking the Project+ exam. Write a two-page paper summarizing what you found.

3. Answer the 20 sample PMP questions in this text or take another sample test, and then score your results. Summarize how you did and areas you would need to study before you could take the PMP exam.

4. Interview someone who has PMP or Project+ certification. Ask him or her why he or she earned the certification and how it has affected his or her career. Write your findings in a two-page paper.

5. Do an Internet search on earning PMP or Project+ certification. Be sure to search for Yahoo! groups or similar sites related to these topics. What are some of the options you found to help people prepare for either exam? If you were to take one of the exams, what do you think you would do to help study for it? Do you think you would need additional information beyond what is in this text to help you pass? Write a two-page paper describing your findings and opinions.

6. Read a recent issue of PMI's *PM Network* magazine. You can order a copy from PMI's Web site, or contact someone from a local PMI chapter to obtain a copy. Summarize all of the ads you find in the magazine related to earning PMP or other project management related certification in a two-page paper. Also, include your opinion on which ad, course, book, CD-ROM, or other media appeals to you the most.

ANSWERS TO SAMPLE PMP EXAM QUESTIONS

1.	c	11.	b
2.	d	12.	c
3.	b	13.	c
4.	b	14.	c
5.	a	15.	d
6.	b	16.	d
7.	d	17.	c
8.	a	18.	a
9.	c	19.	b
10.	a	20.	b

ANSWERS TO SAMPLE PROJECT+ EXAM QUESTIONS

1.	c	6.	d
2.	c, d, a, b	7.	a, c
3.	a, b, d	8.	d
4.	b, d, a, c	9.	a, b, c
5.	d	10.	c, b, a

END NOTES

1 Project Management Institute, "PMI® Certification Programs," (*www.pmi.org/info/PDC_CertificationsOverview.asp?nav=0401*) (January 2007).

2 Project Management Institute Information Systems Specific Interest Group (ISSIG), *ISSIG Bits* (*www.pmi-issig.org*) (February 2003).

3 Becky Nagel, "CertCities.com's 10 Hottest Certifications for 2006," (*www.CertCities.com*), (December 14, 2005).

4 Global Knowledge, "2003 Certification Salary by Certmag," *Global Knowledge E-Newsletter*, Issue #56 (March 2003).

5 Adrienne Rewi, "The Rise of PMP," *PM Network*, (October 2004), p. 18.

6 The Project Management Institute, "PMI Today," (February 2007).

7 CompTIA Web site (*www.comptia.org/pressroom/get_pr.aspx?prid=489*) (October 2004).

8 Microsoft, "Microsoft Advances Its Project Management Technology and the Project Management Profession," Microsoft PressPass (October 20, 2006).

RESOURCES

INTRODUCTION

This appendix summarizes resources you can use to expand your understanding of project management. It describes information provided on the companion Web site, provides a detailed case study (with more available on the companion Web site), and presents a list of additional sites with useful information. You can also go to the author's Web site (*www.kathyschwalbe.com*) to access information related to this text and project management in general.

COMPANION WEB SITE (WWW.COURSE.COM/MIS/PM2/SCHWALBE OR HTTP://LOGIN.COURSE.COM)

The companion Web site for this text includes the following:

- Lecture notes for each chapter created in PowerPoint
- Interactive, multiple-choice quizzes for each chapter where you can test your understanding of key concepts
- Jeopardy games for each chapter created in PowerPoint, another method for testing your understanding of materials
- See the following section for more information on over 50 template files mentioned in this text.
- Sample documents mentioned in the text
- Podcasts for each chapter that include the chapter summary, quick quiz, and key terms. A podcast is a short audio file designed for use on an iPod, MP3 player, or on a PC using iTunes, Windows Media Player, or other digital music players
- Microsoft Project information, including necessary data files and the Guide to Using Microsoft Project 2003 and its data files, similar to Appendix A in this text, but for the previous version of Project
- Links and suggested readings mentioned in each chapter and appendix
- Instructions for accessing and using a 120-day trial for up to five users of VPMi Express, a Web-based enterprise project management software product from Virtual Communications Services (VCS)
- Instructions for using Fissure's project management simulation software, a bundled option with this text
- More ideas for team projects, including real projects, and additional case studies similar to the one in this appendix
- Links to additional resources related to project management, such as those mentioned in the last section of this appendix

CASE STUDIES

Each chapter of this text includes Exercises and Team Projects, but some instructors like to assign more detailed case studies. This section provides one running case study, and more can be found on the companion Web site. You can also find further suggestions for using real projects or other case studies, such as those provided by the Harvard Business Review. See the item called "Teaching Ideas" in the Table of Contents on the companion Web site.

Each running case includes five parts—initiating, planning, executing, controlling, and closing—with scenario-based information and several tasks to complete under each part. Students can refer to the sample documents found in the text to help them complete the tasks. Several of the tasks involve using templates provided on the companion Web site. Instructors can download the suggested solutions for these cases from the password-protected section of Course Technology's homepage. Anyone can use these cases as long as they mention the source. Feel free to modify them to meet your class needs.

New Business Venture Case Study

This case should be interesting to anyone interested in starting a new business. It involves research, marketing, finance, technology, and personal ethics. The main purpose of this and other cases, however, is to help you practice some of the project management skills you are developing as part of your course.

Part 1: Initiating

Background Scenario: You and several of your friends have been working for corporations for over five years, but several of you have a desire to start your own business. You have decided that you are ready to pursue your idea of starting a music academy for children ages 3-16. You all enjoy creating music, and you saw the advantages that some children had from participating in special music programs beyond those available in schools. In particular, you see the need for music training in your area for children interested in voice, guitar, keyboard, and percussion so they can perform in their own bands.

This New Business Venture Project would primarily involve you and three of your friends, who were all part of your high school band:

- You are an excellent bass player, and you were the one who organized your band in high school and got the few paid gigs that you had. You can also play keyboard. You continue to play both instruments occasionally, but your full-time job and new spouse take up a lot of your time. Your current full-time job is working as a business analyst for a large retail store. Although your job is going well, you realize that you would be happier working in your own business and with something involving music. Your strengths are your creativity, organization, and analytical skills. Your spouse is employed full-time and supports your idea to start your own business, as long as you have a detailed plan and financial backing.

- Brian, one of your best friends since sixth grade, played lead guitar in your band. He is a natural musician and has little trouble learning to play very complicated songs. Brian is very quiet, but he would love to work for a successful small business and be able to share his passion for guitar with children. He is also a whiz at music technology, having recorded and edited CDs for several years. He works as a software developer for a large consulting firm. He is married and has one young child, and his spouse works part-time. Brian would not give up his full-time job until he knew he could support his family in this new business venture, but he could do a lot of part-time work.

- Nicole, also one of your best friends since sixth grade, was the lead singer in your band. She has a great voice and really knows how to work a crowd, too. She is currently working as a part-time telemarketer, but she doesn't like her job at all and is ready for something new. Her spouse has a great job and supports her in pursuing a new business oportunity. Her strengths are her vocal talent, professional voice training, and sales ability. She also loves working with children and would be willing to work full-time on this new business venture.

- Andres was the last person to join your band in high school, having replaced your original drummer. He currently works as a music teacher at a local middle school. He has a lot of contacts with local schools and is dying to get this new music academy started. He is single and would want to keep his current job, but he could devote a fair amount of time to the business in the evenings, on weekends, and full-time in the summer. His strengths are his drumming expertise, teaching ability, music technology experience, and contacts with school-age children, parents, and school administrators. He currently gives some private lessons and knows other people who do as well, so he has potential clients and instructors that he could bring into the business.

The main goals of the New Business Venture Project are to prepare a business plan, get financial backing, handle legal issues, develop marketing materials, find a rental space for the music academy, purchase/develop curriculum, hire staff, and open for business by one year from now, September 1, to coincide with the school year. Your team has already analyzed the market, and you know you can make this business succeed. Your goal would be to cover your investment costs after two years in business.

Tasks

1. To become more familiar with the children's music instruction market, do some preliminary research to find out how big this market is, who the main companies are in the market, what the best-selling services are, pricing and marketing strategies, etc. If you do not want to focus on your own geographic area, pick one to focus on for this and future tasks. Write a two- to three-page paper (double-spaced) with your findings, citing at least two references. For example, the author's son took lessons and performed in rock bands from Virtuosos Music Academy in Plymouth, Minnesota (*www.virtuososonline.com*). You can also include a paragraph or two with your team's personal experience in this area, if applicable.

2. Prepare a stakeholder analysis for the project. Include all project team members and make up names and information for at least one spouse, one potential financial backer, and one local competitor. Assume that you and your three friends are all team members, and you each invest $10,000 into the business. Your mother, a retired business professor, has decided to provide a substantial loan ($30,000), so she will be the sponsor. You still need to figure out how to get an additonal $30,000 for the first-year start-up costs. Use the template provided on the companion Web site, and review the sample stakeholder analysis in the text.

3. Prepare a team contract for this project. Use the template provided on the companion Web site, and review the sample in the text.

4. Prepare a project charter for the New Business Venture Project. Assume the project will take one year to complete and cost about $100,000. Recall that the main project objectives are to prepare a business plan, get financial backing, handle legal issues, develop marketing materials, find a rental place for the music academy, purchase/develop curriculum, hire staff, and open for business by one year from now. Your project team will not get paid for the hours they put into this project, but once the business opens, they will be compensated. You will incorporate the business and hire a lawyer to help with this and other legal issues. Use the template provided on the companion Web site, and review the sample in the text.

5. An important part of starting any business is preparing financial projections. Although you will prepare a more detailed financial analysis when you create your business plan, you still want to do rough projections at this stage. Prepare a spreadsheet that can be used to determine the profit potential of starting this business. Include inputs for the initial investment cost, number of customers in the first month, customer growth rate/quarter, average monthly fee per customer, fixed and variable monthly operating costs, and variable costs per customer. Use the most likely, optimistic, and pessimistic inputs as shown in Figure C-1 to generate results for all three scenarios. For each month (Month 1-24), calculate your revenues (number of customers that month X monthly fee/customer) and expenses (fixed monthly salaries plus fixed monthly operative costs plus variable costs/customer/month X number of customers that month). Then determine the cumulative income each month. For example, the cumulative income in Month 1 is the Monthly Revenues - Monthly Expenses for Month 1. The cumulative income for Month 2 is the Monthly Revenues - Monthly Expenses for Month 2 plus the Cumulative Income for Month 1. The first few months for the most likely scenario are filled in for you to check your formulas. Will you be able to recoup your $100,000 start-up costs within two years in each scenario? If so, in what month? There is no template for this example, but you can use the format in Figure C-1. Print out a sheet with results for each scenario, clearly labeling if/when you recoup your investment.

FIGURE C-1 Financial Projections Format

Financial Projections for New Business Venture

Assumptions/Inputs:	Most likely	Optimistic	Pessimistic
Number of customers in month 1	150	175	120
Quarterly customer growth rate	10%	20%	5%
Monthly fee/customer	$150	$175	$125
Fixed monthly salaries	$9,000	$8,000	$10,000
Fixed monthly operating costs	$5,000	$4,000	$6,000
Variable costs/customer/month	$80	$70	$100

Month	Number of Customers	Monthly Revenues	Monthly Expenses	Cumulative Monthly Income
1	150	$22,500	$26,000	($3,500)
2	150	$22,500	$26,000	($7,000)
3	150	$22,500	$26,000	($10,500)
4	165	$24,750	$27,200	($12,950)
5				
6				
7				
8				
9				
10				
11				
12				
13				
14				
15				
16				
17				
18				
19				
20				
21				
22				
23				
24				

6. Prepare a 10–15 minute presentation that you would give to summarize results from the initiating phase of the project. Assume the presentation is for a management review to decide if the project should move on to the next phase.

Part 2: Planning

Tasks

1. Develop a scope statement for the project. Use the template provided on the companion Web site, and review the sample in the text. Remember that the main project goals are to prepare a business plan, get financial backing, handle

legal issues, develop marketing materials, find a rental space for the music academy, purchase/develop curriculum, and hire staff so you can open for business by one year from now. Be as specific as possible in describing product characteristics and requirements, as well as key deliverables. For example, assume that you need to rent a space for your business that is in a desirable part of town near other businesses and schools, has enough room for a reception area, technology lab with five computers, two larger band rooms that have soundproofing or can be sound proofed, and five small rooms for private lessons.

2. Develop a work breakdown structure (WBS) for the project. Break down the work to what you think is an appropriate level. Use the template provided on the companion Web site, and review the samples in the text. Print the WBS in list form as a Word file. Be sure the WBS is based on the project charter, scope statement, and other relevant information.

3. Create a milestone list for this project, and include at least 10 milestones and estimated completion dates for them.

4. Use the WBS and milestone list you developed in numbers 2 and 3 above to create a Gantt chart and network diagram in Project 2007 for the project. Estimate task durations and enter dependencies, as appropriate. Remember that your scheduled goal for the project is one year. Print the Gantt chart and network diagram.

5. Develop a cost estimate for developing just the technology lab for your music academy. Assume that you will purchase five personal computers that can connect to the Internet and run several popular music creation and editing programs. Include the costs of the desks, chairs, microphones, keyboards, soundproofing the room, set-up, testing, etc.

6. Create a quality checklist for ensuring that the business is ready to open its doors. Also define at least two quality metrics for the project. Use the templates and samples provided.

7. Create a RACI chart for the main tasks and deliverables for the project. Use the template and sample provided.

8. Develop a communications management plan for the project. Use the template and sample provided.

9. Create a probability/impact matrix and list of prioritized risks for the project. Include at least 10 risks. Use the template and sample provided.

10. Prepare a request for proposal for the technology lab (including purchasing the hardware, software, installation, soundproofing, testing, and maintenance) for your music academy and describe at least two procurement issues you need to consider for the project.

11. Prepare a 10–15 minute presentation that you would give to summarize results from the planning phase of the project. Assume the presentation is for a management review to decide if the project should move on to the next phase.

> **N O T E**
>
> Remember that the main project goals are to prepare a business plan, get financial backing, handle legal issues, develop marketing materials, find a rental space for the music academy, purchase/develop curriculum, and hire staff so you can open for business by one year from now. Instructors might want to pick just a few of these tasks for students to do, since several could take a while to prepare.

Tasks

1. Write a business plan for this project. Review sample business plans. For example, *www.bplans.com/*, *www.score.org*, and Microsoft Office online (select File, New, Microsoft Online, Plans from within Microsoft Word) provide templates and/or guidelines for preparing business plans. Decide on a name for this business, as well. Include, at a minimum, the following sections in a five- to eight-page paper:

   - Executive Summary
   - Company Description
   - Products and Services
   - Marketing Plan
   - Operational Plan
   - Management Summary
   - Financial Plan

2. Research options for getting small business loans. For example, most governments have a small business administration office that offers loans or loan information. (See *www.sba.gov* for U.S. information.) Several colleges provide loans to alumni. You can also go to banks and credit card companies for funds. Develop a list of at least five different, realistic options for getting financial backing for your new business. Recall that you estimate that you will need $100,000 the first year alone, and you are still short $30,000. Include the source of the funds, interest rates, payment arrangements, etc. Document your results in a two- to three-page paper, including a recommendation on which option to pursue.

3. Create a one-page flier for your new business, a home page for a Web site, and a tri-fold brochure listing key services/courses of the business, and any other marketing materials you think you would need for your business.

4. Research options for a rental space for the music academy. Develop at least five alternative sites. Include a picture of the site, if available, square footage, cost, pros and cons, etc. Document the results and make a recommendation for which site to select in a three- to four-page paper.

5. Assume that you decide to have students sign up for weekly individual instruction on a term basis. You will offer a fall, spring, and two summer terms consisting of 12 hours of instruction in each. Half of the hour will be one-on-one with an instructor, and the other half will be in the music technology lab. You will also have several rock band courses with three to five students each that will meet

weekly for six weeks, followed by a performance. Reseach where to purchase curriculum or what is involved in developing it, if needed, for the following courses:

- Basic, intermediate, and advanced keyboard
- Basic, intermediate, and advanced bass
- Basic, intermediate, and advanced guitar
- Basic, intermediate, and advanced percussion/drums
- Basic, intermediate, and advanced voice
- Basic, intermediate, and advanced rock band

Include a one-page curriculum sheet for each course and a one-page schedule for all of the courses, including times for performances for the rock band. Also include a performance each term for students taking the individual lessons.

6. Create a plan for hiring staff for your new business. Assume that you will work full-time as the main manager, providing some front-desk coverage, giving some lessons, and managing most of the business. Assume that Nicole will also work full-time, heading up the vocal lessons area, marketing, and providing some front-desk coverage. Brian will lead the music technology lab development, outsourcing a fair amount of the work. He will also teach some of the rock band ensembles in the evenings or on weekends. Andres will help with marketing and give percussion instructions as his schedule allows. You will also need to hire a part-time receptionist to always have front-desk and phone coverage. You also need to hire several part-time instructors for all of the classes provided. Include job descriptions for all of the positions, salary/pay information, and a work schedule. Document your results in a four- to six-page paper.

7. Assume that the following has occurred since the project started: As usual, you ended up taking lead of this team, but you're starting to get burned out. You are four months into the project. You are still working your full-time job, and your spouse has been complaining that you work too much and aren't delegating enough. Nicole quit her telemarketing job to focus on this new business, and she is getting nervous about the business actually opening. Andres promised to get a big list of potential students and instructors to you for the past two months, but he still hasn't delivered it. Brian thinks that he can set up the whole music technology lab instead of outsourcing it, as you planned. Write a two- to three-page paper describing how you would handle these challenges.

Part 4: Controlling

Background Scenario: You are six months into the project. You completed the business plan and most of the marketing materials. You had planned to have the location for your business selected and additional start-up funds by now, but you are behind schedule. Brian and Nicole seem to disagree on a lot of key decisions, especially the location. Your mother calls at least three times a week asking how things are going. You are happy that she lives 500 miles away, but you know that she needs assurance that the business will actually open. Andres is in charge of puchasing/developing the curriculum, but he has had very little time to work on it since school is in session. You want him to focus on creating a list of potential students and instructors, so you might hire someone else to help with the curriculum.

Tasks

1. Create a new Gantt chart based on the revised information above, if needed. Briefly describe other plans you have created so far that you think you should update in a one- to two-page paper.

2. Prepare an agenda for a team meeting to discuss several of the issues you are facing. You definitely want to decide on the location at this meeting, since it is down to two and you have to decide soon. Also write a one- to two-page paper summarizing how you will approach particular people during the meeting.
3. Prepare a 10–15 slide presentation to give to potential funders for your business. Use information from your business plan.
4. Write a two- to three-page statement of work to hire someone to help you purchase/develop the curriculum. Use the template and sample provided.
5. Review the Seven Basic Tools of Quality. Based on the current project scenario, pick one of these tools and create a chart/diagram to help you solve problems you are facing. Use the templates and samples provided.
6. Update your list of prioritized risks. Create a risk register entry for two of them. Use the template and sample provided.

Part 5: Closing

Background Scenario: It is one month before you plan to open your new business. You just got into your leased building, and you are busy starting to get it ready to open. You have hired a small construction firm to put in a few walls, do some painting, etc. You also got a lot of help from family and friends. You quit your job, and Nicole is also working every day now on the new business. She did a great job at marketing, and you are getting calls and e-mails from your new Web site every day. Brian's friend, Tom, built the site for you at no charge after Brian said he could come in and use the technology lab when it wasn't busy. Eric, the person you hired to help with the curriculum, was a fantastic resource, even though it cost you $10,000 you had not planned on spending. He did help you expand your list of potential students and instructors, as well, since he knew the local market very well. You did meet your schedule goal, but you had to borrow another $10,000 from your mom. She is only charging you 5% interest, starting when your doors open. She is happy with the results and has already booked a flight to visit for your grand opening celebration, where you and your team will be performing. Your mom loves to cook and bake, so she volunteered to handle the food for the opening.

Tasks

1. You have scheduled a final project presentation two days before your grand opening. Prepare a 10–15 slide presentation to summarize the results of the project. Describe the initial project goals, planned versus actual scope, time, and cost information, challenges faced, and key products produced.
2. Prepare a lessons-learned report for the entire project. Include input from all stakeholders in summarizing the lessons learned. Use the template and sample provided, and be creative in your response.

Resources

3. Prepare a final project report, using information from your final project presentation and the template provided. Be sure to include all of the documents you have prepared as appendices.
4. Document your own list of best practices that you think helped or could have helped you on this project in a two- to three-page paper.

TEMPLATE FILES

As mentioned throughout this text, using templates can help you prepare various project management documents, spreadsheets, charts, and other files. Figure C-2 lists the template name, the chapter where it is used in the text, and the application software used to create it. Be careful to enter information into the templates carefully, and feel free to modify the templates to meet your particular project needs. You can download the files in one compressed file from the companion Web site. You must have the application software to use the templates.

FIGURE C-2 Templates available for download on the companion Web site

Template name	Chapter reference	Application software
Payback period chart	2	Excel
Weighted scoring model	2	Excel
Stakeholder analysis	3	Word
Business case	3	Word
Business case financials	3	Excel
Project charter	3	Word
Kick-off meeting agenda	3	Word
Preliminary scope statement	3	Word
Team contract	4	Word
Project management plan	4	Word
Scope management plan	4	Word
Scope statement	4	Word
WBS	4	Word
WBS dictionary entry	4	Word
Activity list and attributes	4	Word
Milestone list	4	Word
Activity resource requirements	4	Word
Project schedule	4	Project

Template name	Chapter reference	Application software
Cost estimate	4	Excel
Cost baseline	4	Excel
Quality management plan	5	Word
Quality metrics	5	Word
Quality checklist	5	Word
Project organizational chart	5	PowerPoint
RACI chart	5	Excel
Resource histogram	5	Excel
Staffing management plan	5	Word
Communications management plan	5	Word
Project Web site	5	FrontPage
Risk management plan	5	Word
Probability/impact matrix	5	PowerPoint
Risk register	5	Excel
Make-or-buy analysis	5	Word
Procurement management plan	5	Word
Request for proposal	5	Word
Contract statement of work	5	Word
Supplier evaluation matrix	5	Excel
Milestone report	6	Word
Change request	6	Word
Cause-and-effect diagram	6 and 7	PowerPoint
Team roster	6	Word
Team performance assessment	6	Word
Qualified sellers list	6	Word
Contract	6	Word
Earned value chart	7	Excel
Deliverable acceptance form	7	Word
Run chart	7	Excel

FIGURE C-2 Templates available for download on the companion Web site (continued)

Template name	Chapter reference	Application software
Scatter diagram	7	Excel
Histogram	7	Excel
Pareto chart	7	Excel
Flow chart	7	PowerPoint
Performance report	7	Word
Issue log	7	Excel
Customer acceptance-project completion form	8	Word
Final project report table of contents	8	Word
Transition plan	8	Word
Lessons learned report	8	Word
Contract closure notice	8	Word

USEFUL PROJECT MANAGEMENT SITES

Thousands of Web sites provide useful information related to project, program, and portfolio management. This brief listing highlights just a few useful sites, which provide many links to other sites. You can easily link to these sites from the companion Web site for this text, and you can also search the Internet to find other useful sites.

Professional Societies

- *Project Management Institute (www.pmi.org)*: This site includes lots of information related to project management, Project Management Professional (PMP) certification, project management seminars and conferences, and so on. Students throughout the world can join PMI at deep discounts. As a member, you receive a free copy of the *PMBOK® Guide*, subscriptions to the monthly PM Network magazine and quarterly PM Journal, and access to online member resources.
- *Students of Project Management (www.studentsofpm.org)*: This virtual group, sponsored by PMI, supports students studying project management.
- *International Association of Project and Program Management (www.iappm. org)*: This site includes information about the Certified Portfolio Managers (CPM) certification and other services provided by this international professional society for project and program managers.

- *Association for Project Management (www.apmgroup.co.uk)*: This UK-based professional society provides an accreditation, certification, and examination body for key elements of best practice in program, project, and risk management.
- *American Society for the Advancement of Project Management (www.asapm. org)*: This competency-based credentialing organization advocates effective project management practice throughout all organizations.
- *Australian Institute of Project Management (www.aipm.com.au)*: This professional group was organized in 1976 to promote and progress the profession of project management in Australia.

Sites with Project Management Articles (in Alphabetical Order)

- Chief Project Officer (*www.cpo.com*)
- Gantthead.com (*www.gantthead.com*)
- Human Systems International (*www.humansystems.net/newsroom.html*)
- Project Management Boulevard (*www.pmblvd.com*)
- Project Management Control Tower (*www.4pm.com*)
- Project Management Forum, with links to several journals (*www.pmforum.org*)
- ProjectNet (*www.projectnet.co.uk*)
- ProjectReference (*www.projectreference.com*)
- Projects @ Work (*www.projectsatwork.com*)
- The Center for Business Practices (*www.cpbonline.com*)
- The International Research Network on Organizing by Projects (*www.irnop.org*)
- The Project Manager's Home Page (*www.allpm.com*)
- The Tenstep Project Management Process Methodology (*www.tenstep.com*)

activity attributes — Information that provides schedule-related information about each activity, such as predecessors, successors, logical relationships, leads and lags, resource requirements, constraints, imposed dates, and assumptions related to the activity.

activity list — A tabulation of activities to be included on a project schedule.

activity-on-arrow (AOA) approach, or the arrow diagramming method (ADM) — A network diagramming technique in which activities are represented by arrows and connected at points called nodes to illustrate the sequence of activities.

actual cost (AC) — The total direct and indirect costs incurred in accomplishing work on an activity during a given period.

analogous estimates, or top-down estimates — The estimates that use the actual cost of a previous, similar project as the basis for estimating the cost of the current project.

balanced scorecard — A methodology that converts an organization's value drivers to a series of defined metrics.

baseline — A starting point, a measurement, or an observation that is documented so that it can be used for future comparison; also defined as the original project plans plus approved changes.

benchmarking — The process of generating ideas for quality improvements by comparing specific project practices or product characteristics to those of other projects or products within or outside of the performing organization.

best practice — An optimal way recognized by industry to achieve a stated goal or objective.

bid — A document prepared by sellers providing pricing for standard items that have been clearly defined by the buyer.

blogs — Easy-to-use journals on the Web that allow users to write entries, create links, and upload pictures, while allowing readers to post comments to particular journal entries.

bottom-up estimates — Cost estimates created by estimating individual activities and summing them to get a project total.

budget at completion (BAC) — The approved total budget for the project.

buffer — Additional time to complete a task, added to an estimate to account for various factors.

burst — An occurence when two or more activities follow a single node on a network diagram.

business case — A document that provides justification for investing in a project.

capabilities — The incremental steps that lead to best practices.

cash flow — Benefits minus costs, or income minus expenses.

cause-and-effect diagrams — Also called fishbone or Ishikawa diagrams, these diagrams can assist in ensuring and improving quality by finding the root causes of quality problems.

champion — A senior manager who acts as a key proponent for a project.

checklist — A list of items to be noted or consulted.

closing processes — The actions that involve formalizing acceptance of the project or phase and bringing it to an orderly end.

communications management plan — A document that guides project communications.

compromise mode — The conflict-handling mode that uses a give-and-take approach to resolve conflicts.

conformance to requirements — The process of ensuring that the project's processes and products meet written specifications.

confrontation mode — The conflict-handling mode that involves directly facing a conflict using a problem-solving approach that allows affected parties to work through their disagreements.

constructive change orders — Oral or written acts or omissions by someone with actual or apparent authority that can be construed to have the same effect as a written change order.

contingency plans — The predefined actions that the project team will take if an identified risk event occurs.

contingency reserves or contingency allowances — The funds held by the project sponsor that can be used to mitigate cost or schedule overruns if unknown risks occur.

contract closure — The completion and settlement of contracts, and resolution of any open items.

contract statement of work (SOW) — A description of the work that is to be purchased.

contracts — The mutually binding agreements that obligate the seller to provide the specified products or services, and obligate the buyer to pay for them.

control chart — A graphic display of data that illustrates the results of a process over time.

cost baseline — A time-phased budget that project managers use to measure and monitor cost performance.

cost-reimbursable contract — A contract that involves payment to the seller for direct and indirect actual costs.

crashing — A technique for making cost and schedule trade-offs to obtain the greatest amount of schedule compression for the least incremental cost.

critical chain scheduling — A method of scheduling that takes limited resources into account when creating a project schedule and includes buffers to protect the project completion date.

critical path — The series of activities that determine the *earliest* time by which the project can be completed; it is the *longest* path through the network diagram and has the least amount of slack or float.

critical path method (CPM), or critical path analysis — A network diagramming technique used to predict total project duration.

deliverable — A product or service produced or provided as part of a project.

dependency, or relationship — The sequencing of project activities or tasks.

directives — The new requirements imposed by management, government, or some external influence.

discount factor — A multiplier for each year based on the discount rate and year.

discount rate — The rate used in discounting future cash flows.

discretionary dependencies — The dependencies that are defined by the project team.

duration — The actual amount of time spent working on an activity *plus* elapsed time.

earned value (EV) — An estimate of the value of the physical work actually completed.

earned value management (EVM) — A project performance measurement technique that integrates scope, time, and cost data.

effort — The number of workdays or work hours required to complete a task.

empathic listening — The process of listening with the intent to understand by putting yourself in the shoes of the other person.

estimate at completion (EAC) — A forecast of how much the project will cost upon completion.

ethics — A set of principles that guide our decision making based on personal values of what is "right" and "wrong."

executing processes — The actions that involve coordinating people and other resources to carry out the project plans and produce the deliverables of the project.

external dependencies — The dependencies that involve relationships between project and nonproject activities.

extrinsic motivation — A motivation that causes people to do something for a reward or to avoid a penalty.

fallback plans — The plans that are developed for risks that have a high impact on meeting project objectives, and are put into effect if attempts to reduce the risk are not effective.

fast tracking — A schedule compression technique where you do activities in parallel that you would normally do in sequence.

feeding buffers — Additional time added before tasks on the critical path that are preceded by non-critical-path tasks.

fitness for use — The ability of a product to be used as it was intended.

fixed-price or lump-sum contract — A type of contract that involves a fixed price for a well-defined product or service.

flowcharts — The graphic displays of the logic and flow of processes that help you analyze how problems occur and how processes can be improved.

forcing mode — The conflict-handling mode that involves exerting one's viewpoint at the potential expense of another viewpoint.

forecasts — The reports that predict future project status and progress based on past information and trends.

Gantt charts — A standard format for displaying project schedule information by listing project activities and their corresponding start and finish dates in a calendar format.

groupthink — The conformance to the values or ethical standards of a group.

histogram — A bar graph of a distribution of variables.

initiating processes — The actions to begin or end projects and project phases.

integrated change control — The process of identifying, evaluating, and managing changes throughout the project's life cycle.

internal rate of return (IRR) — The discount rate that results in an NPV of zero for a project.

intrinsic motivation — A motivation that causes people to participate in an activity for their own enjoyment.

issue — A matter under question or dispute that could impede project success.

issue log — A tool used to document and monitor the resolution of project issues.

key performance indicator (KPI) — A criterion used to determine whether the outcome associated with a capability exists, or the degree to which it exists.

kick-off meeting — A meeting held at the beginning of a project so that stakeholders can meet each other, review the goals of the project, and discuss future plans.

leader — A person who focuses on long-term goals and big-picture objectives, while inspiring people to reach those goals.

make-or-buy analysis — The process of estimating the internal costs of providing a product or service and comparing that estimate to the cost of outsourcing.

manager — A person who deals with the day-to-day details of meeting specific goals.

mandatory dependencies — The dependencies that are inherent in the nature of the work being performed on a project.

Maslow's hierarchy of needs — A hierarchy that states that people's behaviors are guided or motivated by a sequence of needs (physiological, safety, social, esteem, and self-actualization).

maturity model — A framework for helping organizations improve their processes and systems.

merge — A situation when two or more nodes precede a single node on a network diagram.

methodology — A plan that describes how things should be done to manage a project.

metric — A standard of measurement.

milestone — A significant event on a project.

mind mapping — A technique that uses branches radiating out from a core idea to structure thoughts and ideas.

mirroring — The matching of certain behaviors of the other person.

monitoring and controlling processes — The actions taken to measure progress toward achieving project goals, monitor deviation from plans, and take corrective action.

multitasking — When a resource works on more than one task at a time.

Murphy's Law — If something can go wrong, it will.

Myers-Briggs Type Indicator (MBTI) — A popular tool for determining personality preferences.

net present value (NPV) analysis — A method of calculating the expected net monetary gain or loss from a project by discounting all expected future cash inflows and outflows to the present point in time.

network diagram — A schematic display of the logical relationships among, or sequencing of, project activities.

node — The starting and ending point of an activity on an activity-on-arrow network diagram.

opportunities — Chances to improve the organization.

opportunity cost of capital — The return available by investing the capital elsewhere.

organizational project management — The systematic management of projects, programs, and portfolios in alignment with the achievement of strategic goals.[15]

outcomes — The results of applying capabilities.

overallocation — When more resources than are available are assigned to perform work at a given time.

parametric modeling — A technique that uses project characteristics (parameters) in a mathematical model to estimate project costs.

Pareto chart — A histogram that can help you identify and prioritize problem areas.

Parkinson's Law — Work expands to fill the time allowed.

payback period — The amount of time it will take to recoup, in the form of net cash inflows, the total dollars invested in a project.

phase — A distinct stage in project development.

planned value (PV) — That portion of the approved total cost estimate planned to be spent on an activity during a given period.

planning processes — The actions that involve devising and maintaining a workable scheme to ensure that the project meets its scope, time, and cost goals as well as organizational needs.

portfolio — A collection of projects or programs and other work that are grouped together to facilitate effective management of that work to meet strategic business objectives.

precedence diagramming method (PDM) — A network diagramming technique in which boxes represent activities.

problems — Undesirable situations that prevent the organization from achieving its goals.

process — A series of actions directed toward a particular result.

procurement audits — Reviews often performed during contract closure to identify lessons learned in the entire procurement process.

program — A group of projects managed in a coordinated way to obtain benefits and control not available from managing them individually.

Program Evaluation and Review Technique (PERT) — A network analysis technique used to estimate project duration when there is a high degree of uncertainty about the individual activity duration estimates.

program manager — The person who provides leadership and direction for the project managers heading the projects within a program.

progress reports — The reports that describe what the project team has accomplished during a certain period.

project — A temporary endeavor undertaken to create a unique product, service, or result.

project buffer — The additional time added before a project's due date to account for unexpected factors.

project charter — A document that formally recognizes the existence of a project and provides a summary of the project's objectives and management.

project communications management — Generating, collecting, disseminating, and storing project information.

project cost management — Preparing and managing the budget for the project.

project dashboard — A graphic screen summarizing key project metrics.

project human resource management — Making effective use of the people involved with the project.

project integration management — Coordinating the other knowledge areas, anticipating and dealing with issues, and making decisions each day about what is in the best interest of the entire project.

project management — The application of knowledge, skills, tools, and techniques to project activities to meet project requirements.

project management knowledge areas — The scope, time, cost, quality, human resource, communications, risk, procurement management, and project integration management.

project management office (PMO) — An organizational entity created to assist project managers in achieving project goals.

project management plan — A document, which is a deliverable for the project integration management knowledge area, used to coordinate all project planning documents and to help guide a project's execution and control.

project management process groups — The progression from initiating activities to planning activities, executing activities, monitoring and controlling activities, and closing activities.

Project Management Professional (PMP) — The certification provided by PMI that requires documenting project experience and education, agreeing to follow the code of ethics and professional conduct, and passing a comprehensive exam.

project management tools and techniques — The methods available to assist project managers and their teams; some popular tools in the time-management knowledge area include Gantt charts, network diagrams, critical-path analysis, and project management software.

project manager — The person responsible for working with the project sponsor, the project team, and the other people involved in a project to meet project goals.

project organizational chart — A graphic representation of how authority and responsibility is distributed within the project.

project portfolio management — The grouping and managing of projects and programs as a portfolio of investments that contribute to the entire enterprise's success.

project procurement management — Acquiring or procuring goods and services for a project from outside the performing organization.

project quality management — Ensuring that the project will satisfy the stated and implied needs for which it was undertaken.

project risk management — Identifying, analyzing, and responding to risks related to the project.

project scope management — Working with all appropriate stakeholders to define, gain written agreement for, and manage all the work required to complete the project successfully.

project sponsor — The person who provides the direction and funding for a project.

project time management — Estimating how long it will take to complete the work, developing an acceptable project schedule given cost-effective use of available resources, and ensuring timely completion of the project.

PRojects IN Controlled Environments (PRINCE2) — A project management methodology with eight process groups developed in the U.K.

proposal — A document in which sellers describe what they will do to meet the requirements of a buyer.

quality — The degree to which a set of inherent characteristics fulfill requirements.

quality assurance — The activities related to satisfying the relevant quality standards for a project.

quality audit — A structured review of specific quality management activities that helps identify lessons learned, which could improve performance on current or future projects.

RACI charts — A type of responsibility assignment matrix that shows Responsibility, Accountability, Consultation, and Informed roles for project stakeholders.

rapport — A relationship of harmony, conformity, accord, or affinity.

rate of performance (RP) — The percentage of actual work completed divided by the percentage of work planned to have been completed at any given time.

Rational Unified Process (RUP) framework — A project management methodology that uses an iterative software development process that focuses on team productivity and delivers software best practices to all team members.

records management system — A tool that provides the ability to easily organize, find, and archive documents.

Request for Proposal (RFP) — A document used to solicit proposals from prospective suppliers.

Request for Quote (RFQ) — A document used to solicit quotes or bids from prospective suppliers.

required rate of return — The minimum acceptable rate of return on an investment.

resource histogram — A column chart that shows the number of resources required for or assigned to a project over time.

resource leveling — A technique for resolving resource conflicts by delaying tasks.

resource loading — The amount of individual resources an existing schedule requires during specific time periods.

responsibility assignment matrix (RAM) — A matrix that maps the work of the project as described in the WBS to the people responsible for performing the work.

return on investment (ROI) — (Benefits minus costs) divided by costs.

risk — An uncertainty that can have a negative or positive effect on meeting project objectives.

risk events — The specific, uncertain events that may occur to the detriment or enhancement of the project.

risk register — A document that contains results of various risk management processes, often displayed in a table or spreadsheet format.

root cause — The real or underlying reason a problem occurs.

scatter diagram — A diagram that helps show if there is a relationship between two variables.

scope baseline — The approved project scope statement and its associated WBS and WBS dictionary.

scope creep — The tendency for project scope to continually increase.

scope management plan — A document that includes descriptions of how the team will prepare the project scope statement, create the WBS, verify completion of the project deliverables, and control requests for changes to the project scope.

scope statement — A document used to develop and confirm a common understanding of the project scope.

scope verification — The formal acceptance of the completed project scope by the customer or designated stakeholders.

short list — A list of the top three to five suppliers created to reduce the work involved in selecting a source.

Six Sigma — A comprehensive and flexible system for achieving, sustaining, and maximizing business success; uniquely driven by close understanding of customer needs, disciplined use of facts, data, and statistical analysis, and diligent attention to managing, improving, and reinventing business processes.

slack or float — The amount of time an activity may be delayed without delaying a succeeding activity or the project finish date.

slipped milestone — A milestone activity that was actually completed later than originally planned.

smoothing mode — The conflict-handling mode that de-emphasizes or avoids areas of differences and emphasizes areas of agreement.

staffing management plan — A plan that describes when and how people will be added to and taken off of a project.

stakeholder analysis — A document that provides information on key stakeholders to help manage relationships with them.

stakeholders — The people involved in or affected by project activities.

standard — A document that describes best practices for what should be done to manage a project.

status reports — The reports that describe where the project stands at a specific point in time.

strategic planning — The process of determining long-term objectives by analyzing the strengths and weaknesses of an organization, studying opportunities and threats in the business environment, predicting future trends, and projecting the need for new products and services.

SWOT analysis — Analyzing Strengths, Weaknesses, Opportunities, and Threats.

synergy — The concept that the whole is equal to more than the sum of its parts.

team contract — A document created to help promote teamwork and clarify team communications.

template — A file with a preset format that serves as a starting point for creating various documents so that the format and structure do not have to be re-created.

Theory of Constraints (TOC) — A management philosophy that states that any complex system at any point in time often has only one aspect or constraint that is limiting its ability to achieve more of its goal.

three-point estimate — An estimate that includes an optimistic, most likely, and pessimistic estimate.

time-and-material contract — A type of contract that is a hybrid of both a fixed-price and cost-reimbursable contract.

tracking Gantt chart — A Gantt chart that compares planned and actual project schedule information.

triggers — The indicators or symptoms of actual risk events.

triple constraint — The balancing of scope, time, and cost goals.

Tuckman model — A model that describes five stages of team development (forming, storming, norming, performing, and adjourning).

weighted scoring model — A technique that provides a systematic process for basing project selection on numerous criteria.

withdrawal mode — The conflict-handling mode that involves retreating or withdrawing from an actual or potential disagreement.

work breakdown structure (WBS) — A deliverable-oriented grouping of the work involved in a project that defines the total scope of the project.

work breakdown structure (WBS) dictionary — A document that describes detailed information about WBS tasks.

work package — A task at the lowest level of the WBS.

workarounds — The unplanned responses to risk events.

INDEX

Note: Page numbers in boldface type indicate key terms and their definitions.

A

B

C

O

P

T